# THE MACROECONOMY OF IRELAND

# THE MACRO-ECONOMY OF IRELAND

ANTHONY J. LEDDIN

University of Limerick

BRENDAN M. WALSH

University College, Dublin

GILL AND MACMILLAN

Published in Ireland by
Gill and Macmillan Ltd
Goldenbridge
Dublin 8
with associated companies in
Auckland, Delhi, Gaborone, Hamburg, Harare,
Hong Kong, Johannesburg, Kuala Lumpur, Lagos, London,
Manzini, Melbourne, Mexico City, Nairobi,
New York, Singapore, Tokyo
© Anthony J. Leddin and Brendan M. Walsh, 1990
0  7171 1760 X
Printed by
The Bath Press, Bath

The text of this book was composed by the authors using Microsoft Word. The graphs were generated
on Gem software. The final document was brought to camera ready copy, to the publishers' design
specifications, on Ventura Desk Top Publisher using the facilities of the Department of Information
Technology at the University of Limerick.

To

Celeste and Sophie
A.J.L.

Patricia, Colm, Nessa and Ben
B.M.W.

# Contents

# *Contents*

# *Preface*

This book has been written to introduce Irish students to the study of macroeconomics and to provide those who already have some familiarity with the subject with Irish examples and applications. It is designed to fill a gap which we believe exists in the market. At the present time there are plenty of international textbooks, some of which are used in Irish colleges and universities. We know from experience that Irish students do not find the treatment of macroeconomics in these texts congenial. There are also a number of Irish textbooks geared to the Leaving Certificate syllabus. We believe that this syllabus is over-inclusive and lacking in analytical focus. What is not available is a concise introduction to macroeconomics which combines basic theory with data and equips the reader to analyse Ireland's recent economic experience.

This text is designed to meet this need. We have tried to produce a book that will appeal both to Irish students taking university-level courses in economics and to students in the growing number of post-graduate courses designed to provide mature students with an understanding of applied macroeconomics.

We wish to acknowledge the help provided in the preparation of this book by J. Durkan and J.P. Neary of University College, Dublin, who commented on a draft of some of the chapters. We also thank the staff of the Information Technology Department at the University of Limerick, in particular Martin Leonard, for solving all our technical problems. Finally, we acknowledge successive generations of students in our courses in University College, Dublin, and the University of Limerick who, perhaps unwittingly, helped us improve the presentation of the concepts in this book.

Plassey, Limerick                                                       A.J.L.
Banjul, The Gambia                                                      B.M.W.
February, 1990

# Chapter 1

# *Introduction to Macroeconomics*

## .1 Introduction

Macroeconomics studies whole economies rather than individual markets, which is the concern of microeconomics. It deals with *aggregates* such as national income and economy-wide phenomena such as the price level, the rate of interest, the level of employment and unemployment, foreign exchange and the balance of payments. In many of these areas, macroeconomists draw on the analytical techniques developed by microeconomists. Thus the two branches of economics should not be rigidly segregated. None the less, there is a distinctive body of thought that we call macroeconomics. The best way to learn what the subject consists of is to plunge into it!

## 1.2 National Income, Expenditure and Output

In macroeconomics the most important concept is the level of economic activity in a country. This may be measured in three ways:

1. by adding up all the *income* arising in the country,
2. by adding up all the *expenditure* in the country, or
3. by adding up the value of all the *output* produced in the country.

The student has to grasp the fundamental point that these three approaches to measuring the level of economic activity should yield the same figure. This is usually explained in introductory textbooks in terms of diagrams showing the *circular flow of income and expenditure*. The barest model of this is as follows: with no public sector and international trade, the only economic agents are *firms* and *households*. The households supply labour to the firms: in return they receive income. The firms use the households' labour to produce output (consumption goods). The households spend their income on the output of the firms and the loop is complete.

Many introductory textbooks use some ingenuity to elaborate this basic framework pictorially, to take account of investment spending, the output of the public sector (and taxes!), and imports and exports. We shall defer to Chapter 3 our presentation of this material, preferring first to launch the student on the actual details of the Irish national accounts in Chapter 2. We do wish, however, to emphasise two important theoretical points at this stage.

1. When we measure the value of output in the economy, we must avoid double counting. We can do this by adding up only the *value added* at each stage in the chain of production. In the time-honoured example of a simple economy in which the only product being produced is bread, we should count only the value of the *final* goods (bread) and not the *intermediate* goods (flour, wheat) as well. If we observe this rule, we shall arrive at a value for output that equals the value of all the incomes received in the country: people are paid wages and salaries for adding value! The rent paid to land-owners and the interest received by owners of capital are payments for the contribution of these factors of production to the value of output.

The distinction between intermediate and final output is not always as clearcut as in the example of wheat, flour and bread. A feature of complex societies is the growing proportion of effort that has to be devoted to commuting, security and health care. These are, for the most part, not enjoyed in themselves. They are inputs to the business of producing and enjoying all the other things we really want. Longer traffic jams, higher bills for policing and law enforcement increase GNP (gross national product) as we measure it, but they hardly increase economic welfare.

2. A second basic principle in measuring national economic activity is to include things at their market value or factor cost. (If there are no indirect taxes, the two valuation bases are the same.) Measures such as national income or product are by definition concerned with magnitudes that can be measured using the measuring rod of money. *Non-market activities* are in general excluded, as are the benefits of a pleasant climate or political stability. This can give rise to some unsatisfactory results. An old, somewhat sexist example is that if a man marries his housekeeper, the value of national income falls because her work moves from the market economy to an intra-familial activity. It would be in principle possible to impute the value of this type of work in the national income accounts, but in practice this is only done for the value of farm produce consumed on the farm. We should bear this market bias in mind, however, especially in making comparisons between economies at very different levels of development. At very low levels of income there may be a significant amount of non-market activity, which becomes commercialised as economic development leads to greater specialisation.

A particularly important ramification of the second point is the question of pollution or what economists more generally call *external costs* or *spillover effects*. These are not reflected in the (private) costs of producing national product, which therefore overstate the true value of what is being produced. Ideally, the national

2

accounts should include a negative item reflecting the cost to the environment of the production that has taken place during the year. The value of clean air, water and a healthy environment has every bit as much claim for inclusion in GNP as has the value of cars, radios or clothes. The trouble is that generally the former are not bought and sold, but the latter are. It is very unsatisfactory to ignore the former, while elevating the latter into the goal of existence. Economists are not in general guilty of this mistake, but they leave themselves open to the accusation that they are because of the difficulties of incorporating the value of changes in communally owned resources in the national income accounts.

# 3 The Level and Trend of Irish National Income

Many international bodies, including the *Organisation for Economic Cooperation and Development (OECD),* produce more or less comparable data for national income (or the related *concept of GDP [gross domestic product],* see Chapter 2) in a wide range of countries. To make international comparisons it is, of course, necessary to adjust these figures by dividing by population. It is also necessary to convert the local data into a common currency (usually the US$). GDP per person in US$ is the most frequently used index of the level of economic development and the level of economic welfare in a country. Despite all its deficiencies, it is more comprehensive than alternative indicators such as the level of life expectancy or the number of telephones per 1,000 population.

The most recent comparative data published by the OECD relate to 1987. They show GDP per person in Ireland was $6,914. This may be compared with a level of $20,587 in Switzerland (the richest country in the OECD) or $1,142 in Turkey (the poorest country in the OECD).

There is a problem in using these figures expressed in US$. They have been derived from figures in domestic currencies using current exchange rates. These market exchange rates fluctuate widely. For example, in the first quarter of 1985 an Irish pound was worth only $0.96, but by the first quarter of 1988 it had risen to $1.59. If these exchange rates were used to calculate the level of Irish GDP in dollars, they would imply that we were 66% better off in 1988 than in 1985 (even if no economic growth had taken place). In order to provide data that avoid this kind of misleading implication, the OECD has devoted a great deal of effort to calculating what are called *purchasing power parity (PPP)* exchange rates. The idea behind PPP is that exchange rates should reflect the relative cost of a bundle of goods and services in the different countries. We shall return to this concept at greater length in Chapters 9 and 10, when we discuss exchange rates. At this stage we shall simply accept the OECD's measures and note that when PPP exchange rates are used, Switzerland's GDP per person is reduced to $15,144 and Turkey's is raised to

3

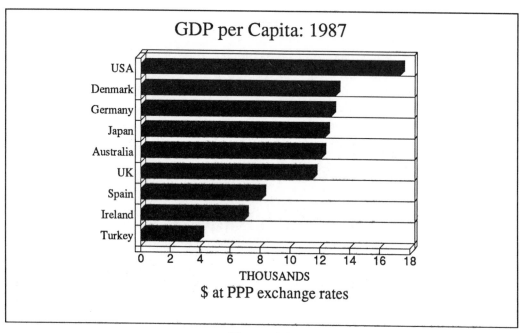

Figure 1.1

$3,924, so that the gap between the two countries is dramatically narrowed, from 18:1 on the basis of current exchange rates to just under 4:1 on the basis of PPP rates. This reflects that fact that in Switzerland most things are expensive, while in Turkey many basic goods and services are cheap.

In Figure 1.1 we show the level of GDP per person, using PPP exchange rates, for a few countries which are of interest to Irish students. The low level of income in Ireland relative to the United States, the United Kingdom and Germany is evident. In fact it is striking that of the 24 OECD member states, only Turkey, Portugal and Greece are poorer than Ireland by this yardstick, and the gap between Ireland and Greece is very narrow.

However, even if we are still relatively poor, we are much richer than we used to be! Even modest growth rates result in substantial increases over the long-run. Such is the power of compound interest that if GNP were to grow at a steady 3% per annum, real income would double in every twenty-five years (roughly the length of a generation). When studying the trend in GNP over the years, care must be taken to concentrate on changes in the *volume* of GNP or *real* GNP and to strip out the increase in money GNP that is due to inflation. (How this is done is discussed in Chapter 2.) Looking back at the period since 1962, the data show that real GNP per person (in 1980 prices) has risen from £1,661 in 1962 to £2,603 in 1987. This 57% increase represents an annual average growth rate of 1.8%. Unfortunately this was one of the lowest of any of the OECD countries over this period. Thus, even though we have made progress over the past quarter of a century, we have not managed to

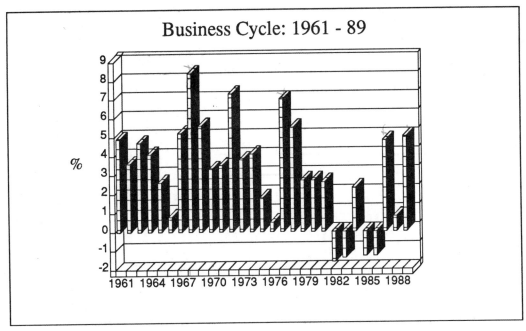

Figure 1.2

close the gap between ourselves and the richest countries of the world. In fact many countries (Spain, Greece, and the newly industrialising countries of Asia) have grown much more rapidly than we have, with the result that our position in the global GNP/population league table has slipped.

# 4 The Goals of Macroeconomic Policy

The most important goal of economic policy is to raise the *living standards* of the population. Clearly this affects almost every aspect of a country's life, including its educational system. Macroeconomic policy as such has a narrower focus. Its primary objective is maintaining *a high and stable level of economic activity*, that is, smoothing out the boom and bust of the business cycle. If it is successful in this objective, it will also minimise the level of unemployment and reduce the incidence of poverty.

In fact the rate of growth of GNP in Ireland has been very volatile over the years. This is illustrated in Figure 1.2, which shows the annual percentage change in real GNP since 1961. Ideally, an economy should expand at a steady growth rate which keeps it close to the trend growth path of *potential output*. The growth path is determined by fundamental factors such as the rate of growth of the labour force and its productivity and its endowment with cooperating factors of production,

5

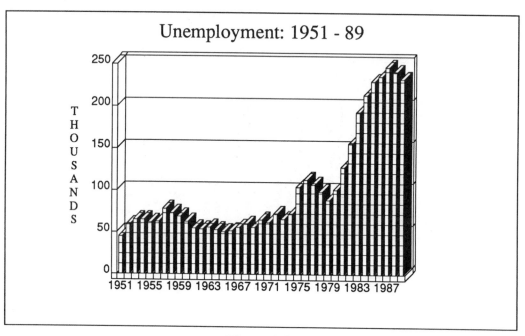

Figure 1.3

notably capital. In Ireland, the growth of the total labour force has not been an inhibiting factor, although the rate of improvement in its skills may have been. An average growth rate of 2.5% a year over the period 1962 - 87 would not have been spectacular by international standards, especially in view of the room for catching up suggested by the low level of income from which we started. If in fact we had achieved this modest target, income per person would now be over £3,000 in 1980 prices, or some 15% higher than its actual level. Moreover, expansion at a steady rate would also have averted the sharp increases in unemployment that were recorded as the rate of growth in GNP declined.

In Ireland we cannot lose sight of the importance of the constraint placed on us by the *balance of payments*. Avoiding chronic deficits is very important and has proved difficult in an economy as open to international trade as ours.

The level and growth rate of GNP are not the only criteria by which an economy should be judged. Two additional considerations of great importance are the rate of *unemployment* and the *rate of inflation*. A high rate of unemployment indicates the existence of widespread hardship due to a failure of the economy to provide jobs for those willing to accept them. A high rate of inflation is very disruptive of economic life. It augurs badly for the longer-term growth prospects and has arbitrary and undesirable effects on the distribution of income. Some commentators combine the rates of unemployment and inflation together into a *misery index*. While this is not very scientific, it has the merit of summarising the combined impact of these two indicators of economic malaise. In Ireland we might also wish to

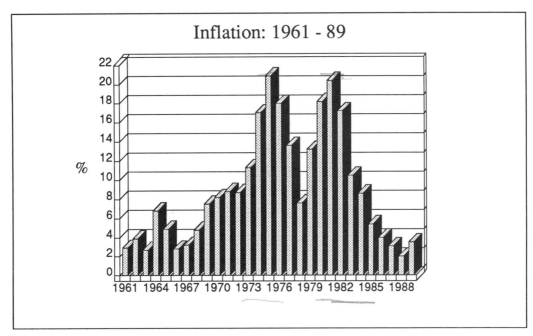

Figure 1.4

include some measure of the rate of emigration which, although it eases the problem of unemployment, is clearly an index of the limitations of the economy's performance.

Figures 1.3 and 1.4 show the rates of unemployment and inflation in Ireland since 1951 and 1961 respectively. The soaring unemployment of the 1980s is clearly our most pressing economic problem. Inflation, which threatened to run away out of control in the mid-1970s and again in the early 1980s, has now been tamed. The misery index reached a peak in the early 1980s, when real income also fell by an exceptional amount. By any criterion, this was a very difficult time for the Irish economy. In the next chapter we shall look in greater detail at how the Irish economy has performed since 1980. In subsequent chapters we shall analyse the reasons for this poor performance.

# Chapter 2

# Measuring the Country's Economic Performance

## 2.1 Introduction

In Chapter 1 we outlined the basic ideas of national income, product and expenditure. In this chapter we shall explore these concepts in much greater detail, focusing on issues that are important in assessing the performance of the Irish economy. As we go through these issues, we shall illustrate them using the data on Ireland's economic performance during the 1980s contained in the latest (1988) edition of *National Income and Expenditure (NIE)*, which should be consulted by the reader.

## 2.2 Basic Definitions: National Product and Income

The national income accountants begin by measuring what is called *net domestic product at factor cost* (NDP$_{FC}$). They obtain data on agricultural income from the experts in that area and details of non-agricultural income (wages and salaries, the income of the self-employed, profits, interest payments and rents) from the Revenue Commissioners and other sources. In this way they build up a picture of the value of what is being produced in the country and what types of income are being received by those producing it. Table 1 of NIE provides data for NDP$_{FC}$, disaggregated into *types of income* (agricultural/non-agricultural; wages and salaries, profits, interest etc.). This table is useful in tracking longer-term trends in the composition and distribution of national income. One ratio of considerable significance is the share of company profits in total non-agricultural income. In 1980 this share was at a low of 13.7%. It had risen to 22.5 % by 1987. This indicates a strong growth in the profitability of Irish business over these years. The other side of this development is the decline in the share of total non-agricultural income represented by remuneration of employees (including employers' contributions to social security), from 77.4% in 1980 to 62.9% in 1988. The rise in the rate of return to capital indicated by the switch in the distribution of income from wages to profits might be expected to give rise to an investment boom. It remains to be seen whether or not this boom will materialise.

Table 2 of NIE provides a breakdown of NDP by *sector of origin* (agriculture etc., industry, distribution, public administration etc.). Not all of the income generated producing $NDP_{FC}$ in a country is available for use by residents of that country. Factor payments are made across national frontiers when, for example, subsidiaries of foreign companies in Ireland repatriate profits abroad or when the Irish government pays interest on its debt to non-residents. These outflows have increased in importance. *Net factor income from the rest of the world* (F) is added to $NDP_{FC}$ to obtain net national product at factor cost ($NNP_{FC}$) which is equal to national income (NI):[1]

(1) $NDP_{FC} + F \equiv NNP_{FC} \equiv NI$

*Note:*

*The student should bear in mind that this is an identity. It holds true by definition and implies nothing about economic behaviour or the equilibrium level of output. This is the significance of the $\equiv$ sign.*

This identity translates into practice the basic idea that all the income received by the factors of production in an economy must equal the value of the final goods and services produced by that economy.

The phrase *factor cost* is used to distinguish $NDP_{FC}$ from net domestic product at *market prices* ($NNP_{MP}$).

(2) $NDP_{MP} \equiv NDP_{FC} +$ indirect taxes less subsidies

Indirect taxes and subsidies drive a wedge between the market value paid for goods and services and the income received by the factors (labour, capital and land) employed in their production. For example, a pint of beer sells for about £1.50, of which about £0.70 represents excise duties and VAT. Only £0.80 goes to pay for the production and distribution of the beer.

The significance of the Net in NDP is that it does not include any allowance for the capital consumed in the production of national product. The depreciation of capital in course of a year is a charge against output and would be reflected in the value of the goods and services produced. For that reason we have to add an allowance for *depreciation,* (D), to $NDP_{FC}$ to obtain *gross domestic product* at factor cost, usually referred to simply as GDP:

(3) $GDP \equiv NDP_{FC} + D$

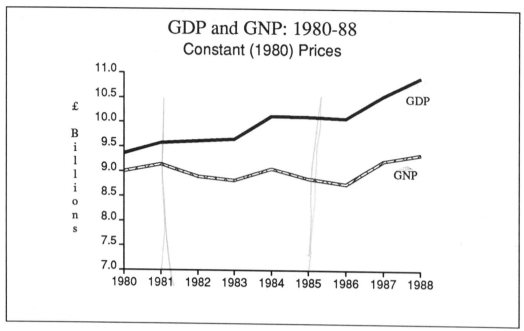

GDP and GNP: 1980-88
Constant (1980) Prices

Figure 2.1

If net income from the rest of the world, (F), is added to GDP, we obtain the familiar concept of *gross national product* (GNP):

(4)  GNP ≡ GDP + F

*net income from rest of world*

There is an element of double-counting in gross measures such as GNP and GDP, due to the inclusion of the value of the capital equipment that is consumed in the production process along with the value of what it produces. These flawed measures of economic activity are widely used because reliable estimates of depreciation are difficult to obtain. GDP is used by international agencies such as the *Organisation for Economic Cooperation and Development (OECD)* in their commentaries on member states' economic performance. We shall use it and related measures in our commentary on the performance of the Irish economy during the 1980s.

In Ireland, F is now a substantial negative figure due to the level of debt service payments to non-residents and to the level of profits repatriated by foreign-owned companies. These outflows have been growing more rapidly than GDP, to the point where they now equal 10% of GDP. As a result GDP provides a misleading guide to the trend in living standards of Irish residents during the 1980s. The figure for GNP is more meaningful as a guide to the resources available to Irish residents to consume or invest. Figure 2.1 shows the trend of both GDP and GNP since 1980.

*Outflows*

10

The growth of the gap between GNP and GDP was most rapid between 1981 and 1985.

GDP comprises the sum of expenditure on personal consumption goods and services (C), public current consumption of goods and services (G),[2] gross domestic capital formation or investment (I),[3] spending by the rest of the world on the output of our economy, or our exports (X) less our spending on the output of the rest of the world, or our imports (M) which have already been included in C, I and G but are clearly not part of our domestic production:

(5)   $GDP \equiv C + G + I + X - M$

Letting the difference between exports and imports, X-M, equal *net exports*, NX, the definition can be rewritten:

(5a)   $GDP \equiv C + G + I + NX$

When examining the trend in a macroeconomic magnitude such as GDP over time it is essential to distinguish between the changes that are due to rises in the *price level* and those that represent *real* or *volume* growth. The measurement of inflation is discussed later in this chapter. At this stage, suffice it to say that our discussion of the economy's performance will be based on the trend in the level of real (or constant price) output, often referred to as the volume of output.

The composition of expenditure on GDP reveals a good deal about the structure of *aggregate demand*. The following sub-totals of GDP are of interest in different contexts, and the student should be familiar with them:

(6) *Domestic consumption expenditure* $\equiv C + G$

that is, the sum of private and public consumption spending.

(7) *Gross domestic expenditure* (GDE) $\equiv C + G + I$

This aggregate is also known as *Absorption* and measures total spending by the Irish residents, both on the output of the domestic economy and on imports.

(8) *Final demand* (FD) $\equiv C + I + G + X$     $\dfrac{M}{C+I+G+X}$     Import penetration

This measures total spending by Irish residents (including spending on imports) plus spending by the rest of the world on the output of our economy. In a sense it represents the total potential market that might be captured by Irish suppliers. Thus, M/FD is a measure of *import penetration*. (Remember that C, I and G include imported components.) A recent study documents how import penetration in Ireland

11

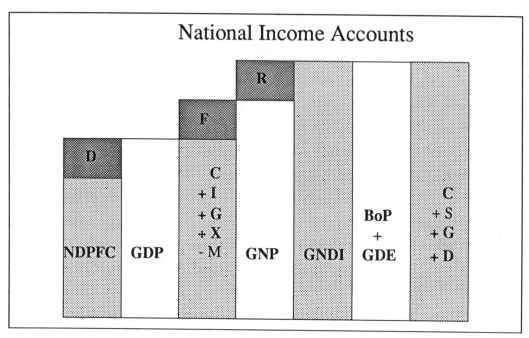

Figure 2.2

rose from 24.9% in 1960 to 40.9% in 1979.[4] It fell back during the depressed years of the 1980s.

Although GNP is preferable to GDP as a measure of the resources available to the residents of the country, it fails to take account of *current transfer payments from the rest of the world* (R), which in Ireland take the form of current grants and subsidies from the European Communities and a smaller amount of emigrants' remittances. If these are added to GNP we arrive at *gross national disposable income (GNDI)*:

(9) $\text{GNDI} \equiv \text{GNP} + \text{R} \equiv \text{C} + \text{I} + \text{G} + \text{X} - \text{M} + \text{F} + \text{R}$

The relationships between $\text{NDP}_{\text{FC}}$, GDP, GNP. GNDI, etc. (equations 3, 4, 5 and 9) are shown in Figure 2.2. The final two columns on the right of this diagram include relationships given in identities 16 and 17. GNDI is the total amount available to Irish residents to consume or to invest. We shall explore in some detail how this income has in fact been allocated between these uses, but before doing so it is necessary to discuss some technical issues arising from the need to adjust for the effects of inflation.

# 2.3 Adjusting for Inflation

Figure 2.1 showed GNP and GDP in constant (1980) prices. It is appropriate at this stage to look in some detail at the process by which the effects of inflation are removed from the macroeconomic data.

The tables in NIE present data in current prices first. But many of the series are also presented in constant (1985) prices. (1985 is the *base year* used in the 1988 edition of NIE.) The link between the current and constant price series is provided by *deflators*, which are not actually published but can be derived from the current and constant price series. Table 2.1 displays the derivation of the *GNP deflator* for 1988. We provide a more detailed example in appendix 1.

*Table 2.1*

**The implicit GNP deflator**

|  | Nominal GNP (billions of current pounds) | Real GNP (billions of 1985 pounds) | Implicit GNP deflator (1985=100) |
|---|---|---|---|
| 1985 | 15.7 | 15.7 | 100 |
| 1988 | 18.8 | 16.8 | 112 |

*Note*: The deflator is the ratio of the current to constant price figure, multiplied by 100.

The data in NIE allow us to calculate deflators for the components of GNP. With 1980 equal to 100 (1980 was the base year in earlier editions of NIE), the following are the values in 1987:

$$P_C = 182, \quad P_G = 190, \quad P_I = 147, \quad P_X = 147.5, \quad P_M = 137$$

where

| | | |
|---|---|---|
| $P_C$ | = | implicit price deflator of personal consumption, |
| $P_G$ | = | implicit price deflator of government consumption, |
| $P_I$ | = | implicit price deflator of investment goods, |
| $P_X$ | = | implicit price deflator of exports, |
| $P_m$ | = | implicit price deflator of imports. |

These deflators are constructed on the basis of information on the consumer price index ($P_C$), the trend in rates of pay in the public sector ($P_G$), the wholesale price index for investment goods ($P_I$) and the unit value indices for imports and exports. A merit of these deflators is the wide range of goods they cover. A drawback is that they are available only annually and appear after a considerable time lag.

It is interesting to note the lower rates of inflation that have been recorded in I, X and M, which are all strongly influenced by world inflation rates and do not reflect the level of indirect taxation in Ireland.

An important issue arises regarding the treatment of import and export prices in the calculation of GNP or GNDI at constant prices.[5] It might seem logical to calculate constant price GNDI by deflating each of the components of expenditure by its respective deflator:

$$(10) \quad GNDI_{CP} \equiv C/P_C + G/P_C + I/P_I + X/P_X - M/P_M + F/P_X + R/P_M$$

However, the use of separate deflators for imports and exports leaves certain problems unresolved.[6] One is the possibility that the trade balance would have different signs in constant and current prices, as in the following data for 1986:

Table 2.2

**Illustration of sign reversal in the trade account**

|  |  |  |  |  |
|---|---|---|---|---|
| X | 10,347 | | $P_m$ | 135.3 |
| M | 9,859 | | $X/P_X$ | 7,051 |
| current prices (X - M) | 488 | | $M/P_m$ | 7,288 |
| $P_X$ | 146.7 | constant prices ($X/P_X$ - $M/P_m$) | -237 |

Source: NIE, 1987

Because of the different rates of inflation in imports and exports, the current price trade balance has the opposite sign from the constant price balance. This paradoxical outcome calls into question the meaning of the *constant price trade balance* when it is measured in this manner.

A second, more philosophical issue is also present. We export in order to import. There is a sense in which the volume of exports, that is $X/P_X$, is irrelevant to the economic welfare of Irish residents. What is relevant is how much our exports will buy in terms of imports. Think of Ireland as a country exporting dairy products and importing petroleum products. If the price of oil rises when that of milk is static, we have to export a larger quantity of milk to finance a given quantity of imported oil. This point is not reflected in the approach to deflating the balance of trade used above.

If, on the other hand, we were to deflate our exports by the price of imports, so that the adjusted trade balance in constant prices equals

(11)    $X/P_M - M/P_M \equiv 1/P_M(X - M)$

this point would be taken into account and inconsistency between the signs of the current and constant price trade balances would be ruled out.

Let us see how we can dovetail definition (11) of the trade balance into our measure of GNDI. The unadjusted constant price trade balance as measured in our definition of GNDI in (10) above was

(12)    Unadjusted constant price trade balance $\equiv X/P_X - M/P_M$

adding and subtracting $X/P_M$ to this we obtain

(13)    $X/P_X - M/P_M \equiv X/P_X - M/P_M + X/P_M - X/P_M$

rearranging we obtain

(14)    $(X/P_M - M/P_M) + (X/P_X - X/P_M) \equiv (X/P_M - M/P_M) + X(1/P_X - 1/P_M)$

Thus our proposed *adjusted constant price trade balance* equals the unadjusted balance plus a term that reflects the difference in the rate of inflation of imports and exports:

(15)    $(X/P_M - M/P_M) \equiv (X/P_X - M/P_M) + X(1/P_M - 1/P_X)$

In other words, if we add a *terms of trade adjustment*, $N \equiv (X/P_M - X/P_X) \equiv X(1/P_M - 1/P_X)$ to the original, unadjusted trade balance, we move from GNDI to GNDI *adjusted for the terms of trade* $\equiv$ GNDI + N.

This provides us with the best basis for measuring the trend in living standards in Ireland over time. Clearly the divergence between the adjusted and unadjusted GNDI depends on two factors (a) the divergence between the rates of import and export price inflation: if $P_M > P_X$ then $1/P_M < 1/P_X$ and $N < 0$, that is, when import prices are rising more rapidly than export prices, there is a trading loss and vice versa, and (b) the magnitude of X (relative to GNDI). The fact that in Ireland exports are exceptionally important relative to income gives N a special place in the measurement of our economy's performance.

In NIE the effect of N is shown cumulatively with respect to the base year, in which it is by definition zero because it is the year when $P_M = P_X$. Table 2.3 shows the magnitude of N between certain years in the 1970s and 1980 (as a percentage of 1980 GNP).

*Table 2.3*

**Terms of trade: effect as a % of GNP**

|       | 1973-75 | 1978-80 | 1981-87 |
|-------|---------|---------|---------|
| N/GNP | -6.0%   | -4.8%   | +7.9%   |

In the mid-1970s and at the end of the decade, there was an enormous loss of disposable income due to rises in oil prices (and some unfavourable developments on the farm price front), while after 1981 there was a very significant gain as farm prices recovered early in the decade and oil prices collapsed in 1986. Over the long run, the gains and losses tend to cancel out. This is certainly to be hoped for, because otherwise we should be in the situation of having to export ever-increasing numbers of cattle in order to import a given number of barrels of oil!

A further technical issue relating to the measurement of national product at constant prices should be mentioned. Two estimates of GNP at constant prices are prepared, one based on the flow of output, the other on the flow of expenditure. Current price expenditure data are deflated by indices such as the consumer price index, etc. Then the current price output data are converted to volume figures, using information on the volume of production in agriculture, industry etc. Not surprisingly, the two approaches result in different estimates of the trend in the volume of GNP. Over the period 1980-87, the volume of GNP increased by 5.7% according to the expenditure series, compared with 2.6% according to the output series. In both 1982 and 1985 the decline in GNP was 2 percentage points less in the expenditure series than in the output series. The magnitude of these discrepancies reduces the confidence that can be placed in either of the series. It also increases the scope for selective use of the statistics to present a particular picture of the economy's performance! The Central Statistics Office takes the average of the two series as the basis for its tables.

# 2.4 Allowing for Population Growth

Living standards are measured by the level of national income per person.[7] In developed countries where the rate of population growth is low there is no need to worry about adjusting for population growth in the analysis of short-run economic performance. Ireland is unusual, however, in having a very volatile rate of population growth. During the 1970s our population was growing at about 1.5% a year, the highest growth rate in Europe, while during the 1950s it declined by over

16

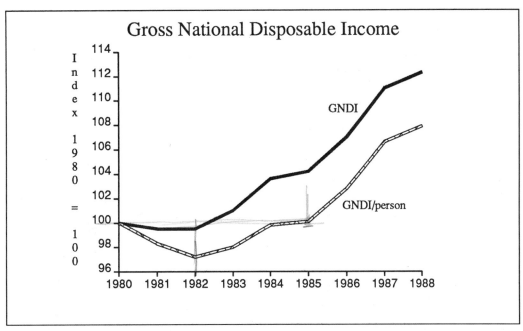

Figure 2.3

1% a year. At the beginning of the 1980s the population was still growing rapidly but it has been static since the middle of the decade. Our view of the country's recent economic performance is therefore distorted unless we take these fluctuations in the rate of population growth into account.

Figure 2.3 shows an index of real GNDI + N (that is, gross national disposable income adjusted for the terms of trade) and GNDI + N per person over the period 1980-88. The latter is the better index of the trend in living standards. (The student should refer back to Figure 2.1 and note the different picture of economic growth that would be obtained from the use of GDP or GNP.) The severity of the recession of the early 1980s may be gauged from the fact that the level of real income per person in 1985 was the same as it had been in 1980. The period 1980-82 was one of the most depressed that has even been experienced in Ireland because the population continued to increase at a time when national income was falling. This was due to the absence of emigration opportunities because of the high and rising level of unemployment in Britain and other countries. In the 1950s, recession in Ireland led to massive emigration and a falling population: this protected the living standards of those remaining at home.

The situation has been transformed since 1983 by three factors, whose importance can be seen from Figures 2.1 and 2.3:

1. The resumption of net emigration in the mid-1980s on a scale sufficient to avert further population growth,

2. The dramatic improvement in the terms of trade in 1986 as oil prices collapsed on world markets, and

3. The resumption of growth in GNP in 1987. This in turn was due to several factors, including the accelerating growth in the UK, the reduction in rates of interest in Ireland, and a marked improvement in agricultural incomes as the weather returned to a more favourable pattern, rates of interest fell and farm prices rose.

The combined effect of these factors has been dramatic. Between 1982 and 1988 real GNDI per person has risen by 11.3%. As we shall note in a later section of this chapter, further growth of about 3.75% is believed to have been achieved in 1989 and a 3.5% growth rate is being forecast for 1990.

# 2.5 The Balance of Payments, National Savings and the Financing of Investment

If a person is spending more than her income, she is borrowing from other people. If a country is spending more than its income, it is borrowing from the rest of the world. This borrowing or lending is recorded in the capital account of the balance of payments. But the excess of spending over income is equal to the current account of the balance of payments, as may be seen from the following relationships.

The sum of the three domestic components of GNDI constitute gross domestic expenditure, $GDE \equiv C + G + I$. The four foreign items, $(X - M + F + R)$, constitute the current account of the balance of payments (BoP).[8] Therefore

(16) $GNDI - GDE \equiv BoP$

When $GDE > GNDI$ there is a current account deficit, when $GDE < GNDI$ there is a surplus.

Figure 2.4 displays the magnitudes of GDE and GNDI in Ireland during the 1980s. The sizeable excess of expenditure over income in the early years was reflected in record BoP deficits. We can see that the gap between expenditure and income has been closed by curtailing expenditure as income grew between 1981 and 1987 the level of real GNDI increased by 12% but the level of GDE fell by 4%. The reduction in expenditure was due to a sharp drop in the volume of C, personal consumption expenditure, which fell by 7.6% in 1982 alone, and in I, capital formation, which was over 20% lower in 1987 than in 1981. Public sector consumption, G, on the other hand rose slightly between 1980 and 1986. It was not

18

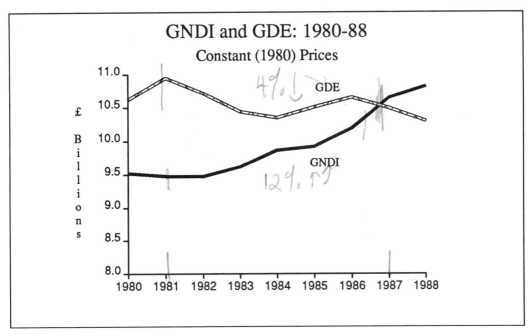

Figure 2.4

until 1987 that the imbalance between public and private sector expenditure began to be redressed by a sharp drop in the level of public consumption.

The current account BoP is a record of all the current transactions involving the purchase and sale of Irish pounds for foreign currencies. The sum of all (current and capital) transactions in foreign exchange must balance: for every seller of Irish pounds there must be a buyer. It follows, therefore, that the balance on the capital account must be equal to, but opposite in sign from, the current account balance. If there is a current account deficit it must be matched by a capital account inflow. Such an inflow can come from

1. private capital inflows,
2. official capital inflows (e.g. government foreign borrowing), and
3. reductions in official external reserves.

*Note:*
*If there is a surplus on current account, it is reflected in capital outflows or increases in reserves.*

All of these ways of financing a deficit involve increasing the country's international indebtedness (or, equivalently, reducing its international net assets), so the current account deficit is also referred to as the country's *net foreign borrowing*. However, the components of the capital inflow have different implications for the economy. For example, there may be a case for treating private

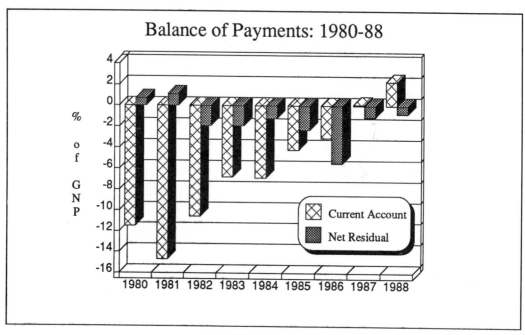

Figure 2.5

capital inflows as *autonomous* and adding them to the current account. Then the BoP deficit thus defined would equal the increase in official net indebtedness to the rest of the world.[9]

In all countries, data deficiencies give rise to discrepancies between the totals of the current and capital accounts. For this reason a *balancing item* is included in the capital account and referred to as

4. the *net residual*.

Despite a major revision to the Irish BoP statistics in the mid-1980s, the net residual on the capital account has remained (a) persistently negative since 1982 and (b) relatively large. It is possible that this residual includes significant current account debit items that are under-recorded (due for example to unrecorded cross-border transactions) in addition to unrecorded capital flows.[10] Because of this, care must be exercised in interpreting changes in the level of BoP. Figure 2.5 shows the level of BoP and the net residual (as a percentage of GNP). It may be seen that the reduction in the BoP deficit was accompanied by a sharp rise in the net residual in 1986. The fall in the current account deficit may well be overstated if the rise in the residual is ignored. However, by 1987 the improvement in the current account was unambiguous in the sense that even if the residual is treated as part of the current account deficit, the deficit nonetheless fell to only 1% of GNP.

An important extension of the national income accounting framework allows us to document how the country finances its investment, I. The nation has only two possible ways of using up its disposable income, by consuming it or saving it. Domestic consumption consists of C + G, hence

(17)  $GNDI \equiv C + G + S + D$

where

(18)  gross national saving (GNS) $\equiv S + D$,

(19)  net national saving (NNS) $\equiv S$

and D = the allowance for depreciation.

Now from (16) above we know that $GNDI \equiv C + G + I + BoP$. Hence,

(20)  $C + G + I + BoP \equiv C + G + GNS$,

and

(21)  $I \equiv GNS - BoP$,

that is, domestic capital formation equals (is financed by) gross national savings plus the balance of payments *deficit*. If D is subtracted from both sides we obtain the following:

(22)  $I - D \equiv$ net investment $\equiv NNS - BoP$

We may see from these identities that in a closed economy, where the BoP = 0, investment must equal national savings.[11]

It is possible to disaggregate GNS into public sector net (dis)savings and private sector savings, and the latter can be further disaggregated into household and company savings. Considerable interest attaches to the contribution of each of these sectors to the total available for investment in the country. International discussions of macroeconomic policy in the 1980s have been very concerned with the emergence of a large BoP deficit in the US and the fact that US investment has increasingly depended on the rest of the world's (and especially Japan's) savings. The figures for Ireland tell an interesting story, as may be seen from Figure 2.6. In the early 1980s the level of capital formation was exceptionally high relative to GNP. Much of this exceptional level of investment was financed through a BoP deficit. Net national savings fell to 3.5% of GNP in 1981, because the very high level of public

21

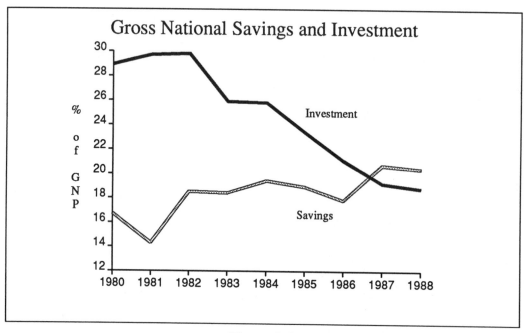

Figure 2.6

sector dissavings (equal to 8.2% of GNP) offset much of the private sector's savings. Since then there has been a remarkable change. Investment has declined and national savings have risen relative to GNP. The second development has been due primarily to the increase in public sector savings (or reduction in the public sector deficit). As a result the country has moved into a BoP surplus: GNS > I and the excess is being invested in the rest of the world.

In looking back at the situation that prevailed in Ireland early in the decade, the question of the *sustainability* of a BoP deficit naturally arises. Sustainability depends on the uses to which the funds that are being borrowed from the rest of the world are put. From the identity GNDI ≡ GDE + BoP we see that the BoP deficit equals the excess of absorption over income. But absorption consists of domestic consumption (C + G) and capital formation (I) and it matters whether the BoP deficit is being used to finance the former or the latter. This consideration has led to the view that a BoP deficit is sustainable if two conditions are met, namely,

(1)     I > -BoP

(If I < -BoP, then GNS < 0 and at least some of the deficit is being used to finance current consumption, which by definition cannot help repay the foreign debt that is being incurred.)

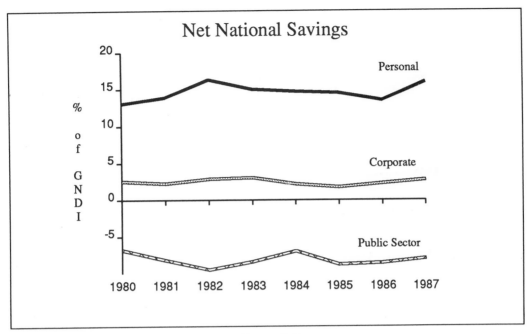

Net National Savings

Figure 2.7

(2) the additional capital formation that is facilitated by the BoP deficit is productive
enough to remunerate the foreign borrowing associated with it.[12]

The national income accounts provide details of the distribution of national
saving not just between public and private sectors, but also within the private sector
between companies and households. The main component of company saving is
the retained earnings of the larger corporations. Household savings are calculated
as a residual, namely, the difference between household disposable income and
household consumption. As a residual it is particularly subject to measurement
errors.[13] Personal savings ranged between 15% and 20% of personal disposable
income during the 1980s. While the Japanese save an even higher proportion of their
income, in the US the corresponding ratio is now below 4% and in the UK it fell
from 16% in 1980 to a mere 2% in 1988. In addition to being affected by
measurement errors, however, it should be borne in mind that household savings,
as defined by the national income accountants, do not reflect the value of changes
in the value of assets owned by households. The level of savings would be lower if
account were taken of the capital losses on stocks and liquid assets during periods
when inflation was accelerating, such as 1975 and 1981.[14] Similarly, the sharp fall
in the savings ratio during periods of rising house prices (e.g. the UK during the late
1980s) would be modified if the growth of households' wealth were included in
measured savings.

One of the features of the recent behaviour of the components of national savings in Ireland and other countries has been an apparent tendency for private sector, and in particular household, savings to increase in periods when public sector savings are falling (or the public sector deficit is rising). The Irish experience is summarised in Figure 2.7. The significance of this phenomenon is discussed in Chapter 4.

## 2.6 The Distribution of National Income

The data discussed up to this point in this chapter all relate to national totals or averages. As we noted in Chapter 1, averages give a very incomplete picture of the well-being of the population. Additional information on the distribution of income should be considered, where available. One indicator of income distribution that is readily available is the rate of unemployment. We shall be discussing the problem of unemployment in some detail in a later chapter. At this point our interest in it lies in the fact that those who are unemployed have no earned income.[15] During the recession of the early 1980s the rate of unemployment in Ireland soared from under 8% of the labour force to over 18%. While the real value of the rates of unemployment benefit and assistance rose significantly during the 1980s, the standard of living of those who became unemployed fell sharply. Those who remained out of work for long enough to exhaust their entitlement to the higher rates of benefit also suffered increasing hardship. The recession and the consequent rise in unemployment has almost certainly made the distribution of income less equal. The evidence shows that there has been an increase in the incidence of poverty, whether this is measured in absolute terms (with reference to a predefined minimum standard of living) or in relative terms (as the proportion of the population falling below a certain fraction of national income per person).[16] This problem could even intensify during the initial stages of the recovery that is now underway, due to the persistence of long-term unemployment and the difficult structural problems created by the recession.

## 2.7 International Comparisons

Before ending this chapter, it is of interest to compare Ireland's recent economic performance with that of Britain and the US. As a small open economy, we are strongly influenced by external forces. Indeed, over the very long run, our rate of economic growth has been very similar to the British.[17] During the 1980s however, the close link between the Irish and British economies began to be weakened by our

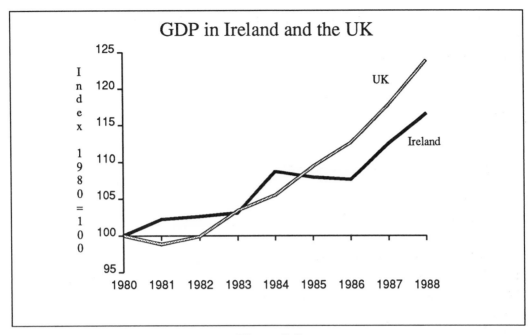

Figure 2.8

full membership of the European Monetary System (discussed in Chapter 10). There were also significant divergences of approach to economic policy in Ireland and Britain, especially in the early years of the Thatcher revolution when we continued to implement less *monetarist* policies.

Our economic performance fell significantly behind that of the OECD countries during the 1980s. To illustrate this point Figure 2.8 shows the trend of Irish and British GDP between 1980-88. The shortfall in growth in Ireland between 1981 and 1986 is very striking. The underperformance of the Irish economy during these years will preoccupy us in several later chapters, as we explore both its consequences and some possible explanations for it.

# .8 Short-term Forecasting

There is always a time lag before official data for the main macroeconomic series become available. For example, the official NIE data for 1988 was published in September 1989 (the main national income aggregates were however published earlier in the year in the Department of Finance's *Economic Review and Outlook)*. Moreover, the data for 1988 and even 1987 in the edition of NIE published in 1989 will be subject to significant revision, so that some uncertainty surrounds the precise details of our most recent economic performance. Government and business economists, on the other hand, are mainly concerned with the very recent past and the prospects for the future. A great deal of effort is devoted to the preparation of estimates of the main macroeconomic variables for the current year and forecasts for the coming year. The Department of Finance, the Central Bank, the Economic and Social Research Institute (ESRI) and a growing number of private sector firms prepare forecasts. These may be used to update the official estimates in NIE.

Forecasters in Ireland do not reveal the methods they apply to arrive at their view of the future course of the economy. This is partly because there is an element of rivalry between different agencies and partly because forecasting is an imprecise art rather than an exact science. While some forecasters may use econometric models as an aid in the preparation of their tables, none would rely rigidly on the numbers churned out by a model. There is a large element of hunch and intuition in every forecast.

A review of the track record of forecasting in all areas of economics and the social sciences reveals that estimates are strongly influenced by current conditions. Foreseeing turning points is the most difficult part of the exercise and one which few people get right. We should always be sceptical, therefore, of any forecast that simply extrapolates the recent past.

The standard way of presenting forecasts for the macroeconomy is to build up to GDP through the expenditure components, C, G, I, X and M. A forecast of the growth in the nominal value of these components is prepared and disaggregated into price and volume components. As an example of this approach, Table 2.4 reproduces the relevant table from the November 1989 *Quarterly Economic Commentary* of the ESRI. It may be seen that continued recovery is foreseen, with a growth in real GNP of 4.75% being forecasted for 1990. The high growth rate in the volume of investment and exports is notable. The volume of G, public sector consumption, is expected to be unchanged in 1990, while the significant increase in the *price* of this component of GNP reflects the continuing growth of public sector rates of pay.

One of the most difficult components of GNP to forecast is personal consumption expenditure, C. While it may be possible to anticipate the trend in private sector incomes with some accuracy, the link between income and consumption is the savings ratio, which is volatile and subject to many measurement errors. There is some feeling, for example, that the growth in C foreseen by the ESRI in the data contained in Table 2.4 may be on the low side because with the improving economic climate the personal savings ratio may fall and personal consumption grow even more rapidly than anticipated by the ESRI's forecasters. By the time this book is published, the reader should be in possession of more up-to-date information on this point!

*Table 2.4*

**Forecasting the components of GNP for 1989 and 1990**

|  |  | 1989 forecast £m | % change in 1990 Volume | Price | 1990 forecast £m |
|---|---|---|---|---|---|
| C | Consumer expenditure | 13,510 | 4.75 | 3.75 | 14,672 |
| G | Public net current expenditure | 3,693 | 0.0 | 6.0 | 3,915 |
| I | Domestic capital formation | 4,127 | 12.0 | 4.0 | 4,805 |
| X | Exports | 16,028 | 7.25 | 3.75 | 17,845 |
| S | Change in stocks | -30 |  |  | 100 |
| FD | Final demand | 37,328 | 6.5 | 4.0 | 41,337 |
| *less* |  |  |  |  |  |
| M | Imports | 13,751 | 9.0 | 3.25 | 15,486 |
| GDP | Gross domestic product | 23,577 | 5.0 | 4.5 | 25,851 |
| *less* |  |  |  |  |  |
| F | Net factor payments | 2,902 | 6.75 | 3.75 | 3,213 |
| GNP | Gross national product | 20,675 | 4.75 | 4.5 | 22,638 |

*[handwritten note: Public Sector Pay Rates.]*

*Source: Quarterly Economic Commentary*, November 1989, Table A, p. 7

# 2.9 Conclusion

In this chapter we have explored Ireland's economic performance during the 1980s using the data published by the Central Statistics Office on national income and expenditure. Among the key points that have been presented are:

- The concepts of NI and NNP at market prices and factor cost

- The distinctions between GDP, GNP and GNDI

- The division of GNDI between savings and investment

- The role of the balance of payments in financing domestic investment

27

- How *constant price* series are constructed

- The importance of the terms of trade adjustment

- The impact of population growth on living standards

- The importance of the distribution of national income

- Ireland's economic underperformance during the 1980s

- Some of the issues related to the preparation of short-term forecasts.

# Notes

1. The convention is to *add* F, which will be positive if there is an net inflow, negative if there is an net outflow.

2. Which does not include the public sector's *transfer payments* (pensions, unemployment benefits, etc. and national debt interest paid to Irish residents).

3. Investment includes the value of changes in stocks, a small but important item for which seperate data are provided in NIE. A fall in the level of stocks is a negative contribution to investment, a rise is a positive contribution.

4. John D. FitzGerald, *The Determinants of Irish Imports*, The Economic and Social Research Institute, Research Paper 135, October 1987.

5. Some of the pioneering work on this topic was done by the Irish econometrician R. C. Geary (1896-1983), who made important contributions to the theory of national income accounting and index numbers while director of the Central Statistics Office in Dublin and of the United Nations Statistical Office in New York. For a detailed discussion of alternative approaches to adjusting for the terms of trade see Aidan Punch, "Real Gross National Disposable Income Adjusted for the Terms of Trade: 1970-1984", *Quarterly Economic Commentary*, April, 1986.

6. The export price index is used to deflate F in years when the net flow is negative, the import price index in years when it is positive, on the grounds that a net outflow can be used to purchase imports and a net outflow has to be paid for with increased exports.

7. The phrase income *per capita* is firmly embedded in economics, even though it does not mean '"per person" but refers to a legal method of transferring property. The correct Latin for "per person" is *per caput* !

8. The (X - M) component of this is the trade balance, which is widely quoted because timely data are available for it. Even more up-to-date information can be obtained for the balance of merchandise trade, which relates to the physical (i. e. excluding services) components of X and M. A small adjustment should be made to take account of capital transfers from the rest of the world, which are not included in R, but are part of BoP. We have ignored this in the text.

9. If there were no capital movements, either private or offical, then the BoP  deficit/surplus would be reflected in changes in the country's *reserves of foreign exchange*. This was more or less the case in the 1950s.

10. Estimates are actually made of the "normal" amount of smuggling. Because there are so many mysterious outflows in the net residual it has become known as the *black hole*. The Irish balance of payments data are given in Table 30 of NIE.

11. Two items complicate this identity in the NIE tables. Net foreign capital transfers (e. g., the grants we received when we joined the European Monetary System) are added to BoP and an adjustment for stock appreciation is made to NNS to remove the effect of changes in the price of non-agricultural stocks.

12. These ideas were discussed by the National Planning Board in their report, *Proposals for Plan*, published in April 1984 against the background of the extraordinary BoP deficits of the early 1980s.

13. In Ireland this problem is complicated by the further consideration that personal consumption is it self a residual and bears the brunt of errors in the measurement of the other components of expenditure on GNP.

14. The disaggregated data for savings are unadjusted for stock appreciation and therefore in the early 1980s contained a significant inflationary component. For a discussion of the behaviour of savings in Ireland, see D. Rodney Thom, *The Taxation of Savings*, Dublin: Foundation for Fiscal Studies, Research Report No. 2, October, 1988.

15. This is generally a legal requirement of entitlement to benefit or assistance. The reality is more complex. A further complication arises from the fact that the unemployment data refer to individuals, but the basic consuming unit in the economy is the household. Some unemployed individuals live in households where other individuals are employed.

16. See B. Nolan and T. Callan, "Measuring Trends in Poverty Over Time, Some Robust Results for Ireland 1980-87", *The Economic and Social Review*, Vol. 20, No. 4, July, 1989, p. 329-352.

17. This has meant, of course, that we have not caught up with the continental European countries that have enjoyed more rapid growth than Britain.

Chapter 3

# *Introduction to the Theory of Income Determination and Fiscal Policy*

## 3.1 Introduction

As discussed in Chapter 1, the primary objectives of macroeconomic policy are:

1. to achieve a high growth rate in real output or national income
2. to achieve a low level of unemployment
3. to achieve a low and stable inflation rate.

All three objectives should be aimed at simultaneously, but, however difficult it is to hit any one of them, to hit all three simultaneously can be an exceptionally difficult task.

There are no *absolute* levels of GNP growth, inflation and unemployment which can be set as hard and fast targets for an economy. We saw in Chapter 2 that over the long run the Irish economy has achieved a growth rate of less than 3% a year in real terms - a disappointing performance and one which it should be possible to improve on through the choice of suitable *supply side* policies. Perhaps the ideal with respect to inflation would be a zero rate, that is, *price stability*, but no country has attained this for any length of time since the Second World War. We have come to think of an inflation rate of 3% as acceptably low, but we should bear in mind that if prices rise at this rate over a 23-year period they will double. Over a century the price index would rise from 100 to 1922! Even modest rates of inflation entail serious long-term adjustments.

Defining a target for unemployment is the most difficult, and controversial, aspect of formulating economic policy. We are no longer sure what we mean by *full employment*. Under the conditions that obtain in most countries, the idea of completely eliminating unemployment is unrealistic: there has to be some *frictional* unemployment as people move between jobs and the economy adjusts to changes in the pattern of demand. But what is an *acceptable* level of frictional unemployment? Clearly this depends on a host of considerations, such as the size of the economy, the density of its population (a small labour force distributed over

30

a large area is likely to have higher frictional unemployment than a more compact, high-density population), the level of social welfare payments and the way the housing market functions, as well as on the skills and motivation of the working population. In the US, for example, it is now accepted that with about 5% of the labour force unemployed the economy is close to full employment and there are signs that the labour market is beginning to overheat due to shortages of many types of workers. Even in Britain, with 6% of the labour force still unemployed, there is clear evidence that shortages of some types of workers in some areas are constraining the growth in the economy.

In Ireland a rate of unemployment in the region of 5% seemed very normal throughout the 1960s, but since the recessions of 1974/5 and 1981/2 a much higher rate of unemployment has prevailed and the rate of unemployment has not come back down to the levels that obtained in the past. We shall return to the factors behind these developments in Chapters 4 and 7. At this stage, it is enough to point out the present unemployment rate of 17% is clearly unacceptable and bringing it down must have a high priority in Irish economic policy.

Finally, it is important to draw attention to the fact that the goals of economic policy (growth, price stability and employment) are interrelated and may be in conflict with each other. Faster growth will usually tend to increase employment and lower unemployment, but progress towards these objectives could jeopardise the third objective, price stability. As unemployment falls, there is increasing pressure on wages and other costs of production; employers are anxious to recruit more workers, and willing to pay above the odds to do so. They believe that it is possible to pass their higher costs of production on to consumers in a buoyant market. The result could be inflation, even a rising rate of inflation. A key question that has confronted economic policy makers again and again is: how much additional inflation should be tolerated in return for additional growth? In answering this question, attention has to be paid to the underlying issue of whether the growth that is achieved by allowing inflationary pressures to build up is sustainable. It could be argued that price stability and growth are not really conflicting objectives after all because the best foundation for long-run growth is confidence in the currency and this will only come about in an environment of low inflation.

We shall return to the issue of the existence of a *trade-off* between the objectives of price stability and growth, in the long-run and in the short-run, when we discuss the Phillips Curve in Chapter 8.

A further complication is that the achievement of the objectives is subject to a balance of payments constraint (the balance of payments is discussed in Chapters 2 and 9). Deficits or surpluses on the balance of payments can result in exchange rate depreciation or appreciation and this in turn will have an effect on output, unemployment and inflation. The international dimension of macroeconomics adds considerably to the complexity of the analysis.

# 3.2 Macroeconomic Models

The standard approach to analysing the goals of macroeconomic policy is to develop or construct a *model* of how macroeconomic variables interact. There are a large number of macroeconomic variables, for example, wages (W), government expenditure (G), interest rates (r), the money supply ($M^S$), unemployment (U) and the exchange rate (E). The idea is to theorise about how these variables are related and then see how certain *policy variables*, such as government expenditure, can be used to improve the economy's performance. Put another way, the objective is to take a complex economy and attempt to reduce its workings down to a few manageable principles.

*Note:*

*Economic variables are usually denoted by some letter or symbol. It is a good idea to open up a glossary of terms accompanied by the symbol for each of the variables mentioned in the text.*

All models are *theories* which can be used for policy analysis if:

1. the model can explain economic events. The model is not much use if, for example, it cannot explain why a particular country is experiencing high unemployment.
2. the model can help analyse the effectiveness of alternative remedies for current problems.

Macroeconomic theory has developed at a rapid pace in recent years with the literature becoming increasingly fragmented and inaccessible to the general reader. While it is probably true to say that economists now know more than they ever did about the way the economy works, there is still no clear-cut consensus on some of the more important issues. Broadly speaking, there are two main schools of thought: Keynesians and monetarists. However, even here, there is no clear-cut divide between these two schools of thought as a number of important issues continue to be unresolved and highly controversial.

The model developed in this chapter is based on the so-called *Keynesian model* named after the British economist J. M. Keynes (1883-1946). Keynes first published his theory in 1936 as the *General Theory of Employment, Interest and Money*.[1] That book is still very relevant not just for the concepts it introduced but because it remains controversial. The Keynesian model provides the basis of much of the macroeconomic literature today.

The approach we have taken in developing the Keynesian model is initially to make a number of simplifying assumptions. As these assumptions are dropped the

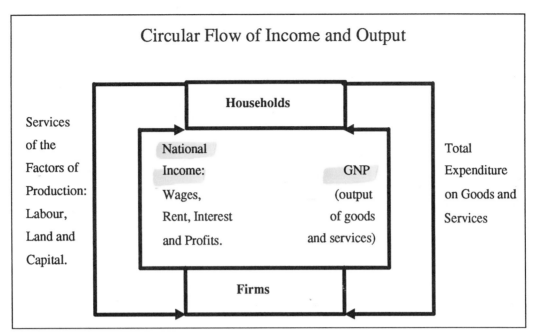

Circular Flow of Income and Output

Households

Services
of the
Factors of
Production:
Labour,
Land and
Capital.

National
Income:
Wages,
Rent, Interest
and Profits.

GNP
(output
of goods
and services)

Total
Expenditure
on Goods and
Services

Firms

Figure 3.1

complexity of the model increases, but it gains in realism and relevance to the real world.

# .3 The Basic Keynesian Model

The *Theory of Income Determination* is essentially the Keynesian theory of how the level of output or income is determined in the economy. One way of introducing the model is to start with the *circular flow of income* model (this model was briefly discussed in Chapter 1). The circular flow model was originally suggested by a court physician to Louis XV, Francois Quesnay (1694-1774) and it is outlined in Figure 3.1.

There are two units in the economy: households and firms. Consider first the two loops on the left hand side of the diagram. It is assumed that Households own the *factors of production*: land, labour and capital which are made available to Firms in return for rent, wages, interest and profit. The sum of rent, wages, interest and profit equals national income. In microeconomic terms (ignoring land and capital), the two loops on the left hand side are equivalent to somebody going to work and receiving a salary or wage at the end of the week for his or her labour.

Consider now the two loops on the right hand side. Firms, using the factors of production, produce the total output of goods and services (GNP) in the economy.

We do not go into detail about firms' production techniques. Inputs of land, labour and capital simply enter a *black box* called the *production function* and outputs of goods and services emerge on the other side. To complete the circle, households, using national income, purchase the goods and services produced by firms (total expenditure).

The essential message of the simplified circular flow diagram given in Figure 3.1 is that, in the aggregate, we consume what we produce. A person goes to work and gets paid a wage. That person can then use his wages (income) to purchase a range of goods and services.

The circular flow diagram highlights several important relationships in macroeconomic theory and provides the key as to how to the authorities could influence output, income, unemployment and inflation. Suppose, for example, that the economy was operating at less than full capacity so that the growth rate in output and income is stagnant and unemployment is relatively high. How could output and income be increased? The Keynesian answer to this question is to increase total expenditure which is situated on the outer loop, right hand side, of Figure 3.1.

The process is as follows. An increase in total expenditure will be followed by an increase in output (GNP). If people are buying more goods and services there is an incentive for firms to increase production. Firms will recognise the greater level of expenditure as order books fill up and stocks fall. Profit maximising firms will respond to the additional expenditure by producing more goods and services. However, to increase output, firms must use more factors of production. In the short run, land and capital are relatively fixed and firms will necessarily use more labour (thereby reducing unemployment). The money received from selling the extra goods and services will be used to compensate households for the extra labour used. As a result of an increase in total expenditure, both output and income rise and unemployment falls.

*Note:*

*It does not matter at this stage how total expenditure is increased. This issue will be examined below.*

The circular flow diagram therefore suggests that the following variables are closely related:

(1)   NI $\leftrightarrow$ GNP = total expenditure (TE)

Reading (1) from right to left:

$\uparrow$ TE $\rightarrow$ $\uparrow$ GNP $\rightarrow$ $\uparrow$ NI

*Notes:*
*1. $\uparrow$ and $\downarrow$ indicate an increase and a decrease respectively and $\rightarrow$ means "leads to". The symbol*

$\leftrightarrow$ indicates that the variables are closely related. In the above example, an increase in GNP will be quickly followed by a rise in NI. We will use this notation throughout the text.

2. In the discussion on the national income accounts in Chapter 2, GNP equalled total expenditure by definition. As a result, there could never be an excess demand or supply for goods and services. Implicit in that discussion was the notion of a "desired" level of stocks. If output equalled expenditure and stocks were at the desired level, the goods market was in equilibrium. The discussion here takes stock levels into account. If expenditure exceeds output, stocks will fall below the desired level, which is a signal for firms to increase production. It is in this sense that there is an excess demand for goods and services. Similarly, if output exceeds expenditure, stocks are above the desired level and this is a signal for firms to cut production. There is now an excess supply of goods and services. It is the actual level of stocks in relation to the desired level that enables us to speak of an excess supply or an excess demand for GNP. We return to this point later in the text.

Consider now the total expenditure variable in more detail. As pointed out in Chapter 2, total expenditure can be divided into five categories:

1. Consumer expenditure       (C)
2. Investment                 (I)
3. Government expenditure      (G)
4. Exports                     (X)
5. Imports                     (M)

In short:

Total expenditure $\equiv$ C + I + G + X - M

where the symbol $\equiv$ denotes an identity. Inserting this classification of total expenditure into (1) above gives:

NI $\leftrightarrow$ GNP = TE $\equiv$ C + I + G + X - M

Consider again the steps involved in increasing output and income. If government expenditure (G) is increased, by definition, total expenditure (TE) must also increase but the level of GNP has not as yet changed. In effect the government has created an excess demand for goods and services.

As before, firms will recognize the excess demand through falling levels of stocks and respond by producing the extra goods and services (GNP) demanded. However, in order to do so, firms must hire more labour, so unemployment will fall. To compensate households for the extra labour, more wages will be paid (NI increases).

In summary:

$$\uparrow G \quad \rightarrow \quad \uparrow TE \quad \rightarrow \quad \uparrow GNP \quad \rightarrow \quad \downarrow U \rightarrow \uparrow NI$$

*Note:*

*This sequence assumes that more labour can be hired. We shall see that a lot depends on this assumption and the underlying model of labour supply.*

When government uses its own expenditure (or/and taxation) to influence total expenditure, it is referred to as *fiscal policy* (in this case, an expansionary policy). This type of policy raises a number of questions such as how government spending is financed and how it is spent. These questions will be discussed below. The government could also influence total expenditure by attempting to increase C, I or X or to reduce M. It can, however, be difficult to change these variables. For example, how do we get foreigners to buy more Irish goods and services (X)? For that reason governments usually concentrate on the component of total expenditure that is directly under their control, that is government expenditure (G) and/or taxation (T).

# 3.4 Aggregate Supply and Aggregate Demand

*Expenditure is demand.* When you spend your money on a particular good or service you contribute to the demand for that good or service. In macroeconomics, total expenditure is referred to as *aggregate demand* (AD). This is one of the key concepts in macroeconomics. Similarly, GNP is the supply of goods or services and is referred to as *aggregate supply* (AS). These two concepts, AD and AS, lie at the heart of the Keynesian model.

The first step in outlining basic Keynesian economics is to develop a graphical representation of AD and AS. Before doing so however, recall from Chapter 2 that nominal GNP is equal to the price level (P) multiplied by real GNP. That is:

Nominal GNP = P * real GNP

*Note:*
*\* indicates "multiplied by".*

In appendix 1, we show how real GNP can be calculated given data for nominal GNP and the price level.

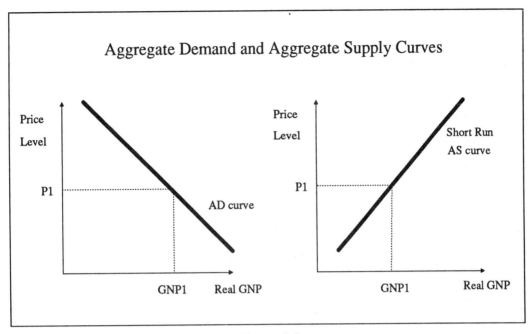

Figure 3.2

In Figure 3.2, the price level (henceforth P) and real GNP are measured on the vertical and horizontal axis respectively. The aggregate demand (AD) curve is shown as downward sloping, indicating that a fall in P will increase the demand for the volume of goods and services and vice versa. The aggregate supply (AS) curve is upward sloping indicating that an increase in P will increase the real supply of goods and services.

*Note:*
*When we speak of real output we mean the volume or quantity of goods and services produced or consumed.*

It is not possible at this stage to give a complete explanation of the factors underlying these two curves. While an upward sloping supply curve and a downward sloping demand curve will be familiar to students who have already studied microeconomics, the factors influencing the AS and AD curves are quite different from those encountered in microeconomics. For example, monetary variables, which are introduced in Chapters 5 and 6, have an important bearing on both the slope and the location of the AD curve. We can, however, give a brief, somewhat intuitive explanation as to why the AD and AS curves slope downwards and upwards respectively.

Consider first the AS curve. On the supply side of the economy, an increase in output prices (P) will increase firms' profits if input prices, and in particular money wages, remain constant. Higher profits, in turn, act as an incentive for firms to increase the volume of output. As a consequence, as P increases, the volume of output supplied increases and the AS curve slopes upward.

*Note:*

*A firm's profit is equal to total revenue minus total cost. An increase in output prices therefore increases total revenue and profits. The crucial assumption is that input prices, and wages in particular, remain constant as output prices change. This assumption is certainly not valid in the long run. It would imply that people were willing to work for a falling real wage.*

The AS curve is drawn for a given level of total costs or input prices. If these costs change, for a given output/price level, then the AS curve will shift to the right or to the left. For example, if the student selects a certain level of real GNP, he or she can read up and bounce off the AS curve to get the associated P level. If costs now increase and firms pass this on to customers in the form of higher P, the new P/real GNP combination is a point above the original AS curve. This point indicates the position of the new AS curve. In general, an increase in wages or any other input price, or a fall in productivity, will shift the AS curve upwards. Conversely, a fall in wages or any other input price, or an increase in productivity, will shift the AS curve downwards.

*Note:*

*Productivity is the amount of output produced by a unit of input. If productivity increases because of improved technology, for example, more output is produced from a given amount of inputs. In other words, costs are reduced and this is reflected in a downward movement of the AS curve. Conversely, lower productivity implies higher costs, and the AS curve shifts upwards.*

Consider now the AD curve. On the demand side of the economy, a fall in prices relative to foreign prices increases competitiveness and this in turn will increase exports and reduce imports. As a result, a fall in P leads to an increase in the demand for real goods and services. Conversely, an increase in P leads to a fall in the demand for goods and services.

*Note:*

*A change in prices may also affect aggregate demand through a real balance effect. The argument is that a fall in prices will increase individuals' real wealth and this in turn will lead to an increase in consumer expenditure (C). Conversely, an increase in prices lowers real wealth and reduces consumer expenditure. This real balance effect is sometimes referred to as the Pigou effect after the British economist, and contemporary of Keynes at Cambridge, A.C. Pigou.*

Assuming that P is constant, an increase in C, I, G or X or a fall in M will shift the AD curve to the right and vice versa. For example, suppose that P is constant;

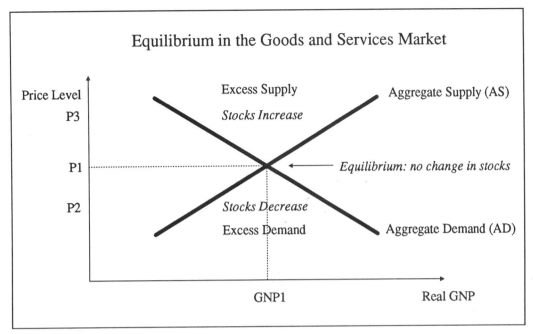

Figure 3.3

an increase in I will increase real output demanded and this is reflected in the diagram by a shift to the right of the AD curve. The student should experiment by drawing AD curves for different levels of expenditure to convince him or herself that this is the case.

In Figure 3.3, the AS and AD curves are superimposed on each other in order to give the equilibrium price (P1) and real output (GNP1) combination. At this point, actual stock levels equal desired stock levels. If the price level is greater than P1, say P3, AS exceeds AD and there is an excess supply of goods and services. In this case, stocks will increase above the desired level. Firms will respond by cutting production and lowering prices. The economy will move back towards equilibrium. Similarly, if the price level is below P1, say P2, AS is less than AD and there is excess demand. Firms will recognise the excess demand as stocks will be falling below the desired level and they will respond by increasing production and raising prices. Again the economy moves towards equilibrium. Stock changes therefore act as a signal to firms as to whether production should be increased or reduced. If stocks are above or below the desired level, firms respond by reducing or increasing production. It is firms in response to changes in stocks that move the economy 𝒥17 towards equilibrium. At the same time, excess demand is likely to lead to a rise in the price level, while excess supply will put downward pressure on prices.

Figure 3.4 illustrates how shifts in the AS and AD curves affect P and real GNP. In the case of the AD curve, prices and output move in the same direction. For example, a shift of the AD curve to the right increases P and increases real GNP. In

39

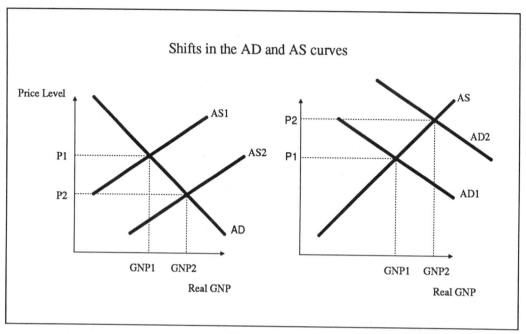

Figure 3.4

contrast, a shift of the AS curve leads to opposite movements in prices and output. For example, a shift to the right reduces P and increases real GNP.

A policy that shifts the AS curve to the right may be regarded as highly desirable because a lower price level is combined with higher real output. Equally, a policy or event that shifts the AS curve to the left has a particularly harmful effect on the economy. The resultant combination of rising prices and falling output has been labelled *stagflation*. A leftward shift of the AS curve is what occurred when the price of energy inputs rose sharply in the 1970s.

It should be noted that the relative changes in P and real GNP depend crucially on the slope or steepness of the AS and AD curves. For example, if the AD curve is relatively flat, a shift to the right of the AS curve will result in a large increase in real GNP and a small change in prices. On the other hand, if the AD curve is steep, a shift of the AS curve to the right leads to a large fall in prices and little change in real GNP.

One of the important insights of Keynesian economics is that the slope of the AS curve is *not uniform*. In particular, it is argued that the AS curve is relatively flat at low levels of real GNP and relatively steep when the economy is approaching full capacity or full employment. At full employment, the AS curve will be vertical. Figure 3.5 gives an example of a *kinked* AS curve. When unemployment is high and there is a great deal of excess capacity, the AS curve is relatively flat or elastic. A shift in the AD curve to the right will lead to an increase in real GNP and leave prices relatively unchanged. This is shown in the diagram as a movement in AD from AD1

40

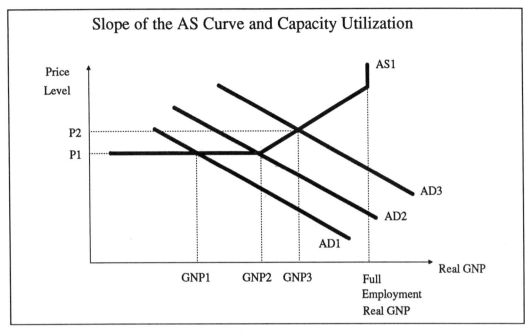

Slope of the AS Curve and Capacity Utilization

Figure 3.5

to AD2. The reason is that with a great deal of excess capacity, firms can easily produce the extra goods and services demanded and there is little scope for price increases. In this situation the level of output is said to be *demand determined.*

However, as the economy approaches *full employment*, the slope of the AS curve becomes increasingly steep (inelastic). Now price increases accompany any expansion in real output. This is shown in Figure 3.5 as the AD curve shifts from AD2 to AD3. When the economy reaches the full employment point, the AS curve becomes perfectly vertical. In this case, any increase in AD simply increases prices and does not affect real output. The only way to increase output in this situation is through an increase in supply (that is, a rightward shift in AS). This could occur through growth in the labour force and its productivity, technical progress and similar developments.

*Note:*

*The classical school of economics, as opposed to the Keynesian school, argues that the AS curve is vertical. This means that in the long run the economy will always revert back to the full employment level following some disturbance. This theory is based on an automatic adjustment mechanism namely, flexible prices and costs. One implication of this theory is that fiscal policy can not have any long run effect on real GNP. Much of the controversy in modern macroeconomics boils down to a disagreement as to how much of an increase in AD will be reflected in higher real GNP, and how much in higher prices. We examine these issues in detail in Chapter 8.*

41

The increase in prices brought about by a shift of the AD curve is referred to as *demand pull inflation* because aggregate demand is pulling up prices. This is in contrast to *cost push inflation* where increased costs push up prices. A leftward shift of the AS curve due to, for example, higher oil prices, is a example of cost push inflation.

Keynesian economics did not emphasise the AS curve or the supply side of the economy. If the economy was operating at less than full capacity and unemployment was relatively high, the Keynesian solution was to shift the AD curve to the right (using fiscal policy). It was recognised, of course, that the price level would increase as the economy approached full employment (the AS curve would become increasingly steep). The relationship between increasing real GNP (falling unemployment) and rising prices is examined in Chapter 8 under the *Phillips Curve*.

# 3.5 The Multiplier

The concept of the multiplier theory has become an integral part of Keynesian economics. The basic idea is that an increase in any of the components of total expenditure (AD) will raise equilibrium GNP by a *multiple* of the initial increase in AD. The multiplier is simply a *number* that relates the initial change in expenditure to the final change in equilibrium GNP.

The idea of the multiplier increased the appeal of Keynesian theory in the 1950s and 1960s. After all, if the government need only spend £1m in order to boost GNP by some multiple of £1m, it would seem foolish not to do so. But how valid is the concept of the multiplier? And, assuming there is such a thing, how large is it under Irish conditions? To answer these questions we need to explore the derivation of the multiplier in Keynesian theory.

*Table 3.1*

**The multiplier process**

$$\uparrow4 \qquad \uparrow3 \qquad\quad \uparrow2 \quad \uparrow5 \qquad\quad \uparrow1$$
$$NI \leftrightarrow GNP \;=\; AD \equiv C \;+\; I \;+\; G \;+\; X \;-\; M$$

Consider the basic Keynesian model given in Table 3.1. The arrows indicate which direction/athe particular variable moves and the numbers indicate the steps in the sequence of events. The basic objective is to compare an initial increase in government expenditure (G), step 1, with the final change in GNP, step 5.

In the first round, an increase in G (step 1) raises AD (step 2) by definition. There is now an excess demand for goods and services. Assuming the AS curve is not vertical, firms respond to the higher level of demand by producing more goods and services, and GNP (step 3) and NI (step 4) both increase. At the end of this first round the multiplier is 1 as GNP has increased by exactly the initial increase in G. That, however, is not the end of the process. In the *second* round, the increase in NI raises C (step 5) and this sets off further increases in AD, GNP and NI. The main point is that GNP has increased in the second round. The link between income (NI) and consumer expenditure (C) is of crucial importance and is discussed below under the heading of the *consumption function*. The NI-C link is, however, intuitively easy to understand. If a person receives an increase in income he or she will normally increase expenditure. The same is true at the macro or aggregate level. If the nation's income increases, consumption will also increase.

This process will continue into third, fourth and successive rounds because the economy has entered into a rising NI-C spiral. Every increase in NI leads to an increase in C which in turn increases NI and so on. As we explain below, the process will of course come to a halt (otherwise we would all be very rich!).

The multiplier is that number that relates the initial increase in G to the final change in GNP (or NI). Suppose, for example, the initial increase in G was £1m and the final (after all the rounds are taken into account) increase in GNP was £5m, the multiplier is 5.

In short:

$$\uparrow G \rightarrow \uparrow AD \rightarrow \uparrow GNP \rightarrow \uparrow NI$$

In the *second* round:

$$\uparrow NI \rightarrow \uparrow C \rightarrow \uparrow AD \qquad \text{and so on.}$$

# Leakages

The size of the multiplier depends on two links: (1) how much of the increase in NI is passed on through an increase in C and (2) how much of the increase in C is spent on domestically produced goods and services. The size of these links depends on the size of the savings, taxation and import leakages. That is, how much of each round of increases in NI leaks out of the stream of AD into savings, taxation or imports. The greater the overall leakage, the smaller the multiplier. We shall now consider the leakages in turn.

## Savings and consumption

Consider first the relationship between C and NI. This link is subject to a savings and a taxation leakage. If all of the extra income is saved or taxed, expenditure will not increase and there will be no multiplier effect.

Ignoring taxation, the relationship between income and expenditure is given by the consumption function.

$$C = \alpha + MPC * NI$$

where $\alpha$ is the intercept term and MPC is a coefficient known as the *marginal propensity to consume*. The MPC is a positive number equal to or less than one. In short, $0 < MPC \leq 1$. An MPC of 0.9 means that for every £1 increase in income, spending increases by £0.90. If the MPC is 0.7, expenditure increases by £0.70. Closely related to the consumption function is the *savings function*: $S = \psi + MPS * NI$, where $\psi$ is an intercept term and MPS is the *marginal propensity to save*. The MPS also lies between 0 and 1. Because extra income must be spent or saved, the MPC and the MPS must sum to 1. Hence

$$1 = MPC + MPS.$$

*Note:*
*It also follows that* $\psi = -\alpha$.

## Multiplier formulae

Assuming no taxation or imports, the multiplier depends on the MPC (or MPS). The multiplier formula (derived in appendix 2) is:

Over-simplified multiplier formula

---

Multiplier $= 1/(1 - MPC)$

---

*Examples:*

| If | MPC | = | 0.9 | Multiplier | = | 10 |
|----|-----|---|-----|------------|---|----|
| If | MPC | = | 0.8 | Multiplier | = | 5 |
| If | MPC | = | 0.5 | Multiplier | = | 2 |
| If | MPC | = | 1.0 | Multiplier | = | Infinity |

In general:

Change in equilibrium GNP = Multiplier * Initial change in expenditure

Because MPS = 1 - MPC, the multiplier formula can also be written as:

Multiplier = 1/MPS

It is easy to see that the multiplier is large whenever the MPC is large. Put another way, the multiplier is large whenever the MPS (savings) is small. More generally, the multiplier is equal to [1/marginal leakages out of income].

# Taxation

If there is a flat rate of tax on income, the relationship between taxation (T) and NI is given by the *marginal propensity to tax* (MPT). That is: $T = \beta + MPT * NI$, where $\beta$ is the intercept term and $0 < MPT < 1$. Allowing for taxation, the multiplier formula becomes:

Multiplier formula with savings and taxation leakages

---

Multiplier = 1/(MPS + MPT)

---

This formula is derived in appendix 3. It is clear from the formula that the greater the savings and taxation leakage, the smaller the multiplier.

# Imports

The third possible leakage is due to the relationship between NI and imports: $M = \chi + MPM * NI$ where $\chi$ is an intercept term, MPM is the *marginal propensity to import* and $0 < MPM < 1$. If all of the extra spending goes on imports, GNP will not increase. We show in appendix 4 that the multiplier with savings, taxation and import leakages is:

Multiplier formula with savings, taxation and import leakages

---

Multiplier = 1/(MPS + MPT + MPM)

---

It should be noted that the multiplier formula depends on the structure of the macroeconomic model. For example, if C depends on disposable income, rather

45

than gross income (recall from Chapter 2 that, disposable income = gross income - direct taxation), the multiplier formula will be quite different from that given above. We derive this multiplier formula in appendix 5. Similarly, if the model contains a money market, the formula will contain more terms and will be more complex. We do not want to derive all the different formulae here. Instead we wish to discuss the relevance of the multiplier concept for a small open economy such as Ireland.

In the Irish context, a survey of the literature would suggest that MPS = 0.2, MPT = 0.3 and MPM = 0.4 are realistic values for the parameters that enter into the calculation of the multiplier. Inserting these values into the simple formula given above:

Multiplier = $1/(0.2 + 0.3 + 0.4)$ = 1.11

An increase in G (or C, I, X or a reduction in M) of £1m would raise GNP by £1.11m. In a sense, *multiplier* is a misnomer under these conditions. The leakages in the Irish economy are so large that a given change in expenditure will only marginally increase GNP. One of the more attractive aspects to Keynesian economics does not apply in the Irish economy. But, at least on the basis of our survey so far, increased AD *does* increase the equilibrium level of national income. (However, this would not happen if the economy was already at full employment.)

*Note:*

*In appendix 4, we derive the multiplier formula when consumer expenditure depends on disposable income. If the above values for the MPS, MPT and MPM are inserted into this formula, the multiplier is 1.19. This emphasises the point that the actual value for the multiplier depends on the structure of the model as well as on the three marginal propensities.*

In recent years, multiplier analysis has lost much of its prominence in the economic literature. The reason is not simply that large tax and import leakages give rise to small multipliers. Rather, there is the more fundamental question of whether fiscal policy can have any long lasting effect on GNP. In subsequent chapters, we will discuss the *crowding out* effect and the *natural rate of unemployment* theory. In section 3.7 of this chapter we discuss the *Barro-Ricardo Equivalence Proposition*. These theories or propositions, if they are correct, not only further reduce the multiplier, but call into question the effectiveness of fiscal policy in achieving any sustained increase in GNP.

# 5 Stabilisation Policy

The growth of Irish GNP has been very irregular over the years. These fluctuations in the growth rate, with alternating periods of boom and recession, are known as the business cycle. Figure 1.2 in Chapter 1 shows the Irish experience since 1960. One of the principal tenets of Keynesian economics was that fiscal policy could be used to eliminate the business cycle by stabilising the behaviour of GNP over time.

In particular, Keynes emphasised *potential* GNP and argued that fiscal policy (changes in government expenditure and taxation) should be used to keep *actual* GNP close to the potential level. Potential GNP is sometimes referred to as *full employment* GNP. It is that level of output where there is full employment.

*Note:*
*The actual level of unemployment corresponding to full employment is not constant over time or between countries. We shall discuss this issue in the Irish context in Chapter 7.*

In Figure 3.6 the *growth rate* of potential GNP is indicated by the horizontal line. It assumes that the Irish economy is capable of growing by about 3 % a year. Faster growth than this would not be sustainable due to, for example, the emergence of shortages of skilled labour. However, *supply side* policies (e.g. retraining of

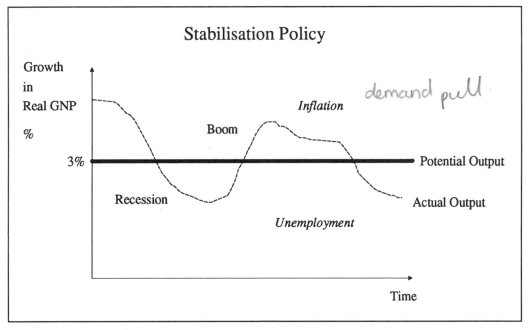

Figure 3.6

47

unskilled unemployed workers) could be used to raise the growth rate of potential GNP.

Actual GNP is shown as swinging above and below the 3% line over time. Since the economy is operating near full capacity along the potential GNP line, demand-pull inflation occurs above the line and unemployment increases below the line. The objective of stabilisation policy is to keep actual GNP as close to the potential level as possible and thereby avoid inflation and unemployment.

Recall that in the short run, with unemployed resources, we assume that GNP is demand determined, and that aggregate demand (AD) is broken down into C + I + G + X - M. A down-swing (recession) or up-swing (boom) can occur if there is a change in any of the components of AD. If, for example, the economy moves into a recession (because of, say, a fall in exports) the government could offset the fall in demand by increasing its own expenditure (G). Alternatively, it could reduce taxes or increase transfer payments. The government will raise aggregate demand by raising G - NT, where NT = taxes less transfers. As a result, AD and GNP might remain close to the potential level. Similarly, if prices are rising because of an excess demand for goods and services, the Keynesian prescription is for the government to cut expenditure or raise taxes.

When Keynes published the *General Theory* in 1936, most of the industrial nations were in the depths of the Great Depression. Unemployment in the US, for example, was over 25%. Some economists at the time were advocating an increase in government expenditure but they lacked a theoretical justification for their views. Classical economics, which dominated the economic literature at the time, could not explain persistent unemployment. Keynesian theory seemed to show how to understand and cure the problem of unemployment.

A stabilisation policy necessarily involves running a fiscal surplus or deficit at various times. However, over the longer term, the government's accounts should be balanced. It is not possible for a government, no more than it is for a household, to run a *permanent* budget deficit. Why this is so is illustrated, in the Irish context, in Chapter 4.

By the late 1980s, scepticism about the scope for an effective stabilisation policy had become widespread. In the following sections we outline some of the reasons for this loss of faith in the original Keynesian view.

# 3.7 Difficulties in Implementing a Stabilisation Policy

In theory, *fine tuning* the economy may seem like a straight-forward idea. In practice, however, it is very difficult if not impossible to implement. The basic problems are (1) inside and outside lags, (2) measuring the magnitude of the government's response, (3) the political dimension and (4) the uncertain effect of fiscal policy on output. Before examining each of these problems, two general points should be borne in mind when discussing fiscal policy.

First, disturbances or shocks to the economy can be either *permanent* or *temporary*. If a disturbance is temporary the government should do nothing. If the government mistakenly identifies a temporary disturbance as a permanent one and reacts by running a budget surplus or deficit, then the effect is to amplify the business cycle instead of dampening it. Secondly, government expenditure financed by borrowing should at all times be productive. The rate of return should at least be sufficient to repay the principal and interest on the debt incurred in financing it. However, there are numerous difficulties in assessing the costs and benefits of government expenditure. Because of this uncertainty, the type of project implemented may have more to do with politics than economics. The impact on the economy of creating thousands of unproductive jobs in the civil service or subsidising unproductive state firms is obviously very different from that of building a new motorway. Increasing transfer payments such as unemployment benefits could have serious implications for the supply of labour in the productive economy. The way in which the government increases AD is an important, but often neglected, aspect of fiscal policy.

## Inside and outside lags

It takes time for the government to respond to movements in the business cycle. First there is a *recognition lag*. Economic statistics are anything up to six months or a year out of date. Hence the government may not be immediately aware that the economy is over-heating or moving into a recession. Secondly, there is a *decision lag*. If the government decides to increase expenditure, a decision has to be taken on the type of project. Should the money be spent on health, education, roads...? Should a committee be set up to examine the options? Thirdly, there is an *implementation lag*. If the government decided to increase expenditure on, say, roads, the project will have to be advertised and it will take time for contractors to submit tenders. On the revenue side, tax changes are generally made only once a year at budget time.

These three types of lags are referred to as *inside* lags and can result in considerable delays. There is also an *outside* lag. That is the time between implementing a policy and when it takes effect on the economy. Typically, the impact on the economy will not be confined to a single year but will be spread out over several years, by which time the underlying conditions may well have made the policy inappropriate.

The upshot of these lags is that the policy could be inappropriate by the time it becomes effective and end up *de-stabilising* the economy. This would happen if the economy suddenly changed direction. For example, if a fall in exports were

49

superseded by a consumer boom, recession would give way to boom before the policies designed to deal with the recession had begun to take effect.

## Quantifying the government's response

A second problem is deciding *how much* demand the government should inject or withdraw. To counter, for example, a fall in investment the policy maker needs rather exact knowledge of both the investment and fiscal multipliers. But calculating multipliers entails estimating a model of the economy. This raises a number of questions. Which model, for example, should be used? Even minor differences between models can result in different policy prescriptions. Also macroeconomic models contain a subjective or judgemental element and this can have an important bearing on the conclusions. Consequently, the magnitude of the policy maker's response to a disturbance can vary considerably depending on the model used for analysis.

*Note:*

*As discussed in Chapter 2, the three most important forecasting institutions in Ireland are the Department of Finance, the Central Bank and the Economic and Social Research Institute (ESRI). A number of private firms also publish forecasts. The really difficult task in forecasting is recognising turning-points, e.g. the move from recession to recovery.* eg. US 1990 Recession?

## The political business cycle

If increases in government expenditure or tax cuts are used to try to influence the voting behaviour of the electorate, there will be a correlation between elections and policy. This can result, as happened in Ireland in 1978, in the implementation of an expansionary fiscal policy when the economy is moving into a boom. In addition, the Irish experience in the early 1980s suggests a ratchet effect in government expenditure. Governments find it easy to increase expenditure but very difficult to reduce it. This does not concur with the principle of stabilisation policy, which requires a balance between strategic surpluses and deficits.

## The uncertain effect of fiscal policy on aggregate demand

As mentioned in section 3.5 of this chapter, basic Keynesian theory suggests that the fiscal multiplier is likely to be very small in Ireland. This clearly reduces the scope for fiscal policy in stabilising the economy. We now discuss two other issues which may further undermine the effectiveness of fiscal policy.

A budget deficit can be financed from four sources. The government can borrow from (1) abroad (2) the Central Bank (3) the licensed banks and (4) the non-bank public. If the government borrows from sources (1) to (3), the money supply in the economy is increased. This form of borrowing is referred to as *government monetary financing (GMF)*. If the government borrows from the non-bank public the money supply is not affected. Borrowing from this source is called *debt financing*.

The impact of an expansionary fiscal policy on aggregate demand depends crucially on whether the deficit is financed through an expansion of the money supply or through borrowing. Monetary financing will be examined in Chapter 6 in the context of monetary policy. Here we mention two issues relating to debt financing. First there is the problem of *crowding-out*. Briefly, debt financing involves the government selling bonds to the public. The difficulty is that the sale of bonds can result in higher interest rates and this in turn may reduce private sector investment. In terms of the components of aggregate demand, the increase in G or cut in taxes has led to a fall in I. Government expenditure has crowded out private sector investment. If this is the case, the overall impact of fiscal policy on aggregate demand will be even smaller than is suggested by a multiplier of 0.9! This issue is examined in detail in Chapter 6.

The second issue relates to the effect of debt financing on consumer expenditure and the so-called *Barro-Ricardo Equivalence Proposition*. Suppose the government lowers taxes and finances the deficit by selling bonds to the public. Consumers' holdings of bonds will increase. If consumers regard the bonds as wealth, then it is possible that consumer expenditure will increase. This will happen because wealth is an important determinant of consumer spending.

However, in calculating wealth, consumers may make an adjustment for future tax liabilities. Given that taxes must be raised some time in the future in order to retire the debt (permanent deficits are not possible), the lower taxes may be seen as only temporary. In other words, consumers may take a life-cycle or even inter-generational perspective on the issue and in calculating their wealth realise that the increase in income to-day will have to be repaid sometime in the future. Over the longer term, wealth has not increased. Consumers may therefore save the current gain in income and not increase their expenditure.

*Note:*

*It is possible to take the argument a stage further and argue that consumers expected the debt to be retired in some future generation. In this case, the tax cut could be regarded as permanent as the future generation will repay the debt. Consumers' wealth has therefore increased and so will consumer expenditure. This line of argument, however, assumes that consumers are not particularly concerned about the future generation. But people do save for their children, which indicates that they are concerned about posterity. Hence, even on an inter-generation basis, it is possible that people save the tax-induced increase in income. The increase in wealth is perceived to be temporary and saving is increased to provide for the essential day of reckoning.*

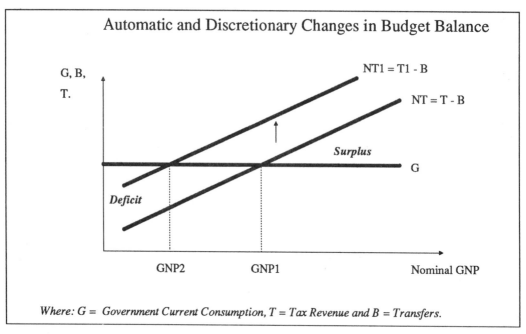

**Automatic and Discretionary Changes in Budget Balance**

G, B, T.

$NT1 = T1 - B$

$NT = T - B$

Surplus

G

Deficit

GNP2        GNP1                    Nominal GNP

Where: G = *Government Current Consumption, T = Tax Revenue and B = Transfers.*

Figure 3.7

The effect of debt financing on consumer expenditure was first raised by the classical economist David Ricardo in the nineteenth century (who discounted its practical significance) and more recently by the Harvard economist Robert Barro. The proposition is clearly of some importance in assessing the impact of fiscal policy on aggregate demand. If consumers react to a budget deficit/surplus by increasing/decreasing savings, the impact of fiscal policy on the economy is further reduced. In this case, changes in (G - NT) are offset by changes in C and have no net effect on AD. We present some relevant evidence for Ireland in Chapter 4.

# 3.8 Full Employment Budget

There are two *built-in stabilisers* which have a cushioning effect on the business cycle. First, the *income tax system* makes people pay more tax as nominal income rises. Moreover, a progressive income tax intensifies this effect. People who were previously liable at, say, a 48% tax rate become liable at the 56% rate as income increases. This is referred to as *bracket creep* and occurs whenever tax brackets are not indexed to inflation. Over the business cycle, as the economy expands and nominal income increases, the government automatically withdraws more money from the system. Conversely, during a recession the fall in disposable income is less than the fall in national income.

*1. The revenue buoyancy effect of the tax system on growth is known as "fiscal drag".*
*2. An "inflation tax" occurs when inflation increases nominal income and pushes people into a higher tax bracket if these are not adjusted.*

Secondly, government *transfer (social welfare) payments* automatically change with movements in economic activity and the unemployment rate. If the economy moves into a recession, government transfer payments automatically increase. The effect is to dampen the business cycle.

The effect of the income tax system and transfer payments on the government's budget is illustrated in Figure 3.7. The diagram shows government expenditure and *net taxes* (tax revenue minus transfers) on the vertical axis and nominal GNP on the horizontal axis. Government expenditure is assumed constant as output changes and is therefore represented as a horizontal line. The net taxes line, (NT), on the other hand, is positively sloped indicating an increase in NT as output rises and vice versa. At GNP1, the budget is balanced as G = NT. To the left of GNP1 there is a budget deficit and to the right a budget surplus. It is clear from the diagram that changes in GNP can automatically result in budget deficits or surpluses even if government expenditure is fixed.

In Figure 3.7 we also distinguish between an *automatic* and a *discretionary* change in the budget balance. An increase in net taxes from NT to NT1 due to a tax increase or a reduction in transfers moves the NT curve to the left. The budget will now be balanced at a lower level of nominal GNP.

Suppose the government decides to follow a policy of "balancing the budget". The correct budget to balance is the "full employment budget" (also referred to as the structural, high-employment or cyclically-adjusted budget). That is, the government should choose the levels of tax rates and expenditure that results in a balanced budget when the economy is at full employment. At all other levels of national income the government should allow for the effect on the budget of the built-in stabilisers. A policy of balancing the "full employment budget" means there should only be "cyclical deficits". Discretionary or deliberate deficits would be avoided. Hence in times of recession there should be a budget deficit and a surplus in boom periods. This will tend to dampen the business cycle.

# 9 Taxation and the Supply Side of the Economy

Changes in taxation can affect the demand side of the economy by influencing the components of total expenditure, most notably consumer expenditure and private sector investment. However, some recent literature on taxation has argued that

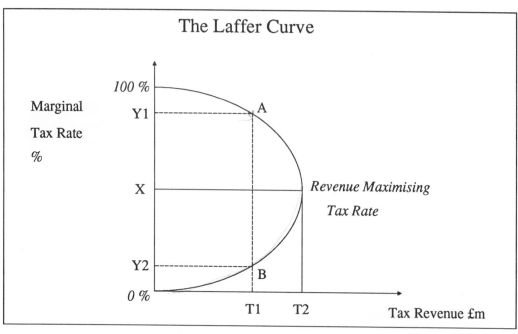

Figure 3.8

taxation will also affect the supply side of the economy. The reason is that taxation affects the *incentive* to work and this in turn affects output and income. This line of argument can lead to the attractive proposition that tax cuts can increase, not decrease, tax revenue.

Figure 3.8 shows the *Laffer Curve* (named after the Californian economist Arthur Laffer, who apparently drew the curve on a napkin in a Washington restaurant to explain a point to a reporter), which depicts the relationship between the marginal tax rate (vertical axis) and tax revenue (horizontal axis). There are two points on the vertical axis where tax revenue is zero, the 0% tax rate and the 100% tax rate. In the latter case, all income is taken in tax so that there is no incentive to work and consequentially tax revenue is zero. Between these two extremes, it is argued, tax revenue first increases and then declines as the marginal tax rate is raised.

The diagram indicates a tax rate (X) where tax revenue is maximised (the revenue-maximising tax rate). If the tax rate is anywhere above this rate, a lowering of the tax rate will generate extra tax revenue. For example, if the government were to lower the tax rate from $Y_1$ to the X rate, tax revenue would increase from $T_1$ to $T_2$. The Laffer Curve also suggests that the same amount of tax revenue can be obtained at high or low tax rates. Tax rates $Y_1$ and $Y_2$ in Figure 3.8, for example, generate the same tax revenue, $T_1$.

While the importance of tax incentives has gained increased recognition in macroeconomic policy (notably under the Reagan administration in the US), the ideas underlying the Laffer Curve remain very controversial. There are a number of reasons why tax cuts may not have the predicted effect. It is possible, for example, that lower taxes might encourage people to work less for the same level of net pay. In other words, people may prefer to enjoy more leisure rather than more income. *Unemp, High?* Alternatively, people could opt for some in-between combination of more leisure and more pay.

A more fundamental point is that the reduction in taxes has to boost output to a level where total tax revenue (at lower tax rates) more than compensates for the initial loss of tax revenue. Suppose, for example, that national income is £10,000m and the tax rate is 35%. Total tax revenue is initially £3,500m. If the government lowers the tax rate to 30%, total tax revenue falls to £3,000m. National income will now have to increase to £11,667m before tax revenue returns to its initial level (£11,667m * 30% = £3,500m). But this represents a 14.2% increase in national income, and this large an expansion may not be forthcoming in response to the tax cut. While there may be particular sectors of the economy where tax cuts increase tax revenue, it is by no means certain, even at very high levels of taxation, that this will happen in the overall macroeconomy. However the openness of the Irish economy does imply that we cannot afford to move too far out of line from UK tax rates. High excise tax rates on spirits and petrol led to serious cross-border flows in the mid-1980s. At lower tax rates more was spent in the Republic and revenue rose. There is now a serious loss of qualified people to the UK and the US, encouraged by the low rates of income taxes in those countries. These effects of higher taxation are consistent with the basic idea underlying the Laffer Curve.

# 10 Debt Management

We have seen how Keynesian theory assigns an important role to budget deficits as an instrument of stabilisation policy. We shall now consider the important issue of how these deficits are financed. Table 3.2 shows a summary statement of the Irish government accounts for 1989. The overall budget is divided into current and capital accounts. The essential difference between these two accounts lies in the type of expenditure. Current expenditure is "day to day" expenditure where no fixed asset is created. The public sector pay bill is part of current expenditure. Capital expenditure, on the other hand, creates a fixed asset such as an improved road or a new school. The distinction is, of course, an accounting convention and does not correspond with the productive/unproductive distinction an economist would make. Some current expenditure is more productive than some capital expenditure, for example, paying doctors' salaries compared with building an uneconomic fertiliser factory.

In 1989 the government had a deficit on both the current and capital accounts.

*Table 3.2*

**Government current and capital budgets: 1989**

| | | | £m |
|---|---|---|---|
| A. *Current budget* | | | |
| | 1. Expenditure | | 8,019 |
| | 2. Revenue | | 7,756 |
| | Tax | 7,443 | |
| | Non-tax | 313 | |
| | 3. *Current budget deficit* | | *263* |
| | | | |
| B. *Capital budget* | | | |
| | 4. Expenditure | | 1,433 |
| | 5. Revenue | | 1,217 |
| | 6. *Capital budget deficit* | | *216* |
| | | | |
| C. | 7. Exchequer borrowing requirement (EBR) | | 479 |
| | 8. EBR as a % of GNP | | 2.4% |

*Source*: Exchequer Returns, 1990

The sum of these two deficits (line 7) is referred to as the *exchequer borrowing requirement (EBR)*. This is the amount of money the government had to borrow in 1989 to make ends meet. Line 8 in Table 3.2 shows the EBR as a percentage of GNP.

As was pointed out in section 3.7, the EBR can be financed from four sources: abroad, the Central Bank, the licensed banks and the non-bank public. Table 3.3 shows the composition of borrowing in 1989. All of the funding came from abroad as foreign investors purchased IR£1,369m of Irish government stock (offical foreign borrowing was only IR£29m). In contrast, the relaxation in exchange controls in early 1989 encouraged both the banks and the non-bank public to sell IR£688m of Irish government stock and move the proceeds to overseas markets. However, this outflow of funds was more than offset by the capital inflow due to foreign residents and the "over-funding" of the EBR enabled the government to reduce Central Bank debt by IR£202m.

Government borrowing from abroad, the Central Bank or the licensed banks is referred to as government monetary financing (GMF), because borrowing from these sources increases the money supply. When the government borrows from the

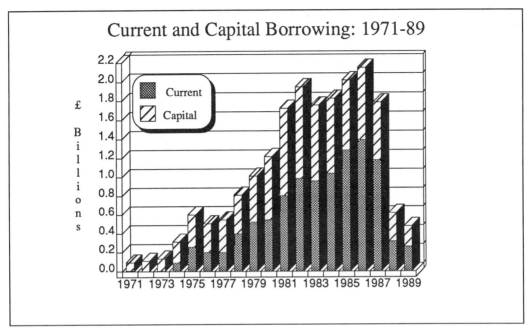

Figure 3.9

non-bank public (pension funds, life assurance companies, the general public...etc) the money supply is not affected. We return to this issue in Chapters 6 and 12.

Allowing for repayments of principal, the sum of each year's EBR gives the stock of national debt at any point in time. Figure 3.9 shows the EBR, as well as its composition between current and capital borrowing, for each year over the period 1972 to 1989. We will examine in detail this borrowing in the context of Keynesian

*Table 3.3*
**Financing the EBR: 1989**

|  | £m | % |
|---|---|---|
| *Borrowing from:* |  |  |
| Abroad | 1,369 | 285.6 |
| Licensed banks | -323 | -67.4 |
| Central Bank | -202 | -42.1 |
| Non-bank public | -365 | -76.1 |
| *Total* | 479 | 100.0 |

*Source:* Exchequer Returns, 1990

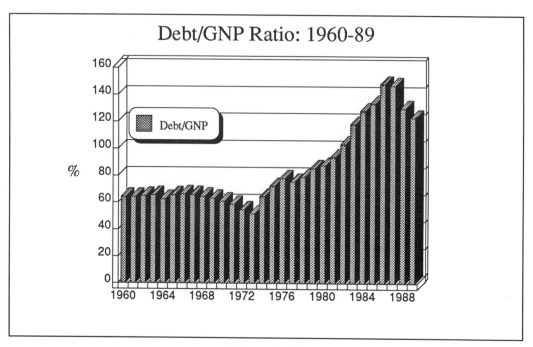

Figure 3.10

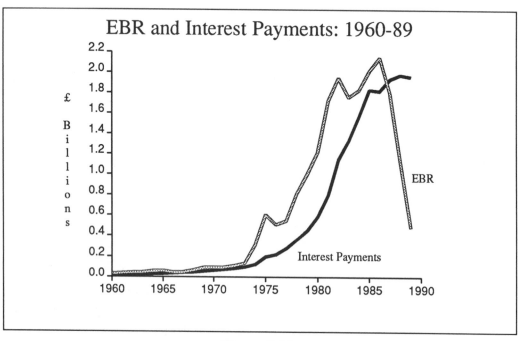

Figure 3.11

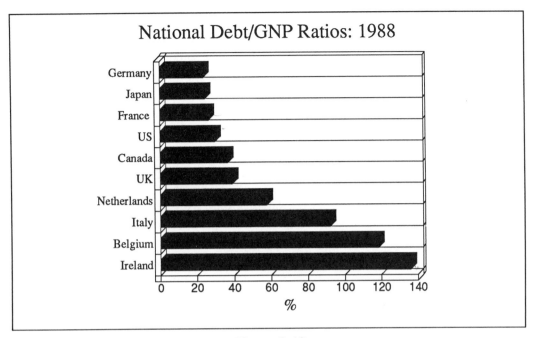

Figure 3.12

stabilisation policy in Chapter 4. At this stage we simply wish to make the point that the cumulative borrowing by the government and the semi-state bodies over the period raised the national debt from £1,009m in 1970 to £29,467m in 1988.

Rather than discussing the absolute amount of debt, it is more useful to express the debt as a percentage of nominal GNP, that is, to calculate the debt/GNP ratio. This is because GNP is a measure of the size of the economy and gives a good indication of the country's ability to service the debt. A national debt of £29,467m, for example, would be very small for a country like the US where GNP in 1988 was IR£3,200 billion. It is, however, very large when expressed as a percentage of Irish GNP. Figure 3.10 shows the Irish debt/GNP ratio between 1960-89. The sustained rise in the ratio after 1975 followed by the down-turn after 1987 are the most noticeable features of the graph. One of the important issues in debt management is to establish the conditions under which the debt/GNP ratio will stabilise. We examine this issue in Chapter 4.

It is evident that the debt/GNP ratio cannot grow indefinitely and without limit. After a time, the mounting debt and the associated rise in interest repayments would result in a debt crisis. By 1982, for example, there was a sharp rise in arrears in debt service in the less developed countries, cumulating in a panic when Mexico announced it could no longer pay interest on its massive outstanding loans. The political economy of "debt fatigue", "debt re-scheduling" and "debt forgiveness" has preoccupied the International Monetary Fund (IMF) since this episode. For a country that has acquired the habit of large fiscal deficits, reducing or stabilising the debt entails significant increases in taxation and/or cuts in government expenditure. Rectifying the government finances would have to take priority over all other macroeconomic problems, including the problem of unemployment. That is the sort of situation Ireland faced in 1981 when there was a very real possibility that the rise in our debt/GNP ratio would lead us into the predicament facing many less developed countries today.

To put the situation in perspective, Figure 3.11 compares the EBR and interest repayments on the national debt over the period 1960-89 (the EBR figure for 1988 excludes revenue received owing to the tax amnesty). By 1987 interest repayments were virtually equal to the budget deficit. In other words, nearly all government borrowing was been used to pay the interest on the debt. If there was no interest repayments, there would have been a small budget surplus by 1987. The continued reduction in the EBR in 1988 and 1989 meant that were it not for the burden of debt there would have been a substantial budget surplus in those years.

Figure 3.12 compares the Irish debt/GNP ratio with that prevailing in other countries. It is clear that Ireland's indebtedness is quite exceptional. Among the countries of the OECD, only Belgium and Italy are anyway close to the Irish level. (However, numerous less developed countries faced a much more serious problem of external debt servicing and stagnant foreign exchange receipts.) Ireland got into this situation by the pursuit of expansionary fiscal policies in the 1970s. We now turn to a detailed examination of these policies.

# 3.11 Conclusion

Some of the main points discussed in this chapter include:

- The Keynesian theory of income determination and the concepts of aggregate supply and aggregate demand

- The multiplier effect and how its size depends on savings, tax and import leakages

- Keynesian stabilisation policy and the difficulties in implementing such a policy. The exchequer borrowing requirement, the national debt and the debt/GNP ratio.

Note:

1. J.M.Keynes, *The General Theory of Employment, Interest and Money*, Macmillan, 1936.

# Chapter 4

# Fiscal Policy: the Irish Experience

## .1 Introduction

As we saw in Chapter 3, the theory of fiscal policy suggests that the public sector may be able to use its contribution to aggregate demand, (AD), to offset fluctuations in private consumption, investment and export demand. If successfully pursued, this approach will move output closer to its long-run trend growth path and help to keep it on this path. In this chapter we examine the record of fiscal policy in Ireland over the years since 1972. We shall explore whether the changes in fiscal policy have been well-timed, that is, whether they have dampened rather than amplified the business cycle, and what contribution they have made to the goal of maintaining a high level of output and employment.

## .2 The Growth of Government Spending and Taxation

As background to the main subject of this chapter we shall first outline the level and trend of government receipts and expenditure over the period 1972-86. In describing the broad trend since 1962 we shall use the data for the "public authorities" (that is, central government and local authorities)[1] contained in the national accounts publication NIE (national income and expenditure). These data are more comprehensive, and are classified in a more meaningful manner, than the annual budgetary data presented by the Minister for Finance (which relate primarily to the central government). Later in this chapter we shall, however, use the budgetary data because of their familiarity to commentators on the public finances and their more timely availability.

The data in Table 4.1 show the main components of public sector receipts and expenditure in 1962, 1972, 1980 and 1986, all expressed as percentages of GNP in current prices. Up to 1972 current receipts actually exceeded current expenditure: on a national accounts basis, there was a small current budget surplus. By 1980, however, this had turned to a current budget deficit amounting to 6.4% of GNP. Between 1980 and 1986 there was little change in the size of this deficit. We shall

*Table 4.1*

**Public sector receipts and expenditure (as a percentage of GNP)**

|  | *1962* | *1972* | *1980* | *1986* |
|---|---|---|---|---|
| *Current receipts* | | | | |
| Taxes on income | 7.2 | 11.9 | 18.1 | 23.6 |
| Taxes on expenditure | 14.9 | 18.4 | 16.4 | 19.1 |
| All other current income | 4.0 | 4.2 | 5.0 | 6.4 |
| *Total* | 26.1 | 34.5 | 39.5 | 49.1 |
| *Current expenditure* | | | | |
| Current subsidies | 3.6. | 4.2 | 4.0 | 3.3 |
| National debt interest | 2.8 | 3.7 | 6.8 | 11.0 |
| Transfer payments | 6.2 | 9.3 | 13.4 | 19.5 |
| Expenditure on goods and services | 12.8 | 15.9 | 21.7 | 22.8 |
| *Total* | 25.4 | 33.1 | 45.9 | 56.6 |
| *Capital receipts* | | | | |
| Net borrowing | 5.2 | 5.3 | 14.5 | 13.2 |
| Other | 1.8 | 1.3 | 2.1 | 2.0 |
| *Total* | 7.0 | 6.6 | 16.6 | 15.2 |
| *Capital spending* | | | | |
| Grants to enterprises | 1.0 | 1.6 | 2.0 | 0.9 |
| Gross domestic physical Capital formation | 3.2 | 4.5 | 6.1 | 4.1 |
| *Total* | 4.2 | 6.1 | 8.1 | 5.0 |

*Source*: NIE (1988) and Department of Finance databank of economic time series

examine the recent trend of the budget balance in greater detail later in this chapter. The growth in the share of government current expenditure in GNP from 25% in 1962 to 46% in 1980 and 57% in 1986 occurred because transfer payments trebled, and national debt interest increased fourfold, relative to GNP. The share of current expenditure on goods and services in GNP increased less dramatically, from 13% of GNP to 23%. Subsidies declined relative to GNP. There was a slight fall in public capital spending relative to GNP, comparing 1986 with 1972, but between 1972 and 1980 the ratio rose by about one third. After 1980 the level of capital grants to enterprises (e.g. Industrial Development Authority grants) and direct investment by the public sector declined.

On the revenue side, the most striking development has been the growth of taxation relative to GNP. The share of income taxes (including social security contributions) in GNP more than doubled between 1972 and 1986 and more than trebled between 1962 and 1986. This is all the more remarkable in view of the low level of taxation on certain types of income (corporate profits, farmers' incomes, etc.) and has led to an exceptionally heavy burden of taxation on employees liable to PAYE, who contributed almost 80% of all income tax paid in 1987. Moreover, our indirect tax system is highly selective. Very heavy excise taxes have been placed on a narrow range of goods including alcohol, petrol and tobacco. During the 1980s this led to major cross-border smuggling and importation from Northern Ireland. The high level of taxation, and its uneven pattern, imposes a considerable *dead-weight burden* on the economy and entails a serious *welfare loss.*[2]

# .3 An Informal Account of Recent Fiscal Policy

Before we discuss alternative approaches to measuring the stance of fiscal policy, we provide a brief account of the way fiscal policy has been conducted in Ireland since the beginning of the 1970s.[3]

The year 1973 was a watershed in western economic history. The *Organization of Petroleum Exporting Countries* (OPEC) raised crude oil prices from $3 to $12 a barrel. This severe shock affected both the demand and the supply sides of economies dependent on imported energy. On the demand side, the enormous price increase led to a massive increase in expenditure on imports because there was little scope for reducing dependence on imported energy in the short run. The surge in imports had a deflationary impact on the Irish economy. On the supply side, the dramatic change in relative prices rendered a large amount of capital equipment obsolete and reduced the effective productive capacity of the economy.

Governments were quicker to recognise and respond to the deflationary implications of the oil price shock than to its implications for the supply side of the economy. In fact it was not until after the second oil price shock, at the end of the

1970s, that effective measures were put in place to reduce the energy-intensity of economic growth.

In Ireland the immediate reaction to the first oil price shock was to try to maintain the level of aggregate demand in the face of a sharp increase in the level of imports by increasing government spending without any corresponding increase in the level of taxation. A sizeable current budget deficit was recorded in 1974, the first time that this happened. In 1975 the deficit rose to 7% of GNP. In response to the rising rate of inflation the government introduced a mini-budget during 1975 and used food subsidies and tax cuts to try to moderate the inflationary wage claims that were building up, at the cost of a further widening of the budget deficit. However, in 1976 the Minister for Finance (Richie Ryan) raised taxes and curbed expenditure as the economy began to recover. The measures announced in the 1976 budget, together with the unexpectedly rapid growth of the economy during the year, reduced the deficit by over 2% of GNP. By 1977 it had fallen to 3.6% of GNP. Even though policy had wavered from subsidies and tax cuts to tax increases, it seemed as if the economy had weathered the first oil crisis in good order. But in fact the structural problems created by the oil price shock remained unresolved.

The general election of 1977 destroyed the chances of further progress towards restoring order in the public finances. The parties vied with one another in promising to cut taxation. (Both major parties claim credit for having been the first to promise to abolish rates on private houses and put nothing in their place.) In the event, the incoming Fianna Fáil government exceeded their manifesto promises on tax cuts and expenditure increases. The measures introduced by George Colley in the 1978 Budget added about 1.5% of GNP to the current budget deficit. This occurred at a time when the economy was already growing at an unsustainable rate (6.0% in 1977) and was forecast to continue to grow rapidly even if there had been no fiscal stimulus. The policy was rationalised by reference to the need to reduce the level of unemployment, which was still above its 1973 level.[4] It was argued that the increase in the deficit would lead to increased private sector investment which would sustain the economic expansion. According to this view, the increased tax revenue that would follow would eventually lead to the elimination of the budget deficit.

Events between 1978 and 1980 confounded these hopes. Real GNP grew by 5.1% in 1978 but the rate of growth fell to under 3% in 1979 and 1980. The current budget deficit remained above 6% of GNP and the balance of payments current account deficit grew to 11% of GNP. By the end of the decade it was clear that the Irish economy was plunging into a balance of payments crisis. But even when it became clear that the logic of the *self-financing fiscal boost* was flawed, no serious attempt was made to restore balance to the public finances through discretionary increases in taxes or cuts in expenditure. We were, therefore, particularly ill-prepared to cope with the second oil price shock, which occurred in 1979.

As a result of the increase in the price of oil to over $40 a barrel, in 1981 all OECD countries experienced rising unemployment and inflation and widening public sector deficits. The Irish budgetary situation left no scope for trying to offset the deflationary impact of the oil price increase through an expansionary fiscal policy. As a result of the persistent budget deficits incurred after 1973, and our resort to external borrowing to finance them, by 1980 we had become a *net debtor country*: the level of our external public debt had reached £2,207 million, whereas our official external reserves were only £1,346 million. While some argued that further (external) borrowing was warranted because our credit rating was still sound on international financial markets and the money could be used to generate employment and create valuable assets in Ireland, the reality was that much of the public capital programme was spent on projects with a very low rate of return and that further borrowing for such purposes was not warranted.

In July 1981 the new coalition government introduced a mini-budget to try to correct the budgetary situation. This relied mainly on tax increases to reduce the deficit and thereby set the pattern for many subsequent attempts to restore order to the public finances. However the absence of revenue buoyancy during the year resulted in an increase in the current budget deficit. This outcome - higher taxation leading to larger rather than smaller deficits - was to be repeated in subsequent years. By the time of the General Election of November 1982 (the third within 18 months), the main political parties were agreed that the need to restore order to the public finances had to take precedence over other objectives, such as trying to reduce the level of unemployment. The only disagreement concerned the speed with which the current budget deficit would be phased out and the appropriate balance between increased taxation and reduced expenditure.

The coalition government tried to tackle the problem over the period 1982-86 primarily by raising the level of taxation and reducing the level of borrowing for capital purposes. However, their attempts to reduce the level of government current expenditure on goods and services by imposing a ban on recruitment in the public sector proved ineffective. Under the momentum of rising unemployment and accumulating debt, both transfer payments and national debt interest continued to increase relative to GNP. Thus, although Mr Dukes' 1983 budget set a record by the magnitude of the tax increases it contained, the severity of the economic decline during the year offset this attempt to bring down the level of borrowing. In the government's White Paper on the economy *Building on Reality 1985-87,* published at the end of 1984, the target for fiscal rectitude was changed from the *elimination of the current budget deficit* to the *stabilisation of the debt/GNP ratio*. While in fact this was a more meaningful short-term objective than one that focused exclusively on the current budget deficit, the switch of emphasis entailed an admission that the ambitious targets that had been espoused during the 1982 election campaigns would not be attained in the foreseeable future.

No immediate progress was made towards either reducing the current budget deficit or stabilising the debt/GNP ratio. Between 1983 and 1986 the current budget deficit rose from 7.1% to 8.6% of GNP and the debt/GNP ratio rose from 86% to 113%. During the third quarter of 1986 disappointing exchequer returns led to a loss of confidence in the economy's prospects, which was manifested by nervousness on the foreign exchanges and a 3% increase in the Irish/UK interest rate differential. This episode marked the beginning of the end of the attempt to reduce the level of borrowing through higher taxation. It had become clear to all but a small minority that this strategy was proving self-defeating. Higher taxes had put the economy on a downward spiral of reduced revenue and higher deficits. Under Irish conditions, the predictions derived from the Laffer Curve (see Figure 3.8, Chapter 3) seem to be broadly correct. The alternative approach to correcting the budget deficit through drastic cuts in expenditure had to be taken. The Coalition government split and eventually fell on this issue. The current expenditure cuts proposed by the Minister for Finance, John Bruton, in the draft Book of Estimates in October 1986 were not acceptable to his Labour Party colleagues, who still favoured the strategy of increased taxation.

The formation of a minority Fianna Fáil government in January 1987 occasioned increased uncertainty about the likely future course of economic policy, because while in opposition the party had vehemently attacked what they had labelled the "monetarist" or "Thatcherite" policies of the Coalition government. However, in office the new government, with the support of the main opposition parties, tackled the problem of curbing government expenditure head-on. In Ray MacSharry's 1987 budget the level of current government spending was reduced below the level that had been proposed by Fine Gael in the draft Book of Estimates that led to downfall of the Coalition.

External factors, including the collapse of oil prices, lower interest rates, higher farm prices and accelerating growth in the United Kingdom, contributed to a recovery in the economy and helped the government to achieve its fiscal targets. The move towards fiscal rectitude gained momentum with the publication of the Book of Estimates for 1988 in the autumn of 1987. This proposed a 3% reduction in the value of current government spending, the first cut in the level of spending in the post-war period. In the January 1988 budget these estimates were accepted by the Dáil. The support, or abstention, of the main opposition parties enabled a minority Fianna Fáil government to get its budget adopted.

The 1987 budget also proposed a tax amnesty, with the objective of collecting £30 million in unpaid taxes. In fact during 1988 over £500 million was raised from this source and from the application of a new system of self-assessment tax to the self-employed. Moreover, other sources of revenue (VAT and excises) were buoyant, and expenditure was held below the level projected in the budget. As a result of these developments the current budget deficit fell to 2.2% of GNP and the PSBR to 5.3%. The unexpectedly rapid progress in restoring order to the public

66

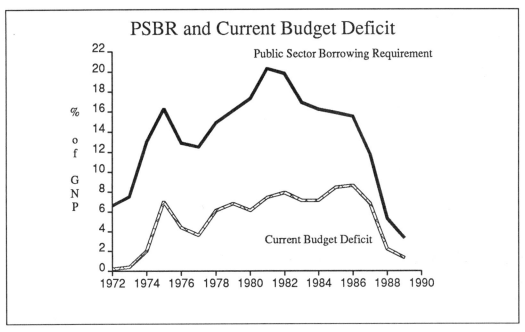

Figure 4.1

finances, and the rise in the pound sterling relative to the EMS currencies, facilitated further reductions in Irish rates of interest even as rates rose sharply in Britain.

In the early 1980s there was a particular concern with the current budget deficit, based on the view that whereas borrowing for capital purposes might be acceptable, it was not justifiable to borrow for day-to-day expenses. The validity of this distinction depends on the rate of return achieved by the public sector's capital spending. The public capital programme grew very rapidly in the late 1970s as spending was increased on "sectoral economic development" and "productive infrastructure" projects that had very long pay-back periods and low, even negative, rates of return, and on "social infrastructure" (housing, schools and hospitals) that did not yield any immediate return to the exchequer. During the 1980s, as may be seen from Figure 4.1 and Table 4.2, there was a very sharp decline in the level of borrowing for capital purposes, from almost 13% of GNP in 1981 to only 2.3% in 1989. This was due to the completion of many of the large projects started in the early 1980s, such as the Moneypoint power station, the Dublin-Cork gas pipeline and the DART, and the reduction in capital injections to ailing state-sponsored bodies. Reducing the current budget deficit proved much more difficult than allowing the public capital programme to shrink. The attempt to curb public current spending could only be said to have finally begun to take effect in 1987 and 1988. The volume of current government expenditure is estimated to have declined by almost 10% between 1986 and 1989.[5]

The performance of the Irish economy during 1987, 1988 and 1989 was extraordinary. The PSBR was reduced by 10% of GNP but the rate of growth of GNP increased. This would seem to refute the Keynesian belief that the public sector contribution to aggregate demand is the key influence on short-term performance of the economy. As far as interest rates and the level of confidence in the economy are concerned, the decisive factor seems to have been the credibility of the government's commitment to restoring order to the public finances. Lower interest rates and increased confidence led to a recovery in private sector investment and consumption spending which more than offset the contractionary effects of fiscal retrenchment. This could be viewed as a clear example of "reverse crowding out" which we discuss on a theoretical level in Chapter 6.

# 4.4 Measuring the Stance of Fiscal Policy

The public sector's contribution to AD comprises, on the current side, G - NT, where G is government current expenditure and NT is taxes less transfer payments, and on the capital side, borrowing for capital purposes, including the borrowing of state-sponsored bodies. These three components constitute the *public sector borrowing requirement (PSBR)*. Table 4.2 shows this, and its components, as a percentage of GNP, for the period 1972-89. Also included is a measure called the "primary" deficit, that is the PSBR less the cost of servicing the public debt. We discuss this concept below.

A comprehensive measure of changes in the public sector's contribution to AD is provided by the changes in the PSBR. Several refinements are, however, required in order to obtain a true picture of the *stance* of fiscal policy.

In the first place, it should be recalled that the PSBR is an *ex post* magnitude. That is, it reflects the impact of changes in the level of economic activity (and the rate of unemployment in particular) on the level of government receipts and expenditure. In assessing the stance of fiscal policy, it is desirable to net out these effects, usually referred to as "built-in stabilisers", and to isolate the components of changes in the deficits that are due to *discretionary* fiscal policy. For example, a significant proportion of the reduction in the borrowing requirement that followed Richie Ryan's 1976 budget was due to the accelerating growth of the economy. Similarly, Alan Dukes' very deflationary 1983 budget achieved only a slight reduction in the borrowing requirement because of the decline in the level of economic activity during the year, some of which was due to the measures taken in the budget.

Another point that should be taken into account during periods of rapid inflation is the effect of this inflation on the real value of the outstanding government debt. The hypothetical data in Table 4.3 illustrates this point.

*Table 4.2*

**Indicators of the stance of fiscal policy**

All data expressed as a percentage of GNP

| | *Current budget deficit* | *Borrowing for capital purposes* | *Public sector borrowing requirement* | *"Primary" deficit* | *Deficit excluding external interest* |
|---|---|---|---|---|---|
| | (1) | (2) | (3)=(1)+(2) | (4) | (5) |
| 1972 | 0.2 | 6.4 | 6.6 | 3.0 | n.a. |
| 1973 | 0.4 | 7.1 | 7.5 | 3.9 | n.a. |
| 1974 | 2.0 | 11.0 | 13.0 | 9.0 | n.a. |
| 1975 | 7.0 | 9.3 | 16.3 | 11.7 | n.a. |
| 1976 | 4.4 | 8.5 | 12.9 | 6.9 | n.a. |
| 1977 | 3.6 | 8.9 | 12.5 | 6.5 | n.a. |
| 1978 | 6.1 | 8.8 | 14.9 | 8.5 | 12.9 |
| 1979 | 6.8 | 9.3 | 16.1 | 10.7 | 14.2 |
| 1980 | 6.1 | 11.2 | 17.3 | 10.0 | 14.7 |
| 1981 | 7.4 | 12.9 | 20.3 | 12.1 | 16.9 |
| 1982 | 7.9 | 11.9 | 19.8 | 10.4 | 14.6 |
| 1983 | 7.1 | 9.8 | 16.9 | 6.1 | 11.4 |
| 1984 | 7.1 | 9.1 | 16.2 | 4.6 | 10.2 |
| 1985 | 8.4 | 7.5 | 15.9 | 3.1 | 9.5 |
| 1986 | 8.6 | 6.9 | 15.5 | 3.2 | 9.7 |
| 1987 | 6.8 | 5.0 | 11.8 | -0.4 | 7.6 |
| 1988 | 1.7 | 2.3 | 4.0 | -9.4 | -0.6 |
| 1989 | 1.3 | 2.0 | 3.3 | -9.3 | -1.2 |

*Source*:  Budget Book  1990  and Exchequer Returns, 1990

n.a. = not available

*Notes*:

(1) Borrowing for capital purposes includes borrowing by state-sponsored bodies.

(2) The "Primary" deficit equals the PSBR minus the cost of debt service.

(3) Data for 1988 includes once off tax amnesty receipts.

*Table 4.3*

**Inflation and government debt**

| Debt at start of year | Rate of inflation | Capital loss on outstanding debt | Borrowing during year | Real borrowing during year |
|---|---|---|---|---|
| £1,000 | 20 % | £200 | £100 | -£100 |

While the figure for "real" borrowing is a hypothetical calculation, the point made by these figures gains in relevance when it is recalled that the rate of interest paid by the government on its debt reflects the rate of inflation. If, in our example above, the government were paying a 23% nominal rate of interest (3% real plus 20% for expected inflation), then £200 of its current spending would be due to compensation of holders of government debt for the fall in its capital value, which is tantamount to advance repayment of principal. If this idea had been applied to the Irish situation during the early 1980s, the inflation adjustment would have reduced the deficit by over 10% of GNP. However, while this calculation is of interest from the perspective of getting an accurate measure of changes in the real level of government indebtedness, it is not directly relevant to the measurement of the impact of the deficit on aggregate demand.[6]

There have been several attempts to measure the stance of fiscal policy, taking account of the distinction between automatic and discretionary, real and nominal, changes in taxation and expenditure. For example, an estimate of the effect of *cyclical factors* on the level of the deficit was published in *Proposals for Plan*.[7] The approach taken in this document was to see how cyclical factors ("built-in stabilisers") would have changed the level of the deficit in a reference year (1979), which is called the "structural deficit". The actual deficit is then compared with the cyclically-adjusted deficit. This analysis showed that between 1979 and 1983 the actual deficit fell from 9.9% to 8.3% of GNP, while the *structural deficit* fell from 7.1% to 3.8%. Thus cyclical factors (i.e. the rise in unemployment) added 4.5% of GNP to the current budget deficit.[8] The stance of fiscal policy over these years was therefore more deflationary than appears from the unadjusted data.

An evaluation of the stance of fiscal policy over the period 1972-81 based on a large-scale econometric model was published by the Economic and Social Research Institute in 1982. The authors concluded that

policy appears to have tended to operate in a pro-cyclical fashion during periods of expansion. For example, in 1973 and again in 1977 and 1978 it seems that fiscal policy was reinforcing the

70

autonomous growth that was already underway. During the downturn of 1974/75 policy was strongly counter-cyclical as it has been in the most recent recession.[9]

*Note:*
*"Counter cyclical" means "tending to dampen the business cycle", whereas "pro-cyclical" means "tending to amplify the cycle".*

A similar assessment is contained in Bradley *et al.*[10] They present measures of the extent to which each budget over the period 1972-80 deviated from "fiscal neutrality" or "fiscal indexation", that is the level of receipts and expenditure that would have occurred if all rates of taxation and rates of social welfare benefit etc. had been held at the real levels that obtained in the base year (1967). Comparing the actual, historical level of receipts and expenditure with these hypothetical amounts provides a measure of the stance of fiscal policy: if actual expenditure is higher, or tax receipts lower, than the hypothetical levels, discretionary fiscal policy is deemed to have been expansionary. On this basis they characterise discretionary fiscal policy in the following manner:

|         |         |
|---------|---------|
| *pre-1974:* | relatively inactive and neutral |
| *1974-75:* | fiscal activism, counter-cyclical |
| *1976:* | counter-cyclical contraction |
| *1977-79:* | an unbridled fiscal expansion which was strongly pro-cyclical. |

These two evaluations concur in the low marks given to the timing of the major fiscal stimulus in 1978. If the same methodology were applied to later years, discretionary fiscal policy since 1982 would be characterised as sharply *contractionary* and strongly *pro-cyclical*. Thus, the timing of Irish fiscal policy has continued to be very inappropriate from the point of view of stabilisation policy.

## Primary deficit

Another concept that is important in the evaluation of the stance of fiscal policy is the primary deficit. In the fourth column of Table 4.2 the level of the primary deficit is shown. A graphical representation is given in Figure 4.2. Government borrowing during a year has two components, one of which is the amount that has to be used to service the debt outstanding at the start of the year, the other is the balance between the rest of expenditure and tax revenue.

71

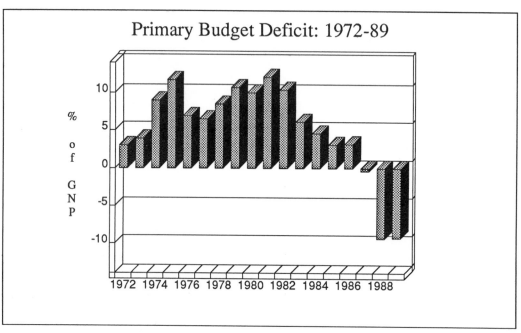

Figure 4.2

| | | | |
|---|---|---|---|
| If | r | = | the rate of interest, |
| and | $D_t$ | = | the national debt at the start of the year, |
| then | $rD_t$ | = | debt service during the year |
| and the "primary" surplus is | P | = | $rD_t$ - PSBR |

*Note:*

*We define a positive primary balance as a surplus and a deficit as a "negative surplus".*

This magnitude has a significance in relation to the dynamics of the debt that will be explained below. If there is a primary deficit, that is, if PSBR > $rD_t$ then the government is not raising enough in revenue to cover its spending exclusive of debt service. It is borrowing more than is needed simply to service past borrowing. From Table 4.2 it may be seen that the primary deficit reached a peak in 1981 at 12% of GNP. By 1987 it had fallen to almost zero: all of the PSBR was accounted for by borrowing to service accumulated debt. In 1988 a primary surplus equal to 6.6% of GNP was recorded. This illustrates the dramatic change in fiscal policy over the period.

*Note:*

*A graph of the exchequer borrowing requirement (EBR) and interest payments is given in Chapter 3, section 3.10.*

Increased government spending paid directly to non-residents has no impact on AD in Ireland. The growth of foreign borrowing up to 1982 led to a rapid increase in interest payments to non-residents, but net external borrowing fell sharply after 1982 and interest payments to non-residents levelled off in 1983. As was pointed out by the OECD in its *Survey of Ireland,*

... the current budget deficit excluding external debt interest - a better indication of the demand impact of the deficit - actually fell appreciably from its 1981 peak and by 1984 was little over 1 per cent of GNP.
(OECD, *Survey of Ireland*, December 1987, p. 54.)

Thus 1981-82 marked a watershed after which the impact of fiscal policy on the economy became increasingly *deflationary*. This is clear when the figures for the primary deficit and the deficit adjusted for the growth of interest payments to non-residents are examined, but is masked in the data on the current budget deficit, which went on rising mainly because of the operations of built-in stablisers until 1987. The discretionary measures that were taken to reduce the current budget deficit after 1981 were reinforced by the drop in the level of borrowing for capital purposes.

# 5 The Effects of Deficits

## The growth of debt

The Keynesian model provides a rationale for counter-cyclical deficit spending to mitigate the effects of private sector shocks on AD. In theory, these strategic deficits should be matched by surpluses during periods of overheating, so that over the medium-term the budget will be balanced. In reality, the political process makes this ideal unattainable and all governments that have embarked on the expedient of deficit spending to alleviate unemployment during a recession have found it extremely difficult to re-impose the norm of a balanced budget, let alone to generate surpluses in good times. (The Conservative government in Britain has, however, moved from a large public sector *borrowing requirement* to public sector *debt retirement*.) The Irish experience at the end of the 1970s shows how perilous it can be to rely on the prospect of abundant tax revenue in the future to cancel deficits. Unless a large multiplier applies to the expansionary fiscal policy, automatic revenue buoyancy will not generate sufficient additional revenue to restore a balanced budget. The most immediate effect of deficit spending, therefore, tends to be an accumulation of debt.

The traditional (pre-1973) emphasis on fiscal rectitude in Ireland extended only to the concept of a balanced current budget; borrowing for capital purposes was condoned. As a result we had accumulated a significant national debt even before we embarked on a more active fiscal policy after 1972. However, due to the combination of moderate levels of borrowing, fairly rapid growth in GNP and low real rates of interest, the ratio of debt to GNP declined from over 70% in the early 1960s to under 60% in 1974. Between 1970 and 1987, however, the level of national debt rose *24-fold*, and the ratio of debt to GNP doubled.[11] Moreover, external debt rose from virtually nil to just under £10 billion or over 50% of GNP. Interest paid on the outstanding debt rose to over 10% of GNP, accounting for over one quarter of total public sector current expenditure and one third of total tax revenue. A measure that is used by the International Monetary Fund in conjunction with the third-world debt crisis is the ratio of interest paid on external debt to export earnings. This ratio peaked at 9.1% in Ireland in 1982. It has now fallen to below 5%.

*Note:*
*A graph of the debt/GNP ratio was given in Chapter 3, section 3.10.*

There is no well-defined limit beyond which these ratios cannot rise without causing economic catastrophe. But it is clear that they cannot be allowed to rise indefinitely. The high level, and uneven pattern, of taxation in Ireland undoubtedly gives rise to important *dead-weight costs*, which increase rapidly at the margin as further taxation is imposed. This is the case even when the tax receipts are being used to pay interest to Irish residents (many of whom are, of course, themselves tax-payers). When interest is being paid to non-residents there is the additional consideration that it pre-empts export earnings and siphons demand off the economy. Early in the 1980s all the debt ratios were moving in the wrong direction. The situation at the end of the decade was clearly far more reassuring.

The dynamics of debt accumulation have been studied by economists, starting with Evsey Domar who analysed the implications of the US war-time borrowing in an article written in 1944.[12] The algebra he used allows us to derive the following condition for a decline in the debt/GNP ratio in the steady state:

D/GNP will decline if
$P/(r - g) > D/GNP$
or
$P > (D/GNP)(r - g)$

*where*

| | | |
|---|---|---|
| P | = | the primary surplus as a percentage of GNP |
| r | = | nominal rate of interest |
| g | = | the rate of growth of GNP (in current prices) |
| D/GNP | = | the present ratio of debt to GNP |

74

This formula says that in the long run the debt/GNP ratio will decline if the primary surplus is greater than the product of the debt/GNP ratio and the difference between the rate of interest and the rate of growth of GNP. Applying this formula to present Irish circumstances, the debt/GNP ratio is about 1.4, the growth rate of GNP is about 8% and the rate of interest on the national debt is about 9%, so a primary surplus equal to, or greater than, about 1.5% of GNP is required to stabilise the debt/GNP ratio. In 1988 this condition was easily met, but once-off revenue from the tax amnesty accounted for a significant part of this surplus. However, preliminary data for 1989 indicate that the primary surplus will once again be large enough to ensure that the debt/GNP ratio continues to decline. Accelerated growth in GNP and relatively stable interest rates are contributing to a rapid improvement in the situation, but with our large overhang of debt, there is no scope for removing the fiscal discipline that has been gradually put in place since 1982 if we wish to maintain the downward trend in the debt/GNP ratio.

To summarise, deficit spending that is not offset by counter-cyclical surpluses results in an exponential growth in the national debt. The debt will grow more rapidly the higher the rate of interest relative to the rate of growth of GNP. The only way of preventing the debt/GNP ratio from exploding is to run a primary surplus, that is, a surplus of tax revenue over non-interest spending. Ireland entered a vicious circle in which the debt was rising faster than GNP in the 1970s. This led to a rising burden of taxation to pay interest on the outstanding debt. It proved very difficult to get to the point where the debt is declining relative to income. An increase in the rate of interest or a slowing down in our growth rate would put us back on the path of a rising debt/GNP ratio. Even if these set-backs are avoided, we shall have to shoulder a considerable tax burden for some time to come to service the domestic and foreign debt accumulated through past deficits.

## Effect on the level of GNP

Many American macroeconomic textbooks use multipliers of three or four to illustrate the basic Keynesian model. We have outlined in Chapter 3 the reasons why the large multipliers used in these examples are not relevant in the Irish context. With a marginal propensity to import of about 0.5 and a marginal tax rate of about 0.4, it is clear that the leakage from the circular flow of spending is very high. In addition to the tendency of these high leakages to curtail the circular flow of spending, there are other forces that may further reduce the size of the multiplier.

The first is the *Ricardian Equivalence Effect*, according to which an increase in the public sector deficit results in an offsetting increase in personal savings. This theory is based on the idea that public sector deficits imply higher taxation sometime in the future, and the private sector anticipates these taxes by increasing their savings. While this degree of foresight and prudence may seem implausible, figures for the 1970s and 1980s show some tendency for private sector savings to rise as public sector borrowing increases (see Chapter 2). It does seem as if the rise in the PSBR in the early 1980s, and the uncertainty associated with this episode in our economic history, led to an increase in the level of personal savings. If this effect does operate, than changes in fiscal policy cause a fall in private sector demand, so the net increase in AD is less than suggested by the change in the stance of fiscal policy.

Another factor that has to be taken into account in assessing the effectiveness of fiscal policy is the impact of increased public sector borrowing on the level of interest rates and/or the rate of exchange. Increased public sector borrowing may put upward pressure on domestic rates of interest and "crowd-out" private sector investment and consumption spending. Alternatively, if the deficit is financed through foreign borrowing, this will tend to raise the foreign exchange value of the domestic currency, and the resultant loss of competitiveness tends to reduce the value of net exports. While it is difficult to evaluate the importance of these considerations from the historical evidence, the scale of public sector borrowing in the early 1980s was so large that its effect on the Irish exchange rate and rate of interest cannot be dismissed. To the extent that either interest rate or exchange rate crowding-out occurs, the impact of fiscal policy on AD is offset by reductions in private sector spending.

Finally, increased government spending will result in a higher burden of taxation, either immediately if the budget is balanced or in the future if the extra spending is deficit-financed. This is very clear from the Irish experience in the 1980s, where the expansionary fiscal policy of the period 1978-81 was followed by a sharp increase in the ratio of taxation to GNP, to the point where the level of debt service payments now equals 80% of the receipts from income tax. In their evaluation of fiscal policy in Ireland, Bradley et al. describe how increased government spending led to higher levels of taxation, which were passed on in the form of higher wages and prices because of the tendency of workers to bargain in terms of net-of-tax income. The result of the higher taxation was, therefore, a reduction in the competitiveness of the traded sectors of the Irish economy. This sequence of events could be viewed as a type of "taxation crowding-out". As a result of this sequence of events, they claim that expansionary fiscal policy led to no lasting increase in the level of employment.

A summary analysis of the impact of fiscal policy on real output is contained in Walsh (1987). Using a reduced-form model,[13] he attempted to explain the growth of real GNP in Ireland in terms of the following variables: the rate of growth in EEC GNP and various definitions of the stance of fiscal policy in Ireland. The results reported show that the changes in the *structural budget deficit* are a significant influence on the rate of economic growth and unemployment in Ireland. However, the effect is relatively small:

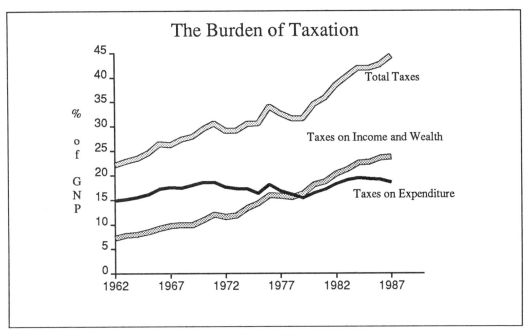

Figure 4.3

the net effect of a reduction in the structural budget surplus of 1% of GNP would be to lower the rate of unemployment by only 0.4% (e.g. from 19% to 18.6%).[14]

His results also indicate that a reduction of 1% in the structural surplus would raise the rate of growth of GNP by about 0.7%. The impact of fiscal policy on GNP growth is greater than on unemployment, but it is still relatively small. Moreover, these are estimates of the short run effects; in the longer run the expansionary effect of fiscal policy is likely to be smaller as crowding-out of one type or another occurs.

# Effect on the structure of GNP

Sudden expansions and contractions in the level of government spending affect the composition of GNP as well as its level. Increased public sector employment played a major role in the fiscal stimulus that was administered at the end of the 1970s. Employment in the health services and in education increased by 27% and 22%, respectively, between 1977 and the early 1980s. Total public sector employment rose by 17% between 1977 and 1982. It is reasonable to suspect that the *marginal productivity* of these large increases in employment was low. However, it has proved extremely difficult to reduce employment to its pre-expansion level. Since 1986, hard-fought cuts in public expenditure have only resulted in a decline of about 10,000 or about 3% in the level of employment in the public sector. During the general election campaign of June 1989, the size of the public health services became a major political issue.

An expansionary fiscal policy also tends to have a large effect on the building and construction industry, due to the tendency to rely on the public capital programme and incentives to private house building to provide a stimulus to the economy. The numbers at work in the building industry rose by 23% between 1976 and 1980 and then fell by 32% between 1980 and 1988. (Clearly, those employed in this sector do not enjoy the degree of job security that exists in the public sector!) Instead of dampening the cycle of boom and bust that characterises the construction sector, fiscal policy in Ireland has actually amplified it.

Fiscal expansion also leads to a sharp rise in the level of taxation relative to GNP. The tax burden is shown in Figure 4.3. It can be seen that total taxation as a percentage of GNP increased from 22.1% in 1962 to 42.6% in 1986. The ratio of taxes on income and wealth to GNP *trebled* over the period. The distortions and disincentives created by these developments became a source of growing discontent. High indirect tax rates encouraged increased cross-border imports from Northern Ireland. High rates of personal taxation have become a factor in the high rate of emigration of young people. The decline in real after-tax incomes fuelled inflationary wage claims and militated against maintaining the level of employment. While the upward spiral of taxation has been halted, the level of taxation in Ireland remains very high by international standards, and especially by comparision with other countries of the same level of economic development. The adverse effects of the taxation needed to service our large public debt on the economy will be felt for some years to come.

## Summary

There is now widespread agreement that under Irish conditions fiscal policy is not an effective instrument. Moreover, fiscal policy was implemented in a very ill-judged manner over the period since 1972 and especially since 1977. The mistake was made of stimulating the economy during periods when it was already growing at a satisfactory pace. These mistakes occurred through a combination of analytical errors and expedient use of tax and spending decisions as an adjunct of party politics. Subsequent events show how disruptive an inappropriate fiscal expansion is under Irish conditions.

# 4.6 Conclusion

In this chapter, we have reviewed the following topics:

- The growth of government spending and taxation

- The measurement of the stance of fiscal policy in Ireland, 1970 to 1988

- The effect of fiscal policy on the economy.

We showed that:

- The public sector has increased dramatically relative to GNP

- The timing of fiscal policy since 1978 has been strongly *pro-cyclical*, that is, it has tended to amplify rather than dampen the business cycle

- Fiscal policy has not been effective as a means of maintaining a high level of output and employment

- The most conspicuous effect of deficit spending has been to increase the burden of the national debt

- The sudden fiscal expansion of the late 1970s distorted the structure of the economy. There was a rapid growth of employment in the public sector and in building and construction. While the construction industry shrank rapidly during the 1980s, it is proving much more difficult to reduce the level of public sector employment.

# Notes

1. State-sponsored companies are not included in the public sector in the national income accounts. The transfer of some of the operations of the Department of Post and Telegraphs to the new bodies called An Post and An Bord Telecom in 1984 reduced the size of the public sector. The data presented here have not been adjusted to allow for this change.

2. This topic has been explored by Patrick Honohan and Ian Irvine, "The Marginal Social Costs of Taxation in Ireland", *The Economic and Social Review*, Vol. 19, No. 1, 1987, p. 15-42.

3. Readers should consult T. K. Whitaker, "Fiscal Turning Points", in *Interests*, Dublin: The Institute of Public Administration, 1983, for an insider's account.

4. This illustrates how important it is to have a working definition of the concept of "full employment", a point we shall return to in Chapter 7.

5. While the numbers in the public sector have fallen significantly since 1986, rates of pay in the public sector have risen faster than the rate of inflation over the same period. Those remaining in the sector are increasingly well paid.

6. This statement should be modified to the extent that the capital loss suffered by the private sector holders of public sector debt leads to a fall in their consumption spending (through a wealth effect).

7. The National Planning Board, April 1984.

8. See *Proposals for Plan*, (April, 1984), Chapter II.2, Table A.

9. Peter Bacon, Joe Durkan and Jim O'Leary, *The Irish Economy: Policy and Performance 1972-81*, Dublin, The Economic and Social Research Institute, 1982, p. 58.

10. John Bradley, Connell Fanning, Canice Prendergast and Mark Wynne, *Medium Term Analysis of Fiscal Policy in Ireland: A Macroeconomic Study of the Period 1967-80*, Dublin: The Economic and Social Research Institute, Research Paper 122, 1985.

11. For a discussion of the measurement of these trends see Patrick Honohan, "The Public Debt and Borrowing: Issues of Interpretation", *Irish Banking Review*, March, 1985, p. 3-19.

12. E. Domar, "The Burden of the Debt and National Income", *American Economic Review*, Vol. 33, 1944.

13. This means that instead of trying to estimate a full model of the whole economy, a single equation was used with the rate of growth in real GNP as the dependent variable and a few explanatory variables on the right hand side.

14. See Brendan M. Walsh, "Why is Unemployment So High?", in *Perspectives on Economic Policy*, 1, 1987, Centre for Economic Research, University College, Dublin, p. 19.

# Chapter 5

# *Money and Banking*

## 1 Introduction

In this chapter we examine the functions of money in the economy and explain how money is created. This is followed by a discussion of the role of the Central Bank and, in particular, of how the Central Bank regulates the money supply in the system. The chapter concludes with a brief discussion of the characteristics of Irish banking system.

## 2 Functions of Money

Money performs three basic functions. The most important of these is its role as a "medium of exchange". If there is no money, the economy is operating on a *barter system*, that is goods and services are exchanged for goods and services, and money does not enter into any transaction. A barter system is highly inefficient as it involves looking for a "double coincidence of wants". For example, if someone wants to exchange sheep for cows, he has to find someone willing to exchange cows for sheep. The chances are that a third (or fourth) party will become involved and the transaction could involve trading sheep for pigs and then using the pigs to obtain the desired cows. Clearly a barter system is very cumbersome and inefficient.

Money is basically a cost-reducing invention which acts as a medium of exchange and removes the need for the "double coincidence of wants". Goods and services (including labour) can be exchanged for money and that money can, in turn, be used to purchase a range of goods and services.

One important benefit arising from money acting as a medium of exchange is that people can *specialise* in particular occupations. This specialisation, in turn, leads to greater efficiency and more output being produced in the economy. In contrast, a barter system encourages self-sufficiency with the result that people end up doing virtually everything (very badly) for themselves. Without money, occupations requiring a high degree of specialisation such as doctors, engineers, accountants and skilled trades would more or less cease to exist.

81

Over the centuries, money has taken many forms: whales' teeth in Fiji; dogs' teeth in the Admiralty Islands; shells, silk and salt in China, and cattle in Ireland, to mention only a few. For example, writing about Gambia, the Scottish physician and explorer, Mungo Park, noted:

In their early intercourse with Europeans, the article that attracted most notice was iron. Its utility, in forming the instruments of war and husbandry, made it preferable to all others; and soon became the measure by which the value of all other commodities was ascertained. Thus, a certain quantity of goods, of whatever denomination, appearing to be equal in value to a bar of iron, constituted, in the trader's phraseology, a bar of that particular merchandise. Twenty leaves of tobacco, for instance, were considered as a bar of tobacco; and a gallon of spirits (or rather half spirits and half water), as a bar of rum; a bar of one commodity being reckoned equal in value to a bar of another commodity. Mungo Park, *Travels in the Interior of Africa*, Eland, London, 1983, p. 19.

Whatever commodity or object is used as money, it must first achieve a "circularity in its acceptance". That is the "money" must be generally accepted by everyone in the economy. The only reason people accept paper money today is because they are certain that they can use that paper to purchase goods and services at a later stage. If people had the slightest suspicion that paper money, however well engraved or designed, could not be spent, they would not accept it.

In order for an object or a commodity to be accepted as money, it must satisfy at least two criteria. First, it cannot be easily *reproduced.* People will not accept paper money if the notes can be easily *counterfeited.* In 1987 a number of counterfeited £10 notes circulated in the Irish economy and it became a reasonably common occurrence to see forged £10 notes taped to cash registers in shops. Shopkeepers were no longer accepting £10 notes without a thorough examination of the paper. Money must be uniform in appearance so that inferior money is easily recognisable.

The second criterion is *convenience.* The money unit should be divisible into small and large units and the units should have a high value in order to facilitate purchases of a large amount of goods and services. In this context it is easy to see why gold and silver have been a favoured medium of exchange over the centuries. Gold and silver are limited in supply and cannot be reproduced. They are both divisible and small amounts of them have a high value.

A second function normally performed by money is the *store of value* function. That is, money can be used as an asset in which savings are denominated. However, this is a function not only performed by money. There a numerous other assets such as works of art or government stock or company shares that can be used for this purpose. Money is also used as a *standard of deferred payment.* Banks channel funds from savers to borrowers and the loans, denominated in monetary units, can be repaid over time.

A fourth function performed by money is that it acts as a *unit of account.* Goods and services can be valued in terms of pounds and pence. The money units which are used as a medium of exchange need not, however, necessarily perform this function. There are a number of multinational firms operating in Ireland which use dollars as their unit of account. In horse racing, the old guinea is still used as a unit of account worth £1.05, but there are no guineas in circulation any more.

# Currency in Ireland

Gold and silver were used in Ireland as a medium of exchange in ancient times, although the units took the form of rings and bracelets rather than coins.[1] Monetary units, however, took many other forms as the following quote suggests:

> ... the Annals of the Four Masters, originating from A.D. 106, state that the tribute (*Boroimhe* meaning literally "cow-tax") paid by the King of Leinster consisted of 150 cows, 150 pigs, 150 couples of men and women in servitude, 150 girls and 150 cauldrons.[2]

The first coinage in Ireland can be traced to the Norse settlement in Dublin in the 990s.[3] The amount of coinage in circulation was relatively small and largely confined to the main trading areas such as ports and towns. Coin issues increased at a reasonably steady pace between the arrival of the Normans in 1169 and 1500, when the English monarchy began to actively discourage any minting of coinage in Ireland. By the mid-sixteenth century, the English monarchy had, however, changed its position and allowed an issue of the so-called Harp coinage (sometimes referred to as "white money"). In doing so the monarchy acknowledged the existence of a separate Irish currency unit. This was followed in 1601 by an issue of copper coinage by Queen Elizabeth I.

By the 1680s, when banking-type activities first began to emerge, the currency situation in Ireland was unsatisfactory for a number of reasons. First, there was a general shortage of coins and the economy was operating on both a barter and money system (a few years earlier, James II had melted down cannons to manufacture coins; the so-called "gun money" which gave rise to the expression "not worth a brass farthing"). In addition, the coinage in circulation consisted of Continental (mostly Spanish, French and Portuguese) and English coins which were of different quality and design, and this lack of uniformity probably impaired the medium of exchange function of the coins.

Despite reforms introduced in the 1680s and the issue of paper money associated with the emergence of banking-type activities, a general shortage of coinage continued into the eighteenth century. By now it was common for merchants to issue their own coinage in order to facilitate their trade. Very little was done to alleviate the situation. In the early 1720s a Mr Wood received a patent to issue coinage (Wood's half-pence) which would have increased copper coinage in circulation by about 25%.[4] However, this patent was withdrawn two years later, partly because of the argument used by Jonathan Swift in *The Drapier's Letters* that the increase in currency would raise prices. Modern monetarists would have approved of his reasoning!

In 1797, during the turmoil of the Napoleonic wars, the convertibility of Irish and British specie to gold was suspended. This did not however result in any immediate change in the exchange rate between Irish and English currencies. Over the previous one hundred years, that exchange rate had stood at approximately 13 Irish pence to 12 English pence (or IR£1 = STG£0.92 in today's terms).

In 1803 Irish specie depreciated by approximately 12% relative to English specie and this provoked the establishment in 1804 of a parliamentary inquiry which issued a report known as the *Irish Currency Report*. This report contained many of the ideas in the famous Bullion Committee Report of 1810, the main source for nineteenth-century British monetary orthodoxy. The *Irish Currency Report* concluded that excessive credit expansion caused the 1803 depreciation. It argued that the exchange rate could be stabilised if appropriate credit policies were pursued.

*Note:*

*The bullionist controversy of 1796-1821, like the currency versus banking debate in the 1840s and the bimetallist controversy of the 1880s, was concerned with the implications of an "excessive" growth in paper money for the economy. One view was that an "excess" increase in paper money (the money supply) would lead to an increase in the price level and this, in turn, would make exports less competitive and cause the exchange rate to depreciate. The opposing view was that there was no such thing as an "excessive" increase in paper money, as the amount of money in circulation at any one time supported the amount of business being done in the economy. These controversies provide the historical background to the modern Quantity Theory of Money. We discuss this theory in Chapter 6.*

In the years after 1804, Irish currency regained its value relative to English currency. It depreciated again in 1815 but thereafter gradually stabilised at the old 1797 exchange rate of 13:12. By the time gold convertibility was resumed in 1821, this exchange rate was sufficiently established for the Bank of Ireland to accept responsibility for maintaining the exchange rate of the Irish currency. Following the Act of Union in 1800 there was full political and monetary union between Ireland and Great Britain and in 1826 the Irish currency was abolished. The currency situation now improved significantly as coins and notes in circulation were of high quality and could be obtained on demand.

Following the foundation of the Irish Free State in 1922, the Coinage Act of 1926 was passed in order to enable the Minister for Finance to issue new Irish coinage. A commission (referred to as the Parker-Willis Commission, after its chairman, Professor Henry Parker-Willis of Columbia University) was set up to advise the government on the establishment of an Irish pound. The commission recommended that an Irish pound, backed 100% by sterling and gold reserves, be created.

The recommendations of the Parker-Willis Commission were incorporated into the 1927 Currency Act and a new Irish pound, rigidly set at a one-to-one exchange rate with sterling, was issued. In order to induce confidence in the new currency, the sterling exchange rate could not be terminated without the introduction of additional legislation. In 1928 a Currency Commission was formed and made responsible for the issue of the new legal tender. These coins and notes were used until 1971 when, following the introduction of decimalisation, a new design was introduced.

Over the centuries, the exchange rate of Irish currency to English currency has varied considerably. An approximate summary is given in Table 5.1.

*Table 5.1*

**The Exchange rate of the Irish currency in terms of sterling**

| Date | Exchange rate | Movement relative to previous date |
|------|---------------|-----------------------------------|
| 1200 | Par | |
| 1487 | IR 1.5 silver coins/ UK 1 silver coin | Depreciation |
| 1561 | IR 1.3 silver coins/UK 1 silver coin | Appreciation |
| 1601-1602 | IR 4 silver coins/UK 1 silver coin | Depreciation |
| 1603 | IR 1.3 silver coins/UK 1 silver coin | Appreciation |
| 1650 | Par | Appreciation |
| 1689 | IR 13 pence/UK 12 pence | Depreciation |
| 1797-1826 | Irish currency floated against UK currency. | |
| 1826 | Par | Appreciation |
| 1979 | The Irish currency depreciated following Ireland's entry into the European Monetary System. | |

One of the main reasons why the English monarchy depreciated the Irish currency (or appreciated the English currency) was to lower the cost of the English army in Ireland. A devaluation of the Irish exchange rate meant that the English army in Ireland cost less in English currency terms. It should be noted that a revaluation of a currency in the Middle Ages was a major undertaking. Silver or gold coins had to be withdrawn from circulation and re-issued with a lower or higher silver or gold content. This is in contrast to the situation today when a currency can be revalued within minutes on foreign exchange markets. We return to the issue of exchange rates in Chapter 9.

# 5.4 Creation of Money in a Modern Economy

The main characteristics of the Irish banking system are outlined in section 5.8. At this stage, it is only necessary to point out that the associated and non-associated banks are referred to as licensed banks and to mention two important functions played by these banks in the money creation process. First, banks accept funds from the public in the form of current and deposit accounts. These two types of accounts are an important component of the money supply. Secondly, banks act as *financial intermediaries* in that they channel funds from savers to borrowers. As we will see this is a key function in the money creation process.

In order to explain how money is created, it is first necessary to define money and to examine the balance sheet of a commercial bank. In Ireland, there are two measures of the money supply: M1 and M3.

*Table 5.2*
**Money supply: June 1989**

|  | £m |
|---|---|
| Currency | 1,196.4 |
| + Current accounts | 1,419.0 |
| = *M1* | *2,615.4* |
| + Deposit accounts | 7,891.5 |
| = *M3* | *10,506.9* |

*Source*: Central Bank of Ireland, *Quarterly Bulletin*, Summer 1989

Table 5.2 shows how M1 and M3 are defined. M1 is equal to notes and coins in circulation plus current accounts in banks. Cheques written on current accounts are an alternative to cash as a means of making a payment and are therefore included in the narrow definition of money. M3 is obtained by adding licensed banks deposit accounts to M1. Cheques cannot be written on deposit accounts and as such deposit accounts are not strictly money in the medium of exchange sense. However, funds in deposit accounts can be withdrawn at very short notice and with little inconvenience (simply by going to a bank or cash machine) and are therefore included in the broad definition of money.

*Notes:*
*1. The Central Bank of Ireland at one time published an M2 money supply series. This was defined*

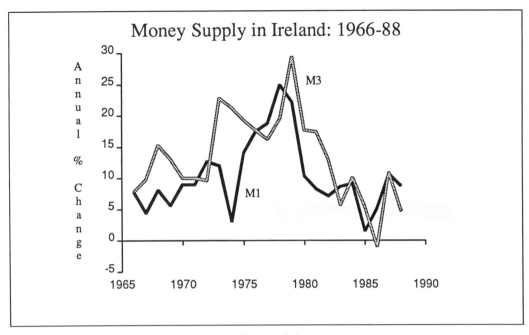

Figure 5.1

as M1 plus associated bank deposit accounts. M3 is obtained by adding non-associated bank deposit accounts to M2. The M2 measure is no longer published.

2. In 1983 the Central Bank re-defined M3. The main change was the exclusion of non-residents' deposits from the new definition. This meant that the old M3 series was no longer comparable with the new M3 series.

3. M3 does not include cash held by the licensed banks, but it does include foreign currency deposits held by residents at within-the-State offices of licensed banks.

Figure 5.1 shows the annual percentage change in M1 and M3 between 1966 and 1988. The variability of both series is the most striking feature of the chart. It should also be noted that the two series do not always move in tandem. This raises an important policy question: which definition of money supply should be of concern to the Central Bank? As we will see in Chapter 6, changes in the money supply can have an effect on the inflation rate and governments therefore consider it desirable to control the growth in money supply. But which definition of the money supply? The government in the UK attempted to control the growth in M3 as part of its economic strategy. However, this definition of money proved very difficult to control and was replaced by a very narrow measure of money, M0, (currency in circulation) in October 1985.

# The fractional reserve banking system

Consider now the simplified balance sheet of a commercial bank as outlined in Table 5.3. The liability side of the balance sheet contains current and deposit accounts and on the asset side, banks reserves and loans. A number of important points can be made in relation to this simplified balance sheet. If you ask someone (not familiar with the operation of a bank) the question; Does the bank have your money? The answer is likely to be yes, or, What do you mean?, or, I sincerely hope so! In fact, banks do not have all of their depositors' money on hand. If £1 is placed in a current or deposit account, the bank keeps only a fraction in reserve and either loans out the rest or uses it to purchase interest-bearing securities such as government stock. This is known as *fractional reserve banking* and it has evolved from the goldsmiths of the Middle Ages.

*Table 5.3*

**Commercial bank balance sheet**

| Assets | Liabilities |
|---|---|
| Reserves | Current and deposit accounts |
| Loans | |
| Total | Total |

*Note:* Reserves comprise the sum of a bank's holdings of notes and coin and deposits with the Central Bank of Ireland.

People used to place gold and other valuables with goldsmiths for safe keeping. At first, goldsmiths simply acted like a left-luggage depot in a railway station or an airport. They stored the gold in a vault for a small fee and issued receipts which could be used at a later stage to reclaim the gold. However, it soon became apparent to goldsmiths that people did not withdraw all of their gold at any one time. It was therefore possible for a goldsmith to increase profits by making loans of gold to people and charging an interest rate.

Modern banking operates on the basis that it is not necessary to keep 100% of deposits in reserve. At any one time, deposits are likely to be matched by withdrawals so that all that is really necessary for the bank is to keep a certain amount of till money to meet predictable daily requirements. If the bank has sufficient reserves to meet normal requirements, and confidence in the bank remains high, the fractional reserve banking system works very well. However, if some contingency does arise, such as the possibility of a prolonged bank strike or the announcement of bank losses on investments, then it is possible that a large proportion of bank customers will converge on the bank and withdraw their money. If that eventful day should ever arrive, a bank (on its own and without recourse to a Central Bank) will not be able to meet depositors' demands. Depositors' money will have been lent out in short-, medium- and long-term loans or invested in securities which cannot be immediately realised. In this case, the bank will have to "close its doors" and its affairs will be wound up.

Could this possibly happen in today's banking system? The answer is yes! As recently as 1984 the Continental Illinois Bank of Chicago, one of America's largest banks, collapsed as a result of investment losses. Even assurances by the Federal Reserve Board, America's Central Bank, failed to prevent "deposit flight".

# Bank profits

Interest paid by banks on deposits (no interest is paid on current accounts) is always lower than the interest charged on loans. In October 1989, the associated banks (AIB, Bank of Ireland, National Irish Bank and the Ulster Bank) paid 4.75% to 8.25% on deposits and charged 16% on term loans (other banks charge even higher lending rates). This interest differential is the main source of bank profits. It should be remembered however that banks incur *bad debts* on loans and this reduces their profits.

# Bank reserves

The licensed banks are required by law to keep a minimum reserve in relation to deposits. These reserves are set by the Central Bank of Ireland through what is referred to as the "required liquidity ratios". The liquidity ratios specify a minimum level of reserves. The banks can keep discretionary or excess reserves if they wish. There are at present two types of liquidity ratios, *primary* and *secondary*. These ratios express primary and secondary liquid assets as a percentage of relevant resources.

*Note:*
*Primary liquid assets consist of banks' holdings of notes and coins and deposits at the Central Bank. Secondary liquid assets comprise mainly government stocks. Relevant resources comprise mainly current and deposit accounts.*

In August 1989 the liquidity ratios relating to the associated banks were (the ratios are slightly different for the non-associated banks):

Primary liquidity ratio = (primary reserves/relevant resources) * 100 = 10%

*Note: the symbol * indicates multiplication.*

This ratio states that for every £1 in current and deposit accounts, the associated banks must keep a minimum of ten pence in a primary reserve (notes and coins plus deposits at the Central Bank).

Secondary liquidity ratio = (government stock/relevant resources)*100 = 25%

This ratio states that for every £1 in current and deposit accounts, the associated banks must purchase at least twenty five pence worth of government stock.

## The relationship between loans and deposits

*Loans create deposits*. When you borrow from a bank, the bank does not give you the amount of the loan in cash over the counter. Instead the bank opens an account for you and credits the amount of the loan to that account. Hence loans automatically create deposits. In the long term, when the borrower draws down the loan and spends the money, it is still true that a deposit will be created. The reason is that the recipient of that money will, very likely, place the money in a bank account. If you borrow a sum of money to purchase a video, the shop owner will, in all probability, lodge your cheque into his or her bank account by the end of the day.

*Table 5.4*
**Money creation**

| | Licensed banks' balance sheet: £m | | | | | |
|---|---|---|---|---|---|---|
| *Assets* | | | *Liabilities* | | | |
| *Increases in round* | 1 | 2 | | 1 | 2 | 3 |
| Reserves | 100 | 90 | Deposits | 1,000 | 900 | 810 |
| Loans | 900 | 810 | | | | |

We are now in a position to explain how money is created in a modern economy. If someone deposits money in a bank, there will be a multiple expansion of the money supply because (1) banks keep only a fraction of deposits in reserve and (2) loans create deposits. These two conditions will lead to a "money multiplier". To illustrate, assume a primary reserve requirement of 10% and no secondary reserve requirement and that there is only one bank in the country (this is a simplifying assumption which does not affect the conclusions). We also assume that banks do not keep any "excess" reserves as it is profitable to loan as much money as possible. Consider now the figures in Table 5.4.

Suppose someone receives £1,000 as a gift from a friend in New York and puts the money into a bank account. The bank, in line with the primary liquidity ratio, keeps only 10% (£100) in reserve and loans out the rest (£900). If the loan is used to purchase a car, the garage will receive £900 and lodge the money with its bank. Hence the car loan has resulted in the creation of a deposit of £900. That, however, is not the end of the matter. In the second round, the bank again keeps a reserve of 10% (£90) and loan out the remainder (£810). As before, the loan will create a further deposit of £810 and so on.

*Table 5.5*
**Money creation**

| Round | ΔM3 | = Δ(Currency + Current and deposit accounts) |
|---|---|---|
| 1 | 1,000 | 1,000 |
| 2 | 900 | 900 |
| 3 | 810 | 810 |
| . | . | . |
| . | . | . |
| n | . | . |
| Total | 10,000 | 10,000 |

In Table 5.5 the figures are inserted into the M3 definition of money. Recall that M3 is equal to notes plus coins plus current and deposit accounts in the banks. It is clear from the table that as bank deposits increase in each round, so too will the money supply. In fact, it can be shown that given a primary reserve ratio of 10%, the initial £1,000 deposit will lead to a £10,000 increase in the money supply.

*Note:*
*This process also works in reverse. If a bank looses reserves, there will be a multiple contraction of*

*credit. This is the reason for our initial assumption that the £1,000 came from a friend in New York, that is, from outside the Irish banking system. If a withdrawal in one bank is matched by a deposit in another bank, the two transactions cancel out and there will be no overall change in the money supply.*

The final increase in the money supply can be calculated by using a simplified formula for the *money multiplier*.

*Money multiplier (m) = 1/reserve requirement*

In the above example, m = 1/0.1 = 10 so that;

| Change in M3 | = | m | * | initial deposit |
|---|---|---|---|---|
| £10,000 | = | 10 | * | £1,000 |

Note that the higher the reserve requirement, the lower the money multiplier. A reserve requirement of 20%, for example, gives a money multiplier of 5 and a reserve requirement of 5% gives a money multiplier of 20. The less money "leaked-out" in the form of reserves, the greater the final increase in the money supply. In practice, bank reserves will not be the only form of leakage. An increase in currency holdings will reduce the size of the money multiplier. Take an extreme example where someone borrows from a bank and "hoards" the money in a box in the attic. The money will not end up back in a bank deposit and the money creation process will come to a halt. In section 5.7, following a discussion of the Central Bank balance sheet and the techniques of money control, we introduce a more realistic money multiplier which takes account of currency holdings by the public.

*Note:*
*Do not confuse the fiscal multiplier, discussed in the Chapter 3, with the money creation multiplier. While the concepts are similar, the fiscal multiplier relates government expenditure to GNP, whereas the money creation multiplier relates a change in a bank deposit to the final change in the money supply.*

# 5.5 Functions of the Central Bank

One way of outlining the functions of the Central Bank is to examine its balance sheet. In Table 5.6 a simplified version of the Central Bank of Ireland's balance sheet for June 1989 is given.

Consider first the liability side of the balance sheet. The Central Bank is responsible for the issue of currency in the system and since this is a claim on the

Central Bank it is recorded on the liability side of the balance sheet. We will examine in a moment what backs domestic currency on the asset side of the balance sheet. The other two entries are licensed bank reserves and the government's account at the Central Bank. The licensed banks and the government keep an account with the Central Bank, just as some individuals keep an account with a commercial bank. The Central Bank pays an undisclosed interest rate on these two accounts (the rate is, in effect, a "state secret" but it is believed to be approximately 3% below market rates). With the exception of the currency item, the liability side of the Central Bank balance sheet is not very different from the licensed bank balance sheet considered earlier in Table 5.3.

*Table 5.6*
**Central Bank balance sheet: £m. June 1989**

| Assets | | Liabilities | |
|---|---|---|---|
| External reserves | 2,497.5 | Currency | 1,196.4 |
| Loans: | | Licensed bank reserves | 1,086.3 |
|    Banks | 1,079.9 | | |
|    Government | 161.5 | Government deposits | 581.4 |
| Other | 344.7 | Other | 1,219.5 |
| | 4,083.6 | | 4,083.6 |

*Source*: Central Bank of Ireland, *Quarterly Bulletin*, Summer 1989

The most important entry on the asset side of the balance sheet is the *external reserves*. This is the country's offical holding of foreign currency, gold and other reserves and is basically what backs the domestic currency. As will be explained in Chapter 9, the Central Bank stands willing to exchange foreign currency, such as sterling, dollars and yen, for Irish pounds, and it is this *convertibility* which maintains confidence in the Irish currency and stabilises the exchange rate.

The next two entries on the asset side show the Central Bank lending to the banks and the government. The Central Bank both accepts deposits and makes loans to the commercial banks and the government and in this sense acts as banker to the banks and the government. Banks normally borrow from the Central Bank if they are short of reserves in relation to the legal primary and secondary reserve ratios. In this regard, the Central Bank is sometimes referred to as "lender of last resort".

We mentioned earlier in the discussion of fractional reserve banking that banks do not keep all depositors' money in liquid assets. It is in this regard that the "lender of last resort" function is important. To put the situation in perspective, consider the case of the *private banks* which operated in Ireland up to the mid-nineteenth century. Private banks extended credit by issuing notes which could be used to purchase goods and services.[5] The size of these banks was limited by legislation passed in 1783 which restricted the number of partners in a bank. Because of an over-reliance on land as collateral, private banks proved vulnerable in times of crisis.

In one month in 1820, thirty private banks failed in Munster alone.[6] The withdrawal of the British navy from Cork following the end of the Napoleonic wars and a general fall in agricultural prices resulted in a number of merchants going bankrupt. This in turn led to speculation that certain private banks in Cork were in trouble owing to bad debts, i.e. their assets were not adequate to cover their note issue. Banking history clearly demonstrates that if people think their deposits are in jeopardy they immediately attempt to withdraw their money. However, if everyone wants his or her money at the same time the banks cannot pay as they keep only a fraction of deposits in reserves and loan out the rest in medium- to long-term loans which cannot be recalled at short notice. The failures in Cork set off a "run" on the other banks throughout the country. By the time the crisis settled, only ten private banks remained solvent outside Dublin and their operations were so restricted that they had, to all intents and purposes, ceased to function.

The private banks in the eighteenth and nineteenth centuries stood alone. There was no Central Bank from which they could borrow in times of crisis and they therefore had no means of stopping a "run" on the banking system. It should also be noted that there was no such thing as "limited liability" at this time. Bankers in Limerick, for example, whose banks had failed lost their town houses and country mansions. To judge from newspaper reports of the day, they would also have lost their lives if their creditors had their way!

Today, the Central Bank essentially acts as a safeguard behind the commercial banks. If a particular bank finds itself unable to meet withdrawals, the funds can be borrowed from the Central Bank and in that way a crisis can be prevented from developing. Banking history also demonstrates that if depositors find they can have their money on demand they do not withdraw it! Reserves are only needed when there is a lack of confidence in the bank. Of course, the banks have to pay interest on the borrowed reserves and eventually repay them. Even though there is a lender of last resort, this does not remove all discipline from the banks.

Central banking in Ireland goes back to 1783 when the Bank of Ireland (now a commercial bank) was founded by Royal Charter. This bank operated on a commercial basis while simultaneously, but in a limited way, performing the functions of a central bank. It issued notes, managed the government's account and acted as (a reluctant) lender of last resort at various times, including during the Munster Bank crisis of 1885.

In 1934 a Commission on Banking, Currency and Credit was formed to report on the possibility of setting up a central bank in Ireland. The commission reported in 1938 and, despite commercial bank opposition, recommended that a central bank be established but that the sterling link be maintained. The recommendations were incorporated into the Central Bank Act 1942, which established a central bank whose primary function was to "safeguard the integrity of the currency". The powers of the new Central Bank were, however, very limited. The bank could act as "lender of last resort" and could use "open market operations" (discussed below) to control the money supply, but it did not act as a banker to either the government or the commercial banks. The government continued to hold its account with the Bank of Ireland and the commercial banks held most of their reserves in the London money markets.

In 1965, the Central Bank first issued "letters of advice" (or credit guidelines) to the banks in relation to credit expansion. Real economic growth was 5% per annum in 1965 and the balance of payments deficit had risen to over 4% of GNP. The "letters of advice" on credit were intended to restrain credit expansion and curtail the growing balance of payments deficit. Also at this time, a number of new banks, such as the North American Banks, began operations in Ireland, and the Allied Irish Bank and Bank of Ireland groups were formed following a series of bank amalgamations. The Central Bank was promoting and developing new markets in foreign exchange, government stocks and money, and it was becoming increasingly clear that the 1942 Central Bank legislation was inadequate. As a response to the changing monetary environment, the Central Bank Act 1971 was passed. This act significantly increased the powers of the Central Bank. Some of the main features were

1. the Central Bank became the licensing authority for banks.
2. the government's account was transferred from the Bank of Ireland to the Central Bank.
3. the commercial banks were required to keep their reserves with the Central Bank and the bank was given the power to issue primary and secondary reserve ratios (these were first issued in August 1972).
4. the new legislation made it possible to break the sterling link by government order, as indeed happened on the 30th March 1979, seventeen days after Ireland joined the European Monetary System.

To summarise: the Central Bank issues the currency and both accepts deposits and makes loans to the government and the commercial banks. The Central Bank is also responsible for monetary policy. Monetary policy normally involves controlling the money supply with a view to influencing nominal GNP. The Bank also plays an important role in the day-to-day operation of the foreign exchange market, but ultimate responsibility for exchange rate policy rests with the Minister for Finance. We will examine the techniques of money control in the next section and monetary policy is discussed in Chapter 6.

# 5.6 The Control of the Money Supply

Central banks typically use the following techniques to control the growth of money in the economy.

A. *Changes in reserve requirements*. If the Central Bank increased the primary reserve ratio from, say, 10% to 20%, this reduces the money multiplier and restricts the growth in money. The banks are required to cover a larger proportion of deposits with reserves and consequentially there will be monetary contraction.

B. *Open market operations*. If the Central Bank buys government stock from the public (individuals, pension funds, life assurance companies) on the open market, that is the normal bond market, this operation increases the money supply in the economy. The Central Bank receives government stock and the public receives a cheque drawn on the Central Bank which, when lodged with the customer's bank, increases the bank's reserves. The money creation process will lead to a multiple increase in the money supply. Conversely, sales of government stock to the general public will reduce the money supply, as funds will be withdrawn from banks in order to pay the Central Bank. There will now be a multiple reduction in the economy's money supply. In general, sales of government stock by the Central Bank reduce the money supply, whereas purchases increase it.

C. *Credit guidelines*. The Central Bank can try to dictate to the banks how much they can lend over some specified period of time. For example, the banks might be allowed to increase lending by, say, 10% in a particular year. Credit guidelines are asymmetrical in the sense that they restrict the growth of credit and therefore money creation in the economy, but they can only permit an expansion of the money supply. We discuss credit guidelines in Chapter 14.

*Note:*
*Refer to the licensed banks' balance sheet in Table 5.3 and note that the three controls mentioned above relate to reserves, deposits and loans respectively.*

D. *The discount rate*. The discount (or bank) rate is the interest rate the Central Bank charges on loans. In Ireland there is also a "short-term credit facility" (STFC) interest rate. This is essentially an overdraft facility for the licensed banks at the Central Bank. If the banks withdraw funds under this facility they are charged the STFC interest rate. An increase in the discount rate discourages the commercial banks from borrowing from the Central Bank and in this way restricts lending in the economy. For example, a commercial bank may wish to borrow from the Central

Bank in order to increase its reserves and lend to the general public. An increase in the discount rate may discourage this lending because the bank will now have to charge its customer a higher rate of interest. More often than not, the Central Bank uses the discount rate to indicate its intentions to the commercial banks. If the Central Bank lowers the discount rate, it would be taken as a signal to increase lending and vice versa. In Chapters 12 and 14 we discuss in greater detail the techniques used by the Central Bank of Ireland to influence monetary aggregates.

# 7 High-Powered Money

The sum of the Central Bank's liabilities (or assets) is referred to as "high-powered money" or the "monetary base". It is called "high-powered" because any change in Central Bank liabilities will have a multiple or expanded impact on the money supply. In this section, we examine the relationship between the money supply and high-powered money.

Ignoring, for simplicity, government deposits and "other liabilities" on the liability side of the Central Bank balance sheet (Table 5.6), high-powered money (H) is equal to currency (CU) plus licensed bank reserves at the Central Bank (RE).

(1) $H = CU + RE$

If we now assume that people hold currency in proportion to current and deposit accounts (D):

(2) $CU = c_p * D$

where $0 < c_p < 1$. That is, $c_p$ takes on fractional values between 0 and 1. If $c_p$ was equal to, say, 0.1, this means that for every £1 held in current and deposit accounts, the public holds ten pence in currency.

Because of the primary liquidity ratio, licensed bank reserves at the Central Bank are also related to current and deposit accounts.

(3) $RE = r_b * D$

Again, $0 < r_b < 1$. If the primary reserve ratio were 10%, $r_b$ would be at least 0.1. The banks can, however, keep excess reserves if they wish. If equations 2 and 3 are inserted into equation 1, we obtain;

(4) $H = (c_p + r_b)D$

Recall now that the M3 definition of money supply is equal to currency plus current and deposit accounts.

(5)  $M3 = CU + D$

Substitute equation 2 into equation 5;

(6)  $M3 = (c_p + 1)D$

The final step in deriving the relationship between M3 and H is to express equation 6 and equation 4 as a ratio.

(7)  $M3/H = (c_p + 1)/(c_p + r_b)$

or

(8)  $M3 = (c_p + 1)/(c_p + r_b) * H$

The ratio $(c_p + 1)/(c_p + r_b)$ is the *money multiplier*. High-powered money (H) is related to the overall money supply (M3) via the money multiplier. Put another way, the money multiplier shows how a change in H will have a multiple effect on M3. This multiplier is a more realistic version of the money multiplier given in section 5.4, as it allows for currency leakages. For example, if the $c_p$ coefficient was zero (the public does not increase currency holdings as deposits increase), we obtain the money multiplier of section 5.4. This clearly is an unrealistic assumption and the earlier money multiplier was grossly oversimplified.

We can calculate the money multiplier in the Irish economy for June 1989 using the data in Tables 5.2 and 5.6.

$c_p = CU/D = 1196.4/9310.5 = 0.128$

$r_b = RE/D = 1086.3/9310.5 = 0.117$

The money multiplier is equal to

$(c_p + 1)/(c_p + r_b) = (0.128 + 1)/(0.128 + 0.117) = 4.6$

This means that an increase of £1 in high-powered money would lead to an increase of £4.6 in the money supply. It is easy to see that an increase in currency holdings in relation to deposits ($c_p$), will reduce the money multiplier. For example, if $c_p$ increased from 0.128 to 0.2, the money multiplier would fall to 3.89. Similarly, an increase in $r_b$ will decrease the money multiplier.

High-powered money is increased whenever the Central Bank increases its assets or its liabilities. It follows therefore that if the Central Bank can control its liabilities then, via the money multiplier, it should be able to control the money supply in the economy. In practice, however, money supply control has proved to be a very difficult task. As recent UK experience illustrates, the problems include $c_p$ and $r_b$ coefficients that vary over time with the result that the money multiplier is not constant. Under these circumstances, control of high-powered money does not translate simply into control of the money supply. None the less, it is not possible to have a sustained expansion of the money supply without an increase in the monetary base.

# Irish Financial Institutions

The banking system in Ireland is similar to that in the UK and Canada in that it is characterised by a few large banks with hundreds of branches. Banking in the US, on the other hand, is characterised by thousands of small, independent and localised banks. Banks and other financial Institutions in Ireland are classified as follows:

*Associated banks* (Allied Irish Bank, Bank of Ireland, National Irish Bank and the Ulster Bank). These banks are often referred to as retail or clearing banks. They are public quoted companies which provide a full range of lending and deposit facilities.

*Non-associated banks*
1. Merchant and commercial banks (Allied Irish Investment Bank, Algemene Bank Nederland, Guinness and Mahon, The Bank of Nova Scotia, Citibank, etc.). These banks tend to cater for large corporate and personal accounts and provide investment advice and consultancy services.
2. Industrial banks (Allied Irish Finance, Bank of Ireland Finance, Bowmaker Bank, Lombard and Ulster, UDT Bank, etc.). These banks largely provide fixed interest loans to the personal sector for consumer durables and to industry for machinery and other equipment.

*Note:*
*The associated and non-associated banks comprise the licensed bank group. The term "associated" bank comes from the Central Bank Act of 1942. It indicates a "special" relationship between these banks and the Central Bank. The remaining banks are simply referred to as non-associated banks. It should be noted that the associated banks have important subsidiaries operating in the non-associated bank categories and in hire purchase finance.*

*State-sponsored financial institutions* (Industrial Credit Corporation and the

Agricultural Credit Bank). These are state-owned banks which have a duty to act as development banks in industry and agriculture.

*The post office savings bank*. This bank is a government owned savings bank. All deposits are lent to the government.

*Trustee savings banks*. Approximately 80% of deposits are lent to the government and the remainder is lent to the public. These banks are owned by trustees on behalf of depositors.

*Building societies* (First National Building Society, Educational Building Society, Irish Permanent Building Society etc.). Building societies lend money for house purchase against the security of the property.

*Hire purchase finance companies* (Allied Finance, Advance Finance etc.). These companies are similar to the industrial banks in that they provide fixed interest loans for the purchase of consumer durables and machinery for industry.

*Credit unions*. Credit unions are localised, co-operative banks whose main business is consumer loans on a non-profit basis.

*Note:*
*We recommended that the reader obtain a copy of a recent issue of the Central Bank of Ireland's Quarterly Bulletin as it contains all the important monetary aggregates. The statistical appendix to the bulletin contains a complete list of financial institutions in Ireland.*

The principal difference between the various institutions lies in the type of service offered and in differences in interest rates charged on loans. For example, the interest rate charged by the industrial banks is roughly double that charged by the associated banks. In October 1989, the associated banks overdraft and term loan rate was 16%. In contrast, the *annual percentage rate* (APR) charged by the industrial banks varied from 19.4% to 28.3%. It should be note that the industrial banks charge interest on the initial sum borrowed right through to the day the entire loan is paid off. Even if there is only a small amount of money outstanding on a loan, the bank continues to calculate the interest on the total amount of money originally borrowed. The associated banks, on the other hand, charge interest on the reducing principal. If there is, say, £50 outstanding on a loan, the interest charged to the borrower is calculated on that £50. The reason for the higher interest rate charged by finance houses etc. is that their loans are riskier and include higher administration costs.

Figure 5.2 shows relative shares in the deposit market for the years 1966, 1976 and 1988. In 1966, the associated banks and the building societies held

## Deposit Market in Ireland: 1966

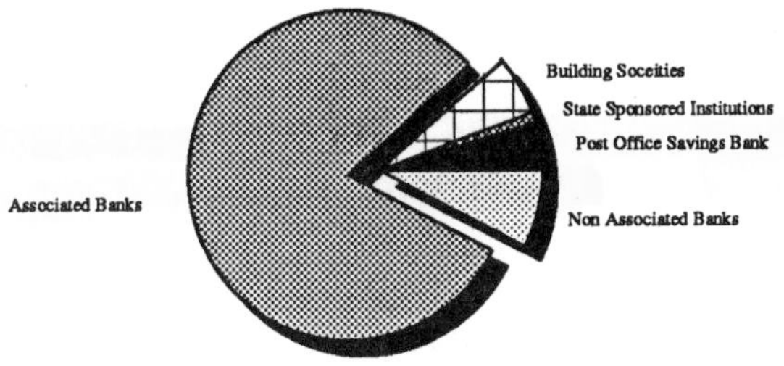

Building Soceities
State Sponsored Institutions
Post Office Savings Bank
Non Associated Banks
Associated Banks

## Deposit Market in Ireland: 1976

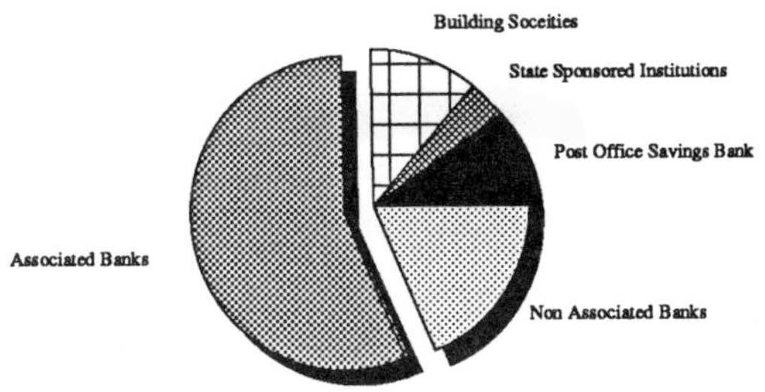

Building Soceities
State Sponsored Institutions
Post Office Savings Bank
Non Associated Banks
Associated Banks

## Deposit Market in Ireland: 1988

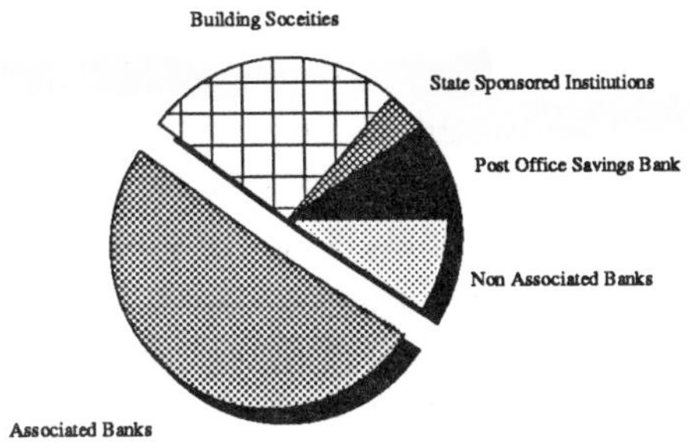

Building Soceities
State Sponsored Institutions
Post Office Savings Bank
Non Associated Banks
Associated Banks

Figure 5.2

101

approximately 80% and 6% of the deposit market respectively. By 1988, their relative share had shifted to 50% and 26% respectively. (The 1988 data for the associated and non-associated banks are slight underestimates because they exclude, due to Central Bank revisions, non-resident deposit accounts). Other financial institutions, such as the post office savings bank and the state-sponsored banks have also gained, but not by as much as the building societies. The building societies gain is partly due to increased demand for housing, confidentiality with regard to ownership of accounts and the favourable tax treatment of deposit interest from this source, up to 1986.

The Finance Act of 1986, however, moved some way towards creating a "level playing field" for all financial institutions. All banking institutions, including the building societies, are now required to deduct a 35% tax on deposit interest. This is the *deposit interest retention tax* (DIRT). This did not involve any change as far as the banks were concerned. However, prior to the introduction of DIRT, the building societies were charging a low "composite tax rate" on deposit interest and the new legislation involved an increase in deposit tax. The Finance Act also removed the disclosure requirements from banks. Banks are no longer required to disclose interest payments to the Revenue Commissioners.

It should also be noted that tax concessions have also been an important factor in the rapid growth of life assurance and pension funds in Ireland. These institutions now attract nearly 50% of total personal savings in the Ireland.

The Irish financial sector is small by international standards. As one commentator on Ireland's financial services has noted " ... the assets of the Halifax Building Society (Britain's largest building society) is (sic) 50% greater than the assets of Ireland's two biggest banks and all the Irish building societies combined."[7] However, while the financial market is relatively small, there are a large number of regulatory bodies in Ireland. The licensed banks and hire purchase finance companies are controlled by the Central Bank. The Department of Finance regulates the post office and the trustee savings banks. The Department of the Environment in conjunction with the Registrar of Friendly Societies controls credit unions and until recently building societies. Legislation passed in 1989 placed building societies under the control of the Central Bank. The Department of Industry and Commerce is responsible for insurance companies and firms operating under the 'Money Lenders' Acts. It is often argued that this lack of uniformity in regulation has resulted in unfair competition in the Irish financial sector.

The years ahead are likely to see important changes in Ireland's financial services. Competition will intensify with the completion of the Custom House Docks site, possible de-regulation and tax harmonisation and the removal of capital and trade barriers proposed for the European Community in 1992.

# 9 Conclusion

In this chapter we introduced money and banking. Some of the main points discussed include:

- Money performs a number of functions. The most important is its role as a medium of exchange

- In Ireland, there are two measures of the money supply, M1 and M3

- Banks keep only a fraction of depositors' money is reserve and either loan out the rest or purchase interest-bearing securities such as government stock

- The licensed banks are required to keep a minimum reserve in relation to deposits. These reserves, known as primary and secondary reserves, are set by the Central Bank

- Bank lending results in an increase in bank deposits

- Because of the fractional reserve banking system and because loans create deposits, a net increase in bank deposits will lead to a multiple expansion in the money supply. Conversely, a net withdrawl of deposits will lead to a multiple contraction in the money supply

- The Central Bank issues currency and both accepts deposits and makes loans to the government and the licensed banks. The Central Bank is also responsible for monetary policy

- Central Banks typically use "open market operations", "changes in the reserve requirements" and/or "credit guidelines" to influence the growth in the money supply

- The sum of the Central Bank's liabilities is referred to as high-powered money. High-powered money is related to the money supply via the money multiplier

- The Irish banking system is characterised by a few banks with hundreds of branches.

# Notes

1. P. Nolan, *A Monetary History of Ireland*, London, 1926.

2. P. Einzig, *Primitive Money*, New York: Pergamon, 2nd edition, 1966, p. 239.

3. See P. Mc Gowan, "Money and Banking in Ireland: Origins, Development and Future", Paper presented to the Statistical and Social Inquiry Society of Ireland, December, 1988, for an extended analysis of money and banking in Ireland.

4. P. Mc Gowan, (*op. cit.*).

5. P. Mc Gowan notes that private banks "... were primarily concerned with facilitating the transfer of agricultural output from the countryside to Dublin and abroad and placing the proceeds of the sale of that output at the disposal of the landlords" (P. Mc Gowan, *op. cit.*, p. 10). Merchants borrowed from the private banks to pay farmers for, say, grain which was sold on the domestic market and exported, expected receipts and other assets being used as collateral. The farmers then paid the notes to landowners as rent and the landowners, in turn, returned the notes to the private banks in exchange for gold, silver or foreign currency. Hence the private banks facilitated a transfer of resources from tenant farmers to landowners. The private banks were superseded by the "joint stock banks" following the banking crises in the early 1920s. In contrast to the private banks, joint stock banks had at least six major shareholders (who accepted unlimited liability) and they were therefore better able to withstand any crises that might arise.

6. E. O'Kelly, *The Old Private Banks and Bankers of Munster*, Cork University Press, 1959.

7. M. Walsh, "Perspectives on the Irish Financial Markets", 5th Annual Lecture, Irish Banks Professorship in Banking and Finance, University College, Dublin, November, 1987.

# Chapter 6

# Monetary Policy in a Closed Economy

## 1 Introduction

Following the discussion in Chapter 5 of the supply of money, we begin this chapter by introducing the demand for money. We then show how the supply and demand for money determine the interest rate in the economy. This is followed by a discussion of monetary policy and in particular of the relative merits of fiscal and monetary policy in influencing output and prices. We conclude the chapter by discussing the Quantity Theory of Money.

## 2 The Demand for Money

At first sight, the concept of the "demand for money" (Md) must appear rather odd. After all, if you ask someone what is their "demand for money", the answer is likely to be infinity or some very large figure. The term "demand for money" is, however, used here in a rather special way and does not refer to the desire to be rich!

People have a choice as to how to store their wealth. Wealth can be kept in money, government stocks, company shares or consumer durables such as works of art or houses. The essential difference between money and the other assets mentioned above is that money is *liquid.* That is, its value can be easily and quickly realised. Unlike the other assets mentioned, however, money does not give a *return* over time. Government stocks, company shares and consumer durables do give a return but they are illiquid in that their values may not be easily realised without incurring a capital loss. The question we wish to address here is why people keep some or all of their wealth in money. That is, why do people demand money?

*Note:*
*Deposit accounts, on which interest is paid, are part of the broader definition of money. In reality, there is a spectrum of assets ranging from the very liquid to the totally illiquid.*

The Keynesian answer to this question, as given in the *Keynesian Theory of Liquidity Preference,*[1] is that people desire liquidity (demand money) for transactions, precautionary and speculative reasons. We now examine each of these motives in turn.

## The transactions and precautionary motives

People hold (demand) money for *transactions* purposes (to pay bus fares, buy petrol or pay for a lunch). This constitutes the transactions demand for money. Related to this transactions motive is the so-called "precautionary" motive. If someone is going away on a holiday or business trip, additional money will be held to cater for any contingency that may arise. This is referred to as the precautionary motive for demanding money.

It is assumed that the transactions and precautionary motives for demanding money depend on the level of national income or GNP. As GNP or national income changes, people need more or less money to purchase goods and services and for precautionary reasons. Hence, an increase in GNP leads to an increase in the demand for money and conversely a fall in GNP reduces the demand for money. The transaction and precautionary motives for holding money may be written mathematically as:

(1) $Md = f(GNP)$

or separating nominal GNP into its real and price components:

(2) $Md = f(\text{real GNP}, P)$

or

(3) $Md/P = f(\text{real GNP})$

Equation (3) states that the real demand for transactions and precautionary balances is a function of real GNP. An increase in real GNP increases the demand for money and conversely, a fall in real GNP reduces the demand for money.

## The speculative motive

*Bonds* issued by a company differ from *shares* in a company in a number of important ways. Shareholders own a proportion of the company and have voting rights, which gives them some control over the operations of the company. Also, shareholders are paid an uncertain dividend which depends on the profits or the performance of the company. In contrast, bondholders simply lend money to a company for a specific period of time and do not have any control over the company's affairs. The bondholder also knows with certainty the return on the bond, as bonds pay a fixed monetary return (*coupon*) until the maturity date. For example, a bond with a face value of £2,000 and a coupon of £100 that matures in 1995 entitles the bondholder to a sum of £100 every year until 1995 as well as the repayment of the initial sum of £2,000 in 1995.

Consider now the data relating to bonds given in Table 6.1. The purpose of the table is to show the effect of changes in interest rates (line 1) on bond prices (line 3). Allowing for brokers' fees, the interest rate received from a bank should be comparable with the yield on bonds. If interest rates exceeded bond yields, investors would move their funds out of bonds into banks and this would have the effect of raising bond yields and lowering interest rates. In other words, *arbitrage* ensures that bank interest rates and bond yields are about the same. Bond yields (line 4) are therefore closely related to the interest rates given in line 1. We shall show that if the yield on bonds is to remain in line with bank interest rates, the price of bonds must rise (fall) as interest rates fall (rise).

Bondholders receive a fixed return, the coupon, on bonds. In line 2, the coupon is assumed to be £10 per annum. If now interest rates vary from 20% to 10% to 5% and the coupon on a bond is fixed at £10, how much will the investor be willing to pay for the bond? Given that the bond yield must equal the interest rate, the price of the bond (line 3) will rise as interest rates fall. (£10/£50)*100 = 20% and (£10/£100)*100 = 10%, and so on.

*Table 6.1*

**The relationship between interest rates and bond prices**

| | | | |
|---|---|---|---|
| 1. Interest rate received from bank | 20% | 10% | 5% |
| 2. Fixed return on bonds | £10 | £10 | £10 |
| 3. Price of bonds | £50 | £100 | £200 |
| 4. Yield on bonds | 20% | 10% | 5% |

The important point is that an increase in interest rates leads to a fall in bond prices and a decrease in interest rates leads to an increase in bond prices. In other words, interest rates and bond prices are *inversely* related.

The relationship between interest rates and bond prices means that bondholders will make a capital gain when interest rates fall and a capital loss when interest rates rise. Investors should therefore buy bonds if they expect interest rates to fall and sell bonds if they expect interest rates to rise. This strategy provides the basis of the Keynesian speculative motive. In reality, the government is the largest issuer of bonds, and government bonds provide a convenient medium for speculators trying to make capital gains.

Keynes assumed a "normal" rate of interest and argued that departures from this "normal" rate would be temporary. If interest rates went above this "normal" rate, the expectation would be that rates would fall at a later stage. Similarly, if interest rates fell below the "normal" rate, the expectation would be that rates would rise again some time in the future.

Suppose, for example, that the "normal" rate of interest is considered to be 10% and interest rates increase from 10% to 20%. An investor holding bonds will have incurred a capital loss. However, the expectation is that interest rates will return to the "normal" level of 10%; that is, interest rates are expected to fall. Investors should therefore reduce their money holdings and purchase bonds in anticipation of making a capital gain sometime in the future.

This means, however, that the increase in interest rates from 10% to 20% has led to a fall in the demand for money. Investors have moved their wealth from money into bonds in order to make a capital gain. The speculative motive therefore provides an explanation for the inverse relationship between interest rates and the demand for money.

Mathematically this relationship can be written:

(4) $Md = f(r)$

An increase in the interest rate reduces the demand for money and, conversely, a fall in the interest rate increases the demand for money.

*Note:*

*There are quite a number of different interest rates, for example, interest rates on short and long term government stocks, on low and high risk company shares, not to mention the different interest rates charged by the banks on deposits and loans. All these interest rates to some degree move together so that we can refer to an average or representative interest rate as "the" interest rate.*

Combining equations (1) and (4), the demand for money equation becomes:

(5) $Md = f(\underset{+}{GNP}, \underset{-}{r})$

Equation (5) states that the demand for money (Md) is a function of GNP and the interest rate (r). The signs underneath the variables indicate how the variables inside the brackets influence the demand for money. There is a positive relationship between GNP and demand for money and an inverse or negative relationship between the interest rate and demand for money.

*Note:*

*Causation runs from the variable inside the brackets to the variable on the left hand side (and not*

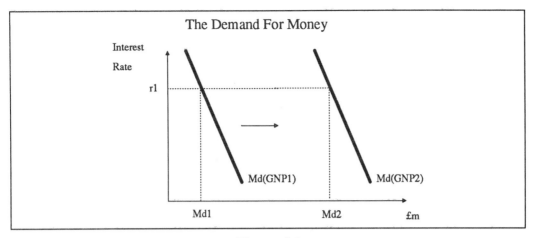

Figure 6.1

*the other way). As a result, the variables inside the bracket are referred to as "explanatory" variables and the left hand side variable as the "dependent" variable. In this case, the demand for money depends on the variables inside the brackets.*

A graphic representation of the demand for money function is given in Figure 6.1. The downward-sloping line shows how the interest rate on the vertical axis affects demand for money on the horizontal axis. An increase in the interest rate reduces the demand for money and conversely a fall in the interest rate increases the demand for money.

GNP on the other hand determines the *position* (*location*) of the demand for money line. An increase in GNP shifts the demand for money line to the right (for constant interest rates) and vice versa. Hence, while the relationship between the interest rate and the demand for money is shown *along* the line, the relationship between GNP and the demand for money is shown by *movements* of the line (parallel shifts to the left and right).

# .3 Money Market Equilibrium

In Figure 6.2, a money supply (Ms) curve is combined with a demand for money (Md) curve. The money supply curve is shown as a vertical line which indicates that changes in the interest rate do not affect the supply of money. This assumes that the money supply is completely controlled by the Central Bank. If changes in interest rates did affect the money supply, the Ms curve would be upward-sloping to the right.

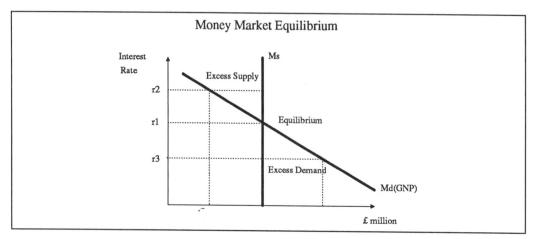

Figure 6.2

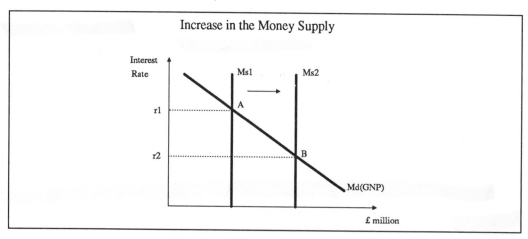

Figure 6.3

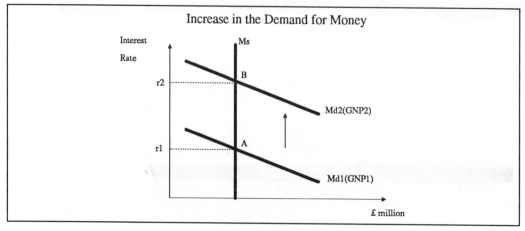

Figure 6.4

110

The important conclusion to be drawn from Figure 6.2 is that *the supply and demand for money determine the interest rate*. The interest rate (r) is simply the "price of money" and, as with other prices, is determined by the forces of supply and demand. At an interest rate of r2, there is an excess supply of money and the interest rate decreases. At an interest rate of r3, there is an excess demand for money and the interest rate increases. In both cases, the interest rate converges towards the equilibrium rate.

*Note:*
*An excess demand for money implies an excess supply of bonds. In an attempt to regain equilibrium the public sells bonds, which drives down the rate of interest.*

Figure 6.3 illustrates what happens to the interest rate when the Central Bank increases the money supply. The money supply (Ms) curve moves out to the right and the interest rate falls from r1 to the new equilibrium at r2. An increase in the money supply therefore reduces the interest rate. Conversely, a reduction in the money supply by the Central Bank leads to an increase in the interest rate.

Figure 6.4 illustrates the case where the demand for money (Md) curve shifts upwards to the right following an increase in GNP (recall that GNP determines the position of the Md curve). The resulting excess demand for money increases the interest rate from r1 to r2. Similarly, a fall in nominal GNP will shift the Md curve downwards and interest rates will fall.

# 4 Monetary Policy

We are now in a position to explain how changes in the nominal money supply can affect nominal GNP. Because money acts as a medium of exchange, the money market may be incorporated into the Keynesian model as underlying the expenditure or demand side of the economy. The expanded Keynesian model is given in Table 6.2.

The model is characterised by two markets: the supply and demand for goods and services (GNP and AD respectively) and the supply and demand for money (Ms and Md respectively). The authorities have two *policy instruments*, government expenditure and taxation (*fiscal policy*) and the money supply and interest rates (*monetary policy*) with which to influence output, income and prices.

The model in Table 6.2 outlines how the principal macroeconomic variables are related. For example, an increase in government expenditure (G) increases aggregate demand (AD) by definition. If the economy is initially in equilibrium, the increase in G leads to an excess demand for goods and services (GNP). Firms recognise this excess demand as stocks will be falling and they respond by producing more goods and services. The resulting increase in GNP leads to an increase in national income (NI) and a reduction in unemployment (U).

*Table 6.2*

**The basic Keynesian model in a closed economy**

---

$$\text{Fiscal policy}$$
$$\downarrow$$

$$\text{U} \leftrightarrow \text{NI} \leftrightarrow \text{GNP} = \text{AD} \equiv \text{C} + \text{I} + \text{G}$$

$$\text{Ms: r :Md(GNP)}$$
$$\uparrow$$

$$\textit{Monetary policy}$$

---

*where:*

| | | | | | |
|---|---|---|---|---|---|
| *U* | = | *Unemployment* | *NI* | = | *National income* |
| *GNP* | = | *Gross national product* | *AD* | = | *Aggregate demand* |
| *C* | = | *Consumer expenditure* | *I* | = | *Investment* |
| *G* | = | *Government expenditure* | *Ms* | = | *Money supply* |
| *r* | = | *Interest rate* | *Md* | = | *Demand for money* |

---

*Notes:*

(1) As already mentioned in Chapter 3, the symbol $\leftrightarrow$ means that the two variables on either side are closely related. Hence an increase in GNP is quickly followed by an increase in NI and this in turn leads to a fall in unemployment. Similarly, we use the identity symbol, $\equiv$, to indicate that aggregate demand and expenditure are one and the same thing and we use a colon (:) to indicate that the interest rate depends on the forces of supply and demand for money.

(2) Because we are discussing policy in a closed economy, imports and exports are omitted from the components of aggregate demand.

---

At this stage the model is rather lopsided in the sense that the emphasis is very much on the demand side of the economy. It is implicitly assumed that there are unemployed resources in the economy, which will come into production to meet an increased demand for output. We develop the supply side on the economy in greater detail in Chapters 7 and 8.

Two points should be noted about the model as outlined in Table 6.2. First, on the supply side, it is assumed that increases in nominal GNP and NI are associated with a reduction in unemployment (U). That is, as firms produce more output they hire more workers and unemployment falls. This is a very tenuous series of events because the effect on U depends crucially on a number of factors, such as the degree of capacity utilisation and the technology used to produce more output. The second point to note is that GNP is placed in brackets after Md to indicate that changes in GNP affect the demand for money.

Consider now how changes in the nominal money supply might affect nominal GNP. In this Keynesian model, changes in the money supply affect GNP and NI via *interest rates (r) and investment (I)*. The sequence is as follows: an increase in Ms lowers the interest rate (r) and this in turn increases investment (I). The increase in I, by definition, increases AD and therefore GNP.

In short:

$$\uparrow Ms \rightarrow \downarrow r \rightarrow \uparrow I \rightarrow \uparrow AD \rightarrow \uparrow GNP \rightarrow \uparrow NI \rightarrow \downarrow U$$

*Notes:*
*(1) Fiscal policy is much more direct as an increase in G increases AD by definition.*
*(2) It is also possible that a change in interest rates will affect consumer expenditure (C) in addition to investment (I). This potentially important link is not considered at this stage.*
*(3) The symbols, ↑, ↓ and → indicate increase, decrease and "leads to" respectively.*

We now turn to a more detailed examination of the important relationship between interest rates and investment. This is followed in section 6.5 by a discussion of the relative merits of fiscal and monetary policy in influencing output and employment.

## Investment and interest rates

The relationship between the interest rate (r) and investment (I) is of considerable importance and requires elaboration. Briefly, if a firm decides to invest in new plant or machinery, there are three potential sources of finance:

1. Borrow from the banks at interest rate r.
2. Sell more shares in the company.
3. Use retained profits.

In general, the most important sources of finance for firms are (1) and (3). Because the interest rate is the cost of borrowing from banks, it is easy to see why changes in interest rates might have an effect on investment decisions. The relationship between interest rates and investment can, however, be more formally explained by introducing the concept of *present value* for use in evaluating an investment project. This involves using the current interest rate to calculate the present value of future returns expected from a project.

113

In order to explain the present value method, consider first the opposite case of an investor who deposits £1,000 in a bank for a period of three years at an interest rate of 10%. We may calculate the future income from the investment as follows:

Year 1 return = £1,000(1 + r) = £1,000(1 + 0.1) = £1,100
Year 2 return = £1,100(1 + r) = £1,100(1 + 0.1) = £1,210
Year 3 return = £1,210(1 + r) = £1,210(1 + 0.1) = £1,331

Each year the investor earns 10% on an increasing principal giving a total return (interest plus principal) at the end of the three years of £1,331. The return in year three could also have been calculated as follows:

$$£1,000(1 + 0.1)(1 + 0.1)(1 + 0.1) = £1,000(1 + 0.1)^3 = £1,331$$

or in general

(6)  Return in year n = $£1,000(1 + r)^n$

where n is the number of years.

This example shows that an investment of £1,000 today at a 10% interest rate will give a total return (interest plus principal) of £1,331 in three years' time. The present value method simply *reverses* this calculation. That is, £1,331 received in three years' time is equivalent to £1,000 today (present value) if the interest rate is 10%.

The present value of a return expected in three years is calculated as:

$$PV = £1,331/(1 + 0.1)^3 = £1,000$$

In general,

(7)  $PV = Return/(1 + r)^n$

*Note:*
*To calculate a return on an investment some time in the future, multiply by $(1 + r)^n$. To calculate the present value of a sum receivable in the future, divide by $(1 + r)^n$.*

In deciding whether or not to invest in, say, a new machine, the investor calculates the present value of the sum of all future expected returns. The present value figure can then be interpreted as the "demand price" of the investment project. If the demand price exceeds the supply price, the investor should go ahead with the project. In the previous example, the project is expected to give a return of £1,331 at the end of three years. The present value of this investment is £1,000. If the cost of the project is less than £1,000, say £800, the project is profitable and should be undertaken.

Suppose the interest rate increased from 10% to 20%, the present value of £1,331 receivable in three years time is now:

$$PV = £1,331/(1 + 0.2)^3 = £643$$

The demand price is now less than the supply price of £800 and the project is not profitable. The investor should not proceed with the project. As interest rates rise, more and more marginal investment projects will become unprofitable and will be abandoned or not undertaken. Similarly, a fall in interest rates will make previously unprofitable projects worthwhile.

It follows from this that an increase in interest rates will decrease investment in new plant and machinery. Conversely, a fall in interest rates should encourage investment. This inverse relationship between r and I is known as the *marginal efficiency of investment (MEI)* curve and is shown in Figure 6.5.

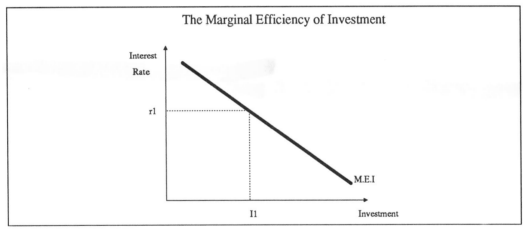

Figure 6.5

*Notes:*

*(1) Keynes in the General Theory[2] did not use the present value method but an alternative technique known as the "internal rate of return method". The internal rate of return is that interest rate that equates the demand price of the capital good to the supply price of the capital good. That is, the interest rate in the present value formula, equation (7), that makes the demand price equal to £800, namely 18.5%. If the computed internal rate of return exceeds the current market rate of interest, the project is profitable and therefore worthwhile. The present value and the internal rate of return methods result in similar conclusions.*

*(2) We emphasise that the interest rate is not the only determinant of investment (I). Sales expectations*

*(managers' perception of what the market will be like next year and the year after) are also very important.*

The next section examines fiscal and monetary policy in the context of the Keynesian, monetarist debate. What is important to bear in mind at this stage is how changes in the money supply affect GNP. The transmission mechanism is money, interest, investment, aggregate demand and then GNP. The important link is between the interest rate and investment. It is assumed for simplicity at this stage that changes in the interest rate do not affect consumer expenditure or exports.

# 6.5 Fiscal Versus Monetary Policy

Basically, the extreme Keynesian position is that fiscal policy is effective and that monetary policy is of little use in influencing GNP. In contrast, monetarists or the neo-classical school (usually identified with Milton Friedman (1912-), formally of the University of Chicago) argue that fiscal policy is ineffective and monetary policy has a strong effect on nominal GNP.

In the simple model, the argument essentially rests on the relationship between the interest rate (r) and investment (I). Keynesians argue that the MEI curve is relatively steep (*inelastic*) over the relevant range. This is illustrated in Figure 6.6,

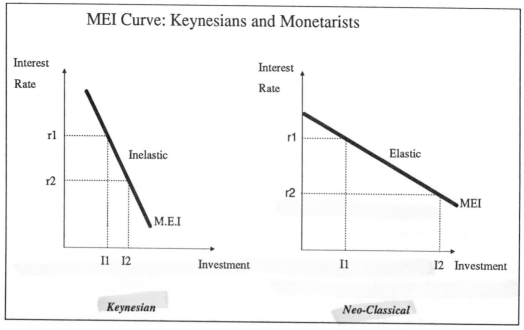

Figure 6.6

left hand side. This means that a given percentage change in r will lead to a small (fractional) percentage change in I. If this is the case, changes in the money supply will have a *weak* effect on GNP.

*Note:*
*The reader should convince him or herself of this by experimenting with different slopes for the MEI curve. A change in Ms leads to a change in r. If that change in r has a "small" effect on I it follows that the initial change in Ms has a small effect on GNP.*

The monetarists on the other hand argue that the MEI curve is relatively flat (*elastic*) over the relevant range. As shown on the right hand side of Figure 6.6, a given percentage change in r will lead to a large percentage change in I. The implication is that changes in the money supply will have an strong effect on GNP.

A second issue of some importance is the monetarists claim that fiscal policy has little or no effect on GNP. At first sight this appears rather odd. After all an increase in government expenditure (G) boosts aggregate demand (AD) by definition and, via the multiplier, GNP. Hence changes in G must influence GNP. The monetarists, however, point to the "crowding-out" effect as one reason why fiscal policy is ineffective. We now turn to this issue.

# 6 "Crowding-Out"

The monetarists agree that changes in G lead to changes in AD and therefore GNP but, they point out, that is not the end of the story. Assuming no increase in the money supply, an increase in GNP will increase the demand for money (Md) and push up interest rates (see Figure 6.4). The rise in interest rates will in turn lower the level of investment. The initial increase in government expenditure has led to a fall in investment. Investment has been "crowded-out" by government expenditure. If the fall in investment equals the initial rise in government expenditure there is said to be 100% "crowding-out". In short:

$$\uparrow G \quad \rightarrow \quad \uparrow AD \quad \rightarrow \quad \uparrow GNP$$

However,

$$\uparrow GNP \quad \rightarrow \quad \uparrow Md \quad \rightarrow \quad \uparrow r \quad \rightarrow \quad \downarrow I$$

If $\uparrow G = \downarrow I$, there is 100% "crowding-out". This is the extreme monetarist position. In this case, AD and GNP revert back to their original level and fiscal policy is completely ineffective. Essentially, increased public sector spending (G) has occurred at the expense of private sector spending (I).

The MEI curve is again of considerable importance here. The monetarists contention that MEI is elastic or flat at and near current interest rates means that a small increase in interest rates has a large effect on investment. If this is the case, the "crowding-out" effect will be important. If, however, as the Keynesians argue, the MEI curve is inelastic or steep, the "crowding-out" effect will not be important, as changes in interest rates have little or no effect on investment. Again we are back to the slope of the MEI curve in deciding which school of thought is correct.

It is important to note that the "crowding-out" effect depends on an unchanged money supply. If the money supply increases as the demand for money rises, the interest rate need not rise and "crowding-out" need not occur. In this regard, the method of financing government expenditure in important. Recall from Chapters 3 and 4 that the government can finance its borrowing requirement from four sources:

1. Abroad
2. Central Bank
3. Licensed banks
4. Domestic public (non-bank)

Sources 1, 2 and 3 are referred to as *government monetary financing (GMF)* as borrowing from these sources increases the money supply. Borrowing from source 4 does not affect the money supply. We explain in detail in Chapter 12 why this is the case.

In Ireland government borrowing has relied heavily on monetary financing. Consequentially, increases in government expenditure have been accompanied by increases in the money supply and interest rates have not been unduly affected. This is one reason that "crowding-out" has not occurred in Ireland on the scale that would be predicted by monetarists. Another is the fact that higher interest rates in Ireland tend to attract capital inflows from the rest of the world, a point to which we return in Chapter 9.

It is interesting to note that in the 1987 general election, Fine Gael emphasised a form of "reverse crowding-out" or "crowding-in". It was acknowledged that cuts in government expenditure would initially lower GNP. However, in the longer term, it was argued that the fall would lower interest rates and stimulate investment. Hence it was argued that cuts in government expenditure to stabilise the national debt would not have a completely adverse effect on output and employment. There is some evidence that this is in fact what happened.

# The IS/LM Model

As outlined in Table 6.1, the Keynesian model (so far developed) contains two markets, the goods and services market and the money market. The IS/LM model is basically a graphic representation which shows the combinations of GNP and interest rates which simultaneously achieve equilibrium in both markets.

Consider first the relationship between the interest rate and GNP in terms of the goods and services market. The equilibrium condition in the goods market is:

(8) $GNP = AD \equiv C + I + G$

where the symbol $\equiv$ indicates an identity. As we have seen, an increase in interest rates (r) leads to a fall in investment (I), and this in turn decreases aggregate demand (AD) and hence the equilibrium level of GNP. Hence, in the goods market, there is an *inverse* relationship between r and GNP. This inverse relationship is shown in Figure 6.7 as a downward-sloping *IS curve*. Each point on the IS curve shows the combinations of r and GNP consistent with equilibrium in the goods market.

Consider now two points not on the IS curve. At point B in the left-hand diagram in Figure 6.7 there is an excess demand for goods and services as GNP is lower than that necessary for equilibrium. Conversely, at point A there is an excess supply of goods and services as GNP is greater than the equilibrium level. The *slope* of the IS curve indicates how a given change in r affects GNP. The slope depends on:

1. the link between r and I (the marginal efficiency of investment [MEI] curve).
2. the link between I and GNP (the multiplier).

An elastic (relatively flat) MEI curve (a change in the interest rate has a strong effect on investment) and a "large" multiplier (investment has a strong effect on GNP) means that there is a close relationship between r and GNP. In this case the IS curve will be relatively flat. Conversely, a steep MEI curve and a small multiplier indicates a weak relationship between r and GNP. In this case, the IS curve will be relatively steep. In general:

Steep MEI curve and a small multiplier    $\Rightarrow$    steep IS curve.
Flat MEI curve and a large multiplier      $\Rightarrow$    flat IS curve.

With regard to the *location* of the IS curve, an increase in consumer expenditure (C), investment (I) (not brought about by a change in r) or government expenditure (G) will shift the IS curve out to the right. GNP increases along the horizontal axis while the interest rate, on the vertical axis, remains constant. The IS curve shifts to

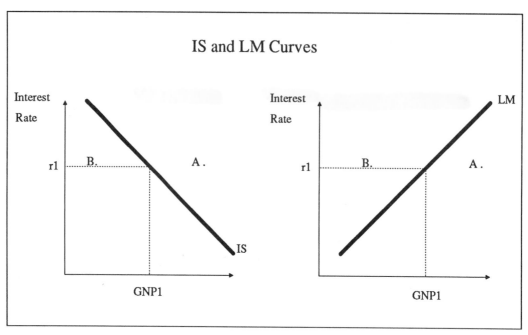

Figure 6.7

the right to show the new GNP, r combination. Conversely, a decrease in C, I (for constant interest rates) or G will move the IS curve to the left.

Consider now the relationship between r and GNP in terms of the money market. The equilibrium condition in the money market is:

(9)  $Ms = Md(GNP, r)$

For a given money supply (Ms), an increase in GNP leads to an increase in the demand for money (Md) and this in turn pushes up interest rates. Hence, in the money market there is a *positive* relationship between the levels of GNP and r that are consistent with equilibrium and this is represented on the right hand side diagram of Figure 6.7 by an upward-sloping *LM curve*.

Consider now two points not on the LM curve. At the point A in the right hand diagram of Figure 6.7, GNP and therefore the demand for money (Md) is greater than that consistent with equilibrium so that there is an excess demand for money. At point B, GNP and Md are lower than is consistent with equilibrium and there is therefore an excess supply of money. The *slope* of the LM curve indicates how r affects GNP in the money market. The slope depends on:

1. how changes in GNP affect Md (this link is referred to as the *income elasticity of the demand for money*).

120

2. the sensitivity of interest rates to changes in Md (the slope of the money supply line).

Consider first the GNP, Md relationship. (Note here that the causation is running from the variable on the horizontal axis (GNP) to the variable on the vertical axis (r), whereas in the case of the IS curve causation ran in the opposite direction.)

An elastic relationship between GNP and Md (i.e. changes in GNP have a large or strong effect on Md) $\Rightarrow$ steep LM curve.
An inelastic relationship between GNP and Md (i.e. changes in GNP have a weak effect on Md) $\Rightarrow$ flat LM curve.

Consider now the second link between Md and r. If, as we have assumed, the money supply curve is vertical, changes in Md are completely reflected in interest rate changes. If, on the other hand, the Ms curve slopes to the right the effect on interest rates is reduced.

Combining the two links, an elastic (strong) relationship between GNP and Md and a vertical money supply curve gives rise to a steep LM curve. Conversely, an inelastic (weak) GNP, Md relationship and a relatively flat money supply curve gives rise to a elastic or flat LM curve. The *location* of the LM curve depends on the level of the money supply. An increase in the money supply shifts the LM curve to the right and a decrease to the left.

*Note:*

*The IS/LM model was first suggested by the Nobel Prize winning English economist J.R. Hicks (1904-1989).[3] The "I" in IS stands for investment and "S" for savings. If the government account is balanced, savings equal investment whenever the goods market is in equilibrium. See for example equation 21, Chapter 2. The "L" in the LM denotes liquidity preference (demand for money) and "M" the money supply and represents equilibrium in the money market.*

We now use this IS/LM model to illustrate the effect of an expansionary fiscal and monetary policy on GNP.

# Fiscal policy

Figure 6.8 illustrates the effect of an expansionary fiscal policy (shift of the IS curve to the right) on r and GNP when the LM curve is flat (left-hand diagram) and when the LM curve is steep (right-hand diagram). It can be seen that fiscal policy has a strong effect on GNP when the LM curve is flat. It will be noticed that there is only a small increase in the interest rate along the vertical axis and as a result there is a small "crowding-out" effect.

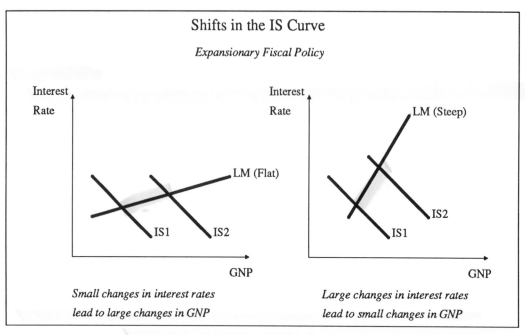

Figure 6.8

In contrast, fiscal policy has a weak effect on GNP when the LM curve is steep. Interest rates rise significantly along the vertical axis and as a result private investment is "crowded-out". In general, the effectiveness of fiscal policy depends on whether interest rates increase by a small (flat LM) or large (steep LM) amount.

# Monetary policy

Figure 6.9 examines the case of an expansionary monetary policy (shift of the LM curve to the right) when the IS curve is both flat and steep. It can be seen that an expansionary monetary policy has a large effect on GNP if the IS curve is relatively flat. In this case, a small change in interest rates has an important effect on investment and, as a result, changes in the money supply have an important effect on nominal output. In contrast, a steep IS curve means that an expansionary monetary policy has a small effect on GNP. In this case, investment is not very sensitive to interest rate changes and, as a consequence, changes in the money supply have a weak effect on nominal output.

# The IS/LM model and the Keynesian/monetarist debate

In terms of the IS/LM diagram, the Keynesian view is represented by a steep IS curve and a flat LM curve. Fiscal policy has a significant effect on GNP and monetary policy has little or no effect on GNP. The monetarist position is largely the opposite, namely a steep LM curve and a flat IS curve. Fiscal policy has a weak

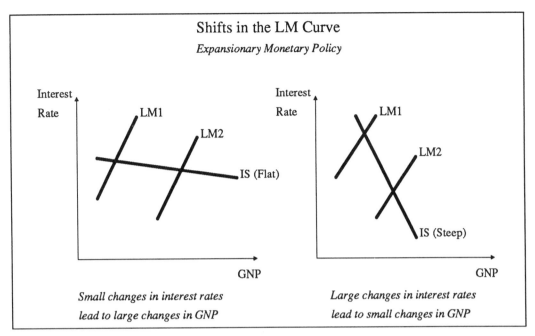

Figure 6.9

effect on GNP because it pushes up interest rates and "crowds-out" investment. In contrast, changes in the money supply will have an important effect on GNP. Both of these views of how an economy works were developed in large economies in which international trade and capital flows were relatively unimportant. These models have to be significantly modified to take account of the special factors affecting small, open economies. We look at these factors in Chapters 9, 11 and 12.

# 3 The Quantity Theory of Money

In emphasising the importance of the money supply as an influence on nominal GNP, monetarists do not stress the links between money, interest rates, investment and AD. Instead the *transmission mechanism* emphasised by the monetarists is that implied by the Quantity Theory of Money. The Quantity Theory is essentially a theory of the price level. In its simplest form it states that the greater the quantity of money in the economy, the higher will be the price level. One way of outlining the Quantity Theory is to begin by defining the *velocity of circulation of money* (V) as being equal to nominal GNP divided by the money supply. That is:

(10)  $V \equiv GNP/Ms$

Using the M3 definition of money, the 1988 figures for Ireland are:

$$V \equiv \text{£18,754m}/\text{£10,421m} = 1.8$$

This means that the average monetary unit or £1 (notes and coins, current and deposit accounts in banks) financed £1.8 worth of expenditure on final goods and services. In other words, the average monetary unit was used less than twice during the year. This is what is meant by "velocity". It is the number of times the "average pound" was turned over or used in the course of the year. Figure 6.10 shows the velocity of circulation of money (calculated using the broad definition of money, M3) for Ireland over the period 1976 to 1988. The reader will note that it has varied within a fairly narrow range over the years, never exceeding 1.9 or falling below 1.6.

If nominal GNP is now divided into the price level (P) and real GNP, identity 10 can be written:

(11) $V \equiv (P * \text{real GNP})/M_s$

Multiply both sides of (11) by Ms:

(12) $M_s * V \equiv P * \text{real GNP}$

Taking the differential of equation (12) and assuming that V and real GNP are constant, it follows that $\Delta M_s = \Delta P$. That is, changes in the money supply lead to proportional changes in the price level. The implication is that the faster the growth of money supply in the economy, the higher the inflation rate. It is in this sense that the Quantity Theory is a theory of inflation. We have seen that, in fact, V has been relatively stable in Ireland. If the economy always tended to the full employment level of output, real GNP would grow at a constant rate. These two points can be used to justify the assumptions made by the monetarists.

*Note:*
*The Quantity Theory is in one sense a kind of "black box" theory. It simply states that if V is constant, an increase in the money supply will lead to an increase in nominal GNP. The exact transmission mechanism is not specified. It also depends crucially on the assumption that real GNP is constant, presumably at full employment.*

The Quantity Theory is a cornerstone of monetarism. The conclusion monetarists draw from the Quantity Theory is that monetary policy should *not* be used to influence GNP or stabilise the business cycle. They argue that a discretionary monetary policy will have a varying and unpredictable effect on the economy (lags can vary, according to Friedman, from six months to two years). Any increase in

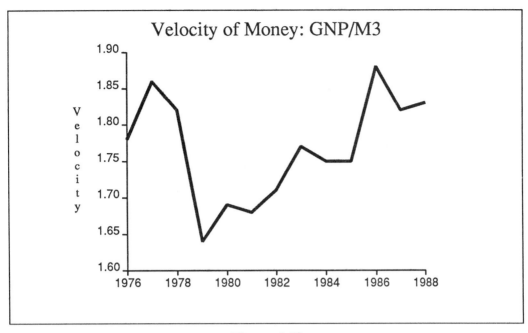

Figure 6.10

the money supply will be translated into an increase in nominal GNP. Since real GNP tends to be close to the full employment level, this means that the price level will rise. Monetarists deny that monetary policy will have any lasting effect on real GNP in the long run. This is because they believe that the economy tends towards full employment if left to its own devices.

As support for the Quantity Theory, monetarists point to a close correlation between inflation and the growth in the money supply. One of Friedman's best known works (written with his wife Anna Schwartz) is *A Monetary History of the United States: 1867-1960*.[4] This book examines the relationship between the US inflation and changes in the money supply and provides support for the monetarist point of view. Friedman also finds support for the Quantity Theory in high inflation countries such as Brazil, Bolivia and Israel. These countries have had fast growth rates in their money supplies and hyper-inflation. The most recent example of this phenomenon is Argentina.

Monetarists argue that there should be no discretionary use of monetary policy. Instead the authorities should maintain the growth in Ms in line with the predicted growth in real GNP. This is the so-called *monetary rule*. In this way, the growth in the money supply would support the growth in the real economy and would not create inflation.

The conclusion that monetary policy should not be used to stabilise the business cycle raises another question; if both fiscal and monetary policy are ineffective in influencing real GNP, what policy or policies should the authorities use to influence the business cycle? The monetarist answer is that the authorities should not attempt a stabilisation policy. Monetarists argue that free markets will automatically result in full employment, that is there is an "automatic adjustment mechanism" whereby deviations of actual GNP from potential GNP are self-rectifying. We return to this argument in greater detail in Chapter 8.

Keynesians, in contrast, argue that the velocity of circulation of money (V) is not constant and that an increase in the money supply may lead to a fall in V. In this case, an expansionary monetary policy will have little or no effect on nominal output. This implies that monetary policy is ineffective. In addition, the Keynesians contend that the economy will take a very long time to revert to potential GNP following a disturbance so that, for all intents and purposes, the "automatic adjustment" does not occur except in the "long-run" when, as Keynes remarked, "we are all dead". (Monetarists would point out, however, that Keynes is now dead and we are stuck with the "long-run"). Thus Keynes believed there was an important role for an active fiscal policy to play in stabilising the level of GNP around its trend level.

One important criticism of the Quantity Theory levelled by the Keynesians is that *causation* may run from nominal GNP to the money supply, rather than the other way around. In other words, the money supply is "demand led". An increase in nominal GNP will lead to an increase Md which in turn increases Ms. This issue of whether changes in the money supply are the cause or simply the consequence of changes in nominal GNP is of fundamental theoretical significance.[5] As we shall see in subsequent chapters, the question of the control of the money supply is even more complex in a open economy.

# 6.9 Conclusion

In this chapter we have extended the basic Keynesian model by incorporating the money market. The extended Keynesian model now consists of a goods and services market and a money market. The authorities can influence aggregate demand by changing government expenditure or taxation (fiscal policy) or by changing the money supply (monetary policy). The key points or concepts covered in this chapter include:

- The transactions, precautionary and speculative demand for money

- How changes in nominal GNP and interest rates affect the demand for money

- The supply and demand for money determine the interest rate

- Changes in the money supply affect aggregate demand and GNP via interest rates and investment

- The link between interest rates and investment is known as the marginal efficiency of investment curve (MEI)

- The slope of the MEI curve is of crucial importance in the Keynesian/monetarist debate

- Keynesians argue that fiscal policy has an important effect on GNP, whereas monetary policy has a small or weak effect on GNP

- Monetarists argue that monetary policy has a large effect on GNP but fiscal policy, because of the "crowding-out" effect, has a small effect on GNP

- The IS/LM model shows the combinations of GNP and interest rates that give a simultaneous equilibrium in the goods and money markets

- The Quantity Theory of Money and the concept of the velocity of circulation of money.

We have left to later chapters the task of modifying this analysis to allow for the special factors that influence a small open economy.

# Notes

1. J.M. Keynes, *The General Theory of Employment, Interest and Money*, London: Macmillan, 1936.

2. J.M. Keynes, op. cit.

3. J.R. Hicks, "Mr. Keynes and the "Classics": A Suggested Interpretation", *Econometrica*, Vol. 6, p. 147-159, April, 1937.

4. M. Friedman, and A. Schwartz, *A Monetary History of the United States: 1867 - 1960*, Princeton University Press, 1963.

5. See for example Kaldor, N., *The Scourge of Monetarism*, Oxford University Press, 1982. It is important to note that recent studies of Keynes's work argue that his ideas have been mis-interpretated by his followers. See for example, A. Leijonhufvud, *On Keynesian Economics and the Economics of Keynes*, Oxford University Press, 1968 and A.H. Meltzer, *Keynes's Monetary Theory: A Different Interpretation*, Cambridge University Press, 1988. Meltzer argues that Keynes's main concern was economic uncertainty and how this affected the rate of interest and led to permanent deviations of output from potential GNP.

# Chapter 7

# *The Labour Market and the Problem of Unemployment*

## 7.1 Introduction

Unemployment is the most intractable economic problem facing Ireland and many other European countries today. Following the recessions of 1974/5 and 1981/2 the rate of unemployment in most countries of Europe has shown little tendency to return to the level that prevailed in the 1960s. The persistence of high rates of unemployment on this side of the Atlantic contrasts with the fairly rapid return to pre-recession levels in the US and Japan.

A great deal of research has been devoted to exploring the way labour markets function and to trying to understand the behaviour of unemployment. Much of this analysis is set in the context of the debate about the effectiveness of fiscal and monetary policy, but it also raises some special issues regarding the functioning of the labour market. In this chapter we summarise recent research on the problem of unemployment in Ireland against the background of the macroeconomic issues that we have discussed in previous chapters. We start by setting out some background information on the Irish population and labour force and then turn to an analysis of the problem of unemployment.

## 7.2 The Supply of Labour

### Demographic factors

We begin our discussion of the supply of labour by looking at the factors that determine the growth of the labour force. The most important is the growth of the country's *population*. Population growth in turn can be broken down into two components, *natural increase* (the excess of births over deaths) and *net migration*:

Rate of population growth ≡ rate of natural increase + net migration rate

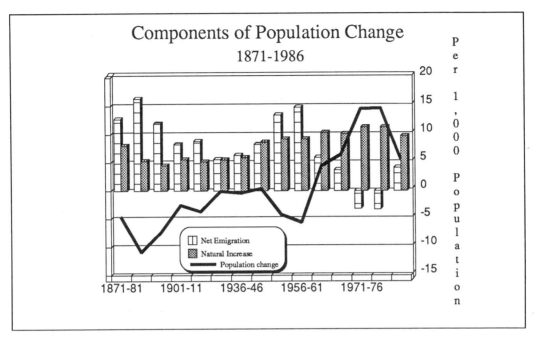

Figure 7.1

*Migration* has had an extraordinary impact on Ireland's population history. During the worst years of the 1950s we lost 2% of our population a year through *emigration,* while during the 1970s *immigration* added about 0.5% a year to our population.[1] In recent years emigration has again risen to the level where it offsets the rate of natural increase, so that our population is now falling.

The annual rate of *natural increase* rose from 0.5% in the 1920s to 1% in the 1960s and peaked at 1.2% in 1980. The main reason for these changes in the rate of natural increase was the behaviour of the birth rate. Whereas in most European countries the birth rate fell sharply in the early 1960s, with the result that their rate of natural increase was very low, or in some cases negative, by the 1980s, the Irish birth rate did not begin to decline until after 1980. The fall in the Irish birth rate since 1980 had reduced the rate of natural increase to 0.8% by 1988.

Figure 7.1 shows the rates of population (using intercensal periods), of natural increase and net emigration over the period 1871-1986. The way fluctuations in the emigration rate have tended to dominate the rate of change in the population is brought out by this graph. This aspect of the Irish situation makes population forecasting a particularly difficult task.

The rate of emigration is to a large extent determined by economic factors, in particular by the rate of economic growth in Ireland relative to Britain and the other countries to which Irish people emigrate. As a result, the rate of population growth, and hence the rate of growth of the labour force, are *endogenous.* This is one of the consequences of being a *small, open economy* (SOE).

The population can be divided into economically *active* and *inactive* age groups. The convention is to refer to the "under fifteen" and "sixty-five and over" age groups as inactive, while those aged fifteen to sixty four are called the population of active age. Obviously, these thresholds are not hard and fast, especially in an era of prolonged schooling and flexible retirement patterns. Moreover, the proportion of women aged fifteen to sixty four who are counted as part of the labour force has been very low in the past but is now rising.

A feature of the Irish population age pyramid has been the relatively high proportions in the young and old inactive age groups. The large proportion of young people reflects our high birth rate, while the large proportion of elderly people is due to the long-run decline in population prior to 1961. For many years about 30% of our population has been in the under-fifteen age group, but this proportion is now falling rapidly due to the decline in the birth rate in the 1980s. The proportion aged sixty-five and over has also been very stable over the years in the region of 11%. Unlike most other developed countries, Ireland will not experience a sharp rise in the proportion of elderly people in the population during the rest of this century: this will not occur here until well into the twenty-first century.

# Labour force participation

The population in the young and old "inactive" age groups amounts to about 40% of the total. Not all of the remaining 60% of the population are in the labour force, however. The labour force is defined[2] as those who are at work and those seeking work:

Labour force ≡ numbers at work + numbers seeking work

The population that is not in the labour force ("not economically active") is classified into the following categories:

in home duties
at school or college
permanently ill or disabled
retired
other

Figure 7.2 shows how the population aged fifteen and over was distributed between the employed, unemployed and non-active categories in the years 1971 to 1987. Note how small are the numbers unemployed relative to the total who are not at work (we return to this point below).

The *labour force participation rate* (LFPR) is the proportion of the population that is in the labour force (whether employed or unemployed).

130

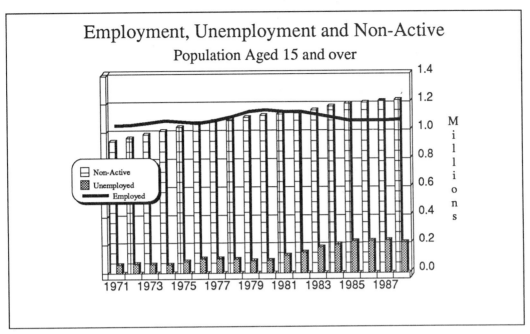

Figure 7.2

LFPR ≡ Labour force/Population

There have been some important changes in labour force participation rates in Ireland in the 1980s. A pronounced tendency has emerged for young people to stay on longer in the educational system, and, as a result, the labour force participation rate has fallen quite sharply among those aged fifteen to twenty-four. There was also a marked move towards earlier retirement among men aged fifty-five to sixty-four. The only significant group in which labour force participation has increased is women aged twenty-five to forty-four. This has been due primarily to the increase in the proportion of married women who are going out to work. These trends are shown in the data in Table 7.1.

These trends in labour force participation can be understood as responses to economic factors. High unemployment undoubtedly encouraged young people to postpone entry into the labour force, while many older people were offered early retirement by firms that were anxious to reduce their labour force. The increasing participation of married women in the paid labour force reflects more complex factors, including the fall in the birth rate and higher levels of educational attainment among women. It also seems that more job opportunities have been available in the occupations where women are traditionally employed. There have also been changes in legislation making it harder to exclude women from employment.

People who stop looking for work because they believe there are no jobs available are not recorded as unemployed, but they constitute a "hidden unemployment". Estimates from the Labour Force Survey show that "discouraged workers" of this type would increase the level of unemployment by about 5% if they were enumerated among the unemployed.[3]

*Table 7.1*

**Labour force participation rates (%)**

| Age | 15-24 | 25-44 | 45-64 | 65+ |
|---|---|---|---|---|
| *Males* | | | | |
| 1979 | 66.1 | 96.4 | 84.7 | 26.0 |
| 1987 | 57.2 | 96.1 | 84.4 | 17.1 |
| | | | | |
| *Females* | | | | |
| 1979 | 54.2 | 28.9 | 22.1 | 4.6 |
| 1987 | 49.4 | 39.8 | 22.8 | 3.0 |
| | | | | |
| *Married Women* | | | | |
| 1979 | 26.9 | 17.3 | 12.8 | |
| 1987 | 45.6 | 28.8 | 16.1 | |

*Source:* Labour Force Surveys and Census of Population.

The population aged fifteen and over that is not economically active has grown since 1979, as have the numbers out of work, while the numbers at work have fallen (Figure 7.2). The result has been a rise in the ratio of dependents to the working population. The combination of a high proportion of the population in the "inactive" age groups and relatively low labour force participation rates in the population in the "active" age groups results in a low overall labour force/population ratio in Ireland.

*Note:*

*In 1987, out of a population of 3,543,000, only 1,312,000, or 37%, were in the labour force. This is one of the lowest proportions economically active in the OECD countries. At the other extreme is a country like Sweden, where there is a low proportion of young children in the population and the labour force participation rate among women is almost as high as among men, so that 52% of total population is in the labour force. Moreover, because we also have a very high rate of unemployment, the ratio of non-employed to employed population is exceptionally high: there are 228 non-employed (that is, unemployed and inactive) people for every 100 employed people in Ireland. In Sweden, the ratio is only 96:100. Thus, our "burden of dependency" is over twice that found in Sweden. This is a fact that should never be forgotten when the levels of benefits and services that are provided for the various categories of the inactive population in Ireland are compared with those available in other countries.*

If the labour force participation rate were stable, then the rate of growth of the labour force would be equal to the rate of growth of the population of working age. To see this, bear in mind the following identity:

Labour force ≡ Population * LFPR

It follows from this that:

Rate of change in the labour force ≡ Rate of change in population plus rate of change in LFPR

When the labour force participation rate falls, the rate of growth of the labour force falls below that of the population, but once the LFPR stabilises again, the rate of growth of the labour force reverts back to that of the population. Thus, reducing the labour force participation rate results in only a temporary reduction in the growth rate of the labour force. This point is often overlooked by those who advocate early retirement or prolonged schooling as ways of reducing the rate of growth of the supply of labour. These strategies cause a once-off reduction in the *size* of the labour force, but have no long-run effect on its *growth rate*.

In the absence of net migration, the population of working age in Ireland would have grown at about 1.5% a year throughout the post-war period. If all of this growth had been absorbed into the Irish labour force, it would have increased by about 80%. However, the labour force is now just 1.3 million, much the same as it was in 1926! It fell sharply during the 1950s because of emigration, and the increase during the 1970s was only enough to restore it to its pre-war level. Further emigration and a fall in the labour force participation rate have caused it to decline again in the 1980s.

# 3 Employment and Unemployment

Figure 7.3 shows the labour force and its two components, employment and unemployment, in Ireland over the period 1971-89. The labour force increased at a rapid pace (over 1.5% a year) in the 1970s. Employment also grew rapidly until 1980. As employment turned down in the early 1980s, the labour force continued to grow and unemployment rose very sharply. This shows what happens when the safety valve of emigration is closed during a recession in Ireland. Large-scale

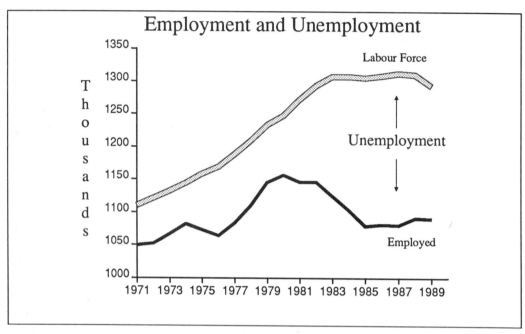

Figure 7.3

emigration started up again in the mid-1980s, siphoning off the potential growth of the labour force. This at least had the effect of stabilising the level of unemployment. In the absence of emigration and further reductions in the labour force participation rate, the labour force would increase by about 1.5 per cent a year until the end of the century (much the same as the potential growth rate in the absence of emigration throughout the post-war period). Where would all these additional job-seekers find employment?

Figure 7.4 shows the level of employment in each sector over the period 1961 to 1989. We can see from this graph the following trends (no distinction is made between public and private sector services in the graph):

*Agriculture*. A long-run decline in employment that has accelerated in recent years and is probably not yet over.

*Industry*. Sustained, if modest, growth from 1961 to 1979, but since 1981 the numbers employed in this sector have declined by over a quarter. Foreign-owned firms have grown steadily, but they are not generating enough extra employment to offset the losses in traditional Irish-owned industry.

*Public sector services*. Long-run growth, with an acceleration in the 1970s, but the state of the public finances necessitated a reversal of trend in the 1980s. There is little prospect of a return to the old expansionary path in this sector.

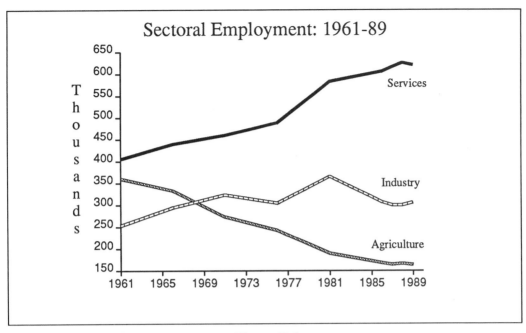

Figure 7.4

*Private sector services.* Steady long-run growth, accelerating in the 1980s. This sector has provided much of the additional employment in the US and in other countries in the 1980s and is expected to continue to be the main growth sector in the 1990s. The jobs that have been created in this sector range from highly skilled occupations in computer software and consulting to low-paid posts in personal services. This sector can act as an employer of "last resort" when no opportunities are available anywhere else in the economy. This is very apparent in low-income countries where there is rapid population growth. Many young people are only able to find jobs like selling cigarettes or polishing shoes on the street corner.

If we extrapolate these trends, it is hard to see how the economy could generate enough jobs, at high enough incomes, to absorb the potential growth of our labour force into employment in Ireland. But we should bear in mind that it is impossible to forecast future patterns of employment. There are too many imponderables. The US economy has generated additional jobs during the past three decades at a rate that puts the economies of Europe to shame. No one could have foretold back in the 1960s that so many people would have been employed in computer services, fast food restaurants or financial institutions. The key lesson that has to be learned from the US experience is that it *is* possible for an economy to generate employment opportunities on a scale sufficient to absorb rapid growth of the labour force into employment. A great deal of research is now underway to explain the contrast

135

between the US and European experiences in regard to job creation. It is clear that the greater flexibility of the US labour force has played an important role.

The growth of employment is not, of itself, a goal of economic policy. What matters, as we stated in Chapter 1, is the rate of unemployment. Obviously, rapid growth in employment will help to keep the level of unemployment down, but in Ireland the rate of migration has also had a very important influence on the trend in unemployment. It would clearly be preferable to reduce unemployment by generating more employment opportunities at home, as opposed to "exporting" our problem through emigration. It is difficult to incorporate the rate of migration into an evaluation of the performance of the Irish economy. We shall therefore concentrate on the rate of unemployment as the key indicator of the performance of the Irish labour market.

# 7.4 The Problem of Unemployment

## Definition and measurement

Our statistics on unemployment come from two sources, the annual *Labour Force Survey* and the monthly *Live Register Statistics*. In the *Survey*, a sample of households is interviewed and each member of the household is classified by "Principal Economic Status". To be classified as unemployed a person has to be (1) not working and (2) actively seeking work. The *Live Register*, on the other hand, is a record of those who qualify under the rules and regulations of the Department of Social Welfare for either unemployment benefits or unemployment assistance. It is to be expected that there would be differences between the two sets of statistics. For example, a married woman who is actively seeking paid employment would be classified as unemployed in the *Labour Force Survey*, but is not likely to show up in the *Live Register Statistics*. On the other hand, a man who has lost his job and gone back to work a family farm could be entitled to unemployment benefits for some time, and hence registered as unemployed on the *Live Register*, but classified as employed in the *Labour Force Survey*. There is also the widespread suspicion, however well- or ill-founded, that some of those claiming "the dole" are not genuinely seeking work because they are work-shy or are not available for employment because they are illicitly working "on the side". The Job Search scheme, introduced in 1987, was designed to eliminate abuses of this sort and has had a significant impact in the areas where it has operated.

A comparison of the trend in unemployment since 1979 as revealed in the *Labour Force Survey* on the one hand and the *Live Register* on the other is shown in Table 7.2. There are some interesting differences between the level of unemployment in the two sources. In 1987 the *Live Register* figure for unemployment among those aged twenty five and over was higher than in the *Labour Force Survey* figure, but the reverse was the case for those aged under twenty-five. The increase in total unemployment over this period is almost identical in the two sources but the increase in male unemployment is much more rapid in the *Labour Force Survey* than in the *Live Register*, while the reverse is true for female unemployment. It is interesting to speculate about the reasons for these contrasts, but the main conclusion that has to be drawn is that the two data sources do not reveal any major inconsistency in the pattern or trend in unemployment. This increases our confidence in the reliability of the statistics.

*Table 7.2*
**Labour force survey and live register data on unemployment**

|  |  | 1979 | | 1987 | | Increase 1979-87 | |
|---|---|---|---|---|---|---|---|
|  |  | LFS | LR | LFS | LR | LFS | LR |
|  |  | (thousands) | | (thousands) | | % | % |
| *Males* |  |  |  |  |  |  |  |
|  | *Under 25* | 20.6 | N.A. | 53.2 | 46.5 | 158 | N.A. |
|  | *25 and over* | 43.6 | N.A. | 123.1 | 133.5 | 182 | N.A. |
|  | *Total* | 64.2 | 72.2 | 176.3 | 180.0 | 175 | 149 |
| *Females* |  |  |  |  |  |  |  |
|  | *Under 25* | 12.6 | N.A. | 32.9 | 28.2 | 161 | N.A. |
|  | *25 and over* | 8.1 | N.A. | 22.3 | 42.5 | 175 | N.A. |
|  | *Total* | 20.7 | 20.3 | 55.2 | 70.7 | 167 | 248 |
| *Both sexes:* |  | 84.8 | 92.5 | 231.5 | 250.7 | 173 | 171 |

*Note*: N.A. indicates that the data are not available.

# The structure of unemployment

It is common to talk of unemployment as a *structural* problem, or at least as having a structural component. By this is meant that certain sectors, industries, regions or demographic groups experience higher than average rates of unemployment and do not benefit from a general decline in unemployment. Table 7.3 illustrates the pattern of unemployment differentials in Ireland today. These *differentials* are not in themselves evidence of a structural problem. A *widening* of differentials would be, however. This would happen if, for example, the country as a whole enjoyed a boom, but a few regions remained in recession. Vacancies would be unfilled in the boom area despite high unemployment in the depressed areas, unless there was mobility from the latter to the former. In general, a structural problem implies a lack of mobility, between regions, occupations or industries.

*Table 7.3*

|  | *Low unemployment rate* | *High unemployment rate* |
|---|---|---|
| *Regions:* | West (Galway, Mayo) | North-West (Donegal, Leitrim, Sligo) |
| *Occupations:* | Unskilled | Skilled, Professional |
| *Industries:* | Building & Construction | Public sector, Banking, Insurance |
| *Demographic groups:* | Teenagers | Adult males |

*Note:*

*An often-cited example of a structural problem of unemployment is the coexistence of labour shortages in the south-east of England with very high unemployment rates in the north of England and parts of Wales and Scotland. Lack of geographical mobility within Britain, encouraged by rigidities in the housing market, contributes to this problem. There seems to be greater mobility from Ireland to the south of England than there is between the north and the south of Britain.*

There is not much evidence that the problem of unemployment in Ireland in the 1980s is structural to any greater extent than in previous periods. While the differentials in unemployment rates between the various categories are always changing, there has been no marked widening of differentials in the 1980s.

*Note:*

*Dublin and some of the other urban centres have suffered very severely from the decline of industry in the 1980s, and there is a very high concentration of unemployment in the large urban local authority housing estates. The designated areas in the west of Ireland that qualify for special industrial grants are no longer the most disadvantaged regions. In response to the changed pattern of unemployment differentials in the 1980s, the inner city areas now qualify for higher rates of grants.*

The structural dimension of the Irish labour market that received most attention as unemployment began to increase was the demographic one. Great concern was expressed about youth unemployment. The link between the large outflow from our educational system and the rise in unemployment was very apparent in the early 1980s when young people had few opportunities to emigrate due to the global recession. A *Youth Unemployment Levy* of 1% on all incomes was introduced in 1981 as a response to this problem. The proceeds were used to help create employment for those aged under twenty-five years old. The *Youth Employment Agency* was merged into the *National Employment and Training Agency* (FAS) in 1988. The levy on income remains in place.

*Note:*

*Taxing the employed to fund special schemes for the unemployed is not a sensible policy. Pay roll taxes tend to increase the cost of hiring workers and hence discourage employment. Moreover, singling out one category of the unemployed for special aid puts others at a disadvantage. It should only be done where there is a clear need to overcome a particular disadvantage, such as lack of skills or employer discrimination.*

The rate of unemployment among young people is much higher than the adult unemployment rate in all countries. However in Ireland the ratio is under 2:1, which is lower than it is in many other OECD countries. Moreover, despite our high rate of demographic growth, this ratio did not rise in Ireland during the 1980s. To some extent this may have been due to the impact of special measures to help school-leavers, as well as the sharp decline in the labour force participation of this age group, noted above. The resumption of large-scale emigration has siphoned off thousands of young people from the Irish labour market, but has had relatively little effect on the older population. It is not surprising, therefore, than over the past two years the decline in registered unemployment has been almost entirely concentrated among the under twenty-fives, especially males.[4]

The most important structural dimension of Irish unemployment is the tendency for shortages of skilled workers to emerge even when the overall unemployment rate is still very high. When this happens it puts upward pressure on wage rates and can curtail the economic expansion long before there is general full employment. This brings us face to face with the question of what we mean by "full employment". We take up this issue in a later sub-section.

# Unemployment and the social welfare system

The problem of unemployment should not be considered in isolation from the social welfare system. As we have seen above, one of our main sources of data on unemployment is the number eligible for unemployment benefit and assistance under the social welfare legislation. There is, therefore, an intimate link between the rules and regulations concerning these benefits and the numbers registered as unemployed. For example, an increasing proportion of school-leavers who are looking for their first regular job are registering as unemployed. Data from the *Labour Force Survey* show that in 1975 only 5% of those whose Principal Economic Status was "looking for first job" were registered as unemployed, but by 1987 this proportion had risen to 52%. Changes in Irish social welfare regulations brought about by EC directives have also increased women's eligibility for unemployment benefits.

We noted in Figure 7.2 that only 43% of the population aged fifteen and over are actually "at work". Of the remanding 57%, only 25% are classified as unemployed. Many of the other categories in the non-employed population are close substitutes for unemployment. Students, for example, can remain in education as an alternative to unemployment. Some of the women who are classified as in "home duties" are available for work should a suitable opportunity arise. Some of those who have retired at an early age during the recession could be interested in taking up employment again. The numbers in these categories are affected by the conditions governing eligibility for unemployment benefits and other types of social insurance entitlements, as well as by more objective economic considerations.

*Note:*

*In the Netherlands, after the revenue from North Sea gas began to flow, a very generous system of classifying people as disabled was introduced during the 1970s. The numbers classified as disabled doubled between 1975 and 1980! By 1984, 13.6% of national income was being spent on sickness and disability benefits. Almost one million people were receiving these benefits out of a population of 14 million. No wonder the phrase "The Dutch Disease" was coined to describe how the Dutch economy reacted to the way the revenue from North Sea gas was spent!*

The idea that the distribution of the population between different labour force classifications is affected by social welfare rules and regulations is hardly controversial. But the question of whether the relative generosity of unemployment benefits affects the behaviour of the unemployed is contentious. The key concept in this context is the *replacement ratio*. This measures the proportion of after-tax income that is replaced by the social welfare payments to which an unemployed person is entitled:

Replacement ratio ≡ Unemployment benefit/After-tax income

Consider a single person whose best employment opportunity offers a gross wage of £120 a week. She will have to pay £19 a week in PAYE and a further £9 a week in PRSI, leaving £92 a week in after-tax income. When unemployed she would be entitled to £45 a week in unemployment benefit (somewhat less if she only qualifies for unemployment assistance). Thus the replacement ratio for this person is just under 50%. However, this comparison does not give a full picture of the relative attractiveness of accepting or refusing an offer of employment. Account should also be taken of several other factors which increase the real income of the unemployed, such as priority for public authority housing, subsidised rents and other means-tested allowances, the pay-related supplement to the basic unemployment benefit, redundancy payments and tax refunds. Moreover, some of the unemployed may be able to earn some income "on the side". On the other hand, the employed may have to incur significant work-related expenses, of which the most important is the cost of travel to work. Thus, there is no such thing as "the" replacement ratio. It varies between individuals, depending on their circumstances and employment opportunities.

A person earning gross pay of £120 a week costs her employer £134.64 because the employer has to pay 12.2% in PRSI in addition to the PRSI paid by the employee. Thus, it costs the employer £132.64 to give an employee take home pay of £92. But the story does not end there. When the employee spends this £92 she will pay about 30% of it in indirect taxes (VAT, excise taxes, etc.). Thus, the net-of-all-taxes income left from the £134.64 is only £66, just under 50%! Moreover, since marginal income tax rates are higher than average, it would take more then £1 of additional income to secure an extra 50p of net-of-tax purchasing power for the employee. This size of the tax wedge is often cited as a factor that lowers the level of employment and raises the level of unemployment. This wedge increased by about 30 per cent between 1979 and 1986 in Ireland. This wedge tends to reduce the level of employment below what it would be if there were no taxes.

The key issue is whether the level of the replacement ratio affects the level of unemployment. It could do this in several ways:

1. By reducing the employee resistance to redundancy.

2. By encouraging those who are looking for employment to "sign on" in order to qualify for benefits. This does not affect the true level of unemployment, but it increases the proportion of the unemployed who are registered as such.

3. By encouraging those who are unemployed to prolong their search for a suitable job. Relatively generous unemployment benefits may raise the "reservation wage", that is, the minimum wage that a job seeker has to be offered before she will accept a job. While this may help her to find a better job, it tends to prolong the time spent in unemployment.

How important are these effects in Ireland? This is impossible to answer with precision. We can say, however, that the replacement ratio has been increasing over time. It has been the policy of successive governments to raise the basic rates of social insurance and assistance faster that the rate of inflation. During the 1980s, the real value of these entitlements increased at a time when real after-tax incomes from employment were declining. The average value of the replacement ratio rose from 46% in 1978 to 58% in 1985. It has been shown that higher levels of the replacement ratio tend to lengthen the typical spell of unemployment.[5] Furthermore, generous redundancy terms seem to have had a major impact on attitudes towards job losses;

in the 1980s most voluntary redundancy schemes were over-subscribed. We can thus conclude that some of the rise in registered unemployment during the 1980s is due to the impact of the social welfare system on the behaviour of job seekers.

The international evidence suggests that the effect of social welfare systems on the level of unemployment is quite striking. In the US, for example, there is no Federal unemployment insurance system, and most state and occupational systems do not provide benefits after six months' unemployment. That there is such a low level of long-duration unemployment in the US is undoubtedly related to these facts. In Sweden those who have been out of work for over six months are required to undergo very intensive counselling and retraining and, when they have completed these courses, steps are taken to place them in employment. The idea of simply paying the long-term unemployed income maintenance is not part of the Swedish social insurance system. The result is a low level of long-term unemployment.[6]

The contrast between Ireland, Sweden and the US is clear from the statistics in Table 7.4.

*Table 7.4*

**Short and long-term unemployment rates in selected countries: 1987**

|  | Short-term unemployment rate % | Long-term unemployment rate % |
|---|---|---|
| *Ireland* | 10.4 | 8.3 |
| *Sweden* | 1.7 | 0.2 |
| *US* | 5.7 | 0.5 |

*Note*: Long-term = one year and over.
*Source*: OECD, *Employment Outlook*, 1988, Tables 1.7 and M.

The difference between the long-term unemployment rate in Ireland, on the one hand, and Sweden and the US, on the other, is far greater than that between the short-term unemployment rates. The high rate of long-term unemployment in Ireland is a particularly serious aspect of our overall unemployment problem. While a higher rate of economic growth would reduce both types of unemployment, changes in the social security system will probably be required if we are ever to get our rate of long-term unemployment down to US or Swedish levels.

# Theories of Unemployment

Having outlined the nature and structure of unemployment in Ireland, we shall now present an overview of economic theories of unemployment and how these relate to the Irish experience.[7]

## Equilibrium unemployment

It is now generally accepted that even when the economy and labour market are in equilibrium there is some "normal" level of unemployment. It is neither feasible nor desirable to eliminate unemployment completely. In a famous article published in 1968, Milton Friedman used the phrase the "natural rate of unemployment" to describe the unemployment that persists even at "full employment". The Nobel Prize winning Yale University economist James Tobin introduced a closely related concept which he called the *non-accelerating inflation rate of unemployment (NAIRU)*. Both of these concepts are attempts to define the level of unemployment that would exist when the economy is in equilibrium.

The existence of unemployment even when the labour market is in equilibrium is due to *frictions* and *imperfect information*.[8] On both sides of the labour market, information is imperfect and costly to obtain. It takes time and effort for job-seekers to find out about job openings. Employers also have to invest in recruiting and screening employees. The fact that there are unemployed people does not guarantee that employers are able to fill the openings they have available: the match between the qualifications of the unemployed and the requirements of employers is not likely to be perfect. People who are looking for jobs do not take the first job that becomes available: they have reservation wages for the type of jobs they are seeking. If a person's reservation wage is above the wage that is being offered for the type of work he wishes to do, he will continue searching until he is lucky enough to get a better-than-average offer or until he lowers his expectations. Clearly, there is an element of choice about this type of job-search unemployment, so it forms part of what is sometimes referred to as "voluntary" or "equilibrium" unemployment.

The magnitude of "equilibrium" unemployment will vary from country to country. It depends on the flexibility and adaptability of the labour force, the appropriateness of the qualifications of those looking for work, the realism of their job aspirations, their geographical and occupational mobility and the level of social welfare benefits.

Imagine two economies, one with an inflexible labour force, a poor match between the qualifications of the unemployed and those sought by employers, and a generous social welfare system, the other with a flexible labour force, a good match between the qualifications of the unemployed and those sought by employers, and a harsh social welfare system. The first would have a high natural rate of

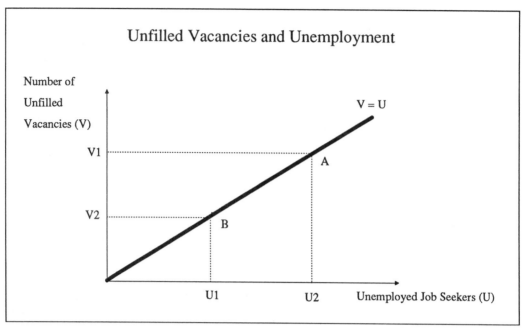

Figure 7.5

unemployment, the second a low rate. The contrast between the two can be illustrated with a diagram (Figure 7.5) that shows the situation in terms of the number of job openings (vacancies) and job-seekers (unemployed).

*Note:*

*The curve linking combinations of the number of vacancies and job-seekers in an economy is known as the Beveridge curve, after the British economist William Beveridge (1879-1963) who is famous as the "father of the British welfare state".*

Assuming that the total labour force is the same size in both countries, and that in both there is full employment in the sense that the number of vacancies equals the number of unemployed, in economy A the rate of unemployment is much higher than in economy B because of the greater efficiency of B's labour market.

*Note:*

*The "natural rate" is not the same in all economies, nor is it immutable over time. In the example in the text, there is obviously scope in economy A for policies to increase the efficiency of its labour market. Examples of these would be training to improve the match between vacancies and the unemployed, incentives for regional and occupational mobility and disincentives for prolonged job search. There is evidence that over time the "natural rate" has tended to increase in many economies. Some economists question the appropriateness of using the adjective "natural" to describe a phenomenon that is so unstable. We return to this issue in Chapter 8.*

# Disequilibrium unemployment

In addition to the sources of unemployment discussed in the previous section, it has to be acknowledged that western economies have exhibited persistent and occasionally severe *disequilibrium unemployment*. Whereas "natural rate" unemployment arises because of frictions and adjustment costs, disequilibrium unemployment occurs because of a *malfunctioning of the macroeconomy*. Many different causes have been blamed for this type of unemployment and it is possible to group these in several ways. We shall concentrate on the distinction between the "classical" and "Keynesian" explanations of disequilibrium unemployment.

# Classical unemployment

Classical unemployment is due to the failure of the labour market to establish the *market-clearing real wage*. To understand what is meant by classical unemployment it is necessary to set out the standard theory of the supply and demand for labour.

Neo-classical economics analyses the labour market in much the same way as any other market: the supply and demand of labour are functions of price (the real wage) and equilibrium occurs where these two schedules intersect, at the market-clearing real wage. The unemployment that exists even in equilibrium is usually depicted in these diagrams as the gap between the supply of labour schedule (sometimes called the "accept job" or AJ schedule) and another schedule, to the right of the AJ schedule, indicating the number of people who enter the labour force and search for a job at each real wage level (called the "labour force" or LF schedule).[9]

In Figure 7.6 the market-clearing wage is $(W/P)_1$ and there is no involuntary unemployment. The unemployment rate is equal to AB/OB, and all of this is equilibrium, voluntary or natural rate unemployment. (Although these phrases do not have exactly the same meaning, they overlap sufficiently to be used interchangeably.) But what happens if the market-clearing wage is not established? In the typical microeconomic setting, an excess supply of a good will lead to a fall in its price. What happens in the labour market if the real wage is too high, leading to an excess supply of labour?

If we start from $(W/P)_2$, which is above $(W/P)_1$, we see that in addition to the voluntary unemployment DE at this wage there is a further gap between the demand for labour schedule and the AJ schedule, equal to FD. This distance measures the number of people who would accept a job at the prevailing wage, $(W/P)_2$, but are unable to obtain a job offer at this wage because only OF jobs are on offer. The unemployed people, represented by the distance FD, are said to be involuntarily unemployed because there is nothing they can do to ensure that they will receive an acceptable job offer; their reservation wage is already at or below the market wage. Despite their willingness to accept jobs paying less than $(W/P)_2$, the market wage remains stuck at this level and employers are only prepared to hire OF workers. The

145

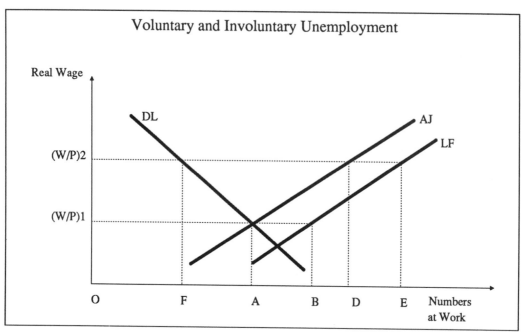

Figure 7.6

remaining FD workers are unemployed because of the failure of the labour market to establish the market-clearing wage.

The magnitude of the gap between the actual wage and the wage at which full employment would be established has been estimated by two economists (one of whom, Michael Bruno, is now governor of the Central Bank of Israel) for eight countries in a recent influential study.[10] They conclude that this gap was very large in the mid-1970s in Belgium and Denmark, but that it has played a smaller role in accounting for unemployment in the 1980s. A recent study[11] applied this methodology to the Irish experience and concluded that, compared to the general OECD experience, the Irish wage gap has been moderate.

What are the sources of this market failure? In other words, why are (real) wages not flexible so that they fall in response to the excess supply of labour, FD? The answer to this question lies in the nature of labour markets and in the myriad ways they differ from commodity markets. In the first place, trade unions exist in part to ensure that real wages *are* rigid. By combining together, workers try to prevent their wages from being undercut by the forces of supply and demand. In inflationary periods unions try to enforce *indexation* of wages, that is, automatic increases in money wages to compensate for rises in the cost of living. But trade unions are not the only reason why the existence of unemployed job-seekers, who would be willing to work for less than the going rate, does not lead to a fall in wages. Employers rarely try to force their existing employees to accept a wage cut by threatening to replace them with new recruits at a lower wage. Especially in the case of workers with firm-specific skills, modern personnel practices are very different from the hiring and firing of labour on an "auction market" that would be required to ensure that the labour market always cleared. Employers and employees tend to enter into long-term (*explicit or implicit*) *contracts* because this ensures a more contented, and productive, labour force than would be achieved by ruthless hiring and firing as demand for the firm's output fluctuated. The Japanese practice of "hiring for life" (*nenko*) is an example of this approach.[12]

*Note:*

*Karl Marx (1818-83) believed that the Reserve Army of the Unemployed was used by capitalists to screw the wages of workers down to the bare subsistence minimum. But modern labour markets are more complex than he realised, and the outsiders (the unemployed who are willing to work at lower wages) are not able to compete effectively for the insiders' jobs.*

*Table 7.5*

**Earnings, employment and unemployment**

|  |  | *1980* | *1986* |
|---|---|---|---|
| *Real earnings:* |  |  |  |
|  | US | 100 | 101 |
|  | EEC | 100 | 113 |
| *Employment:* |  |  |  |
|  | US | 100 | 110 |
|  | EEC | 100 | 98 |
| *Unemployment (%):* |  |  |  |
|  | US | 7.2 | 7.0 |
|  | EEC | 6.4 | 11.3 |

*Source*: OECD, *Main Economic Indicators*

It is generally believed that *real wage flexibility* can make an important contribution to solving the problem of involuntary unemployment. The recent experience of the US may be cited as an illustration. Part of the reason why the US has had a boom in employment in the 1980s, with unemployment quickly falling to its pre-recession level, is that real wages have been static throughout the long recovery in economic activity. This is in marked contrast with most European economies where, despite high unemployment, the real wages of the employed rose rapidly in the 1980s. Employment has stagnated in Europe while it has surged ahead in the US (Table 7.5).

The weakness of trade unions in the US, the harshness of the social security system and the mobility and flexibility of the labour force are the underlying reasons for the contrast between the experiences of the two labour markets. Another factor has been the tendency for US labour unions to enter into relatively long-term (three or four year) collective agreements without full cost of living indexation. In inflationary periods, when the money wage is fixed in this manner, nominal wage rigidity leads to real wage flexibility.

# Keynesian unemployment

The type of unemployment that concerned Keynes in his famous *General Theory of Employment, Interest and Money* (1936) has its origins in cyclical downturns in economic activity. Keynes was concerned in particular with *adverse demand shocks*, on which he blamed the Great Depression of the 1930s. He believed that a collapse of private sector investment and consumption spending had triggered the slump in economic activity. Since the oil price increases of the 1970s we are now very aware that *supply shocks*, caused by cost increases, can also lead to a fall in the demand for labour and a rise in unemployment.

To illustrate the impact of recession on the labour market, we can think of an economy growing at a steady rate, determined by the growth of the fully employed labour force, the rate of capital accumulation and technical progress. We denote this full employment, or potential, output $Q^*$. When an adverse shock occurs, the actual level of output (Q) falls below $Q^*$. The *output gap* is equal to $(Q^* - Q)/Q^*$. The Yale economist Arthur Okun (1928-80) showed that there was a close association between the output gap and the rate of unemployment in the US.

*Note:*

*Okun's law states that, in the US, for every 5% fall in output relative to potential GNP, the rate of unemployment increases by two percentage points. The Irish experience seems to be somewhat worse. If output falls 5% below its trend level, the rate of unemployment rises by about three percentage points.*[13]

Figure 7.7 shows the trend growth rate in GNP (potential GNP) and the *actual* growth rate in GNP for the Irish economy over the period 1970-94. The data for the early 1990s is based on current forecasts. It can be seen that, with the exception of the 1974/5 recession, actual GNP was close to the potential level up to 1980. However, since 1980, a large output gap has emerged reflecting the recession in the Irish economy. Current forecasts indicate that actual GNP will converge towards potential GNP in the early 1990s.

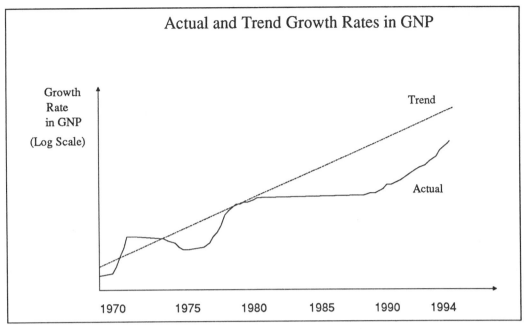

Figure 7.7

*Note:*

*Potential GNP is calculated by fitting a non-linear trend through to the time series for actual GNP. This provides an estimate of what GNP would have been if it had been on a smooth growth path instead of fluctuating from peak to trough of the business cycle. There is a problem in calculating the potential level of output when, as in the mid-1980s, the economy is still in the throes of a recession: until we know where the next peak of the business cycle is, it is difficult to estimate how fast the economy could have grown if the recession had been avoided.*

Figure 7.8 shows the relationship between the output gap and the rate of unemployment in Ireland over the period 1979-86. Clearly these two variables move closely together. During the recession of 1974-76, for example, the output gap rose to 5% and unemployment increased by about three percentage points. The 15% gap between actual and potential output that opened up during the 1980s was associated with an increase of ten percentage points in the unemployment rate, which is consistent with what would have been predicted on the basis of the relationship between the output gap and unemployment in 1970s.

The finding that when the level of output falls below its trend growth path, the rate of unemployment increases, is hardly surprising. It is, none the less, very important because it shows that no special explanation, such as "the death of work", is required to account for the enormous increase in unemployment during the 1980s. If the trend growth rate of the economy had been maintained, the rate of

149

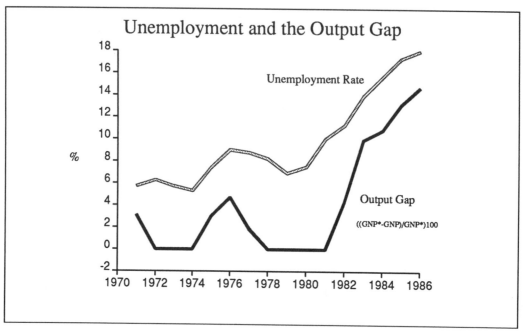

Figure 7.8

unemployment would not have risen. There is also an important message here for those concerned about poverty. Because unemployment is the primary cause of poverty in our society, economic growth, by reducing the rate of unemployment, reduces the incidence of poverty.

A distinguishing feature of the Keynesian type of unemployment that occurs during a cyclical downturn is that firms would be willing to produce more at the existing wage level. The reason they do not do so is that there is a *deficiency of aggregate demand*. Firms are *quantity constrained*, whereas they are *cost constrained* in the case of classical unemployment. Moreover, when there is Keynesian unemployment households would like to buy more, but they cannot because they lack the necessary purchasing power due to the fact that they are unemployed.

A crucial difference between Keynesian and classical unemployment lies in the way firms would respond to an increase in aggregate demand. If there is Keynesian unemployment, an increase in aggregate demand will elicit increased production and employment with no increase in the price level and without a fall in real wages.[14] When there is classical unemployment, on the other hand, firms will not respond to an increase in demand unless there is a fall in real wages. In terms of the AD/AS diagrams discussed in Chapter 3, in the Keynesian case the AS curve is horizontal, where in the classical case it is vertical.

It is not possible to measure with any accuracy the Keynesian and classical components of unemployment. (In the next chapter we discuss one attempt to estimate the NAIRU.) However, evidence of the importance of Keynesian unemployment is available from the responses to a survey of manufacturing industry conducted quarterly on behalf of the Commission of the European Communities. In this survey firms are asked if "production is being held up" and if they respond that it is, they are asked if "deficient demand" is the reason. In the mid-1980s between one quarter and one third of the respondents gave this as the reason for not expanding output.[15]

## Remedies

Unemployment is too complex a phenomenon to admit of a single "solution". While in principle Keynesian unemployment is amenable to an expansionary fiscal policy, we have seen that under Irish conditions there are very narrow limits on the effectiveness of this approach. Faster growth of the world economy that leads to increased demand for our exports would alleviate Keynesian unemployment, but there is nothing we can do to affect the macroeconomic policies of the countries with which we trade.

Classical unemployment is more amenable to domestic policies, although it is not easy to ensure that the right policies will be implemented. Many economists believe that an important contribution can be made by an *incomes policy* to moderating the level (or at least the rate of increase) of real wages. In Ireland there were a number of *National Wage Agreements* and *National Understandings* during the 1970s. These were agreements between employer organisations and trades unions about the rate of increase of money wages. In some cases commitments were also given by the government concerning tax reductions, increases in social welfare payments and even increases in spending on health and education. The contribution made by these arrangements to wage moderation in the long run is debatable. Many believe that at best their effect was short-lived and that they were followed by a period of catching-up. The latest experiment of this type is the *Programme for National Recovery* (October 1987). This provides for pay increases of 2.5% in each of the years 1988, 1989 and 1990. Up to mid-1989 pay increases in the private sector have been held to this guideline, aided by low inflation and some tax reductions. The real test of the agreement will come as the rate of inflation rises significantly above 2.5% and leads to a fall in real incomes.

These experiments with cooperation between the "social partners" (that is, unions, employers and government) are examples of what has come to be known as *corporatism*. There is some evidence that countries with a high degree of corporatism (such as Sweden and Austria) or those with a low degree (such as Japan and the US) have achieved a better economic performance compared with those where a number of relatively powerful, but unco-ordinated, unions and employer organisations, negotiate wage bargains on behalf of their members.

In a small, open economy the rate of exchange has a major role to play in ensuring the *competitiveness* of the economy. For this reason, domestic wage increases should be related to what can be afforded in the light of developments in competitor countries and of trends in the rate of exchange. As an example of this approach, the *Committee on Costs and Competitiveness* in its Report (1981) calculated the *wage norm* that could be afforded by Irish firms in light of the developments in our main trading partners. However, the Committee's calculations had to be quickly revised as it became apparent that sterling was weakening on the foreign exchanges in the last quarter of 1981. If there is a rise in the exchange rate, leading to a loss of competitiveness in the traded sectors of the economy, firms will not find it profitable to maintain output and employment.[16] (We discuss these concepts in detail in Chapter 9.) Suffice it to say at this point that a *devaluation*, if successful, would operate in much the same way as a wage cut. To be successful, however, it is necessary that the rise in the cost of living due to the fact that the devaluation has made imported goods dearer is not fully compensated through cost of living adjustments to wages.

Earlier in this chapter we discussed the way taxes, and payroll taxes in particular, tend to increase the cost of hiring labour and therefore reduce the level of employment. A way of redressing this factor without causing the exchequer undue loss of revenue is to provide *incremental employment subsidies.* These would lower the cost of taking on additional workers without causing any loss of revenue from those already in employment. Different schemes could be used to achieve this result, such as paying a firm a subsidy for each additional worker recruited over and above a benchmark level of employment. Alternatively, these additional workers could be exempted from employee and employer PRSI. Schemes of this type have been tried on a modest scale in Ireland.[17] It has been argued that in view of our very high rate of unemployment it would be appropriate to divert to this use much of the money that is at present devoted to capital grants by the Industrial Development Authority.[18]

# 7.6 The Outlook for Unemployment in Ireland

The survey of the problem of unemployment contained in this chapter makes it clear that no panacea exists. We can, however, list a number of factors that will help to reduce the level of unemployment. These include, first and foremost, a faster rate of economic growth, and then moderation in the rate of growth of real wages, greater flexibility in work practices, increased occupational and geographical mobility, a larger gap between people's standard of living while unemployed and when working at the jobs for which they are qualified, a better match between school-leavers' qualifications and the skills sought by employers, more effective retraining of the long-term unemployed, and a slowing down of the rate of growth of the labour force. This long list is not exhaustive. The level of unemployment in Ireland during the 1990s will therefore depend on many factors, some of which are subject to control by policy-makers and some of which depend on the overall macroeconomic performance of the country. The disastrous consequences of the ill-advised push for a meaningless goal of "full employment" in the late 1970s must not be forgotten.

In this area, to paraphrase St Francis of Assisi, we have to learn to change what we can and to live with what we cannot change, and to recognise the difference between the two.

# Conclusion

The main topics discussed in this chapter include:

- The growth of population, the labour force and employment

- The nature and structure of unemployment in Ireland today. The main differentials in unemployment rates

- The distinction between equilibrium and disequilibrium unemployment. The concept of the natural rate of unemployment

- The sources of disequilibrium unemployment

- The importance of maintaining the economy near its trend growth path in order to avoid Keynesian unemployment

- The labour market policies that would reduce classical unemployment: wage moderation and increased competitiveness. The importance of the exchange rate in this context.

Notes

1. We use the words *emigration* and *immigration* to refer to the net balance, inward or outward, of migration.

2. Most of the data used in this chapter come from the Labour Force Survey. The definition of *unemployed* includes those who are seeking a first job as well as those who have lost their job. Only those who indicate some form of job search are classified as unemployed. Regular monthly data on *registered unemployment* are published from the Live Register returns. We have adopted the usual practice of describing housewifes and others who are engaged in home duties as economically inactive. We do not mean to imply by this that they are not working!

3. OECD, *Employment Outlook*, 1987, Table 6.1.

4. The outflow of population during the 1980s has contained a preponderance of males, which is a change from the more evenly balance emigration of previous years.

5. B., Nolan, "More on Actual versus Hypothetical Replacement Ratios in Ireland", *Economic and Social Review*, April 1988 and J.G.Hughes and Brendan M. Walsh, "Unemployment Duration, Aggregate Demand and Unemployment Insurance", *The Economic and Social Review*, January 1984.

6. It should be noted that a relatively large proportion of the labour force is classified as handicapped. The OECD estimates that the true unemployment rate in Sweden is about 5%, compared with the 1.6% rate used in official statistics. See OECD, *Economic Survey of Sweden*, 1988/89, p. 62.

7. This section has drawn on several textbooks, in particular: Peter Fallon and Donald Verry, *The Economics of Labour Markets*, Philip Allen, 1988; Peter Sinclair, *Unemployment: Economic Theory and Evidence*, Basil Blackwell, 1987; and R.J. Gordon, *Macroeconomics*, Little, Brown and Company, Third Edition, 1984.

8. This type of unemployment can merge into structural unemployment, discussed above.

9. A weakness of this presentation is that it does not depict the level of vacancies in the labour market. At the equilibrium wage there are no unfilled jobs: firms are on their demand for labour scheduals.

10. M. Bruno and J. D. Sachs, *Economics of Worldwide Stagflation*, Basil Blackwell, 1985.

11. P.P. Walsh, F.A. Walsh and E. Woelger, "The Real Wage Gap and its Development over Time: The Irish Experience 1960-1987", *The Economic and Social Review*, Vol. 21, No.1, October, 1989, p. 87-102.

12. This practice applies only to the elite workers hired by the big corporations. The conditions of those working for smaller firms and subcontractors to the big companies are far less secure.

13. For details of these calculations and a discussion of the application of Okun's law in Ireland, see Brendan M. Walsh, "Why is Unemployment So High?", *Perspectives on Economic Policy*, 1, 1987, (Department of Political Economy, University College, Dublin).

14. Keynes even implied that a fall in real wages would reduce aggregate demand and aggravate the problem of unemployment.

15. The way this question is framed does not allow us to explore the possibility that the reason for the firm's lack of demand is that its prices are too high.

16. Keynes argued that the high unemployment in Britain during the late 1920s was due to Mr Churchill's decision to go back on the gold standard in 1925 at the pre-War parity. As Britain had experienced much more inflation than the US since 1914 the result was a misaligned rate of exchange against the dollar. As a result many of the traditional exporting industries became uncompetitive. See J.M. Keynes, "The Economic Consequences of Mr Churchill" in *Essays in Persuasion*, London, Macmillan, 1931.

17. See R. Breen and B. Halpin, *Subsidising Jobs: An Evaluation of the Employment Incentive Scheme*, The Economic and Social Research Institute, 1989.

18. Frank Barry, "Payroll Taxes, Capital Grants and Irish Unemployment", *The Economic and Social Review*, Vol. 21, No.1, October, 1989, p. 107-121.

# Chapter 8

# *Inflation and Unemployment*

## 1 Introduction

The goal of minimising the rate of unemployment has to be interpreted in the light of the way the country's labour market functions and its "natural rate" of unemployment. We argued in Chapter 7 that Swedish or US levels of unemployment are unattainable in Ireland with our present social welfare and labour market structures. Pursuit of an unrealistic target rate of unemployment through an expansionary fiscal policy would destabilise the economy.

These considerations have been incorporated into economic theory by recognising that policy-makers should not pursue the goal of minimising the rate of unemployment without regard for the other objectives of economic policy. In particular, they have to take into account the possibility that lowering the rate of unemployment will tend to increase the rate of inflation.

We take up these issues in this chapter. Our approach is first to expand the aggregate supply-and-demand analysis of Chapter 3. In particular, we introduce a labour market on the supply side of the economy and a money market on the demand side. We then use this aggregate supply and demand framework to examine the relationship between inflation and unemployment. It should be borne in mind that this theory was developed with regard to relatively large and closed economies. In the final few sections of the chapter we discuss how this theory has to be modified to take account of the special considerations that apply in a small, open economy (SOE) such as Ireland.

## 2 Production Function

On the supply side of the economy, land, labour and capital, *the factors of production*, are the three basic inputs in the production process. The *production function* shows the relationship between these three inputs and the output of goods and services. Mathematically the production function can be written as:

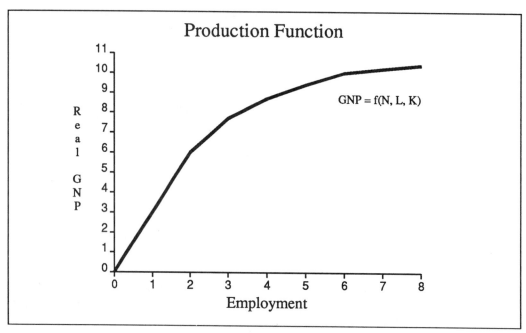

Figure 8.1

(1)   GNP = f(N, L, K)

where , N = employment (or labour), L = land and K = capital. Equation (1) states that output is a function of employment, land and capital. If we now hold land and capital constant, we can examine the relationship between output and employment. In Figure 8.1 an increase in employment on the horizontal axis leads to an increase in output on the vertical axis. It will be observed that the production curve tends to become rather flat at high levels of output. The reason for this is "diminishing returns" from labour. As more and more labour is applied to a fixed amount of land and capital, labour becomes less productive. Output continues to increase, but it does so at a diminishing rate.

# 8.3 Labour Market

As briefly discussed in Chapter 7, the supply and demand for labour determine the wage rate (W) and employment (N). The labour market diagram is shown in Figure 8.2. The labour supply curve (Ns) is upward-sloping, indicating that firms must offer higher wages in order to encourage workers to supply more labour. The

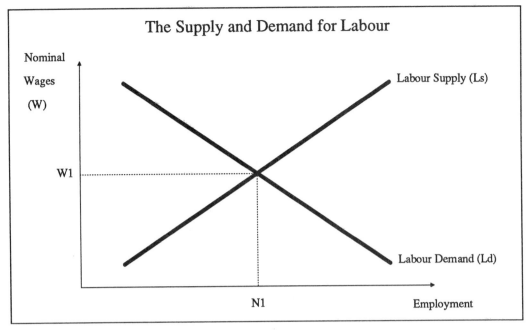

**Figure 8.2**

downward-sloping labour demand curve (Nd) indicates that firms will reduce their demand for labour if wages increase.

Consider now the demand for labour curve in greater detail. Underlying the Nd curve is the *marginal revenue product of labour (MRPL)*, the value of the extra output produced by the firm when one extra worker is hired. The value of the extra output can be broken down into a volume component and a price component. That is:

Marginal revenue product of labour (MRPL) = Marginal product of labour (MPL) * Price of output (P)

Figure 8.3 shows the MRPL for four hypothetical workers, referred to as A, B, C and D. With MRPL measured on the vertical axis, worker B produces less than worker A and worker C produces less than worker B and so on. The reason for this, as mentioned in the previous section, is diminishing returns. As more and more labour is applied to a fixed amount of land and capital, the extra output produced by additional workers decreases. Hence, diminishing returns account for the step reduction in each worker's MRPL. (This is no reflection on workers like D; it is simply due to the fact that they are being hired *after* other workers are already in the labour force.)

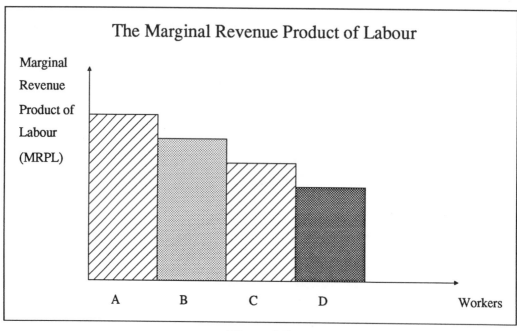

Figure 8.3

The basic rule that firms adopt in hiring workers is hire up to the point where the

Wage rate (W) = Marginal revenue product of labour (MRPL)

Suppose, for example, that the current wage rate is £100 per week and the MRPL for workers A, B, C and D is £150, £100, £80 and £50 respectively. The firm will hire worker A as the value of the output produced by this worker exceeds the wage rate. The firm is indifferent in the case of worker B as the value of the output produced by this worker is equal to the wage rate. We assume however that the firm will hire this worker. The firm will not hire workers C and D as the revenue generated by these two workers is less than the wage rate.

In Figure 8.4, the boxes used in Figure 8.3 are replaced by a downward-sloping MRPL curve and a horizontal line is used to indicate the wage rate of £100. At point X, MRPL = W, and this point is therefore one point on the demand for labour curve. We can repeat this for every conceivable wage rate. If, for example, the wage rate is reduced to £80, the firm will hire workers A, B and C. Hence, point Z is also a point on the demand for labour curve. It follows from this analysis that the MRPL curve *coincides* with the demand for labour curve.

Given that the MRPL curve underlies the Nd curve, an increase in productivity or an increase in the output price shifts the Nd curve upwards to the right. Conversely a decrease in productivity or a fall in output prices shifts the Nd curve downwards

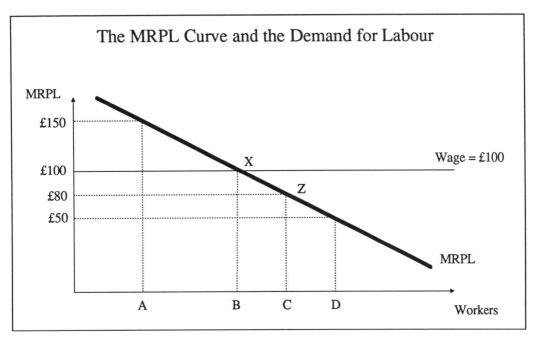

Figure 8.4

to the left. Thus, the Nd curve with the nominal wage on the vertical axis shifts every time the price level changes.

*Note:*
*We could also have drawn the Nd curve with the real wage on the vertical axis. Recall that MRPL/P = MPL and that the profit-maximising firm will set MPL = W/P, the real wage.*

# 4 Aggregate Supply

It will be recalled from Chapter 3 that the aggregate supply (AS) curve showed a positive relationship between prices and real GNP on the supply side of the economy. The process was as follows:

$\uparrow$ Output Prices (P) $\rightarrow$ $\uparrow$ Profits $\rightarrow$ $\uparrow$ Real GNP.

The important assumption underlying this process is that input prices, and wages in particular, remain constant. If input prices remain constant then an increase in output prices leads to an increase in profits and this, in turn, will encourage firms to expand real output. On the supply side of the economy, therefore, an increase in output prices leads to an increase in real GNP and conversely a fall in output prices

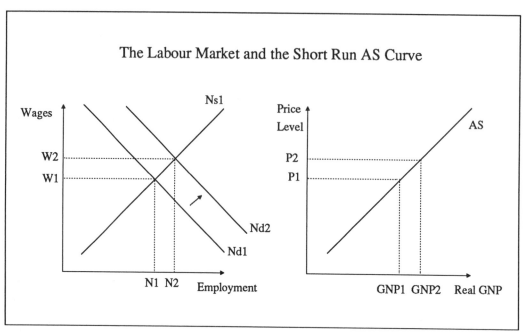

Figure 8.5

leads to a fall in real GNP. If wages or other input prices increase or productivity decreases, the AS curve will shift upwards to the left. Conversely, a fall in input prices or a rise in productivity will shift the AS curve downwards.

We will now develop this relationship between prices and real output in the context of the labour market and the production function. The reader should bear in mind that the supply and demand for labour determine the wage rate and employment, whereas the production function provides the link between employment and the supply of goods and services (GNP).

Suppose output prices increase from P1 to P2. The effect of this is shown in the left hand diagram in Figure 8.5 as an outward shift of the Nd curve (Nd1 to Nd2). This is because the position of the demand for labour curve depends on MPL * P. It can be seen that both wages and employment increase. The increase in employment (N1 to N2), in turn, will increase GNP via the production function. Hence, on the supply side of the economy, there is a positive relationship between prices and real output. This is shown in the right-hand diagram in Figure 8.5 as an upward-sloping AS curve.

*Note:*

*The slope of the AS curve depends on the slope of the labour supply (Ns) curve. The flatter (elastic) the Ns curve, the more elastic will be the AS curve. Conversely, the steeper (inelastic) the Ns curve the more inelastic will be the AS curve.*

So far the analysis is not very different from that presented in Chapter 3. As we have already stated, the rationale underlying the upward-sloping AS curve is the extra profit available to firms as the price level rises. The important assumption is that wages and other input prices remain constant as output prices increase. This results in increased profits and encourages firms to expand production.

At this point we return to the distinction between *nominal* and *real* wages. The real wage is simply the nominal wage divided by the price level (W/P). In Figure 8.5, both nominal wages and prices have increased. However the increase in P *exceeds* the increase in W so that real wages (W/P) have fallen. This means that workers have supplied more labour in response to higher nominal wages but a lower real wage. In a sense workers have been tricked or they have confused nominal wage increases for real wage increases. This is known as *money illusion*. Workers are under the illusion they are being paid more but when inflation is allowed for this is not the case.

After a time workers will catch on that real wages have fallen and will demand an increase in money wages in line with the increase in output prices. This is shown in the left hand side diagram of Figure 8.6 as an upward shift of the labour supply line. Equilibrium in the labour market is now at the point B. The increase in W equals the increase in P so that the real wage (W/P) returns to its initial level. At the point B employment (N) is also back to its original level. The reason for this is that the increase in wages has eroded firms' profits and there is no longer any incentive for firms to produce more output or hire any additional workers. In the long run, the labour market goes back to the original levels of real wages, employment and output. The increase in money wages also shifts the AS curve upwards. In the right hand side diagram of Figure 8.6 this is shown as a shift from AS1 to AS2. Prices have increased on the vertical axis but real GNP is unchanged on the horizontal axis. This means that the upward-sloping AS curves are really only *short-run* aggregate supply curves. They are upward-sloping only for as long as workers suffer from money illusion. As soon as workers demand higher wages to compensate for higher output prices, the upward-sloping AS curves shift upwards. The movement of the short-run AS curves enables us to map out the long-run AS. It can be seen that the long-run AS curve (LRAS) is vertical. The increase in output prices has not led to any increase in real output in the longer term. This is because only N1 workers are willing to accept employment at the real wage level W1/P1 = W2/P2.

The crucial question is: How long before workers realise that real wages have fallen and demand an increase in wages to compensate for the higher output prices? This depends on many factors, including the *change* in the rate of inflation. It takes time for people to become aware that the rate of inflation is rising or falling. Institutional arrangements concerning wage bargaining are also important. Wage contracts can be set for periods ranging from months to years and workers may not be able to negotiate an increase in wages until the contract expires. However, contracts may have cost of living adjustment (COLA) clauses. If this type of

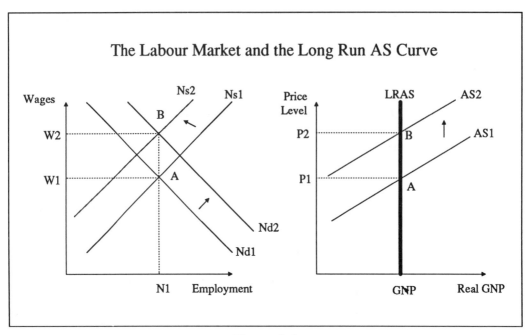

Figure 8.6

*indexation* is complete and automatic, there can be no money illusion. The AS curve will be vertical even in the short run.

So far we have concentrated on the relationship between output prices and wage costs. However, other raw material prices are also important. If raw material prices increase as output prices rise, profits may not increase and firms may not expand production. In what follows we will assume that raw material contracts are set for some period into the future and therefore do not immediately change as output prices change. This assumption allows us to concentrate on the relationship between wages and output prices.

# 8.5 Aggregate Demand

On the demand side of the economy there is an inverse relationship between prices and real GNP. That is, an increase in the price level lowers spending on GNP and, conversely, a decrease in the price level increases spending on GNP. In Chapter 3, we explained this inverse relationship in terms of the link between the price level, competitiveness and the trade account of the balance of payments. An increase in the price level leads to a loss of competitiveness and this results in a decrease in exports and an increase in imports. A trade account deficit therefore emerges which decreases aggregate demand and GNP. Hence there is an inverse relationship between changes in prices and GNP on the demand side of the economy.

In this chapter we are concerned to derive a downward-sloping AD curve without recourse to balance of payments effects. We have not as yet covered the relevant material relating to the balance of payments and until we do so in Chapter 9, our model is that of a closed economy. In this regard, we revise our explanation of the AD curve by ignoring the balance of payments effect and instead emphasising the money market and monetary policy.

In Chapter 6 we explained, in the context of the Keynesian model, how changes in the money supply influenced nominal GNP. Briefly, an increase in the money supply lowered interest rates which increased investment and this, in turn, increased aggregate demand and GNP. Conversely, a decrease in the money supply increased interest rates and reduced investment and GNP. The only adjustment or extension needed at this point to derive a downward-sloping AD curve is to replace the nominal money supply (Ms) by a *real money supply* (Ms/P). With this adjustment it is relatively simple to derive an inverse relationship between prices and GNP on the demand side of the economy. In short, the sequence is as follows:

$$\uparrow P \ \rightarrow \underset{1}{\downarrow} (Ms/P) \ \rightarrow \underset{2}{\uparrow} r \rightarrow \underset{3}{\downarrow} I \ \rightarrow \downarrow AD \ \rightarrow \downarrow GNP$$

An increase in the price level reduces the real money supply. The remaining steps are as before. The reduction in the real money supply increases interest rates and this reduces investment, aggregate demand and GNP. Conversely, a decrease in the price level increases the real money supply and lowers interest rates. Investment, aggregate demand and GNP now increase.

How steep the *slope* of the AD curve is depends on links 1, 2 and 3. That is:

1. The slope of the demand for money (Md) curve. If the slope of the demand for money curve is relatively flat (elastic), a given change in the real money supply will have a small effect on interest rates. Conversely, a steep (inelastic) Md curve means that changes in the money supply have a large effect on interest rates.

2. The marginal efficiency of investment (MEI) curve. If the MEI curve is relatively flat (elastic), a given change in the interest rate has a strong effect on investment. Conversely, a steep (inelastic) MEI curve means that investment is not sensitive to interest rate changes.

3. The multiplier. A large multiplier will mean that a given change in investment has a strong effect on GNP.

A flat (elastic) AD curve means that the initial change in prices has a strong effect on GNP. This will be the case if:

1. the Md curve is steep (inelastic)
2. if the MEI curve is flat (elastic) and
3. the multiplier is large.

Some combination of the above would be sufficient to give a flat (elastic) AD curve. The AD curve will be relatively steep (inelastic) if a given change in prices have a weak effect on GNP. This occurs if

1. the Md curve is flat (elastic)
2. the MEI curve is steep (inelastic) and
3. there is a small multiplier.

The *location* of the AD line depends on changes in consumer expenditure (C), investment (I), government expenditure (G) and the money supply (Ms). An increase in C, I, G and Ms (not brought about by price changes) will shift the AD curve to the right. An expansionary fiscal and monetary policy, for example, shifts the AD curve outwards. Conversely, a decrease in any of these variables shifts the AD curve to the left.

*Note:*

*We confine our discussion here to a closed economy. Hence, we ignore for the moment the effect of changes in exports and imports on the location of the AD curve.*

In Figure 8.7, the AS curve derived in the previous section is combined with the AD curve. The interaction of these two curves determines the price level (P) and real GNP in the economy. This diagram is very similar to that given in Chapter 3. The main difference is that we have expanded the analysis underlying the two curves. A labour market and a production function now underlie the AS curve and the goods and money markets underlie the AD curve.

*Note:*

*We could also express the variables in Figure 8.7 in terms of "rate of change". In this case, the inflation rate appears on the vertical axis and the rate of growth of real GNP on the horizontal axis.*

# The Phillips Curve

As shown in Figure 8.7, a shift of the AD curve to the right leads to an increase in the price level on the vertical axis and an increase in real GNP on the horizontal axis. Assuming unemployed resources, the increase in real GNP, in turn, should lead to a fall in unemployment. More output can only be produced if more labour is employed (see Figure 8.1). Higher levels of employment will tend to be reflected in lower rates of unemployment.

The idea that there is a negative relationship between the rate of unemployment and the rate of increase in prices was first suggested by the New Zealand economist A.W. Phillips (1914-75), working at the London School of Economics in the 1950s. He noted that between 1862 and 1956 in Britain there was a tendency for periods of low unemployment to coincide with periods of rising wage rates.[1] He drew a diagram depicting this inverse relationship, which has come to be known as the "Phillips Curve". Variants of it have appeared in macroeconomic textbooks ever since.

*Note:*
*Phillips originally put the rate of wage inflation on the vertical axis. The relationship between wage inflation and price inflation depends on the rate of growth of labour productivity and the share of labour in national income. If the productivity of labour (that is, output per worker) is growing at a*

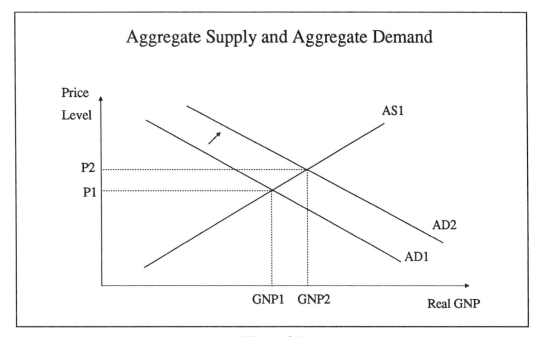

Figure 8.7

165

*constant rate, and labour's share of national income is constant, there will be a linear relationship between wage and price inflation.*

The Phillips Curve can be written mathematically as follows:

(2)  $P^* = f(U)$

where $P^*$ = the inflation rate and U = the unemployment rate. Equation (2) states that the inflation rate is a function of the rate of unemployment. An increase in unemployment leads to a fall in the rate of inflation and conversely a fall in unemployment leads to an increase in inflation.

Phillips suggested that the best fit to the historical data was a non-linear one, as shown in Figure 8.8, because as unemployment fell to very low levels, the increase in the rate of inflation accelerated, whereas at very high levels of unemployment, inflation levelled off or even became negative.

The economic rationale given for this relationship was simple. It did not make use of sophisticated ideas about aggregate supply and aggregate demand! Instead it was argued that the rate of unemployment is an index of the degree of excess supply of labour. When this is high, workers will have difficulty persuading employers to increase their rates of pay, but when it is low, employers will be willing to pay above the odds to attract and retain increasingly hard-to-recruit workers.

The thinking behind the Phillips curve was enormously influential in the 1960s. It led macroeconomic policy-makers to believe, in a phrase used by Paul Samuelson and Robert Solow (both Nobel prize laureates teaching at the Massachusetts Institute of Technology), that there exists a "menu for policy choice". A choice could be made between high inflation-low unemployment or low inflation-high unemployment. There is a *trade-off* between these two evils: it is not possible to enjoy a low rate of inflation *and* a low rate of unemployment at the same time. For example, suppose the economy was initially at the point A in Figure 8.8 where an inflation rate of 2% is combined with an unemployment rate of 4%. If the government now uses fiscal or monetary policy to move the economy to the point B, unemployment is reduced to 2% and inflation rises to 6%. Countries have to decide how much extra inflation they are prepared to tolerate in order to achieve a reduction in unemployment. This is essentially a political decision. Conservatives might prefer low inflation and ignore the high unemployment which this entailes whereas Labour or left-wing parties would opt for low unemployment and accept the consequences in terms of inflation.

Attempts to exploit this trade-off during the 1960s led to increasing disillusionment. It seemed that in many countries the rate of inflation associated with a rate of unemployment was rising. This became to be known as "stagflation". It is a situation where an increase in prices or inflation is combined with stagnant output and rising unemployment. In particular, it appeared that the policies designed

166

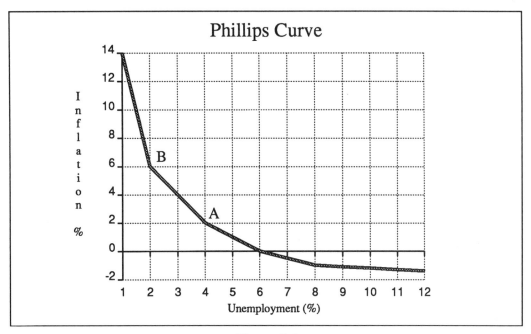

Figure 8.8

to move the economy *along* the Phillips Curve were in fact causing the curve to *shift outwards*.

Hence just as the authorities began to use the Phillips Curve for policy purposes, the inflation/unemployment relationship, which apparently had lasted for over a hundred years, broke down. There was much discussion of possible explanations for this: increased trade union militancy, a mis-match between the skills of the job seekers and the requirements of employers, a more generous social welfare system and so on. However, none of these explanations seemed to go to the heart of the matter.

# 7 The Modern Version of the Phillips Curve: Accelerationist Theory

A fundamental critique of the Phillips Curve analysis was advanced by Edmund Phelps of Columbia University and Milton Friedman[2] in the late 1960s. Their view of how the labour market functioned differed from the one on which the early Phillips Curve analysis relied. These two economists incorporated into the Phillips Curve the concept of the natural rate of unemployment and price (or inflation) expectations and argued that the Phillips Curve was vertical in the long-run. The implication of a vertical Phillips Curve is that there is no trade-off between inflation and unemployment and as a result, the long-run effectiveness of macroeconomic policy is severely limited.

# Natural rate of unemployment

Phelps and Friedman introduced the concept of the *natural rate of unemployment* (Un) and argued that inflation depends not just on the unemployment rate but on unemployment relative to the natural rate. In particular, if:

(U - Un) > 0, this leads to downward pressure on wages and as a consequence the inflation rate tends to fall.

(U - Un) < 0, there is upward pressure on wages as there is "over-full" employment and this will result in a higher inflation rate.

(U - Un) = 0, unemployment will not exert any pressure on wage rates or inflation.

*Note:*

*At the natural rate of unemployment, Un, all those who are willing to accept jobs at the prevailing real wage are employed. The remaining unemployment is essentially "voluntary", consisting largely of people who have entered the labour force in the hope of obtaining a better-than-average job offer and are still looking for such an offer. As we noted in Chapter 7, the level of the natural rate of unemployment depends on factors such as the mobility and flexibility of the population, the rates of social welfare available to support them while looking for work, and their reservation wage. Furthermore we have argued above that the natural rate is not immutable. It can be reduced by labour market policies, such as a harsher social welfare regime, increased spending on job placement and so on.*

# Expected price inflation

The second major strand in the Phelps and Friedman analysis concerns expected inflation. They drew attention to the basic point that workers are not concerned with *money wages* (W) but with *real wages* (W/P), that is the wage rate adjusted for the price level (P). Moreover, they pointed out that because wage contracts last for some period into the future workers will try to anticipate inflation in order to protect their real wage for the duration of the contract. If for example, inflation is expected to be 20% over the coming year, workers will demand a 20% increase in wages to maintain their real wages. In other words, workers are concerned with the change in expected real wages, $(\Delta W/P^{*e})$, where $\Delta W$ is the change in wages and $P^{*e}$ is expected price inflation. Hence *expected price inflation* is of crucial importance because any change in price expectations will be reflected in a change in workers' wage demands.

# The revised Phillips Curve

Given the natural rate of unemployment and inflation expectations the original Phillips Curve, equation 2, can be amended as follows:

(3)  $P^* = P^{*e} - \alpha(U - Un)$

where $\alpha$ is a coefficient, $0 < \alpha < 1$ which indicates how inflation ($P^*$) reacts to the (U - Un) gap.

Equation (3) states that the inflation rate depends on inflation expectations plus an adjustment based on the deviation of unemployment from the natural rate of unemployment. In Figure 8.9 we draw a Phillips Curve that corresponds to equation (3). The natural rate of unemployment is represented by the vertical line labelled Un. For illustrative purposes we assume that Un equals 6%. Note from equation (3) that whenever U = Un, the term in brackets is zero and $P^*$ must equal $P^{*e}$. The Phillips Curve therefore intersects the Un reference line at this expected rate of inflation. For example, at the point A in Figure 8.9, U = Un and both the actual and expected inflation rates are zero. The Phillips Curve labelled PC1 intersects the Un line at the zero inflation rate. If U continues to equal Un and expected inflation increases (for whatever reason) to 4% then the Phillips Curve will shift upwards and intersect the Un reference line at the 4% inflation rate. In Figure 8.9 the curve labelled PC2 corresponds to an expected inflation rate of 4 %. In effect, price expectations ($P^{*e}$) determines the position of the Phillips Curve. An increase in $P^{*e}$ shifts the Phillips Curve upwards and a decrease in $P^{*e}$ shifts the curve downwards.

It is only natural at this stage to ask how workers formulate price expectations. One explanation of the way expectations are formulated is to assume that this year's inflation rate will recur next year. Hence, the rate of inflation anticipated for this year is equal to the rate experienced last year, while this year's rate will be the rate anticipated for next year. Thus, if the inflation rate was 18% this year, this rate would be expected next year. Mathematically:

$$P^{*e}_t = P^*_{t-1}$$

where the subscript t indicates the particular year.

*Note:*
*There are many different ways of formulating inflation expectations. The above mentioned formulation is somewhat simplistic and naive because it implies that individuals and firms do not take into account any new developments in the economy when formulating expectations. This is clearly unrealistic. However, this over-simplified formulation will suffice in order to illustrate the main ideas underlying modern Phillips Curve analysis. In a later section in this chapter we discuss*

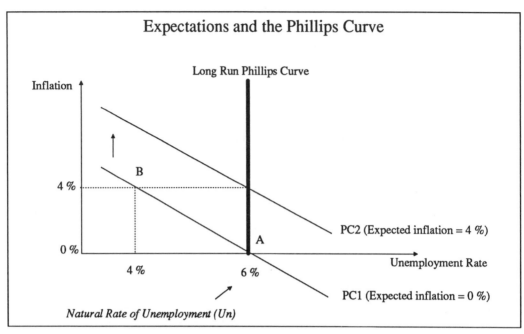

Figure 8.9

*a more sophisticated variant known as rational expectations.*

Substituting into equation 3 we have

(4) $\quad P^*_t = P^*_{t-1} - \alpha\,(U - Un)$

Equation (4) states that the current inflation rate depends on last period inflation rate plus an adjustment based on the deviation of the unemployment rate from the natural rate. We are now in a position to explain the implications of equation (4) for Phillips Curve analysis.

# Vertical (long-run) Phillips Curve

As we will see, the introduction of the natural rate of unemployment and price expectations leads to the conclusion that the long-run Phillips Curve is *vertical*. This means that in the long-run there is *no* trade-off between inflation and unemployment. If this theory, sometimes referred to as the *natural rate hypothesis* or the *accelerationist theory of inflation*, is correct then there are important implications for long-run macroeconomic policy.

Consider first the Phillips Curve given in Figure 8.10 and suppose the economy is initially at the point A, where a zero rate of inflation is combined with a 6% unemployment rate. If the government, using monetary policy (or fiscal policy),

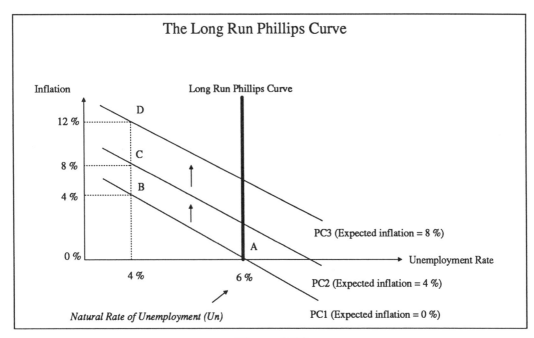

Figure 8.10

increases nominal GNP by, say, 10% the economy moves to the point B where inflation has increased to 4% and unemployment has fallen to 4%.

*Note:*

*We can work out the combination of inflation and unemployment that will result from an increase of 10% in nominal GNP. Recall from Chapter 7 the discussion of Okun's Law. Okun's Law suggests that unemployment will fall by approximately 1% point for every 3% increase in real GNP. That is there is a 3 to 1 relationship between changes in real output and unemployment. In the above example unemployment has fallen by 2% which implies a increase of 6% in real GNP. Hence the increase of 10% in nominal GNP is divided between a 4% increase in inflation and a 6% increase in real GNP.*

This movement from the point A to the point B in Figure 8.10 is a satisfactory outcome from the government's point of view. The expansionary monetary policy has increased real output and lowered unemployment at the cost of a 4% increase in inflation.

The point B is not however a long-run equilibrium point. Inflation has increased from 0% to 4% and as soon as workers realise what has happened, they will revise their inflation expectations ($P^{*e}$) upwards. Recall that $P^{*e}$ determines the position of the Phillips Curve. An increase in $P^{*e}$ from 0% to 4% shifts the Phillips Curve upwards from PC1 to PC2 in Figure 8.10. PC1 corresponds to zero expected inflation whereas PC2 corresponds to 4% expected inflation.

Suppose for the moment that unemployment remained at 4%. In this case, the economy will move to the point C on PC2 where 4% unemployment is combined with an inflation rate of 8%. Why has the inflation rate increased from 4% to 8%? At the point B the inflation rate was 4% but the revision in price expectations from 0% to 4% resulted in an increase in wage demands and this added a further 4% to the inflation rate. Again the point C is not a long-run equilibrium point. Next year, workers will again revise their inflation expectations (this time from 4% to 8%) and the Phillips Curve will again shift upwards from PC2 to PC3. The economy now moves to the point D, where 4% unemployment is combined with a 12% inflation rate.

*Note:*

*The above analysis could also be conducted in terms of the Phillips Curve equation. Recall from equation (4) that:*

$$P^*_t = P^*_{t-1} - \alpha (U - Un)$$

*The expansionary monetary policy reduced U relative to Un and this added 4 % to $P^*_t$ in the first year. In the second year, this increase in inflation feeds back into the $P^*_{t-1}$ term and this pushes $P^*_t$ to 8 %. In the third year the increase in inflation again feeds back into the $P^*_{t-1}$ term and inflation again rises and so on.*

The outcome after a number of years would be very unsatisfactory. In Table 8.1. we show what would happen after a period of 5 years.

*Table 8.1*

**Accelerating inflation**

| Year | Change in nominal GNP % | Change in volume GNP % | Actual inflation % | Change in unemploy-ment. % | Expected inflation $(P^{*e})$ % | Phillips Curve |
|---|---|---|---|---|---|---|
| 1 | 10 | 6 | 4 | -2 | 0 | PC1 |
| 2 | 8 | - | 8 | - | 4 | PC2 |
| 3 | 12 | - | 12 | - | 8 | PC3 |
| 4 | 16 | - | 16 | - | 12 | PC4 |
| 5 | 20 | - | 20 | - | 16 | PC5 |

The figures in Table 8.1 show that if unemployment remains at 4% level, by year 5 inflation will have risen to 20%. The cost of the expansionary policy therefore increases in later years as inflation increases. In the longer term, the price of the original reduction in unemployment is an ever-rising rate of inflation. The expansionary monetary policy has not just caused a once off increase in inflation but has led to an accelerating rate of inflation. This is why this modern version of the Phillips Curve is referred to as the accelerationist theory of inflation.

Eventually, for reasons we explain below, the economy will revert back to the natural rate of unemployment. Given that we started from a point on the natural rate and that we have ended-up back at the natural rate, then it follows that by joining these two points together, the long-run Phillips Curve is *vertical*. This means that there is *no* trade-off between inflation and unemployment in the long term. If expectations are stable there is a short-run trade-off between inflation and unemployment, but as expectations adjust to changing rates of inflation, in the long-run, there is no such trade-off.

But why does the economy revert to the natural rate of unemployment? The answer is that there is a "natural self correcting mechanism" or "automatic adjustment mechanism" which moves the economy back to the natural rate of unemployment. The analysis given in section 8.3 and Figure 8.6 provides the basis for this. For convenience we reproduce the main points here. Consider the AS/AD diagram in Figure 8.11. We have included in this diagram a Un reference line to indicate the natural rate of unemployment. Starting from the point A, the expansionary monetary policy shifts the AD curve outwards and the economy moves to the point B where unemployment has fallen and inflation has increased. (The points A and B correspond to the points A and B in the Phillips Curve diagram of Figure 8.10.) However the point B is not a long-run equilibrium point. Workers' real wages have fallen and they will demand higher wages to compensate for the increase in prices. As a result, the AS curve shifts upwards from AS1 to AS2 and the economy moves to the point C. It is the shift in the AS curve to the left which moves the economy back to the natural rate of unemployment. It is in this sense that there is an "automatic adjustment mechanism" which moves the economy back to the natural rate.

How can the rate of inflation keep on increasing as it did in the Phillips Curve analysis on Figure 8.10? The answer is that accelerating inflation occurs for as long as the government contrives to keep unemployment below the natural rate of unemployment. To see this point, consider again the AS/AD diagram in Figure 8.11. Starting from the point C, the government could regain the 4% unemployment rate by implemented a further expansionary policy. This policy would shift the AD curve outwards until it intersected the AS curve at the point D. This point is directly above the point B and it therefore corresponds to a 4% unemployment rate.

But again the point D is not a long-run equilibrium point. In the next period, workers will demand an increase in wages, the AS curve will shift upwards and the

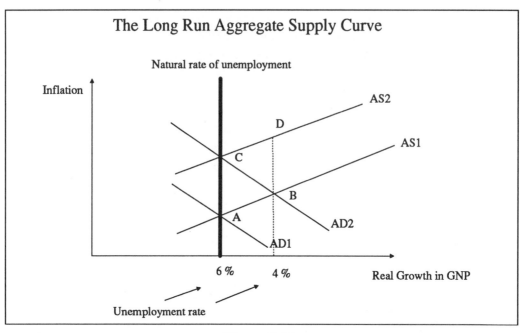

Figure 8.11

economy will revert to the natural rate. If the government is determined to maintain the 4% unemployment rate, further increases in aggregate demand will have to be engineered. As we saw earlier in Figure 8.10, the cost of maintaining unemployment below the natural rate will be an accelerating inflation rate.

*Note:*

*One important point implicit in the above analysis is that the rate of unemployment can only be held below the natural rate by engineering continuous unanticipated increases in inflation. It can be seen from Table 8.1 that $P^{*e}$ continually lags behind $P^*$. Put another way, the only way of increasing the number of people willing to accept employment, and hence to lower the rate of unemployment, is to generate an unanticipated increase in the rate of inflation. Job seekers will then be tricked into accepting job offers at lower real wages. They suffer from a money illusion, confusing increases in money wages with increases in real wages. (Employers, on the other hand, do not suffer from this illusion and rightly see that rising inflation offers them a chance to hire additional workers at lower real wages but to sell the extra output they produce at higher prices.)*

    The Phillips Curve and the AS/AD framework are therefore telling the same story. In the long term there is no trade-off between inflation and unemployment. Unemployment will revert to the natural rate and inflation will increase. This means that the *long-run* Phillips Curve and the *long-run* AS curve are both *vertical* at the natural rate of unemployment. The two Phillips Curves (PC1 and PC2) and the two AS curves (AS1 and AS2) are only *short-run* curves. It is important to note that the

174

time it takes workers to revise their inflation expectations or realise that their real wages have fallen is of crucial importance in both analyses.

It should be noted that attempting to keep unemployment below the natural rate for long periods of time would eventually have to be abandoned in order to curtail inflation. Rising inflation would lead to *hyper-inflation* of the sort experienced in central Europe after the First World War and in many Latin American countries today, with prices increasing by the hour. Such inflation is so disruptive that it provides no basis on which to build economic policy in the long-run.

*Note:*
*There are numerous stories of what hyper-inflation does to an economy. Here are two examples.*

Argentines went on a buying spree yesterday in a race against soaring prices. In a whirl of hyper-inflation, supermarkets are sometimes marking up prices twice a day while the Argentine currency, the Austral, plunges in value. Customers overturned trolleys full of goods at one supermarket after the management announced over loudspeakers that all prices were being immediately raised by 30%. *Irish Times, 26/4/1989.*

*In Germany in the 1920s inflation was running at 3,000% per month or 38,000% per annum. The story told is that if you went into a bar in Germany at that time it would be worth your while to buy two pints of beer rather than one. The reason was that the rate at which the second pint was going stale was slower than the rate at which the price was going up! A nice example of marginal cost analysis!*

On the basis of this critique, therefore, Phelps and Friedman rejected the notion that in the long-run unemployment could be reduced by accepting a higher rate of inflation. Both the Phillips Curve and the AS curve are vertical in the long-run at the natural rate of unemployment.

It should also be noted that if the economy is to the right of the Un reference line, inflation will decrease and this in turn will reduce inflation expectations. The Phillips Curve will shift downward and eventually the economy will converge to the Un rate. Hence, whether U is greater or less than Un, the economy will ultimately revert to the natural rate of unemployment.

# Rational Expectations

The way expectations were formulated in the previous section is *backward looking* in that past inflation is used to predict future inflation. In this sense, this method of formulating expectations has been criticised as being naive as it does not take account of current developments both inside and outside the country.

The "rational expectations" view of macroeconomic policy which has been expounded by economists such as Robert Lucas and Thomas Sargent of the University of Chicago and Robert Barro of Harvard University is that economic agents make use of all available information in formulating expectations. This method is *forward looking*. It is argued that economic agents know what causes inflation. For example, they might infer it from increases in the money supply if they believe in monetarism. Hence by watching the behaviour of the money supply they would be able to predict and anticipate future inflation with reasonable accuracy. Similarly, if the economy is close to full employment and the government pursues an expansionary policy the likelihood is that inflation will increase. The public would realise this and anticipate the inflationary consequences of the expansionary policy.

*Note:*

*The public might anticipate the behaviour of the money supply and other relevant policy variables by studying the announcements made by the monetary authorities and politicians. One implication of this theory is that a credible commitment to fiscal rectitude could break inflationary expectations.*

To the extent that the behaviour of prices is correctly anticipated, there can be no significant unanticipated inflation and hence no trade-off between inflation and unemployment, not even in the short-run. In terms of the AS/AD framework, an increase in the AD curve to the right will be matched, in a very short space of time, by an equal shift of the AS curve to the left. There is no money illusion on the part of workers and unemployment will not fall even in the short-run.

# 8.9 Non-Accelerating Inflation Rate of Unemployment

It is difficult to estimate the "natural rate" of unemployment statistically. The related concept of the *non-accelerating inflation rate of unemployment (NAIRU)* is more amenable to statistical estimation. As its name implies, this is simply the rate of unemployment at which, in the past, the rate of inflation has been stable. To estimate this, following the method used by Layard and Nickell for several OECD countries, *changes* in the rate of inflation ($P^*_t - P^*_{t-1}$) were regressed on the rate of unemployment (U) and a time trend (T), which was included to capture various unspecified influences. The equation obtained was then solved to establish the rate of unemployment that is compatible with a stable rate of inflation. If

(5) $\quad P^*_t - P^*_{t-1} = \alpha - \beta U + \phi T$

then to find the NAIRU set

$P^*_t - P^*_{t-1} = 0,$

Hence

(6)  $0 = \alpha - \beta\, NAIRU + \phi\, T$

where NAIRU has been substituted for U to indicate that this unemployment rate is consistent with a non-accelerating rate of inflation. Rearranging:

(7)  $NAIRU = (\alpha + \phi\, T)/\beta$

*Note:*
*If $\phi > 0$, NAIRU will increase over time.*

Using data for 1961-86, the estimate of NAIRU obtained with Irish data for 1986 was 12.5%.[3] The coefficient of the trend variable (T) was highly significant, so that the estimated NAIRU increases over time. If this result is valid, then the Irish rate of unemployment could fall by more than 5% from its 1989 level without rekindling the fires of inflation. The gap between the actual rate of unemployment and the NAIRU is much greater in Ireland than in the UK, US, Germany or Japan, according to the estimates provided by Layard and Nickell.[4]

Thus, according to this result there would seem to be plenty of scope for reducing the rate of unemployment before we encounter inflationary pressures from the labour market. However, the analysis that has been summarised in this section was developed for large and relatively closed economies. It is debatable whether these theories should be applied to a small open economy such as Ireland. We return to this issue below.

# 0  Why Is Unemployment So High at Full Employment?

Why should a rate of unemployment of 12% or even higher come to be viewed as the "natural" rate or NAIRU? Why is unemployment so high at "full employment"? This is a question has been asked in the US with respect to an unemployment rate of 5%, so it is even more urgent for us to try to answer it if we accept that the NAIRU in Ireland is now in the region of 12%.

An important idea in this context is "hysteresis". This concept has been borrowed from physics to describe the phenomenon of a variable that, once displaced, does not tend to return to its original equilibrium level. It refers to a kind of inertia, where the past history of a phenomenon influences its present behaviour. When applied to the functioning of labour markets, it means that the "equilibrium" or "natural rate" of unemployment is a function of the *actual* level of unemployment in the recent past. Thus if the rate of unemployment rises above the natural rate due to an adverse shock, the longer it remains above the natural rate, the more likely it is that a new, higher "natural" rate will be established.

*Note:*

*Think of what would happen if every time you got a high temperature there was a tendency for your body's normal temperature to rise. As your fever subsided, your temperature would not return to 37 degrees celsius, but would settle down at a higher level. Your body temperature would be exhibiting the phenomenon of hysteresis. It sounds unpleasant!*

There are good reasons for believing that a prolonged period of high unemployment does affect the economy's ability to return to the rate of unemployment that would have been "normal" before the recession. The principal factor is the changing composition of the pool of unemployed people and in particular the increasing proportion of long-term unemployed in the total. We have noted in Chapter 7 that in 1988 in Ireland 46% of all the unemployed have been out of work for a year or more, compared to less than one third in 1979 and only one fifth in the 1960s. The evidence from other countries suggests that the long-term unemployed have in many ways virtually dropped out of the labour market. They are de-motivated and discouraged from looking for work, because they believe there are few vacancies and that employers are unlikely to offer them work because the long-term unemployed are viewed as "unemployable". An analysis of the data for migration and changes in employment and unemployment in Ireland suggests that the long-term unemployed are less likely than the short-term unemployed to emigrate, which is in keeping with this view of their detachment from the process of job search.[5]

The following quotation from James Tobin, who introduced the concept of the NAIRU, summarises the reasons why it may keep changing very clearly:

It is hard to resist or refute the suspicion that the operational NAIRU gravitates towards the average level of unemployment actually experienced. Among the mechanisms that produce that result are improvements in unemployment compensation and other benefits enacted in response to higher unemployment, loss of on-the-job training and employability by the unemployed, defections to the informal and illegal economy and a slower rate of capital formation as business firms lower their estimates of needed capacity.[6]

178

However, the fact that attempts to measure the NAIRU and the "natural rate" have provided estimates that are extremely unstable has cause Robert Solow to question the usefulness of these concepts:

A natural rate that hops around from one triennium to another under the influences of unspecified forces, including past unemployment rates, is not "natural" at all. "Epiphenomenal" would be a better adjective.[7]

*Note:*
*The tendency of the "equilibrium" rate of unemployment to reflect the actual rate of unemployment can be used as an argument for using stabilisation policy to lower unemployment below its equilibrium rate, because this will in due course lower the equilibrium rate. If the hysteresis argument is valid, then it is true in regard to macroeconomic policy that "nothing succeeds like success" and "nothing fails like failure"!*

Because of the tendency for the long-term unemployed to lose contact with the labour market, it has been argued that the measure of unemployment that is relevant from a labour market (or Phillips Curve) perspective is the short-term rate. It has also been suggested that one reason for the wage moderation experienced in the US is that even at relatively low rates of unemployment a relatively high proportion of the labour force experiences some unemployment in the course of the year. The risk of unemployment looms large before a sizeable proportion of the labour force. In Europe, on the other hand, even when the rate of unemployment is very high it is concentrated among the long-term unemployed and most workers disregard the risk of unemployment when they are bargaining for wage increases.

In Ireland in the 1970s we thought we knew what we meant by "full employment". The National Economic and Social Council published studies that explored the implications for job creation of coping with the growth of the labour force at a low rate of emigration and bringing the rate of unemployment down to 2% or 4%. However these targets seem irrelevant when set against the high rates of unemployment that have persisted throughout the 1980s. Official documents have avoided specifying a precise target for employment or unemployment in recent years. In its study of unemployment, published in 1984, the Economic and Social Research Institute simply stated that the goal of economic policy should be "... to redistribute the benefits of growth to ensure viable employment for all who are willing and able to avail of it."[8] This provides no basis for estimating the rate of unemployment that represents full employment.

It may reasonably be argued that the question of what constitutes full employment is not very relevant until the level of unemployment has declined significantly below the 17% prevailing in 1989. However, if it is true that domestic inflationary pressures would begin to build up as soon as the rate of unemployment approaches 12%, it is clear that a great deal of attention will have to be devoted to microeconomic labour market policies if we are ever to bring the rate of unemployment down to the range that would have been considered acceptable in the 1960s (that is, about 5%).

The issue of how labour markets function will have to be studied closely now that the rate of unemployment is at last beginning to fall. It would be inexcusable if our economic recovery were to be threatened by the emergence of inflationary wage pressures while our rate of unemployment was still in double digits. The crude Keynesian policies of trying to cure unemployment by inflating domestic demand, or wholesale recruitment to public sector employment, have been discredited. A reliance on creating favourable conditions for sustainable private sector investment has resulted in a higher rate of economic growth, but has yet to make a marked impact on the level of employment. It is therefore timely to tackle the problem of unemployment by specific labour market policies. Among these the following should figure prominently:

1. Increasing the incentives for job seekers to accept the jobs that are available

2. Improving the match between the skills of the unemployed and the type of jobs that are available

3. Increasing the various dimensions of labour market flexibility, such as geographical mobility, flexible working practices, etc.

*Table 8.2*
**Public spending on labour market programmes, 1987 (% of GNP)**

|  | "Active" measures | Income maintenance | Total |
|---|---|---|---|
| Ireland | 1.45 | 3.66 | 5.12 |
| US | 0.24 | 0.59 | 0.83 |
| Sweden | 1.86 | 0.80 | 2.66 |

*Source:* OECD Economic Survey of Sweden, 1988/89, Table 24

In this context it is interesting to make some international comparisons of levels of expenditure on labour market programmes, distinguishing between "active" measures, such as those listed above, and "income maintenance" or unemployment compensation. Table 8.2 shows expenditure on labour market programmes for Ireland, the US and Sweden. The high level of spending on unemployment compensation in Ireland is due to our high unemployment rate and relatively generous benefits. Both Ireland and Sweden spend much more than the US on "active" labour market measures. Sweden's absolute level of expenditure per unemployed person would be more than 20 times Ireland's! (Remember that Swedish GNP per person is more than twice ours and its unemployment rate less than one tenth of ours.)

# 11 The Relationship between Inflation and Unemployment in a Small Open Economy (SOE)

In Figure 8.12 we show the association between the rates of inflation and unemployment in Ireland during the post-war years. A close inverse correlation between the two variables exists for only the 1980s. Even during these years, this association does not establish that the increase in one of these variables (unemployment) *caused* the other (inflation) to decline. It is striking that the rate of inflation collapsed in most OECD countries at much the same pace in the 1980s, regardless of the level of unemployment that prevailed in individual countries. Declining energy, food and raw material prices, as well as contractionary monetary and fiscal policies, were the reasons for the global decline in inflation.

It is evident from Figure 8.12 that the Phillips Curve, if it can be said to exist in Ireland, has been very unstable over the years. The short-run Phillips Curve seems to have shifted out over the decades. This is consistent with the finding, mentioned above, that the NAIRU has risen markedly over time.

There has always been some controversy in Ireland as to how much of our inflation is "our own fault" and how much is imported, traditionally from Britain, our main trading partner. In fact, the relevance of the idea of a trade-off between inflation and unemployment can be questioned on theoretical grounds in small, open economies (SOEs) such as Ireland. The rate of inflation in the rest of the world is clearly a major influence on the rate of inflation in a SOE. However, we shall see in Chapters 9 and 10, when discussing the theory of exchange rate determination known as *purchasing power parity* (PPP), that the evidence indicates that Irish inflation, even before we broke the sterling link in 1979, was *not* simply a reflection of British inflation *in the short-run.*[9] In the medium or long term however it is possible to explain Irish inflation in terms of the rate of inflation in Britain and in the countries of the European Monetary System. A recent study of Irish inflation concluded:

The SOE model of price determination is appropriate to Irish manufacturing output. Domestic wage costs play only a minor role in price determination, while foreign price influences are dominant.[10]

181

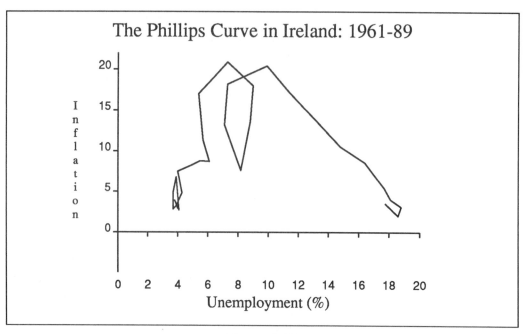

The Phillips Curve in Ireland: 1961-89

Figure 8.12

Thus according to those who espouse the SOE view of inflation, the concept of the NAIRU is irrelevant in a country such as Ireland: it is based on a correlation that loses its significance when account is taken of the influence of external factors on Irish inflation. We return to this issue in Chapter 10, where we discuss Ireland's exchange rate policy in the European Monetary System, and will see that there is some disagreement about the validity of the SOE theory.

At least it is clear that as the labour market tightens and certain categories of skilled labour become scarce, wage rates tend to rise rapidly. Even if this wage inflation does not result in higher rates of price inflation, it will tend to reduce the rate of growth in employment. One of the worrying features of the Irish labour market is the tendency for inflationary wage pressures to appear at relatively high levels of overall unemployment. Unemployed skilled workers tend not to wait for demand to pick up in Ireland when they can readily obtain work abroad. When the Irish economy begins to grow again, it may be necessary to offer these emigrants higher rates of pay to entice them to return to work here. Even if higher wages do not, in the medium term, lead to a higher rate of price inflation, they will tend to impair the country's international competitiveness and militate against lowering the rate of unemployment.

We have come full circle on the issue of the trade-off between inflation and unemployment. According to the evidence, in the medium term, the rate of inflation in a small and open economy such as Ireland is primarily a reflection of inflation in the world outside Ireland. Increases in Irish wage rates under these conditions tend to reduce the growth of employment and to increase rather than lower the rate of unemployment! None the less, the student has to understand the concepts of the Phillips Curve and its critique because of their use in the international economics literature to explore the relationship between inflation and unemployment in large and relatively closed economies. But Irish students should never forget how small and open the Irish economy is and how we have to modify our economic theories to allow for this.

# 12 Conclusion

This chapter has discussed the question of how inflation and unemployment are interrelated. First, we expanded the AS/AD model of Chapter 3 by introducing a labour market on the supply side of the economy and a money market on the demand side of the economy. We then explored:

- The Phillips Curve and the trade-off between inflation and unemployment

- The Phelps-Friedman critique of the Phillips Curve analysis: the trade-off can only occur because of unanticipated inflation. The long-run Phillips Curve is vertical at the natural rate of unemployment. Holding the rate of unemployment below this rate will lead not just to a higher, but to a rising, rate of inflation

- Rational expectations

- The NAIRU

- The concept of hysteresis. Why the "natural" rate of unemployment may vary over time. Why the NAIRU may tend to increase as the actual rate of unemployment increases

We then discussed how to relate these topics to the special circumstances of an SOE. The evidence shows that, in the medium or long term, the main determinants of our inflation are external. None the less, inflationary wage pressures do build up even at high rates of unemployment. This tends to check the rate of economic growth even if it does not result in higher inflation. Under these circumstances, wage inflation tends to increase the rate of unemployment.

# Notes

1. See A.W. Phillips, "The Relation Between Unemployment and the Rate of Change of Money Wages in the United Kingdom, 1861 - 1957", *Economica*, Vol. 25, November, 1958.

2. See E. Phelps, *Inflation Policy and Unemployment Theory*, Norton, 1973 and M. Friedman, "The Role of Monetary Policy", *American Economic Review*, March, 1969.

3. Brendan M. Walsh, "Why is Unemployment so High?", in *Perspectives on Economic Policy*, University College, Dublin, 1987:1, p. 22.

4. See Peter Fallon and Donald Verry, *The Economics of Labour Markets*, Oxford: Philip Allen, 1988, Table 8.21.

5. See Walsh, *loc. cit.*

6. James Tobin, "Stabilization Policy Ten Years After", *Brookings Papers on Economic Activity*, 1:1980, p. 60.

7. Robert Solow, "Unemployment: Getting the Questions Right", *Economica*, 1986 (Supplement), p. S54.

8. Denis Conniffe and Kieran A. Kennedy, (eds.), *Employment and Unemployment Policy for Ireland*, Dublin: The Economic and Social Research Institute, 1984, p. 299.

9. The economic literature relating to the determinants of Irish inflation is discussed in Chapter 10, p. 242-244.

10. Tim Callan and John FitzGerald, "Price Determination in Ireland: Effects of Changes in Exchange Rates and Exchange Rate Regimes", *The Economic and Social Review*, January 1989, p. 184.

# Chapter 9

# *The Balance of Payments and Exchange Rates*

## Introduction

In this chapter we introduce the student to open economy macroeconomics. We begin by discussing the components of the balance of payments and the terms of trade. This is followed in section 9.3 by a discussion of the foreign exchange market in Ireland. Section 9.4 examines the trend in the exchange rate of the Irish currency in recent years and introduces nominal and real effective exchange rate indexes. Section 9.5 identifies some of the main factors influencing exchange rates over time. The concluding two sections discuss the role of the Central Bank in foreign exchange markets and outline some of the advantages and disadvantages of flexible and fixed exchange rate systems.

## The Balance of Payments

The balance of payments is a record of a country's economic transactions with the rest of the world. The basic rule in drawing up the balance of payments is that any transaction that gives rise to a *receipt* of foreign exchange (such as the export of goods) is denoted by a *positive* (+) sign and any transaction that leads to a *payment* (such as the import of goods from abroad) is denoted by a *negative* (-) sign.

*Note:*

*Data recorded on the balance of payments are "flow" data as opposed to "stock" data in that all transactions are recorded over some given period of time rather than at some particular point in time.*

Table 9.1 presents a simplified version of the Irish balance of payments for 1988. As can be seen from the table, the balance of payments contains four main

*Table 9.1*

**Balance of payments, £m, 1988**

| | | |
|---|---:|---:|
| 1.1 Merchandise trade | | 2,025 |
| 1.2 Services | | -42 |
| 1.3 Trading and investment income | | -2,558 |
|     *of which* | | |
|     1.3.1 Net profit, dividends, interest | | |
|           and royalties | -1,908 | |
|     1.3.2 National debt interest | -894 | |
|     1.3.3 Net inflows (other) | 244 | |
| 1.4 International transfers | | 1,011 |
| | | |
| 1 *Balance on current account* | | 436 |
| | | |
| 2.1 Private capital | | -826 |
| 2.2 Official capital | | 523 |
|     *of which* | | |
|     2.2.1 Government foreign borrowing | -282 | |
|     2.2.2 Government securities sold abroad | 867 | |
|     2.2.3 Other | -62 | |
| 2.3 Banking transactions | | 365 |
| | | |
| 2 *Balance on capital account* | | 62 |
| | | |
| 3 Net residual | | -147 |
| | | |
| 4 Change in the external reserves | | 351 |

*Source*: Central Bank of Ireland, *Quarterly Bulletin*, Summer, 1989, Table B8

*Note*: Normally both receipts (or credit items) and payments (debit items) are given for each entry in the balance of payments accounts. In the simplified version given above, we show the balance or net receipts under each of the main headings sub-headings; the *current* and *capital* accounts, a "net residual" entry and a "change in the external reserves" entry.

Consider first the current account of the balance of payments. Within this account there are four sub-accounts: merchandise trade, services, investment income and transfers. Merchandise trade records the export and import of goods only. In 1988, merchandise exports exceeded imports by £2,025m. The services account, on the other hand, records transactions such as international freight, tourism and travel. This sub-account was approximately balanced in 1988. The investment income sub-account records profits, dividends, interest and royalties paid and received by Irish residents during the year. Interest paid by the government on foreign debt is also recorded in this sub-account. As can be seen from the table there was a substantial deficit on this account in 1988. Finally, the international transfers sub-account relates to payments or receipts not in return for any good or service. For example, Irish aid to *less developed countries* (LDC's) or transfers to Ireland from the regional or social fund of the European Community. Current transfers of funds into the country exceed payments by £1,011m in 1988.

Overall, in 1988 there was a surplus of £436m on the current account of the balance of payments. The large deficit on the "trading and investment income" sub-account, due largely to profit repatriation by firms and interest payments by the government on foreign debt, virtually cancelled the surplus on the other three accounts.

The capital account records payments and receipts for "capital" items. Purchases of land, government stock, company shares or works of art are examples of capital transactions. Foreign borrowing by the government, banks or the private sector is also regarded as a capital account item. This means that foreign borrowing by the government is recorded on the capital account whereas repayments of the interest on that debt is a current account entry. As shown in Table 9.1, the capital account is divided into private sector transactions, government transactions and banking sector transactions. In 1988, the surplus on the banking and government (which reflects government foreign borrowing and foreigners' purchases of Irish government stock) sub-accounts was offset by a deficit on the private sector sub-account. There was a small overall surplus on the capital account in 1988.

The "net residual" entry consists of unexplained flows through the balance of payments. Unexplained flows in 1988 amounted to -£147m, down from -£189m in 1987 and an unprecedented -£905m in 1986. As discussed briefly in Chapter 2, some of the unexplained outflow is money leaving the country illegally and has been labelled the "black hole". As we will explain below, the authorities can put a figure on illegal outflows but they cannot say with any great precision *who* is doing it or *how* it is been done. It should be noted however that this residual also reflects "errors and omissions" and all the imperfections in the statistics relating to the other components of the balance of payments.

187

The final entry in Table 9.1 is "change in the external reserves". The offical external reserves are the Central Bank's holdings of foreign currency. They are made up of foreign currencies such as sterling, dollars and yen. We will examine the external reserves in detail in section 9.7. The main point to note at this stage is that an overall surplus (deficit) on the balance of payments will be reflected in an equal increase (decrease) in the external reserves. In 1988, the net balance between the current and capital accounts and the net residual item was a +£351m. The external reserves increased by this amount in 1988. If there was an overall deficit on the balance of payments, the external reserves would have decreased.

The reason why the balance of payments surplus or deficit is mirrored in changes in the external reserves is because the Central Bank of Ireland intervenes in the foreign exchange market to stabilise the exchange rate of the Irish pound. As we discuss in section 9.7, the Central Bank pursues a *fixed exchange rate policy* by maintaining the the exchange rate of the Irish pound in the European Monetary System (EMS). If the Central Bank did not intervene in the foreign exchange market and the exchange rate was allowed to *fluctuate freely*, the external reserves would be more stable. In this case the current, capital and net residual balances would sum to zero. This is because purchases of Irish pounds must equal sales of Irish pounds. If someone wishes to buy Irish pounds on the foreign exchange market, someone else must be willing to sell Irish pounds in order to complete the transaction. We will explain this point in greater detail in section 9.5.

We now return to the calculation of the "net residual item". The Central Bank can put a figure on "unexplained" flows by comparing the current and capital account balances with the "change in the external reserves" entry. Any *legal* international transaction will be documented at point of entry or exit by customs (try importing a car!) and this should give a reasonably accurate indication of the current and capital account balances. In 1988, for example, customs documentation indicated a current and capital account surplus of £436m and £62m respectively which gives an overall balance of payments surplus of £498m. Because of Central Bank intervention in the foreign exchange market, this balance of payments surplus should have been reflected as an equal increase in the external reserves. However, the external reserves *actually* increased by £351m instead of £498m. This means that there is an unexplained outflow of £147m which cannot be accounted for by customs' documentation or from other sources. In order to balance the accounts, the Central Bank simply inserts a balancing entry of -£147 as a residual. In this way, the Central Bank arrives at a figure for unexplained flows. It is not possible, however, to say from this calculation who is moving the money out of the country or how it is being done.

*Note:*

*In the balance of payments accounts a distinction is frequently made between "autonomous" and "accommodating" transactions. An autonomous transaction is an "ordinary" transaction such as an*

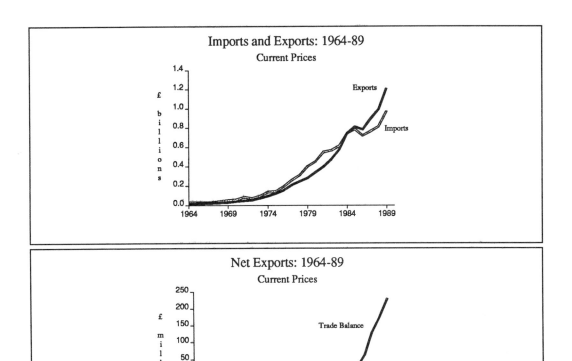

Figure 9.1

*export or an import or purchases of land or government stock by residents or non-residents. Suppose for the moment that the net autonomous transactions resulted in an overall deficit on the balance of payments. The Central Bank has to finance that deficit in some way or, as we will see in section 9.5, allow the exchange rate to depreciate on the foreign exchange market. If the Central Bank chooses to fix the exchange rate, the deficit can be financed by running down the external reserves or by borrowing foreign currency abroad. An overall surplus of autonomous transactions would be reflected in an increase in the external reserves or the repayment of official foreign debt. The change in the external reserves and foreign borrowing are referred to as accommodating transactions. When the net balances on the various sub-accounts are taken together, the accommodating balance ensures that the overall balance of payments adds to zero. Finally, to add to the glossary of terms, in some countries accommodating transactions are referred to as the "official settlements balance".*

## Trade account

Exports and imports of goods and services are of immense importance in a small open economy such as Ireland. These variables have a major impact on aggregate

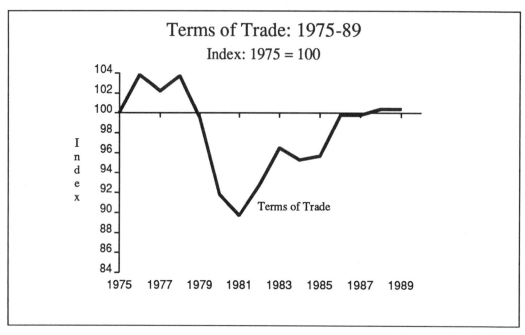

Figure 9.2

demand, output and income in the economy. A deficit on the trade account reduces aggregate demand and a trade surplus increases aggregate demand. Figure 9.1 shows the level of Irish imports, exports and net exports (exports minus imports) over the period 1964-89. Between 1964 and 1984, Ireland's trade account was in deficit, particularly in the years between 1975 and 1980. However since 1984 this trend has been reversed with exports exceeding imports and net exports rising at an increasing rate. We explored some of the links between the domestic and foreign components of aggregate demand in Chapter 2.

In discussing trade flows it is important to distinguish between price changes and quantity changes. Because value equals quantity multiplied by price, we can write:

Value of $X = P_x * Q_x$
Value of $M = P_m * Q_m$

where $P_x$ and $P_m$ denote the price of exports and imports respectively and $Q_x$ and $Q_m$ indicates the quantity of exports and imports.

What matters for domestic production and employment are quantity changes. Firms hire more workers to produce a greater quantity of goods and services. However, prices changes will have a direct effect on the trade account. Starting from an equilibrium position, an increase in $P_x$ relative to $P_m$ will result in a trade account surplus because the value of exports has increased relative to the value of imports.

Conversely, an increase in $P_m$ relative to $P_x$ results in a trade account deficit as the value of imports has increased relative to the value of exports. The *terms of trade* are defined as $P_x/P_m$. An increase is this ratio is referred to as an *improvement* in the terms of trade. The reason is that we need export less goods and services for a given amount of imports. Conversely, if the ratio declines it is referred to as an *adverse* movement in the terms of trade. We must now export more goods and services for a given amount of imports.

Figure 9.2 shows the terms of trade index (1975 = 100) for Ireland over the period 1975-89. There was an adverse movement in the terms of trade between 1978 and 1982, but since then the trend has been reversed. Since 1986 the terms of trade have remained constant at the 1975 level. We explored the impact of these movements in the terms of trade on the population's standard of living in Chapter 2.

# The Foreign Exchange Market

The *foreign exchange market* is a market where one currency is exchanged for another. It exists because countries have different currencies. The Americans use the dollar, the French the franc and so on. If there was only one currency in the world, there would be no need for a foreign exchange market. The vast US economy operates with a single currency; the economy of the European Community (EC) uses eleven different currencies.

The foreign exchange market has no exact location or set opening times. It is a market which spans the globe by means of telephones, computers and telex machines. It is also a market which is open twenty-four hours a day. The opening hours of the markets in New Zealand, Tokyo, Hong Kong, Bahrain, Frankfurt, London, New York, Chicago and San Francisco overlap, so that at any one time a foreign exchange market is open. This means that it is possible to get a price on any of the major currencies at any time of the day or night.

The foreign exchange market can be divided into a *retail* market and a *wholesale* market. The retail market consists of transactions between banks and their clients (individuals and firms). The wholesale market is an inter-bank market where banks transact with each other. The major function of the foreign exchange market is to convert one currency into another currency, that is to transfer purchasing power. If an Irish co-operative sends a shipment of beef to France, the French importer converts francs to Irish pounds on the foreign exchange market and sends the Irish pounds to the co-operative. There has been a transfer of purchasing power from the French importer to the Irish co-operative.

*Note:*

*The foreign exchange market also performs other functions such as providing credit and reducing foreign exchange risk. We will examine these functions in a later chapter.*

Consider now what is meant by the *exchange rate*. The exchange rate is the price of one currency in terms of another. As at 20 September 1989 the dollar/Irish pound exchange rate was $1.3662/IR£1. This means that if you exchanged IR£1 for dollars in a bank you received $1.3662 in return. If the domestic currency falls in value relative to the foreign currency, it is said to have *depreciated*. For example, if the exchange rate fell from $1.3662/IR£1 to $1.3000/IR£1 it means each Irish pound is worth less in dollars. A rise in the exchange rate is referred to as an *appreciation*. In this case more dollars are obtained for each Irish pound. We use the phrases "appreciate" and "depreciate" to refer to movements of a floating exchange rate, and "revalue" and "devalue" to refer to movements of a "fixed" or pegged rate.

In the above example, the exchange rate is expressed as dollars per units of Irish pounds. This is known as an *indirect* quote. The alternative is to express the exchange rate in terms of units of the foreign currency, for example, IR£0.7319/$1 (0.7319 = 1/1.3662). This is known as a *direct* quote. Indirect and direct quotes are, of course, equivalent. One is simply the reciprocal of the other, one is giving the Irish pound price of the dollar, the other the dollar price of the Irish pound.

*Note:*

*In Ireland, the UK and Australia, exchange rates are expressed as indirect quotes, $/£. Most other countries use direct quotes, £/$. The reason for this difference in terminology is that the old pound, shilling and pence monetary units used in Ireland and the UK up to the early 1970s made it cumbersome to express the pound price of a dollar.*

A bank does not charge a commission for converting one currency into another. Instead banks quote different exchange rates for buying and selling foreign currency. These rates are known as the *bid rate* (the rate banks will buy Irish pound or sell foreign currency) and *offer rate* (the rate banks sell Irish pounds or buy foreign currency). The difference between the bid and offer rates is known as the "*spread*". Table 9.2 shows bid and offer $/IR£ exchange rates quoted by the banks for July 1989.

As an example of how a bank earns a profit on foreign exchange transactions consider the case of two different firms, one selling $1m to the bank and the other buying $1m from the bank. The bank is willing to sell dollars at an exchange rate of $1.400/IR£1 and buy dollars at an exchange rate of $1.4020/IR£1.

Bank buys $1m from Firm A at an exchange rate of $1.4020/IR£1 and pays

IR£713,266 to the firm.

Bank sells $1m to Firm B at an exchange rate of $1.400/IR£1 and receives IR£714,285 from the firm.

Profit to the bank from the two transactions is IR£1,019 or 0.1%.

*Table 9.2*

**Bid and offer rates for the Irish pound, dollar exchange rate: July 1989**

| Bid | Offer |
|---|---|
| 1.4000 | 1.4020 |

*Source*: AIB International Department

Converting small amounts of currency is expensive. If, for example, you had IR£1,000 and you converted it into sterling, francs, pesetas etc. until you had done the rounds of the EC currencies and ended up back in Irish pounds, you would be left with only IR£750! The missing IR£250 would have gone to the foreign exchange dealers. An American, on the other hand, can go from Maine to California without incurring any foreign exchange transaction costs.

At the present time, there are 28 banks licensed to trade in foreign exchange in Ireland. Of these banks, the top five banks account for nearly 90% of the business. There are also 4 brokers who act as intermediaries between buyers and sellers. That is, if a customer wishes to sell, say, French francs, the broking house attempts to find someone willing to buy francs. Working for the banks and the broking houses are approximately 100 dealers. Dealing on foreign exchange markets, while financially rewarding, can be a very strenuous occupation because of the large sums of money involved and because small changes in the exchange rate can result in large profits or losses. A large proportion of foreign exchange dealers tend to move on to something else after five or six years service.

In this regard, it is important to distinguish between banks that act as "price-takers" and banks who act as "price-makers". Price-taking banks simply act as intermediaries. If a customer wishes to buy dollars, the bank finds someone willing to sell dollars. The price-taking bank does not take a *position* in the market. That is the bank does not hold an inventory of foreign currency. The spread between the bid and offer exchange rates provides the banks profit from foreign exchange transactions.

The price-making bank on the other hand keeps an *inventory* of foreign exchange and takes a position in the market by standing ready to quote prices on certain foreign currencies. Depending on which way the exchange rate moves, the price-making bank can incur substantial losses or profits on foreign exchange transactions. As an example, suppose a bank buys $1m at an exchange rate of $1.4500/IR£1 so that the Irish pound cost to the bank is IR£689,655. The bank now holds $1m. If during the course of the day or week, the exchange rate falls to $1.4000/IR£1 the bank could exchange the $1m for IR£714,285 and therefore make a profit of IR£24,630. However, if the exchange rate rises to $1.4900/IR£1 the bank would receive only IR£671,140 and therefore incurs a loss of IR£18,515. It should be noted that most banks are not trying to make a profit from this kind of speculation - their interest lies in the profit to be made from the spread between the bid and offer prices. However, at the same time, banks will be very concerned about how exchange rate movements affect their holdings of foreign currency and the implicit losses and profits which this entails.

While banks holding of foreign currency are subject to exchange control regulations in Ireland, in general, price-making banks tend to keep a desired reserve of foreign currencies. If reserves exceed this desired reserve level the bank may feel it necessary to sell the excess reserves of foreign currency. Similarly, if reserves are below the desired level, the bank may find it necessary to buy foreign currency. Exchange rate movements are notorious unpredictable. Dealers who have taken a position in a particular foreign currency and who have an "excess" or "deficiency" in reserves which must be rectified by the close of the market can be in for a very nerve-racking time as exchange rates bob up and down on the foreign exchange market.

*Note:*

*One dealer in an Irish bank tells a story of how he had taken a position in dollars in anticipation of a depreciation of the $/IR£ exchange rate. If the exchange rate depreciated he stood to make a substantial profit on his dollar holdings. During the course of the day, the US presidential car arrived at the White House with a dent on its side and this "news" filtered through to the media. Rumour spread that the dent had been caused by a bullet and that there had been an assassination attempt on the President's life. On the basis of this "news" the dollar fell ten points. The Irish pound appreciated. The dealer ended up losing hundreds of thousands of pounds on his dollar position. It later transpired that the dent was caused by a stone which had fallen on to the road from a lorry. This illustrates how foreign exchange markets react (and over-react) to any "news" that might have a bearing on the future performance of the world's economies.*

Up to the early 1970s there was virtually no foreign exchange market in Ireland. The sterling/Irish pound exchange rate was fixed at par, a very large proportion of Irish trade was with the UK and the associated banks held their reserves in sterling in London. As a result, the banks had little need of a foreign exchange market in Ireland. Foreign exchange transactions could be easily conducted on the London foreign exchange market. In 1969, the Money Market Committee under the chairmanship of Professor W.J.L. Ryan (this committee had been set up by the Directors of the Central Bank) issued a report which became known as the *Money*

*Market Report.* One of the recommendations was that the Central Bank of Ireland take steps to develop a foreign exchange market.

In the early 1970s, licensed bank reserves were transfered from the London markets to the Central Bank of Ireland and the banks were requested to conduct their foreign exchange business directly with the Central Bank. In 1976, the Central Bank refused to quote for small amounts of foreign exchange and this encouraged the banks to hire and train dealers and to conduct more of their business between themselves and on world foreign exchange markets.

In 1979 following Ireland's entry into the EMS and the subsequent termination of the sterling link, the foreign exchange market in Ireland came of age and the associated banks moved from being price-takers to price-makers. (The first non-par deal was done for STG£500,000 at an exchange rate of STG£0.9975/IR£1 on the 30th March 1979). The banks were now quoting an sterling/Irish pound exchange rate, something that had not been required before. In retrospect, the banks coped very well with the new arrangements although many firms with large sterling borrowings lost heavily when the Irish pound unexpectedly depreciated against sterling.

It might be expected that most of the business conducted on the Irish foreign exchange market involves Irish pounds. This is not however the case. Table 9.3 shows that in 1987 only 13% of total turnover involved Irish pounds. Most of the business involves sterling, deutsche marks (DM) or dollar transactions.

*Table 9.3*
**Transactions on the Irish foreign exchange market: 1987**
**Purchases or sales: IR£m**

| | | | | |
|---|---|---|---|---|
| 1. *Irish pound turnover* | | | 74,950 | (13%) |
| 2. *Non-Irish pound turnover* | | | 506.082 | (87%) |
| *of which* | | | | |
| $/DM | 151,824 | (30%) | | |
| Sterling/DM | 111,338 | (22%) | | |
| Sterling/$ | 111,338 | (22%) | | |
| ECU | 75,912 | (15%) | | |
| Other | 55,669 | (11%) | | |
| 3. *Total turnover (1 +2)* | | | 581,032 | (100%) |

*Note*: ECU denotes European currency unit. The ECU is discussed in Chapter 10
*Source*: AIB, International Department

One reason for the large foreign currency turnover in Ireland is that the Irish pound market has little "depth". Dealers are unwilling to act as price-makers and take a position on the Irish pound when they cannot spread the risk with other dealers or banks and, of course, foreigners have little interest in buying and selling Irish pounds, other than small amounts to finance foreign trade. As a result, dealers find it easier and safer to deal in foreign currencies.

# 9.4 Exchange Rates

Figure 9.3 shows the dollar, DM and sterling exchange rates for the Irish pound over the period 1977 to 1989. It is evident from the diagrams that there has been a sustained depreciation of the DM/IR£ exchange rate over the period. In contrast, the $/IR£ exchange rate depreciated up to 1985 but since then has appreciated. The STG£/IR£ exchange rate, on the other hand, has moved fairly widely in both directions without showing any clear long-run trend. We will examine in section 9.5 the important issue of what causes the exchange rate to fluctuate. In this section we elaborate on different measures of the exchange rate.

As shown in Figure 9.3, since 1985, the Irish currency depreciated against the DM, appreciated against the dollar and fluctuated up and down against sterling. The volatility relative to sterling reflects the fact that the currency does not participate in the exchange rate mechanism (ERM) of the EMS (we discuss the EMS in Chapter 10). It would be useful if a single statistic could be derived that summarised all of this information. The summary statistic that is most widely used is the *trade-weighted exchange rate index* sometimes referred to as the *effective exchange rate index*. This index is essentially the *average cost* of foreign currency. The index is weighted so that countries which are not very important in a country's external trade are given little weight and countries which are important are given a large weight.

In Table 9.4 we explain how the trade-weighted exchange rate index is calculated. Column 1 lists Ireland's trading partners according to their importance in external trade, that is, the share of that country in Ireland's imports and exports. Only nine countries are used in compiling the index because they account for virtually all our trade. Column 2 shows the trade weight for each country. The UK has a trade weight of 0.43 (43 % of Ireland's trade is with the UK), West Germany has a weight of 0.14 and so on down to Denmark which has a weight of 0.02. These weights sum to 1.0.

The first step in deriving the trade-weighted exchange rate index is to express exchange rate movements in terms of an index. Choose a base year and set each exchange rate at that time equal to 100. It is now possible to calculate the index for subsequent years. For example, if the DM/IR£ exchange rate was DM3/IR£1 in 1988

# Irish Pound Exchange Rate

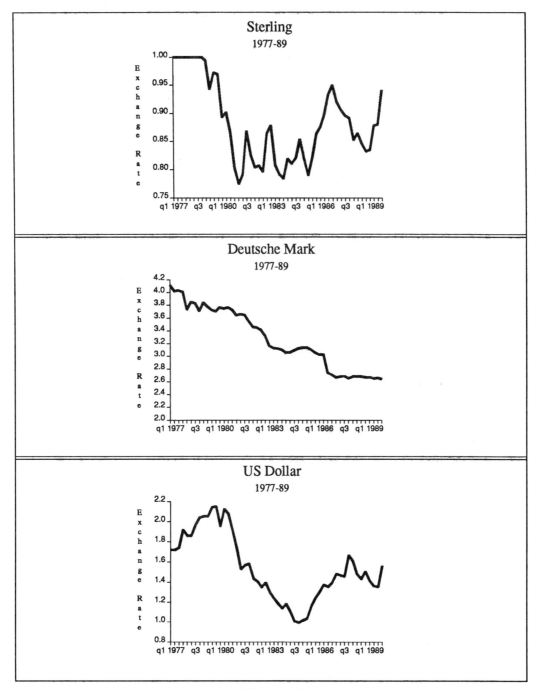

Figure 9.3

and DM2/IR£1 in 1989, the exchange rate index would be 100 in 1988 and 66.6 in 1989. The exchange rate index is calculated for each of our trading partners in columns 3 and 4 in Table 9.4. It can be seen that the Irish pound depreciated (the index fell below 100) against the UK, West German, Dutch and Belgium currencies but appreciated (the index rose above 100) against the other countries in the list.

The trade-weighted exchange rate index is calculated by multiplying each exchange rate index by the associated trade weight and summing for all the countries. This is done in columns 5 and 6 for years 1 and 2 respectively. Column 6 shows that in year 2 the trade-weighted exchange rate index had fallen slightly to 99.4. This indicates that on a trade-weighted basis there was, on average, a small depreciation of the Irish currency over the two years.

*Table 9.4*

**Trade-weighted exchange rate index**

| Country | Trade weight | Exchange rate index | | Trade-weighted exchange rate index | |
|---|---|---|---|---|---|
| | | Year 1 | Year 2 | Year 1 | Year 2 |
| *1* | *2* | *3* | *4* | *5* | *6* |
| UK | 0.43 | 100 | 96.0 | 43.0 | 41.3 |
| WG | 0.14 | 100 | 97.4 | 14.0 | 13.6 |
| US | 0.14 | 100 | 106.8 | 14.0 | 14.9 |
| France | 0.10 | 100 | 100.7 | 10.0 | 10.1 |
| Holland | 0.06 | 100 | 99.5 | 6.0 | 5.97 |
| Italy | 0.04 | 100 | 104.4 | 4.0 | 4.17 |
| Belgium | 0.04 | 100 | 99.5 | 4.0 | 3.98 |
| Japan | 0.03 | 100 | 111.4 | 3.0 | 3.34 |
| Denmark | 0.02 | 100 | 101.9 | 2.0 | 2.04 |
| Total | 1.0 | 900 | 917.6 | 100 | 99.4 |

Figure 9.4 shows Ireland's trade weighted exchange rate index (1971 = 100) over the period 1977-89. It can be seen that the Irish pound depreciated by approximately 40% between 1971 and 1984. Between 1984 and 1986 the Irish pound appreciated by approximately 5%. In recent years the index has been relatively stable, but it rose sharply during the second half of 1989.

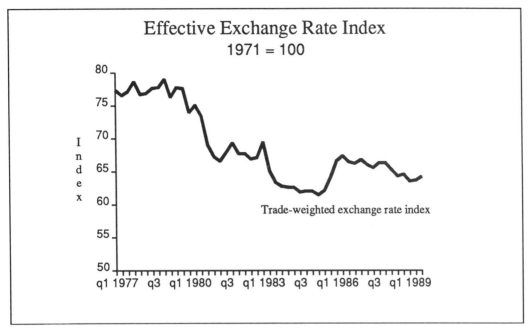

Figure 9.4

*Note:*

*The trade weighted exchange rate index graphed in Figure 9.4 is based on data published in the Central Bank of Ireland, Quarterly Bulletin. It is not possible to calculate this index because the Central Bank does not publish the trade weights used in the calculation. These weights may or may not differ from the weights given in Table 9.4.*

## Real exchange rates

So far we have discussed exchange rates in terms of converting one currency into another. We will now go a stage further and discuss exchange rates from the point of view of *competitiveness*. If we wish to compare prices in two countries we must make an adjustment for the exchange rate. We cannot compare the price of petrol in Dublin and Frankfurt without taking account of the DM/IR£ exchange rate. For example, in 1989, a Big Mac hamburger cost IR£1.30 in Dublin and DM4.30 in Frankfurt. Are Big Mac hamburgers more expensive in Ireland or West Germany? The exchange rate in September 1989 was DM2.667/IR£1. We can compare the two prices by converting the Irish price to DMs or alternatively converting DMs to Irish pounds. Consider first converting Irish prices into DMs.

| $P_{irl}$ | * | E | ? | $P_{wg}$ |
|-----------|---|-------|---|----------|
| £1.30 | * | 2.667 | ? | DM4.30 |

199

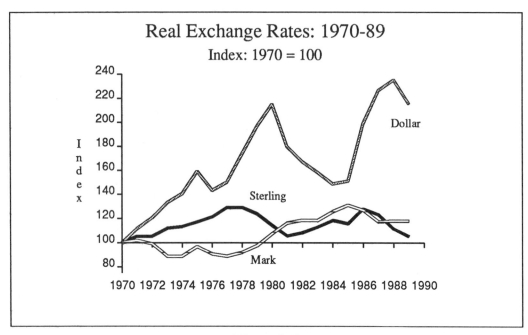

Figure 9.5

where $P_{irl}$ and $P_{wg}$ are Irish and German prices respectively and E is the exchange rate (DM/IR£). Because 1.30 * 2.667 = 3.467, Big Mac hamburgers are cheaper in Ireland. Alternatively the same result could be obtained by converting German prices into Irish pounds:

| $P_{irl}$ | ? | $P_{wg}$ | * | (1/E) |
|---|---|---|---|---|
| £1.30 | ? | DM4.30 | * | 0.3749 |

We see that because 4.3 * 0.3749 = 1.61, a Big Mac in Germany costs the equivalent of IR£1.61. Big Mac hamburgers are approximately 31 pence dearer in Germany.

The above example illustrates how to convert prices using the exchange rate. We can now use this example to define the real exchange rate.

(1)  Real exchange rate index = $(P_{irl} * E)/P_{wg}$ = 100 in the base year.

The real exchange rate is simply the ratio of Irish and German prices expressed in a common currency. Movements in this ratio over time are expressed in terms of an index.

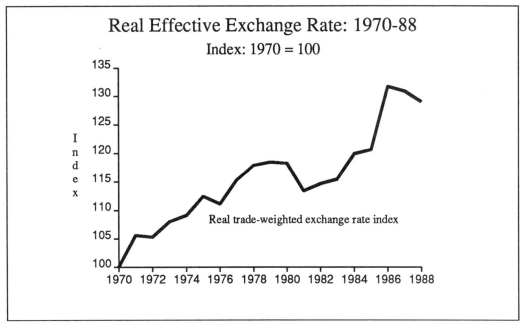

Figure 9.6

Put another way, the real exchange rate is the nominal exchange rate adjusted for relative prices. This is a particularly useful measure as it indicates whether a country is becoming more or less competitive relative to its trading partners over time. If Ireland's real exchange rate index, equation (1), increases it implies a loss of competitiveness because either the domestic price has risen relative to foreign prices and/or the exchange rate has appreciated. Conversely, a fall in Ireland's real exchange rate implies a gain in competitiveness.

*Note:*

*This definition of the real exchange rate is closely related to the concept of purchasing power parity (PPP) which we discuss in Chapter 10. We also discuss in that chapter the effect on output, income and unemployment of a loss or gain in competitiveness.*

Figure 9.5 shows Ireland's real exchange rate index for the dollar, sterling and the DM over the period 1970 to 1989. Note that these indexes are set equal to 100 in 1970. This does not mean that all four countries were exactly "competitive" with one another in that year. What it does mean is that a rise or fall in the index measures a loss or gain of competitiveness *with reference to* the situation in 1970. The large fluctuations that have taken place in the three exchange rates is very apparent from the graph. By the end of the period, Ireland has suffered a loss in competitiveness against all three countries. This is most noticeable in the case of the dollar.

Figure 9.6 shows Ireland's *real trade-weighted exchange rate index* over the period 1970 to 1987. This index is calculated by trade-weighting real exchange rates over time. This is identical to the calculation in Table 9.4 except that nominal exchange rates have been replaced by real exchange rates. Figure 9.6 shows that Ireland has suffered a sustained loss in competitiveness against its main trading partners over the period 1970-87. There were only one or two short periods such as 1975 and 1981 when Ireland's competitive position improved.

*Note:*

*In deriving the real exchange rate index, the choice as to which price to use is somewhat arbitrary. There are a number of exchange rate indexes based on consumer prices, manufacturing output prices, retail prices and input prices. They are closely related but they do not always increase or decrease to the same extent. The point is that a different picture can emerge depending on which "price" is used. The real exchange rates given in Figures 9.5 and 9.6 were calculated using wage rates. Wage rates are one of the most important input prices. We return to this issue in a later chapter. Note also that the choice of base year can be very important. In Figure 9.5, for example, the dollar real exchange rate for 1989 appreciates if the base year is 1970 but remains unchanged if the base year is 1977.*

# 9.5 Exchange Rate Determination

What causes the exchange rate to appreciate or depreciate? Why are exchange rates so volatile? Are fixed exchange rates preferable to flexible exchange rates? At the present time, there is little consensus in the literature on the answers to these questions. While exchange rate economics has developed at a rapid pace in the last twenty years, some of the main issues remain highly controversial and unresolved. In this section we discuss exchange rate determination in terms of the supply and demand for Irish pounds on the foreign exchange market. In other words we view the exchange rate as a price (the price of foreign currency). Like all other prices it is determined by supply and demand forces. It is important to keep in mind that we are discussing supply and demand forces in the *foreign exchange market*. Earlier, in Chapter 6 we examined how the supply and the demand for money determined the interest rate. Domestic money markets and foreign exchange markets are closely related but they are distinct markets. Interest rates are determined on the money market while exchange rates are determined in the foreign exchange market.

In deriving the demand and supply curves for Irish pounds (IR£) on the foreign exchange market, the following points should be noted:

1. Any transaction that gives rise to a *receipt* of foreign currency (for example, exports of goods or services) leads to a *demand* for Irish pounds on the foreign exchange market.

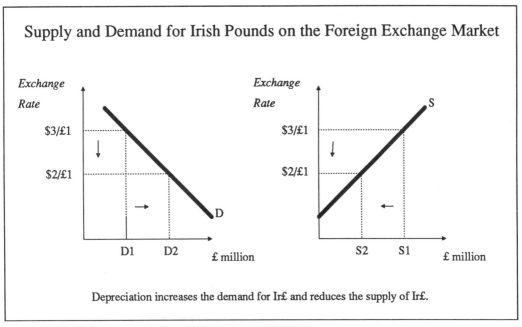

Supply and Demand for Irish Pounds on the Foreign Exchange Market

Depreciation increases the demand for Ir£ and reduces the supply of Ir£.

Figure 9.7

*Note:*
*An exporter sells goods in, say, the UK and receives sterling in return. When the sterling receipts are exchanged for Irish pounds at the foreign exchange desk in a bank, the exporter is "demanding" Irish pounds.*

2. Any transaction that gives rise to a *payment* by Irish residents (for example, payment for imports of goods or services) leads to a *supply* of Irish pounds on the foreign exchange market.

*Note:*
*Suppose an Irish importer needs to obtain sterling to pay his UK supplier. When Irish pounds are exchanged for sterling in a bank, the importer is supplying Irish pounds on the foreign exchange market.*

A graphical representation of the supply and demand curves for Irish pounds on the foreign exchange market is given in Figure 9.7. With the exchange rate (E) on the vertical axis and IR£ million on the horizontal axis, the demand curve is downward sloping and the supply curve is upward sloping.

A downward sloping demand curve means that exchange rate depreciation increases the demand for Irish pounds. Conversely, exchange rate appreciation decreases the demand for Irish pounds. The reason is that a depreciation makes

203

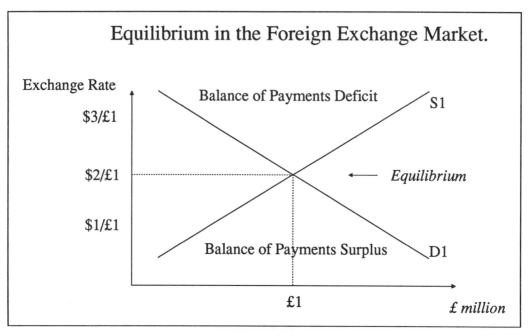

Figure 9.8

exports of goods and services more competitive by enabling exporters to reduce prices abroad. As a result, more goods are exported and the demand for Irish pounds increases. As an example, suppose the exchange rate is $3/IR£1. Ignoring transport costs, taxes etc, if the price of an Aran jumper is IR£10 in Dublin, the equivalent price in New York is $30. Suppose now the Irish pound depreciates to $2/IR£1, the Dublin price continues to be IR£10 but the exporter could afford to lower the New York price to $20. The lower price in New York makes the goods more competitive and a greater quantity of jumpers will be sold. Exports therefore increase and so does the demand for Irish pounds on the foreign exchange market.

However, the exporter could decide to leave the New York price at $30, which is now worth IR£15. In this case he allows his profits to absorb the full benefit of the depreciation. In the long-run, higher profits would attract more exporters into the New York market and increased competition should lower the dollar price of jumpers.

*Note:*

*A depreciation tends to raise the prices (in domestic currency) of both imports and exports or internationally traded goods. The prices of goods not entering international trade ("non-tradeables"), on the other hand, do not change so there relative price falls. This should attract resources away from the non-traded into the traded sector.*

The supply curve for Irish pounds is upward sloping indicating that exchange rate depreciation reduces the supply of Irish pounds on the foreign exchange market. Conversely, an appreciation of the exchange rate will increase the supply of Irish pounds on the foreign exchange market. The reason is that a depreciation makes imports more expensive and consequentially less imports are sold. For example, suppose the exchange rate is \$3/IR£1 and there are no transportation costs or taxes or any other impediment to trade. A pair of jeans manufactured in the US sell for \$30 in New York or IR£10 in Dublin. If the exchange rate depreciates to \$2/IR£1, the Dublin price become IR£15. This price increase reduces the competitiveness of imported goods. Imports of goods into Ireland will fall and this will be accompanied by a reduction in the supply of Irish pounds on the foreign exchange market.

*Note:*
*In the longer run, higher import prices will tend to spill over to domestic costs and prices, so that there will be a tendency for the initial impact of the depreciation on relative prices to be eroded.*

In Figure 9.8 the demand and supply curves are brought together. At an exchange rate of \$2/IR£1 the foreign exchange market is in *equilibrium*. The supply and demand for Irish pounds are equal. At an exchange rate higher than this, say, \$3/IR£1, there is an *excess supply* of Irish pounds. This is the equivalent of a balance of payments current account deficit. The country is importing more than it is exporting. At a lower exchange rate, say \$1/IR£1, there is *excess demand* for Irish pounds. In this case, there is a balance of payments current account surplus.

Under floating exchange rates the market must clear. If there is an excess demand the exchange rate will appreciate and if there is an excess supply the exchange rate will depreciate. This appreciation or depreciation continues until such time as supply equals demand. It is in this sense that the balance of payments must balance. Hence if there is a deficit on the current account of the balance of payments there must be a matching surplus on the capital account.

The foreign exchange market is noted for the rapid changes in prices that occur. This is because the speculative demand for a currency can shift widely in the course of a day. As a result, it is difficult to find a situation where exchange rates are allowed to float completely free of government interference. Even when currencies are not part of a fixed exchange rate system, governments and Central Banks covertly influence rates by intervening in the foreign exchange market. This is known as "dirty floating".

In Figure 9.8 we have drawn the supply for foreign exchange curve with a positive slope. Consider now Figure 9.9 where the supply curve for Irish pounds is downward sloping. The supply curve slopes downward if a depreciation increases the value of imports. Recall that:

Value of Imports = $P_m * Q_m$

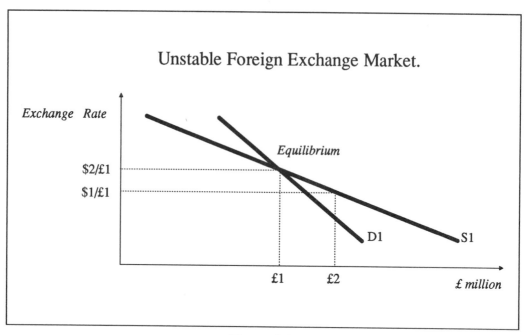

Figure 9.9

where $P_m$ and $Q_m$ are the price and quantity of imports respectively. A depreciation will increase $P_m$ relative to the price of import-competing goods and services and this in turn should reduce $Q_m$ by an amount sufficient to reduce the total value of imports. However suppose that a large proportion of imports are *necessary* goods for which there are no domestically produced substitutes. A good example in Ireland would be oil products. In this case, the quantity of imports may not change very much as the exchange rate falls (the price elasticity of imports is inelastic) and the value of imports and hence the supply of Irish pounds on the foreign exchange market may actually increase. The supply curve of Irish pounds is downward sloping under these circumstances. As we have drawn it in Figure 9.9 the foreign exchange market is *unstable*. If the market was initially in equilibrium, exchange rate depreciation results in an excess supply of Irish pounds and the exchange rate will move away from the equilibrium rate. Similarly, exchange rate appreciation will lead to an excess demand for Irish pounds and the exchange rate will continue to appreciate.

The demand for imports is likely to be inelastic in the short-run but to increase with the passage of time. For this reason, the downward sloping supply of Irish pounds curve is likely to be a short-run phenomenon: in the long-run a depreciation is likely to reduce the demand for imports.

Another way of making this point is to show how the balance of payments changes after a depreciation or devaluation. Figure 9.10 depicts the situation where

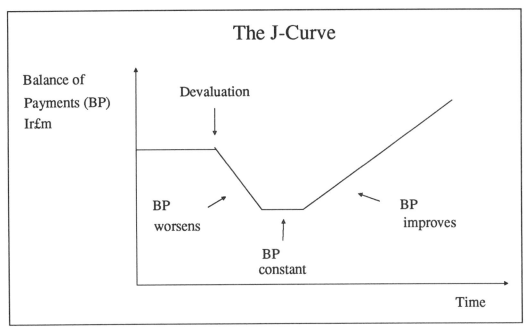

Figure 9.10

there is a deterioration in the balance of payments in the short-run, followed by an improvement in the long-run. Because of the shape of the curve, this effect is known as the J-curve effect.

*Note:*
*The famous Marshall-Lerner condition states that in order for a depreciation to increase the trade balance the sum of the import and export elasticities must be greater than 1. The import elasticity is the percentage change in imports following a one per cent change in $P_x/P_m$. The export elasticity is the percentage change in exports following a one per cent change in $P_x/P_m$. In the long-run the Marshall-Lerner condition stands a good chance of being met. But note that it is a precondition that a change in the exchange rate passes through to the relative prices of imports and exports and that this change in relative prices is not eroded by the effects of the change on domestic costs and prices.*

The supply and demand curves for Irish pounds indicate how the *flow* of imports and exports respond to changes in the exchange rate (recall that imports and exports are a flow in that they are measured over some given period of time). Any change in the flow of imports or exports, not brought about by a change in the exchange rate, will be reflected in a *movement* of the two curves. A change in receipts (not brought about by a change in the exchange rate) affects the demand curve. An increase in receipts shifts the demand curve to the right and a decrease shifts the demand curve to the left. On the other hand, a change in payments (not brought about by a change in the exchange rate) affects the supply curve. An increase in

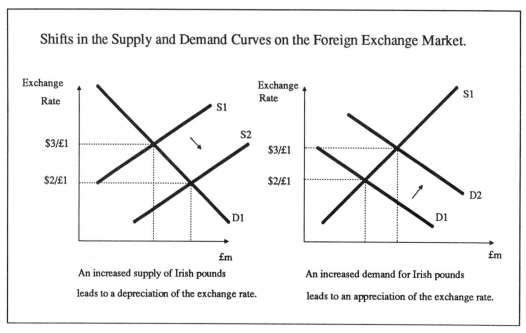

Shifts in the Supply and Demand Curves on the Foreign Exchange Market.

An increased supply of Irish pounds leads to a depreciation of the exchange rate.

An increased demand for Irish pounds leads to an appreciation of the exchange rate.

Figure 9.11

payments shifts the supply curve to the right and a decrease in payments shifts the supply curve to the left.

In Figure 9.11 an increase in imports due for example to higher oil prices shifts the supply curve to the right and the exchange rate depreciates from $3/IR£1 to $2/IR£1. The right hand panel shows how an increase in exports (due for example to a successful marketing campaign for Irish exports in the US) shifts the demand curve to the right. In this case the exchange rate appreciates from $2/IR£1 to $3/IR£1.

Similar comments apply to transfer payments/receipts and capital account flows. Transfer or capital account transactions that result in a receipt or a payment affects the demand curve and supply curves respectively.

The following examples help clarify how a particular transaction might affect the exchange rate.

1. An increase in purchases by Irish residents of UK government stock is a payment which is recorded on the capital account of the balance of payments. The supply curve shifts to the right and the Irish pound exchange rate depreciates.

2. An increase in foreigners buying land in Ireland is a receipt which is recorded as a capital account transaction. The demand curve shifts to the right and the Irish pound exchange rate appreciates.

3. A decrease in exports due to, for example, a fall in aggregate demand in the UK, is a receipt which is recorded as a current account transaction. The demand curve shifts to the left and the Irish pound exchange rate depreciates.

4. An increase in foreign borrowing by Irish banks, the private sector or the Irish government is recorded on the capital account as an increase in receipts. The demand curve shifts to the right and the Irish pound exchange rate appreciates.

5. An increase in Irish aid to Less Developed Countries (LDC's) is recorded on the current account of the balance of payments. Aid to LDC's is a payment so that an increase will shift the supply curve to the right and cause the Irish pound exchange rate to depreciate.

A change in the exchange rate will affect imports and exports *along* the supply and demand curves. In deciding how a particular transaction affects the exchange rate, first identify whether the transaction will result in a receipt to an Irish resident or a payment by an Irish resident. Changes in receipts affect the demand curve and changes in payments affect the supply curve of Irish pounds.

# Factors Influencing the Exchange Rate in the Longer Term

We now examine the most important factors influencing the exchange rate in the medium or long term. Over time the balance of payments and therefore the exchange rate is influenced by four main factors.

1. *Interest rates.* Internationally mobile funds are very responsive to interest rate differentials. In general, higher interest rates in Ireland relative to interest rates in other countries will lead to a capital inflow into Ireland. Conversely, lower interest rates in Ireland relative to interest rates available elsewhere will lead to a capital outflow, provided there are no exchange controls, that is, provided there is free international mobility of capital.

$r_{irl} > r_{foreign} \Rightarrow$ Capital inflow
$r_{irl} < r_{foreign} \Rightarrow$ Capital outflow

An increase in, say, UK interest rates relative to Irish interest rates leads to a capital outflow from Ireland. This is a payment so that the supply curve for Irish pounds on the foreign exchange market shifts to the right and the exchange rate depreciates. On the other hand, an increase in Irish interest rates relative to UK interest rates leads to a capital inflow. The demand curve moves to the right and the exchange rate appreciates.

*Note:*

*In comparing international interest rates a very important consideration is the expected movement in the exchange rate over the investment period. We discuss this point in detail in Chapter 12.*

2. *Inflation.* If Irish inflation consistently out-paces inflation in our main trading partners, the demand for Irish exports will decrease and imports into Ireland will increase because of a loss of competitiveness. In this case, the demand curve shifts to the left (reduction in receipts) and the supply curve shifts to the right (increased payments). Under a floating exchange rate system, the exchange rate will depreciate. Conversely, lower inflation in Ireland relative to inflation in other countries will result in exchange rate appreciation.

This relationship between inflation and the exchange rate is normally referred to as the theory of *purchasing power parity (PPP)*. This is one of the most important theories of exchange rate determination. It is due to the Swedish economist Gustav Cassel (1866-1944).[1] The theory states that inflation is the overriding determinant of movements in the exchange rate. Refer back to section 9.4 and the discussion of real exchange rates. The real exchange rate was defined as

$$(P_{irl} * E)/P_{foreign}$$

where $P_{irl}$ and $P_{foreign}$ are Irish and foreign prices respectively. If PPP theory holds, the real exchange rate will be constant over time. Put another way, PPP theory states that an increase in $P_{irl}$ relative to $P_{foreign}$ will *cause* the nominal exchange rate, $E$, to depreciate until the real exchange rate reverts back to its initial level. An increase in domestic prices relative to foreign prices will be matched by an equal depreciation of the Irish pound exchange rate. Alternatively, a decrease in $P_{irl}$ relative to $P_{foreign}$ will result in $E$ appreciating so that over time the real exchange rate remains constant. We saw however in Figures 9.5 and 9.6 that Ireland's real exchange rate has not been constant over the last twenty years. This seems to suggest that PPP theory does not hold for the Irish economy. There are however a number of qualifications or adjustments that must be made before PPP theory can be properly tested. We discuss PPP theory and the empirical evidence in Chapter 10.

3. *Speculation.* If speculators expect a depreciation of the exchange rate they will move funds out of the country in anticipation of making a capital gain. For example, suppose the current exchange rate for the Irish pound is DM4/IR£1 and, for whatever

reason, speculators expected a depreciation to DM2/IR£1. If a speculator converts IR£1m at an exchange rate of DM4/IR£1 into DM's, he receives DM4m. Suppose his expectations are proved correct and the exchange rate depreciates to DM2/IR£1. The speculator can now convert his holding of DM4m back into Irish pounds and receive IR£2m. The net result is that the speculator has doubled his money. In practice exchange rates do not depreciate by 50% in the short-run. However the above example does illustrate that simply by converting money out of a currency that is expected to depreciate and into a currency that is expected to appreciate, large speculative profits can be made. By trying to avert a depreciation through intervention in the foreign exchange market, Central Banks often offer speculators the opportunity to make profits in the manner outlined above and furthermore, by buying up a currency that is going to depreciate, they waste tax-payers' money!

In terms of the supply and demand curves, a capital outflow will be reflected in a shift to the right of the supply curve and this will result in a depreciation of the exchange rate. Hence speculative outflows can have the effect of fulfilling expectations!

Countries sometimes introduce exchange controls in order to try to prevent speculative inflows or outflows. However speculation is very difficult to stop as it can take different forms. For example, *leading* and *lagging* by companies has been cited as being an important factor in Ireland. Suppose an exporter to the UK expects the Irish pound to be devalued in the near future. If he delays (lags) converting his sterling receipts into Irish pounds until after the depreciation has taken place, he will make a capital gain. Similarly, an importer may speed-up (lead) payments to his UK supplier in order to avoid paying more after the depreciation. Because of the size of Ireland's trade account in relation to GNP, leads and lags in payments and receipts can put tremendous pressure on the exchange rate in the foreign exchange market. This was very apparent during 1986, for example, and showed up in the balance of payments statistics as a large drop in the Central Bank's external reserves.

Exchange rate expectations are of crucial importance in analysing exchange rate movements. Expectations are however very difficult to analyse. A rising inflation rate or a growing government borrowing requirement may lead to speculation that the exchange rate will be depreciated. If a currency depreciates, for whatever reason, this can encourage expectations of further depreciations especially if there is a suspicion Central Banks are intervening to try to "prop-up" the currency at a target level.

4. *Growth rate in real GNP*. Changes in GNP will have a direct affect on imports of goods and services (the relationship between these two variables is summarised by the marginal propensity to import). As the economy expands we import more raw materials and buy more finished goods from abroad. It follows from this that countries with a relatively fast growth rate in real GNP will increase imports relative to slow growth countries. This increased flow of imports will be reflected in a shift

211

of the supply curve to the right and the exchange rate will depreciate. Conversely, a fall in imports relative to other countries will lead to a rise in the exchange rate.

# 9.7 Fixed Exchange Rates: The Role of Central Banks

The European Monetary System (EMS) is an example of a fixed exchange rate system. The basic objective of fixed exchange rate systems is to *stabilise* exchange rates over time. The argument put forward by exponents of fixed exchange rates is that freely floating exchange rates create uncertainty and discourage international trade. If exchange rates are fixed, uncertainty is reduced and trade between member states is promoted. This in turn should have a positive effect on a country's output and employment.

When countries agree to fix their exchange rates they do so by keeping exchange rates within a narrow *band*. The exchange rate is allowed to move around freely within this band. It is only when the exchange rate approaches the "floor" or "ceiling" of the band that Central Banks *intervene* to stabilise the exchange rate.

In order to explain how Central Banks intervene in the foreign exchange market, it is first necessary to explain what is meant by the offical external reserves. These are Central Bank holdings of foreign currency, gold and other reserves which can be converted into foreign currency. Table 9.5 gives a break-down of Ireland's external reserves as at June 1989.

*Table 9.5*
**Ireland's offical external reserves: June 1989**

|  | £m | % |
|---|---|---|
| Foreign exchange | 2,045.6 | 81.9 |
| Gold | 73.2 | 2.9 |
| SDRs | 94.8 | 3.8 |
| Reserve position at IMF | 86.6 | 3.5 |
| ECU | 197.2 | 7.9 |
| Total | 2,497.5 | 100.0 |

*Source:* Central Bank of Ireland, *Quarterly Bulletin*, Summer, 1989

It can be seen from the table that the external reserves consist largely of foreign currency. There are other components of the reserves which are created by international agencies like the *International Monetary Fund (IMF)*. *Special drawing*

212

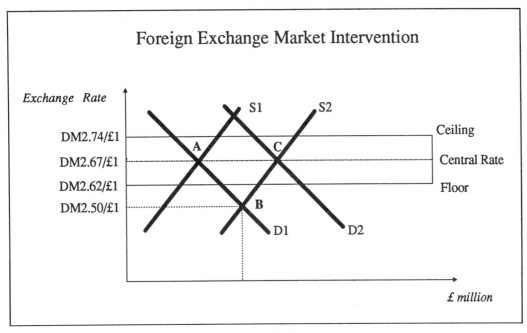

Figure 9.12

*rights* or SDRs, sometimes referred to as "paper gold", are reserve assets created by the IMF and issued every year to member countries. SDRs are an abstract form of reserve in that they are only a book-keeping entry in a special IMF account. The IMF first began issuing SDRs in 1970 to supplement international reserves. The way the SDR system operates is roughly along the following lines. If the Central Bank of Ireland needs to borrow foreign currency in order to stabilise the exchange rate (we discuss this issue below), Ireland's SDR allocation at the IMF can be used to purchase foreign currency from a country with spare or excess reserves. The IMF simply debits Ireland's SDR account and credits the other country's SDR account. In this way, Ireland's holding of foreign currency is increased and its SDR allocation at the IMF is reduced.

The *ECU (European Currency Unit)* is the numèraire of the European Monetary System. It is calculated as a weighted basket of the currencies participating in the EMS. We defer a discussion of the exact calculation of the ECU until Chapter 10 when we examine the EMS in detail. The ECU is similar to the SDR in that it is used by European Central Banks as a reserve currency. Any borrowing or lending involving ECUs is supervised by the *European Monetary Co-operation Fund (EMCF)* which is the European equivalent of the IMF.

Figure 9.12 illustrates the principles underlying Central Bank intervention. The first thing to note is the band within which the exchange rate is to be stabilised. At the start of the fixed exchange rate system, participating Central Banks agree on a *central exchange rate* and on *upper* and *lower* limits for the exchange rate

213

fluctuations. For example, suppose it is agreed that the central exchange rate for the DM/IR£ is DM2.67/IR£1 and that exchange rate fluctuations will be kept within a range or band of plus or minus 2.25% of this central rate. The upper limit to the band is therefore 2.74 and the lower limit is 2.62. The exchange rate can move freely between these two limits and the Central Bank will not interfere. It is only when the limits are about to be breached that the Central Bank intervenes.

In Figure 9.12 the market is in equilibrium at the point A and this point corresponds with the central exchange rate of DM2.67/IR£1. Suppose now the supply curve for Irish pounds shifts to the right (S1 to S2) because of, say, an increase in imports. The new equilibrium is at the point B and the exchange rate has depreciated to DM2.50/IR£1. This exchange rate is below the agreed lower limit of DM2.62/IR£1. The Central Bank of Ireland will respond to this depreciation by *buying* Irish pounds on the foreign exchange market, using its external reserves. This has the effect of shifting the demand curve for Irish pounds to the right (D1 to D2). The new equilibrium is at the point C and the exchange rate has appreciated back into the agreed band.

The Central Bank has purchased Irish pounds using its holdings of foreign currency and in effect has created an *artificial demand* for Irish pounds. The external reserves are lower but the exchange rate has been stabilised within the band. As we pointed out above, this may be a waste of tax-payers' money. If fundamental forces are operating to drive the Irish pound below the central rate in the longer run, the currency will depreciate so that the Bank is selling the appreciating currency and buying the depreciating one!

Suppose now the exchange rate appreciates above the agreed upper limit of the band (not shown in Figure 9.12). Starting at point A in Figure 9.12, this would happen if the demand curve for Irish pounds shifted to the right. In this case, the Central Bank buys foreign currency with Irish pounds and this shifts the supply curve to the right. In effect the Central Bank has created an *artificial supply* of Irish pounds and in doing so has depreciated the exchange rate back into the band. Once again this could be costly, as the Bank is buying a currency whose value is falling!

*Note:*
*Figure 9.12 exaggerates the situation by suggesting that the Central Bank only responds once the exchange rate has gone outside the band. In practice, the Central Bank will intervene before this happens to try to keep the exchange rate within the band.*

It is important to note that a Central Bank cannot create an artificial demand for its currency unless it has sufficient external reserves. If a country should run out of external reserves (because of persistent balance of payments deficits), the Central Bank will not be able to continue to intervene. The options are either to borrow foreign currency from other countries, the IMF or EMCF or to allow the exchange rate to depreciate. Exchange rate appreciation does not put nearly as much pressure

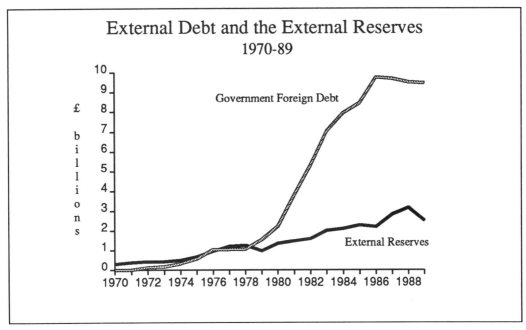

Figure 9.13

on a Central Bank as does depreciation. The Central Bank can always print money and in that way create an artificial supply of the domestic currency on the foreign exchange market. However, the growth of external reserves has the effect of expanding the domestic money supply.

In recent years, the Central Bank of Ireland has intervened heavily to maintain the exchange rate of the Irish pound on the foreign exchanges. Some idea of the extent of this intervention can be got by considering that between 1971 and 1989 the Government borrowed approximately IR£10,000m abroad. However, the external reserves only increased from IR£381m to IR£2,499m over the same period. Figure 9.13 shows the trend in government foreign indebtedness and the level of the external reserves between 1971 and 1989. The difference between the growth in foreign indebtedness and the increase in the level of external reserves gives some indication of the degree of Central Bank intervention in the foreign exchange market over the period.

In order to understand this point note that when the government borrows foreign currency abroad, foreign currency is exchanged at the Central Bank for domestic currency. The Central Bank adds the foreign currency to its external reserves and credits the governments account at the Central Bank with Irish pounds. The government then spends the Irish pounds. The important point is that foreign currency borrowed by the government is added to the Central Bank external reserves. *All other things being equal,* if the Central Bank was not intervening in the foreign exchange market, the external reserves would rise by an amount equal to government foreign borrowing. Figure 9.13 shows clearly that this has not happened. The Central Bank has in effect used a large proportion of its external reserves to stabilise the Irish pound exchange rate on foreign exchanges. In this regard, the Irish pound could be said to have been over-valued for much of the period. This is consistent with the appreciation of the real exchange rate as shown in Figures 9.5 and 9.6.

*Note:*
*The private sector, state-sponsored bodies and the banks have also increased their external indebtedness over the period 1971-89.*

The implication is that without government foreign borrowing, Ireland's external reserves would have been depleted a long time ago. This is of course precisely why the government borrows abroad in the first place. Without corrective action (such as a deflationary fiscal policy), the Central Bank would have had to borrow on its own account from other countries or the IMF or allowed the exchange rate to depreciate. In a very real sense, the exchange rate of the Irish pound in recent years would have been much lower but for government foreign borrowing and Central Bank intervention.

Intervention, as we have pointed out, is a waste of tax-payers' money if it does not succeed in its goal of propping up the exchange rate. The value of the Irish pound has fallen over the years (see Figures 9.3 and 9.4). Hence we have been using foreign exchange whose value is rising to buy Irish pounds whose value is falling! The only real justification for intervention is to smooth out short term fluctuations in the exchange rate.

*Note:*
*We discuss the effectiveness of a devaluation in greater detail in Chapter 11.*

# 9.8 Fixed Versus Floating Exchange Rates

As already mentioned the basic argument in favour of fixed exchange rate systems is that exchange rate uncertainty and volatility are reduced and this encourages international trade and investment. However the success of fixed exchange rate systems depends crucially on participating countries having similar inflation, interest rates and growth rates. This in turn requires similar fiscal and monetary policies. If these policies are not in line, persistent balance of payments deficits and surpluses will arise and Central Banks are ultimately powerless to prevent currencies from realigning.

In practice, countries do not always follow similar fiscal and monetary policies and this results in strains under a fixed exchange rate system. For example, in 1983 in the EMS system, France was pursuing an expansionary fiscal policy while Germany was implementing a deflationary monetary policy. The net result was an increasing balance of payments deficit in France and an increasing surplus in Germany. Speculators anticipating a devaluation of the French franc converted large amounts of funds from francs into DMs in order to make a capital gain. Eventually the French franc was devalued and it was only after France abandoned its expansionary fiscal policy that the speculation subsided. The basic point is that fixed exchange rate systems can only reduce exchange rate uncertainty if there is policy co-ordination between member states.

An advantage of flexible exchange rates is that, in theory at least, there is no need for Central Banks to hold large amounts of external reserves. This means there is no liquidity problem, something which fixed exchange rate systems suffered from in the past. We examine this liquidity issue in Chapter 10 when we discuss the gold standard.

A second advantage to flexible exchange rates is that the exchange rate at any given time is the "true" exchange rate. It is true in the sense that it is determined by supply and demand forces and there is no Central Bank interference. As we have seen, under fixed exchange rate systems, governments stabilise their currencies and this can result in the exchange rate being under- or over-valued or misaligned. We will examine the implications for the economy of under- or over-valued exchange rates in Chapter 11. Here we mention a related problem called the "adjustment problem". That is how governments resolve an under- or over-valuation of the exchange rate. If a balance of payments deficit or deviations from PPP is taken as an indication that the exchange rate is over-valued, the government should introduce measures to reduce domestic costs and prices. However, governments are very reluctant to do this because deflationary policies inevitably have an adverse effect on output, incomes and employment. If governments do not take appropriate actions, the result is prolonged balance of payments disequilibrium.

One potentially important disadvantage of flexible exchange rates is that depreciation may provoke a depreciation-inflation spiral. This occurs when the initial depreciation increases costs and prices in the economy. The increase in inflation in turn results in further depreciation and so on. We examine the effect of depreciation from the point of view of the Irish economy in Chapter 11.

# 9.9 Conclusion

In this chapter we have discussed a number of topics relating to the balance of payments and exchange rate theory. Some of the main issues and concepts covered include:

- The balance of payments is a record of a country's economic transactions with the rest of the world. The current and capital accounts are the main sub-accounts within the balance of payments

- The trade account

- The terms of trade

- The characteristics of the foreign exchange market in Ireland

- Trade-weighted exchange rates and the real exchange rate

- The trend in Ireland's nominal and real exchange rates in recent years

- The supply and demand for Irish pounds on the foreign exchange market determines the exchange rate

- Over time, the main factors influencing exchange rates are relative movements in inflation, interest rate, speculation and the growth rate in the economy

- The external reserves held by the Central Banks consist of foreign exchange, gold and other reserves such as ECUs and SDRs

- The Central Bank uses its external reserves to stabilise the exchange rate of the Irish pound in the EMS

- In recent years, the Central Bank has intervened in the foreign exchange market to support the exchange rate of the Irish pound and this intervention has in large part been financed by government foreign borrowing

- Fixed exchange rate systems depend crucially on the participating countries having similar inflation, interest rates and growth rates. This in turn requires similar fiscal and monetary policies

- One advantage of flexible exchange rate systems is that the exchange rate at any one time is the "true" exchange rate. Fixed exchange rate systems, on the other hand, reduce uncertainty when there is policy co-ordination between member states and this promotes international trade.

# Note

1. G. Cassel, "Abnormal Deviations in International Exchanges", *Economic Journal*, 28, December, 1918. J.M. Keynes, *A Tract on Monetary Reform*, Macmillan and St Martin's Press, 1971, Chapter 3, suggests that purchasing power parity theory can be traced to the writings of David Ricardo in the nineteenth century.

# Chapter 10

# *The International Monetary System and Irish Exchange Rate Policy*

## 10.1 Introduction

We reviewed the history of the Irish monetary system in Chapter 5. We saw that almost complete integration of the Irish and British banking systems was maintained for many decades after Independence. The Irish or Saorstat Pound did not come into existence legally until 1942 and it had virtually no economic significance until we joined the European Monetary System (EMS) in 1979. The decision to join the EMS was the most important event in the monetary history of the Irish State, and in this chapter we shall explore the reasons why it was taken and the impact it has had on the economy. We shall also explore the prospects for closer monetary union in Europe in the 1990s and how this might affect the Irish economy.

## 10.2 Previous International Monetary Systems

### Gold standard

Between the end of the Napoleonic wars in 1815 and the start of World War 1 in 1914, the international monetary system moved towards the "gold standard". The system was fully operational around 1880. Under the gold standard, the value of currencies was fixed in terms of gold and hence in terms of each other. For example, if the gold values of the dollar and of the pound sterling were both fixed, then the dollar/sterling exchange rate was also fixed.

*Note:*
*Under the full gold standard, money was backed 100% by gold. People could convert coins or paper money into gold on demand.*

The gold standard incorporated an "automatic mechanism" whereby balance of payments surpluses or deficits were corrected. If, for example, a country was experiencing a balance of payments deficit, gold would flow out of the country. This in effect would reduce the money supply and lower prices (see the discussion of the quantity theory in Chapter 6). Lower prices would in turn improve competitiveness and increase exports and reduce imports. The incipient balance of payments deficit would be eliminated. Similarly, a country with a balance of payments surplus would experience an increase in the money supply and rising prices. The loss in competitiveness would move the balance of payments towards equilibrium.

*Note:*
*This "automatic mechanism" is behind the modern "Monetary Approach to the Balance of Payments" (MAB) which we discuss in Chapter 14. Versions of it were outlined by Richard Cantillon, who was from County Kerry, in his "Essai Sur la Nature du Commerce en General" (published in 1755 but written 20 years earlier) and by David Hume in "Political Discourses" (1752).*

The main reasons why the gold standard came to an end were:

1. As international trade increased there was an associated increase in the demand for money to act as a medium of exchange. The gold supply, however, increased erratically as new discoveries occurred in California, South Africa and Australia and consequentially there was a tendency for periodic shortages of "liquidity" to develop.

2. Governments were not willing to tolerate the prolonged deflationary or expansionary effects on their economies of outflows or inflows of money as balance of payments disequilibria were corrected. Moreover, the system was too rigid to withstand the shocks of war and depression. The gold standard was suspended during World War 1, but the US, France and eventually Britain went back on it after the war. However, first Britain, and then the US, suspended the convertibility of their currencies into gold in the 1930s and the system collapsed, never to be re-established in its original form, under the strains caused by the Great Depression of 1929-33.

*Note:*
*Keynes regarded Mr Churchill's decision to re-establish the pre-war gold value of sterling in 1925 as a quixotic blunder that imposed a severe deflation on the economy. In fact he regarded the obsession with gold in general as a "barbarous relic". When, in September 1931, Britain abandoned the gold standard, Keynes wrote: "There are few Englishmen who do not rejoice at the breaking of our gold fetters. We feel that we have at last a free hand to do what is sensible. The romantic phase is over, and we can begin to discuss what policy is for the best".*
J.M. Keynes, "The End of the Gold Standard" in *Essays in Persuasion*, London, Rupert Hart-Davis, 1952.

However, the outcome of the new system of adjustable exchange rates was by no means favourable. During the 1930s, country after country pursued a policy of "beggar my neighbour" devaluations in an attempt to gain a competitive advantage. Countries devalued their currencies in order to boost output and employment and the countries that were adversely affected retaliated by devaluing their currencies. The net result was that no one country gained a lasting competitive advantage.

# The Bretton Woods system: 1945-71

Bretton Woods is a small resort town in New Hampshire. It was here that representatives of the major Allied countries met in 1944 to discuss the arrangements for the post-war world monetary system. They hoped that when the war ended, there should be no going back to the chaotic international financial system that had prevailed in the 1930s. They believed that only a system of fixed exchange rates could provide the stable framework required for economic reconstruction. By this time, the US held most of the western world's gold reserves. Consequentially it was natural that the dollar should assume the role of the new reserve currency for the rest of the western world. It was agreed that the dollar would be fixed in terms of gold at $35 an ounce, which had been its value up to 1933, and that all other currencies would fix their values in terms of the dollar. Only central banks would be able to convert their holdings of dollars into gold. This *dollar exchange standard* was, therefore, an attenuated form of the old gold standard.

*Note:*
*The principal architects of the new system were John Maynard Keynes and an American economist, Harry Dexter White. Keynes had deplored the effects of the gold standard on Britain during the inter-war period, so there is some irony in the fact that his last achievement before his death in 1946 was the re-establishment of a new system of fixed exchange rates!*

At the same time the *International Monetary Fund (IMF)* was also set up to provide funds to countries experiencing balance of payments difficulties. Countries could borrow foreign exchange from the IMF and intervene to stop the exchange rate depreciating. If however a country was experiencing a "fundamental disequilibrium" in the balance of payments, that country was expected to devalue its currency. This provision marked a crucial difference between the new system and the old gold standard. No longer did countries have to suffer the protracted deflation of the "automatic adjustment mechanism" in order to correct a balance of payments problem.

The Bretton Woods system worked well during the 1950s and 1960s. The major currencies held to fixed exchange rates for long periods of time. For example, between 1949 and 1967, sterling and the Irish pound were worth $2.80. This was a fact of economic life, and no one bothered to look up the newspapers to see if there had been any change. Trade and investment between the nations of the western world grew rapidly under this arrangement. However, strains began to be felt as the 1960s wore on. In particular, the rising rate of inflation in the US, which was printing money to fight a War on Poverty at home and a War on Communism in South-East Asia, undermined confidence in the US currency and led to massive US balance of payments deficits. With exchange rates fixed, there was no scope for realignments to help to eliminate this deficit. German and Japanese central banks became reluctant to continue to absorb the dollars flooding onto world foreign exchange markets. If these countries cashed in their dollar reserves, American gold reserves would have been completely depleted. Something had to give. In August 1971 President Richard Nixon terminated the convertibility of the dollar at $35 an ounce of gold. In December 1971, at the Smithsonian Institute in Washington, an attempt was made to patch-up the Bretton Woods system at a new gold price. However the new arrangements did not succeed and the system finally came to an end in 1973. It is of interest to note that the 1989 price of gold is over $400 an ounce. The dollar is worth less than 10% of its former value in terms of gold.

# 3 The Road to European Monetary Union

My annals have it so:
A thing my mother saw,
Nigh eighty years ago
With happiness and awe.

Sight never to forget:
Solemn against the sky
In stately silhouette
Ten emus walking by.[1]

*Economic and Monetary Union (EMU)* has been sought since the foundation of the European Community, as is clear from the following time-table of events.

- 1957. The Treaty of Rome referred to the desirability of achieving international monetary stability.

- 1962. A Commission memorandum proposed that European currencies should be irrevocably fixed and that a reserve fund be established.

- 1969. At a conference of European Governments in the Hague, the German Chancellor Brandt called for economic and monetary union. This followed the devaluation of sterling in 1967 and the realignment of the French franc and German mark in 1969. His proposal was adopted by the European Council and a working party chaired by Mr P. Werner (former Prime Minister of Luxembourg) was set up to examine the issues.

- 1971. The Werner Report was published. The report was a compromise in that it called for "parallel progress", involving co-ordination of fiscal and monetary policies at the same time as progress was being made towards fixing exchange rates. The report suggested that economic policies be co-ordinated and exchange rate fluctuations be reduced so that after a period of ten years exchange rates be irrevocably fixed.

- 1973. Following the Werner report, the "snake" system commenced. This was the first stage towards EMU. As discussed in the following section, the snake system did not succeed in stabilising European exchange rates and the remaining stages proposed in the Werner report were postponed.

- 1977. In Florence, the President of the Commission, Roy Jenkins, called for a new initiative in creating EMU.

- 1978 (April). At the European Council meeting in Copenhagen, the German Chancellor Schmidt and the French President Giscard d'Estaing proposed the European Monetary System (EMS).

- 1978 (July). The European Council meeting in Bremen agreed on the structure of the EMS.

- 1978 (December). The European Council meeting in Brussels agreed on the conditions of operation.

- 1979 (March). The EMS commenced operation.

The Single European Act, ratified in 1987, referred to the desirability of a monetary union. More detailed proposals were produced in the Delors Report, published early in 1989 and signed by the governors of all the EC central banks. The Delors plan envisages three stages towards an united Europe.

*Stage 1*. All twelve countries, including the UK, Portugal and Greece, to abide by the exchange rate mechanism (ERM) of the EMS. (We discuss the ERM in section 10.5.) The free movement of capital between countries and the completion by 1992 of a programme for a barrier free internal market. This stage of the Delors plan was adopted by all EC leaders at the Madrid summit in June and will come into effect in July 1990.

*Stage 2*. The Central Banks of member states to join in some form of system to formulate a common EC monetary policy. This stage involves moving from independent national monetary policies to a common European monetary policy.

*Stage 3*. Exchange rates to be irrevocably fixed, leading to a switch to a common European currency. Fiscal and monetary policy would also be controlled at the European level. To this end, some form of European Central Bank would be set up to formulate monetary policy in Europe and the Council of Ministers would be given powers to constrain national budgets.

Stages 2 and 3 require a special inter-governmental conference to amend the Treaty of Rome. Following the decision at the Strasbourg summit in December 1989 to go ahead with EMU a special meeting has been arranged in 1990 to discuss the issues. However, Mrs Thatcher made it clear that she regards the Delors Report as only one of several possible ways forward. In fact, disagreement about whether Britain should participate in the ERM of the EMS was one factor behind the resignation of Mr Nigel Lawson as Chancellor of the Exchequer in October 1989.

Full-blown EMU would involve:

1. Irrevocably fixed exchange rates.
2. Free movement of capital between countries.
3. A common pool of reserves.
4. Some form of European Central Bank.

If these steps were taken by the time the programme for "completing the internal market" - removing all remaining non-tariff barriers, abolishing exchange controls, equalising indirect tax rates and dismantling customs posts - is implemented in 1993, the European Economic Community would have transformed itself into a United States of Europe. However, these steps would involve a substantial surrender of sovereignty and this could prove to be the stumbling block for Britain, who, as one politician put it, is not yet ready to have its economic policy formed by the governor of the Bundesbank. On the other hand, poorer countries, including Ireland, argue that EMU would expose them to competition from much stronger countries, and that therefore there would have to be further large-scale transfers of funds from the tax-payers of rich countries to make the adjustment less painful.[2] The richer countries are tiring of these repeated claims for further assistance.

In view of these obstacles, it is perhaps more likely that the EC will settle in the medium term for something less ambitious than full EMU. A reduction in changes in exchange rates within the EMS, removing all remaining exchange controls and permitting more general use of the ECU (European currency unit) as a unit of account would be possible with a minimum loss of sovereignty. It would create a sort of European gold standard and bring many of the benefits that are expected from an EMU without all of its problems. The western world would then comprise three large currency zones, based on the ECU, the dollar and the yen. The next challenge would be to find a satisfactory mechanism for dealing with relations between these zones and with the rest of the world.

In order to understand the prospects for further progress towards EMU, we propose to review in some detail the working of the Snake and of the EMS.

# 10.4 The Snake: 1973-78

Between 1971 and 1973 most countries operated a "managed float". Their exchange rates were allowed to float but Central Banks intervened on foreign exchange markets to keep currencies within certain target ranges. (See Chapter 9 for a discussion of the drawbacks to intervention along these lines.) In 1973, a number of European countries reached a formal agreement to hold their exchange rates within a band, which was not, however, rigidly fixed. This combination of flexibility and rigidity was called the Snake for obvious reasons!

The Snake enjoyed little success. The UK joined, but left after two months because it proved impossible to maintain the value of sterling at the target level. (Because the Irish pound was locked to sterling, we entered and left the Snake along with it.) France left, rejoined, left and joined again, as its currency rose and fell against the DM.

The main reason the Snake failed was the same as that which led to the downfall of the gold standard and the Bretton Woods system. There was a lack of *economic policy co-ordination* between the participating countries. If countries do not have similar rates of inflation and growth rates in real GNP, they cannot hope to maintain their balance of payments in equilibrium. Chronic surpluses and deficits in the balance of payments will eventually lead to the break-down of any system of fixed exchange rates. During the Snake period, France and the UK tended to pursue much more expansionary fiscal and monetary policies than Germany. It was inevitable that balance of payments deficits and surpluses would arise and force exchange rate changes that went beyond what was permissible under the rules of the Snake.

Thus, the lesson that should be learned from the history of the various experiments with international systems of fixed exchange rates is that countries cannot maintain fixed parities unless their economic policies are closely co-ordinated or at least very consistent. However, such consistency is difficult to achieve as long as national governments believe they can improve their countries' economic performance by pursuing independent monetary and fiscal policies. At the end of the day, if a system of fixed exchange rates is to be successful, it requires a significant sacrifice of economic sovereignty. How significant a loss this would be is open to question. Mrs Thatcher resisted any dilution of Britain's freedom of manoeuvre in the central policy areas throughout the 1980s and kept sterling out of the ERM of the EMS. The results have not been very impressive.

# .5 The European Monetary System: 1979-

Following the collapse of the Snake, the Commission of the EC pressed ahead with its plans for a more ambitious European monetary integration. The interim goal was to create a "zone of monetary stability" in Europe. After long and difficult negotiations, the EMS commenced on the 13th of March 1979. It has survived and to some extent flourished since then, confounding those sceptics, including many economists, who thought it would quickly suffer the fate of its predecessor, the Snake. To understand what the EMS has achieved, and what remains to be done, let us examine the technicalities of the system in some detail.

At the heart of the EMS is a system of quasi-fixed exchange rates. The Central Banks of the countries that participate in the ERM intervene to keep exchange rates within a narrow band (see Chapter 9 for a discussion of intervention). The participating countries are: Germany, France, Italy, The Netherlands, Belgium, Luxembourg, Denmark and Ireland. Spain joined the system in June 1989. The UK, Greece and Portugal are also members of the EMS but these countries do not participate in the ERM.

Significant exchange controls have been in operation between the participating currencies since the EMS was formed. These have insulated currencies from the full effects of speculation, and are an obstacle to moves towards full-blown monetary union. Paradoxically, the Conservative government in the UK, which kept sterling out of the ERM throughout the 1980s, completely dismantled exchange controls early in the decade. Mrs Thatcher has made the removal of all exchange controls in Europe a precondition of British entry to the ERM.

At the centre of the system is the European currency unit (ECU) which is a weighted basket of the currencies. Table 10.1 shows the currencies and the associated weights as at September 1989. The amount of a particular currency in the ECU was fixed at the start of the system in proportion to each country's GNP and has been changed by the Council of Ministers on two occasions (September 1984 and September 1989). The DM has by far the largest weight reflecting the importance and size of the German economy. The Irish pound has a weight of only 1.1%.

A currency's ECU exchange rate is calculated by converting each currency in the basket to that currency and then adding to obtain the value of the ECU in terms of that currency. For example, in Table 10.2, the currencies are converted to Irish pounds using the exchange rates prevailing on 21/11/1989. The sum of the currencies in the basket is worth IR£0.7727. Hence, 1 ECU = IR£0.7727 or using a direct quote, IR£1 = ECU1.2942. A similar calculation can be performed for all other currencies.

*Table 10.1*

**The European currency unit (ECU): September 1989**

|  | Units of currency | Weight (%) |
|---|---|---|
| 1.  German mark (DM) | 0.6242 | 30.1 |
| 2.  French franc (FF) | 1.332 | 19.0 |
| 3.  Dutch guilder (HFL) | 0.2197 | 9.4 |
| 4.  Belgian franc (BFR) | 3.30⌉ | ⌉ |
| 5.  Luxembourg franc (LFR) | 0.13⌋ | ⌋ 7.9 |
| 6.  Italian lira (LIT) | 151.8 | 10.15 |
| 7.  Danish krone (DKR) | 0.1976 | 2.45 |
| 8.  Irish pound (IR£) | 0.0085 | 1.1 |
| 9.  Pound sterling (STG£) | 0.0878 | 13.0 |
| 10. Spanish peseta (PTA) | 6.885 | 5.3 |
| 11. Greek drachma (DR) | 1.15 | 0.8 |
| 12. Portuguese escudo (ESU) | 1.393 | 0.8 |
|  | 1 ECU | 100.0 |

*Notes:*

1. Although the pound sterling, Greek drachma and the Portuguese escudo are used to calculate the ECU, these currencies do not participate in the ERM of the EMS. The Spanish peseta and the Portuguese escudo were added to the list of currencies used to define the ECU on the 21st September 1989.

2. A realignment changes the % weights of each currency in the ECU basket.

The values of each currency in terms of the ECU are know as "central rates" and may be used to calculate "cross rates" between individual currencies. For example, if the DM/ECU and IR£/ECU exchange rates are known, the cross rate DM/IR£, can be calculated. The central rates are known as the "parity grid". The maximum permissible deviation from the central rates is plus or minus 2.25%. That is, the sum of the deviations from their central rates of the strongest and weakest currencies in the grid cannot exceed 2.25%. (The Spanish peseta is allowed a 6% spread. The countries committed to the 2.25% band are described as being in the narrow band of the ERM). The EMS grid is shown in a graph in the Central Bank of Ireland, Quarterly Bulletin, and the position of the various currencies in the grid is published daily in the newspapers.

*Table 10.2*

**Calculating the ECU exchange rate**

| | *1*<br>*Basket* | *2*<br>*Exchange rate*<br>*21-11-1989* | *3*<br>*Converted to*<br>*IR£* |
|---|---|---|---|
| DM | 0.6242 | 2.642 | 0.2362 |
| FF | 1.332 | 8.999 | 0.1480 |
| HFL | 0.2198 | 2.981 | 0.0737 |
| BFR ⎤ | 3.30 | | |
| LFR ⎦ | 0.13 | 55.49 | 0.0618 |
| LIT | 151.8 | 1945.8 | 0.0780 |
| DKR | 0.1976 | 10.258 | 0.0192 |
| IR£ | 0.0085 | 1 | 0.0085 |
| STG£ | 0.0878 | 0.927 | 0.0946 |
| PTA | 6.885 | 169.77 | 0.0405 |
| DR | 1.44 | 238.44 | 0.006 |
| ESU | 1.393 | 228.71 | 0.006 |
| | 1 ECU | | 0.7727 |

Table 10.3 shows the central rate and the *intervention margins* (that is, the upper and lower levels beyond which intervention would be required) for the Irish pound. As discussed in Chapter 9, the Central Bank purchases or sells IR£ on the foreign exchange market to ensure the Irish pound exchange rate remains within these limits. For example, if the DM/IR£ exchange rate fell to 2.60, the Central Bank would buy Irish pounds and thereby move the exchange rate back into the band.

Incorporated into the system is a "divergence indicator", which is a kind of early warning device. The indicator is set at 75% of the allowed intervention margins. In other words, once an exchange rate has moved 75% of the way to the ceiling or floor, there is a presumption that Central Banks will intervene.

*Note:*

*The ECU resolved one problem associated with the Snake system. If a realignment was necessary in the Snake system, the onus of intervention nearly always fell on the weak currency even if that currency was not at the root of the problem. The ECU (because it is a basket of currencies) makes it easy to see which currency is causing the divergence. That country's Central Bank is then required to take appropriate action.*

*Table 10.3*

**Central rates and intervention margins for IR£: January 1990**

|              | HFL  | B/LFR | DM   | DKR   | FF   | LIT    | PTA   |
|--------------|------|-------|------|-------|------|--------|-------|
| + 2.25%      | 3.08 | 56.49 | 2.73 | 10.44 | 9.18 | 2050.0 | 184.5 |
| Central Rate | 3.02 | 55.25 | 2.67 | 10.22 | 8.98 | 2004.9 | 174.1 |
| - 2.25%      | 2.95 | 54.0  | 2.61 | 9.98  | 8.77 | 1959.8 | 163.6 |

*Notes:*

1. If all the other currencies in the system are at the central rate the Irish pound could potentially move by a maximum of 4.5%. This would occur if the Irish pound was at the top of the band (+2.25%) and fell to the bottom of the band (-2.25%). However, at any one time, no two currencies can be more than 2.25% apart. Hence if the French franc was at the bottom of the band, the Irish pound could not move above the central rate.

2. The maximum margin of fluctuation for the peseta is + or - 6%.

An important part of the system is the *European Monetary Co-operation Fund (EMCF)*. At the start of the system, the EMCF received 20% of each member's gold and foreign exchange reserves. In return, each member was credited with a similar amount of ECUs. The objective of the EMCF is to make available reserves to countries experiencing balance of payments difficulties.

# 10.6 Realignments of EMS Currencies

Although the EMS is, as we have said, basically a system of fixed exchange rates, it contains important elements of flexibility. The first is the margin of variation around the central rates that we described in the previous section. A much more important provision is that Finance Ministers can agree to realign the central rates when it becomes clear that these are no longer appropriate. This is akin to the IMF notion of a "fundamental disequilibrium", but the procedure for agreeing on an EMS realignment is much less cumbersome than the one that was required by the IMF in the 1950s and 1960s to change the Bretton Woods parities.

Realignments occurred frequently in the early years of the EMS. There were two every year between 1979 and 1983. By the end of January 1990, there had been a total of 12 realignments. Too frequent realignments would have undermined the System. Since the beginning of 1987, however, the system has enjoyed a period of stability. Table 10.4 gives details of the realignments. It is of interest to examine the reasons for them. Realignment number 11 arose because of the impact of the weakness of sterling on the System. When sterling, the dollar or the yen is weakening, there is a tendency for speculative funds to flow into DMs. This causes the DM to appreciate, and puts a strain on the parity grid. One way out of this problem would be to establish complete capital mobility between the currencies of the EMS. This might remove the tendency to seek out one "strong" currency: the ERM currencies as a group would move up against the non-participating currencies.

*Table 10.4*
**EMS realignments: % changes in bilateral central rates**

| No. | | Date | DM | B/LF | DKR | FF | IR£ | LIT | HFL |
|---|---|---|---|---|---|---|---|---|---|
| 1 | 1979 | 24/9 | +2 | | -2.86 | | | | |
| 2 | | 30/11 | | | -4.76 | | | | |
| 3 | 1982 | 3/3 | | | | | | -6 | |
| 4 | | 5/10 | +5.5 | | | -3 | | -3 | +5.5 |
| 5 | 1982 | 22/2 | | -8.5 | | -3 | | | |
| 6 | | 14/6 | +4.25 | | | -5.57 | | -2.75 | +4.24 |
| 7 | 1983 | 21/3 | +5.5 | +1.5 | +2.5 | -2.5 | -3.5 | -2.5 | +3.5 |
| 8 | 1985 | 22/7 | +2 | +2 | +2 | +2 | +2 | -6 | +2 |
| 9 | 1986 | 7/4 | +3 | +1 | +1 | -3 | | | +3 |
| 10 | | 4/8 | | | | | -8 | | |
| 11 | 1987 | 12/1 | +3 | +2 | | | | | +2 |
| 12 | 1990 | 6/1 | | | | | | -3.75 | |

Realignments number 1, 2, 3, 5, 8 and 10 were in response to the desire of individual smaller countries to offset the effects of high inflation, and to reduce balance of payments deficits, by devaluing. One of the reasons the system has survived is that it has permitted such corrections to be made fairly quickly.

Realignments number 4, 6, 7, and 9 were of fundamental importance as they arose from the differing performances of the German and French economies. Following the election of a socialist president and government in 1982, France pursued an expansionary fiscal policy that was incompatible with the conservative German policies. The resulting spurt of inflation in France created major tensions in the system, which survived only because compromises were worked out between France and Germany which allowed the French franc to fall and the DM to rise. Gradually French and German economic policies came more into line, reducing the need to resort to realignments.

*Note:*

*Speculators have on occasions anticipated EMS realignments and reacted by moving considerable amounts of money between countries in the hope of making a capital gain. Although it is generally clear which currencies are likely to be devalued, speculators have not always gained. In March 1983, the French authorities deliberately delayed a realignment against the DM and hoisted interest rates on the Euro-Franc market to unprecedented rates of five and six thousand per cent. Speculators who had borrowed on this market and converted their borrowings into DMs hoping to make a capital gain badly lost out. "Once speculators' fingers looked memorably burned, the (interest) rate was allowed to subside to a mere three to four hundred per cent" (Irish Times, 19/3/1983, p. 18).*

At most realignments, the Irish pound went "through the middle", that is, its central rate was not changed as the DM rose and the French franc fell. However, the Irish pound was devalued on two occasions: March 1983 and August 1986. We discuss Irish policy in the EMS in more detail below and the effectiveness of devaluation as a means of increasing output and employment in Chapter 11.

With the except of lira realignment in January 1990, there has been no realignment since January 1987. This has been made possible by the much lower, and more uniform, rates of inflation in the member countries, due in turn to the more compatible economic policies that are being followed. However, the persistence of the large German current account balance of payments surplus suggests that another realignment may be needed eventually. In fact some economists (notably those aligned with the British Conservative Party) point to the persistence of this deficit as a sign that the EMS is a flawed concept.

# 10.7 Convergence in the EMS

The motivation for trying to achieve exchange rate stability is the belief that it will bring tangible economic benefits. These are expected to take the form of increased trade and investment between countries whose exchange rates are relatively stable, and a convergence of rates of inflation towards that being experienced in the leading or hegemonic country of the system. It has always been clear that in the case of the EMS that Germany occupies this role. Thus, more inflation-prone countries, such as Italy, France and Ireland hoped to enjoy the German rate of inflation by accepting the discipline implied by membership of the system.

*Note:*

*One of the problems that has bedevilled attempts at exchange rate unions in the past is known as the nth country problem. It arises from the fact that there is always one fewer exchange rate than there are countries in a union. If there are two countries, as under the old sterling link, there is only one exchange rate, namely, that between the Irish pound and sterling. Under these circumstances, it is sufficient for one country's central bank to intervene to hold a target exchange rate. (If they both intervene, they have to co-ordinate their intervention so that they are working towards the same target rate!) More generally, in the EMS there has to be an nth country, whose exchange rate is passively determined as a result of the decisions of others. This country is free to pursue its own monetary policies and the other n-1 countries have to intervene in foreign exchange markets to maintain the target rates of exchange. By intervening, they lose control of their own money supplies. Thus, their monetary policies come to be dictated by those of the nth country, just as British policy dominated Ireland under the sterling link. Under the "dollar exchange standard" that operated until 1971, the US was happy to be the nth country, but as it relaxed its grip on its money supply, other countries became increasingly unhappy at leaving it in that role. The reason why Germany is generally acceptable as the dominant country in the EMS is ultimately that other countries have more faith in the ability of the Bundesbank to control the German money supply than they have in the ability of their own central banks to control their money supplies! The Economist put this point in characteristic prose: "Tory gentlemen may like appointing City gents as governors of the Bank of England, but Mr Karl Otto Poehl [governor of the Bundesbank] would do a better job." (21/9/1988).*

The experience of the first ten years of the EMS has been mixed in regard to the fulfilment of the hopes that attended its birth. Exchange rates have been more stable inside than outside the system, but surprisingly this has not led to an upsurge in intra-EMS trade. In fact, trade between Britain and the rest of the EC has grown more rapidly than, for example, trade between France and Germany, despite the volatility of sterling as a non-member of the ERM.

With regard to inflation, there certainly has been a significant convergence of European rates towards German rates (see Table 10.5). But inflation subsided throughout the western world during the 1980s. For example, between 1979-87, certain countries not participating in the ERM (such as Austria, Canada, Japan, Sweden, US and Switzerland) have, on average, a *better* inflation record than the EMS countries. The key issue is to what extent did participation in the ERM help countries like France, Italy and Ireland bring their inflation under control? The evidence to-date is somewhat mixed. One view is that "there has been no particular influence of the EMS on inflation convergence".[3] An alternative view is that membership of the ERM has had an effect on inflationary expectations. Governments that participated in the ERM were strengthened in their fight against inflation. They used their membership of the EMS to justify unpopular domestic anti-inflationary policies. There was a steady convergence in the fiscal and monetary policies being pursued by the member states. Britain, on the other hand, which does not participate in the ERM, is now experiencing a higher rate of inflation than any other major European country.[4] We discuss this issue in detail in section 10.10.

*Table 10.5*
**Annual average rates of inflation**

| Annual Average | Belgium | Denmark | France | Germany | Ireland | Italy | Holland |
|---|---|---|---|---|---|---|---|
| 1979-82 | 6.8 | 10.9 | 12.4 | 5.3 | 17.2 | 17.9 | 5.8 |
| 1983-85 | 6.3 | 6.6 | 7.6 | 2.6 | 8.1 | 11.4 | 2.8 |
| 1986-88 | 1.4 | 4.1 | 2.8 | 0.8 | 3.0 | 5.2 | 0.2 |

*Source*: Commission of the EC, *European Economy*

# 10.8 Monetary Policy in Britain

Because of the close connection between British and Irish financial markets, and the major developments in this relationship during the 1980s, we outline briefly in this section macroeconomic policy in the UK since 1979.

In order to understand why the UK did not pursue a fixed exchange rate policy in the early 1980s it should be borne in mind that under fixed exchange rates and perfect capital mobility, the Central Bank cannot control the domestic money supply. We explain this point in detail in Chapters 11 and 12. One implication is that if a government wishes to adopt a monetarist policy, as was the case in the UK in 1978-79, then the exchange rate must be allowed to float on foreign exchanges. It will be recalled from discussion of the Quantity Theory of Money in Chapter 6 that one of the main tenets of monetarism is that the money supply must be controlled if the government is to succeed in curtailing the inflation rate. The British government had opted to pursue a monetarist strategy incorporating flexible exchange rates rather than the alternative policy of fixing the exchange rate in the EMS. The decision to adopt a monetarist policy was one of the main reasons why the UK chose not to join the exchange rate mechanism of the EMS in 1979.

In 1978, the Labour government had made it clear in its "Green Paper" on the EMS that controlling inflation was the main priority of economic policy and that this objective would be achieved by controlling the money supply.[5] This policy was given even greater emphasis by the newly elected Conservative government in 1979. Accompanying this monetarist policy were other measures designed to foster free enterprise, increase competition and reduce State intervention in the economy. In terms of the "natural rate hypothesis" discussed in Chapter 8, these policies were designed to speed up adjustment and move the economy as quickly as possible towards the natural rate of unemployment. Some of the main policies introduced include:

- The introduction of a medium term financial strategy (MTFS) which set out five year plans for government expenditure with the aim of controlling the government's borrowing requirement. By 1988-89, the government's borrowing requirement was a negative STG£14.3b; that is, a repayment of public debt.

- Tax reforms designed to create incentive and promote enterprise. The basic rate of income tax has been reduced from 33 pence in the pound in 1979 to 25 pence in the pound in 1988. Also both higher rates of income tax and corporation tax have been significantly reduced.

- The introduction of legislation to restrict the power of trade unions. It was argued that trade unions, through excessive wage demands and restrictive practices, had impeded UK competitiveness. Legislation was passed between 1980-88 relating to picketing, trade unions immunity to civil actions, secret ballots and closed shops.

- Privatisation of the nationalised industries on the grounds that the private sector would provide a better and cheaper service than the public sector. The former Conservative Prime Minister, Harold Macmillan, described privatisation as "selling the family silver". By the end of the 1990s, over 40% of the 1979 nationalised industries will have been sold to the private sector. These include British Gas, British Petroleum, British Telecom and British Steel. There are current proposals to sell both the water authorities and the electricity supply industry. Privatisation has been criticised by economists for confusing a *means* to the goal of greater competition with the goal itself.

When the government introduced its monetarist policy and reduced the growth rate of money in 1979, this, coupled with the reduction in government expenditure and an appreciation of sterling on foreign exchanges (due in part to the increase in oil prices and the high interest rates associated with the government's monetary policy) intensified the recession of 1980-81. GDP fell by nearly 3% in two years and unemployment increased from 1.1m in 1979 to 3m in 1984. Inflation fell from 18% in 1980 to 4.5% in 1983. However, between 1982-89 real GDP has grown at an average of 3% per annum and unemployment has fallen to under 2m. Reflecting the upsurge in economic activity and the loss of control over the money supply, inflation increased to over 8% in 1989, approximately double the German rate.

In October 1985, the government announced that it was ceasing to target the broad definition of money, M3. The main reason given was that changes in international finance had made the money supply indicators unreliable. In practice, the targeted definition of money, M3, had proven very difficult to control. (The M3 definition of money has now in fact been abolished.) From 1986 onwards a narrow definition of money, M0 (currency in circulation), would be the target variable. This in effect downgraded money supply targets as an instrument of policy and heralded the end (for the moment at least) of monetarism in the UK. In its place the government adopted a policy of tracking sterling to the DM. Officially, the UK would not join the exchange rate mechanism of the EMS but unofficially sterling would be tied to the DM. During 1987 and 1988 the DM/STG£ exchange rate was kept in the DM2.94-3.00 range. (If the Irish pound is pegged to the DM and sterling is [unofficially] pegged to the DM, then of course the STG£/IR£ exchange rate is more or less fixed.) During this period, speculation mounted that sterling would become a full member of the EMS. However Mrs Thatcher remained opposed to such a move.

By 1989, the policy of tracking sterling to the DM proved to be unsustainable. Following the termination of targets for broad money, the money supply increased very rapidly in the UK. Between 1986-89 the money supply (M3 definition) increased by an average of 20% per annum compared to an annual rate of 6% in Germany. This increase in the money supply coupled with the tax cuts introduced in the 1988 budget lead to a consumer boom, notably in the housing market. Inflation increased to over 8% and the deficit on the current account of the balance of payments increased to over STG£17bn by 1989. The German inflation rate, on the other hand, remained below 3.5% and the surplus on the trade account of the balance of payments increased to STG£48bn reflecting the conservative policies adopted in Germany.

As we have already mentioned, countries cannot hope to fix their exchange rates if there is a lack of policy co-ordination. With the UK pursuing an expansionary policy and Germany pursuing a conservative policy the inevitable happened and in the second half of 1989, sterling depreciated on foreign exchanges. By December 1989, the DM/STG£ exchange rate had fallen to 2.797.

Note:

*The weakness of sterling on foreign exchanges in October and December of 1989 led to a capital outflow from Ireland and the trade account worsened as Irish companies purchased sterling at the new "cheap" exchange rate of STG£0.94/IR£1 (up from STG£0.83/IR£1 in early 1989). The result was a substantial fall in the external reserves (a 13% decrease in October alone). In December 1989, the Central Bank of Ireland permitted a 1% increase in domestic interest rates to stem the outflow of capital and to allay any fears that the Irish pound might be devalued in an EMS realignment. This episode shows that even after ten years of EMS membership, Ireland is still very much influenced by developments in the UK.*

At the present time monetary policy in the UK is very uncertain. There is continued pressure for the UK to become a full member of the EMS. However Mrs Thatcher remains entrenched in her view that sterling will participate "only when the time is right". Disagreement on this issue led to the resignation of her Chancellor of the Exchequer, Nigel Lawson, in October 1989. Moreover, the UK continues to oppose moves towards EMU. The UK wishes to stop at stage one of the Delors plan for monetary union. One of the arguments advanced by the UK is that the current exchange rate mechanism of the EMS could prove a more effective framework for curtailing inflation than full-blown EMU. The argument is that participating countries compete with one another to maintain their exchange rates in the upper half of the EMS band and thereby avoid the humiliation of a devaluation. To do this countries must pursue a tight monetary policy and keep their inflation rate close to the lowest inflation rate in the EMS (i.e. Germany). Hence, the current system incorporates an incentive for participating countries to control their money supplies. In contrast, it is pointed out that in EMU, European monetary policy and therefore European inflation would be determined by the European Central Bank. It is argued that there is no particular reason why the European Central Bank might be more successful than the present EMS arrangement in achieving low inflation.

# Ireland's Decision to Join the EMS

On the 5th December 1978, the British Government announced that the UK would not participate in the ERM of the EMS. Their objections to joining were based mainly on the fear that the commitment to a fixed exchange rate would involve loss of control over the domestic money supply, which they claimed was indispensable in the fight against inflation. Ten days later, the Irish Government announced that Ireland would participate in the ERM and imposed exchange controls on movements of funds from Ireland to Britain. This in effect signalled the end of Ireland's 153 year-old sterling link.

The actual break with sterling came on 30th March 1979, when the rise of sterling relative to the European currencies forced Ireland to chose between leaving the ERM or breaking the sterling link. We stayed with the ERM and for the first time since the Napoleonic Wars, the Irish pound and sterling diverged in value. For the first time ever the two parts of Ireland were separated by an exchange rate.

*Note:*

*One of the witnesses to the Banking Commission (1934-38) claimed that there were only two catastrophes that Ireland had been spared, earthquakes and an exchange rate! We got an exchange rate with sterling in March 1979 and on the morning of 19th July 1984 an earthquake measuring 5.4 on the Richter scale was recorded in Dublin!*

The strength of sterling during 1979 confounded the forecasts, which were unanimous in predicting that it would continue to depreciate relative to the DM. Sterling's sudden change of fortunes has been attributed to the rise in oil prices and the fact Britain was becoming a net exporter of petroleum. However, the election of a Conservative government in May 1979 had a major bearing on subsequent economic policy. Mrs Thatcher's government was for some years an ardent believer in a rigid form of monetarism. In order to bring inflation under control, the real money supply was sharply reduced in 1980-81 and this drove the exchange rate to an unsustainable high level. Even when sterling returned to a more sustainable level in 1983, the Conservative government continued to refuse to bring sterling into the ERM.

The reasons why Ireland was prepared to join the ERM, even at the cost of breaking the sterling link, were set out by the then Governor of the Central Bank of Ireland, Mr C.H. Murray, as follows:[6]

- The inappropriateness of continuing the sterling link. He believed "... that a floating, unstable (but generally depreciating) pound, and a steady fall in (Ireland's) trade with the UK, had diminished the attractiveness and appropriateness of the link."

- "The benefits in terms of a reduction in inflation to be obtained from adherence to a hard currency regime. It would be prudent to assume that, in the longer-run at any rate, membership of the EMS involves a harder currency regime than non-membership."

- Ireland should make a commitment to a major Community initiative.

- Community support would be forthcoming in the form of a "transfer of resources", that is, a subsidy from the tax-payers of Germany and France.

One of the main reasons, therefore, why we chose to enter the EMS was an expected reduction in Irish inflation to the relatively low German inflation rate. In the next section we discuss purchasing power parity (PPP) which is the theory that explains why Irish inflation should fall to the German rate. For the moment we note that the EMS was, in effect, seen as a powerful disinflation device which offered a kind of "credibility bonus". If our commitment to the EMS was seen as credible and the markets believed that Irish inflation would fall to the German rate then Irish price and wage expectations would be revised downwards and low inflation would be combined with low unemployment. The more credible our commitment to the EMS, the quicker inflation and wage expectations would be revised downwards and the lower the cost of disinflation in terms of lost output and employment.

To see this argument refer back to the AS/AD model of Chapter 8 and suppose that the economy was initially experiencing high inflation and an unemployment rate above the natural rate. One way of lowering inflation would be to implement a deflationary fiscal or monetary policy. Such a policy would shift the AD curve down to the left and inflation would fall along the vertical axis and output along the horizontal axis. Unemployment would increase. Eventually, workers would revise wage expectations downwards and the AS curve would shift down to the right. After a time, the economy could be expected to move to the natural rate of unemployment where a new low inflation rate is combined with "full" employment. The crucial question however is, How long before the economy moves to the natural rate? If workers are very slow to revise their wage expectations, then the government's disinflation policy will involve considerable costs in terms of lost output and employment. Conversely, if wage expectations are revised very quickly, the cost in terms of lost output will be small.

The EMS offered an alternative strategy for reducing inflation. If firms and workers believed that Irish prices would quickly fall to the German level, then wage and price expectations would be quickly revised downwards. The AS curve would shift down to the right and low inflation would be combined with low unemployment. In comparison to deflationary fiscal and/or monetary policies, the EMS offered a way of lowering inflation at a much lower cost in terms of lost output and employment. The more credible our EMS commitment the lower the costs in terms of lost output and employment.

In the short-run, however, it was acknowledged that the Irish economy could expect to experience a loss in competitiveness. In this regard, the Irish Government White Paper, published in December 1978, stated:

... the discipline involved in membership of a zone of monetary stability acts as a powerful aid in the fight against inflation . . .[however] in the initial period of operation of the EMS, the parity of our currency might be higher than it otherwise would be. This could impose severe strain on Ireland's competitiveness, leading to a possible loss of output and employment. (p. 9-10).

To overcome these misgivings the Irish Government sought additional aid from the Community to finance an enlarged programme of infrastructural and industrial development. This came in the form of interest rate subsidies from the Germans and the French. (Similar arguments were to be used to seek an increase in our aid from the Regional and Social Funds in the approach to the implementation of the Single European Act in 1992.)

Obviously, if we were going to enjoy lower inflation and additional subsidies through joining the EMS, it was a very attractive proposition. If Britain had also joined the ERM, it would have been even more attractive, because we would have simply extended to continental Europe the exchange rate stability we already enjoyed with sterling. If joining involved breaking the link with sterling, this was deemed not to be too high a price to pay for getting out from under the shadow of the high British rates of inflation and interest.

Thus expectations were high early in 1979 that we could "... contemplate the prospect of an early and sustained return to inflation rates comfortably back into single figures."[7] This expectation was based on a view of the causes of inflation that can best be described as "reverse purchasing power parity". To understand the influence of this model on Irish thinking with regard to the benefits that would flow from joining the EMS, we must review the theory of purchasing power parity (PPP).

## Purchasing power parity

In Chapter 9, we briefly outlined the theory of purchasing power parity (PPP). PPP is a theory of exchange rate determination.[8] The strong version of PPP (referred to as *absolute* PPP theory) can be written:

(1)  $P_{irl} * E = P_{uk}$

where $P_{irl}$ and $P_{uk}$ are Irish and UK prices respectively and E is the exchange rate expressed as STG£ per units of IR£: STG£/IR£. Equation (1) states that the Irish price level (converted using the exchange rate, E, to UK prices) is equal to the UK price level. We could also re-arrange equation (1) by using the reciprocal of the exchange rate, 1/E, and express the UK price level in terms of Irish prices.

The strong version of PPP relies on the "law of one price". That is, prices of similar goods expressed in a common currency should be the same. Abstracting from the exchange rate for the moment, consider the case of two shops in the same street selling the same range of products. If prices in the two shops are not the same, customers will switch their expenditure to the shop with the lower prices. The high priced shop will be forced to cut prices or go out of business. Competition therefore forces a convergence of prices. The same principle applies between countries. An example is the Northern Ireland border. In the 1980s, prices, expressed in a common currency, of a whole range of consumer goods including petrol, drink and electrical equipment were cheaper in the North than they were in the South. As people switched their expenditure to the Northern side of the border, garages and supermarkets in the South, unable to cut their prices, went out of business and similar businesses sprang up in the North. In order to prevent the situation deteriorating further, the Minister for Finance, Ray MacSharry, introduced a 48 hour rule in 1987 to curtail shopping in the North. The 48 hour rule specified that people had to be resident outside the country for at least 48 hours before they could avail of duty free allowances. This rule combined with long queues at customs check points succeeded in stabilising the situation.

In a broader context the mechanism by which the "law of one price" or PPP is supposed to work is simply goods *arbitrage*, that is, the tendency for people to spot the opportunity of making a profit by buying cheap in one market and selling dear in another. If Irish goods are good value at the going exchange rate, it will pay people to buy them and sell them abroad. Irish exports will boom and Irish imports will slump, leading to a balance of payments surplus and eventually either a rise in Irish prices and/or an appreciation in the exchange rate. Hence, PPP predicts that *the exchange rate will adjust to offset differences in relative prices*. If, for example, prices in the US are higher than prices in Japan, PPP theory predicts that the dollar exchange rate will depreciate. Conversely, if US prices are lower than prices in Japan, PPP theory predicts that the dollar exchange rate will appreciate.

*Note:*
*An example is the German hyper-inflation of 1921-22. In 1921 the mark, dollar exchange rate was M270/$1. Following the rise in prices in Germany, by October 1922 the mark exchange rate had depreciated to M25,000million/$1!*

At any point in time however we would not expect absolute PPP to hold between different countries. Transport costs, tariffs and quotas, lack of information, goods that are too costly to trade, etc. are all reasons why prices will differ between countries. This is why the absolute version of PPP is referred to as the strong version of PPP.[9]

Assuming that equation (1) holds, it will also be true that the rate of change in the exchange rate must equal the difference between the rates of inflation in the two countries:

(2)  $\Delta E = \Delta P_{uk} - \Delta P_{irl}$

$$\left[ \text{Should be:} \quad \frac{\Delta E}{E} = \frac{\Delta P_{uk}}{P_{uk}} - \frac{\Delta P_{irl}}{P_{irl}} \right]$$

*Note:*
*The symbol $\Delta$ denotes rate of change so that $\Delta$ Pirl indicates the Irish inflation rate. The student can confirm that (2) is implied by (1) by taking the natural log of (1) and differentiating.*

Equation (2) is referred to as the *relative* or weak version of PPP and it says that if PPP holds, the nominal exchange rate should rise if British inflation exceeds Irish inflation. Conversely, the exchange rate should decrease if British inflation is less than Irish inflation. PPP implies that nominal exchange rates will adjust to offset differentials in inflation rates between countries. If transport costs, tariffs and quotas remain constant, equation (2) circumvents these considerations and for this reason is referred to as the weak version of PPP.

We can also examine PPP theory in terms of the real exchange rate. In Chapter 9 we defined the real exchange rate as

(3)  Real exchange rate = $(E * P_{irl})/P_{uk}$

It can be seen that equation (3) is simply a re-arrangement of equation (1). If PPP holds, the real exchange rate will be constant. For example, if an increase in $P_{irl}$ relative to $P_{uk}$ is offset by a depreciation (fall) in the exchange rate, the real exchange rate remains constant. In Figure 9.5, Chapter 9, we show the real exchange rate for the Irish pound against the dollar, sterling and the DM since 1970. It can been seen from the graph that the real exchange rate has not remained constant and we could conclude from this that absolute PPP does not hold in the Irish case. We return to this issue below.

PPP theory, which was first proposed by the Swedish economist Gustav Cassel in 1918 (see footnote 1, Chapter 9) as a way of deciding what the appropriate dollar/pound exchange rate should be in the aftermath of war-time inflation, was revived during the 1970s as floating exchange rates came back into fashion. There are basically two reasons why PPP theory receives so much attention in the economic literature. First, PPP can be used to calculate the "equilibrium exchange rate" at any point in time. The problem of identifying the equilibrium exchange rate between the world's major currencies has been centre-stage since the collapse of the Bretton Woods system. In a world where the majority of foreign exchange transactions are driven by speculative, rather than trading motives, the real exchange rates of all the major currencies have fluctuated widely. PPP is best viewed as a anchor point or benchmark from which to judge whether a currency is under- or over-valued.[10] The second reason why PPP is considered important is that it can be used to forecast movements in exchange rates. PPP predicts that the currencies of high inflation countries will depreciate. We return to this issue later in this chapter.

However, it was soon realised that there could be significant departures from PPP exchange rates, persisting into the medium term. For example, between 1980 and 1985 the Irish pound value of the dollar doubled; then between the beginning of 1985 and the end of 1987 it fell by 67%. Clearly these enormous swings in nominal exchange rates were not simply a reflection of differences between Irish and US rates of inflation. Similar *volatility* in nominal exchange rates of all the major currencies gives rise to wide swings in real exchange rates.[11]

## Purchasing power parity and inflation in a SOE

The relevance of PPP to the Irish decision to join the ERM may be seen by turning it on its head and changing it from a theory of the determination of exchange rates to a theory of inflation in a small open economy (SOE). To see how this can be done, re-arrange equation (2):

(4)   $\Delta P_{irl} = \Delta P_{uk} - \Delta E$

If E is fixed, as it was under the sterling link, then PPP says that Irish inflation must equal British inflation. Since there is no question of Ireland *causing* British inflation, because our firms are *price-takers* with little or no market power, the causation must run in the other direction. This leads to the conclusion that, as long as our exchange rate was pegged to sterling, we were forced to experience the same rate of inflation as Britain.

*Note:*
*While this reasoning applies only to traded goods, it can be extended to the whole economy by arguing that there cannot for long be a divergence between the rates of inflation in the traded and non-traded sectors of an economy. If the prices of one class of goods are rising consistently more rapidly than those of another, the pay (including profits) of those working in the production of the former would tend to rise more rapidly than that of the rest of the labour force. This trend could not continue indefinitely.*

Our experience under the sterling link seemed to confirm these theories. Over the long-run, Irish inflation had in fact diverged very little from British inflation, and early econometric studies supported the view that inflation was transmitted to Ireland from abroad, as suggested in the SOE model. Oddly enough none of the papers published during this period actually estimated PPP, as for example specified in equation (1). The estimated equations inevitably included a wage or productivity variable. The basic conclusion, however, was that Irish inflation was more or less equal to UK inflation.[12]

However, it is one thing for there to be a strong link between prices in two countries such as Ireland and Britain, with a long tradition of close economic and financial links, but another to believe that if we transferred our exchange rate commitment from sterling to the EMS, we would almost automatically enjoy the benefits of German rates of inflation. Yet this was implicit in our thinking in 1979 and indeed was made explicit in one commentary written at that time:

... so long as we maintain a fixed exchange rate with any major country with which there is relatively free trade, we will tend in the long-run to have that country's rate of inflation. The reasoning amounts to little more than recognising that markets do exist.[13]

However, not everyone accepted this view of the causes of inflation. During the 1960s and into the 1970s some economists maintained that, although much of our inflation was imported, a significant proportion was still "our own fault". For example, the Central Bank commented in its 1973-74 Annual Report:

It is a fallacy, even for the open Irish economy, that inflation is due more to external than to internal causes and that it is beyond our power to curb or control it ... The fact is ... that even during 1973 when basic commodity and energy prices soared spectacularly and food prices continued to rise, imported inflation accounted directly for no more than half the rise in Irish retail prices ... [14]

An input-output study of the causes of inflation published in 1970 concluded that "wage-push seems to be the major cause of inflation since 1966". [15] Moreover recent empirical evidence does not support PPP theory. Leddin (1988) tested for absolute PPP using quarterly data for both consumer and manufacturing output prices and found that *in the short-run* PPP theory did not hold between Ireland and the UK and Ireland and Germany. PPP was found not to hold between Ireland and Britain even during the sterling link period. [16] This finding that PPP does not hold in the short-run is supported by the findings in Callan and Fitzgerald (1989). [17] These authors go a step further and test whether or not PPP holds in the long-run. They find that long-run PPP did hold between 1979-87 (i.e. the post-EMS entry period) but not between 1976-87. The results also indicate that Irish prices respond much more slowly to changes in the exchange rate than they do to changes in foreign prices. Moreover, the findings indicate that a change took place in the pricing behaviour of Irish firms after 1979 and that changes in German prices now have a stronger effect on Irish prices that the trade-weight would suggest. Changes in German and UK prices now appear to have an equal influence on Irish prices. Returning to the issue of whether or not PPP holds in the long-run, Thom (1989) tests if there is a long-run equilibrium between the nominal exchange rate and the foreign/domestic price ratio. [18] Using the co-integration technique, the results suggest that PPP did not hold between Ireland and its main trading partners, namely, the UK, Germany and the US (the results are not decisive in the case of Germany). In summary, the consensus at this point in time seems to be that short-run PPP does not hold. While the jury is still out on the question of whether or not PPP holds in the long-run, the evidence seems to marginally favour the prosecution, that is it does not hold. Finally, economists working in the Central Bank of Ireland have produced the following apportionment of the blame for Irish inflation, 1977 to 1985: foreign inflation 52%, domestic demand 26%, exchange rate movements 9%, indirect taxes 3% and "drift" 9%. [19]

As we document in the next section, in the light of our experience since 1979, no-one can now claim that the adjustment of domestic prices to international influences is smooth or automatic.

# 10 Ireland's Experience in the EMS

The actual outcome during our first ten years of membership of the ERM contained many surprises, and was much more complicated than was anticipated at the time we decided to join. We shall summarise this experience under a number of different headings.

Distribution of Imports by Area

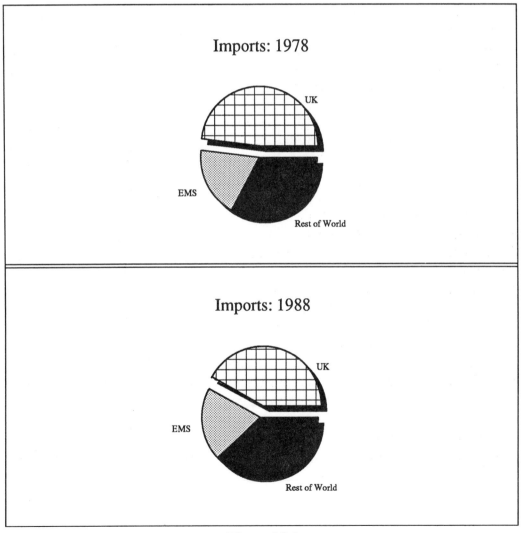

Figure 10.1

# The pattern of trade

It was expected that following the stabilising of our exchange rates with European countries, there would be a significant shift in the pattern of our trade away from Britain towards these countries. In fact, as may be seen from Figure 10.1 and Figure 10.2, the UK has remained surprisingly dominant in both our import and our export markets. After ten years of participation in the narrow band of the EMS, the other participants still account for only 20% of our imports and 33% of our exports. It is

Distribution of Exports by Area

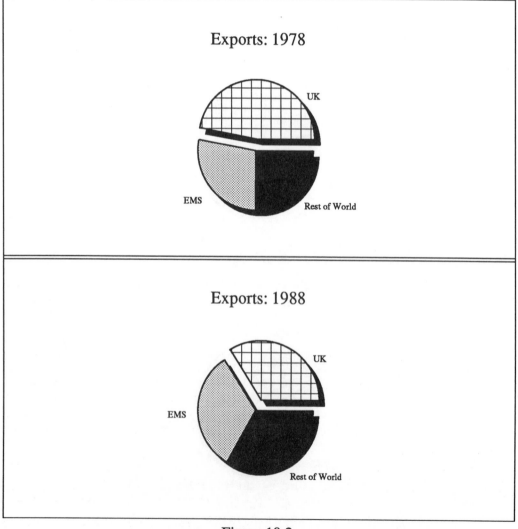

Figure 10.2

246

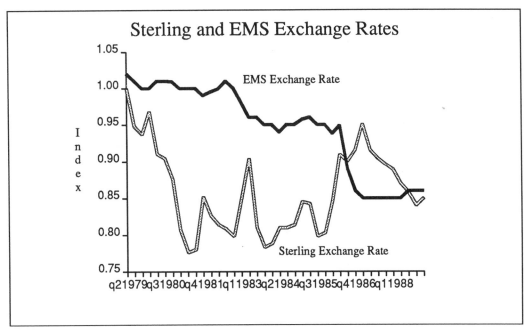

## Sterling and EMS Exchange Rates

Figure 10.3

most unusual for a country to peg its currency to the currencies of a group that accounts for such a small proportion of its trade.

## Nominal exchange rates

In Figure 10.3 we show the behaviour of Ireland's nominal exchange rates against (a) the narrow band EMS currencies and (b) sterling since 1979. Apart from the devaluations in 1983 and 1986, it is striking how stable the Irish pound has been against the narrow band EMS currencies. In fact, during the first four years of the system's operation, the Irish pound was the most stable currency in it. However, as a consequence of the 1983 and 1986 devaluations the Irish pound is now about 15% below its 1979, quarter 1, value relative to these currencies. It is worth one whole DM (or 28%) less than it was at the start of the EMS. Clearly, the decision to join the ERM has not been interpreted by the Irish authorities as committing us to a rigid peg. This has made it easier for us to remain in the system, and it also accounts for some of the divergences between our expectations of the benefits of membership and the out-come.

The sterling/Irish pound exchange rate has been much more erratic than the EMS rate. This reflects the volatility of sterling relative to the EMS. The strength of sterling between January 1979 and January 1981 coincided with the period of exceptional stability of the Irish pound in the EMS. When sterling depreciated during 1982 and 1983, pressure to devalue the Irish pound built up and we availed of the opportunity of the March 1983 realignment to bring our pound back to a more sustainable level relative to sterling by devaluing within the EMS. Similarly, the sterling/Irish pound exchange rate rose from 0.79 in February 1985 to 0.95 in July 1986. At the same time the dollar was falling relative to the Irish pound. Our trade-weighted exchange rate Index rose by 12% over this interval. It was against this background, and growing anxiety about our loss of competitiveness in the British market in particular, that the decision was taken to devalue unilaterally in August 1986.

Thus, our commitment to a "hard currency peg" in 1979 has had some curious results. The value of our pound fell by 25% relative to sterling in the first two years, and we have deliberately tried to keep it under 0.90p ever since. The overall external value of our currency is now some 18% lower than it was in 1979.

## Real exchange rates

Nominal exchange rates adjusted for inflation differentials reveal the trend in real exchange rates. If PPP held rigidly, these rates would be stable but, as we have seen, this has not been true for the major currencies of the world throughout the 1970s and 1980s. An informative way of studying the behaviour of real exchange rates is to plot the nominal exchange rate and the ratio of foreign to domestic prices on the same diagram. To see this note that equation (1) above can be re-arranged as:

(5)  $E = P_{uk}/P_{irl}$

We can plot the exchange rate, E, and the price ratio, $P_{uk}/P_{irl}$. If these two lines move together, then the real exchange rate is constant. If $P_{irl}$ increases faster than $P_{uk}$, the price ratio line slopes downwards. The exchange rate should now fall by an equal amount to compensate for the higher $P_{irl}$. If this does not happen there is a loss of competitiveness. Hence if the E line lies above the $P_{uk}/P_{irl}$ line there is a loss of competitiveness. Conversely, if the E line lies below the $P_{uk}/P_{irl}$ line there is a gain in competitiveness.

*Note:*
*A loss of competitiveness means that the real exchange rate is rising and a gain in competitiveness means that the real exchange rate is falling.*

It may be seen from Figure 10.4 that during the first two years of the EMS we gained an enormous competitive advantage relative to sterling. However, this was eroded between 1981 and 1983 and again in 1986-87. The strength of sterling between 1987 and early 1989 widened the gap in our favour before sterling again weakened late in 1989. Figure 10.6 shows that, relative to the DM, since 1980 our exchange rate has fallen steadily, but not by enough to offset the higher inflation in

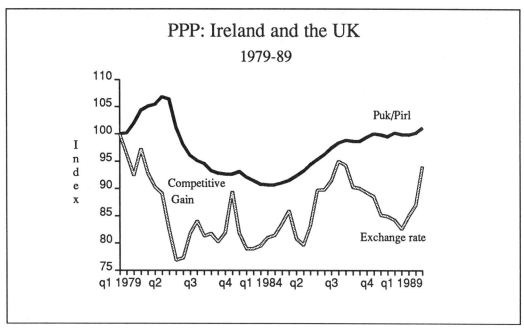

## PPP: Ireland and the UK
### 1979-89

Figure 10.4

Ireland than in Germany. There has therefore been some loss of competitiveness relative to the DM, with the gap narrowing sharply at the devaluations of 1983 and 1986.

*Note:*
*The price lines in Figures 10.4 and 10.5 use wholesale or manufacturers' output prices. Other indices could have been used. The consumer price index is influenced by indirect tax changes and includes the prices of many non-traded goods and services. (However, it is wrong to ignore these prices completely: they affect the competitiveness of tourism, for example, which is an important component of our international trade. They also enter into the cost of traded goods.) Another possibility would be to use an index of wages, as a measure of the cost of the main component of domestic value added. This would show much the same picture as that shown by wholesale prices. Finally, some would argue that unit labour costs are the best measure, but for reasons discussed below, we believe they can be quite misleading in an Irish context.*

If the Irish authorities had simply allowed our pound to fall by the excess of our inflation rate over Germany's, we would in effect have been operating a "crawling peg". This would have meant that there was no attempt to use the discipline implied by membership of the ERM to moderate our rate of inflation. As may be seen from Figure 10.5, we have not done this. Our exchange rate policy has been "non-accommodating" in the sense that we have been prepared to suffer some loss of competitiveness relative to the DM. This acts as an anti-inflationary

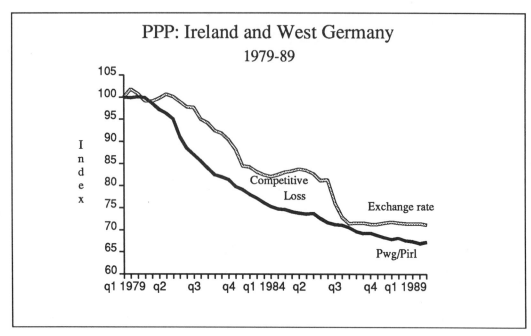

Figure 10.5

discipline and helps put us on a virtuous circle where an appreciating real exchange rate leads to lower inflation, which in turn makes it easier to maintain a high exchange rate.

If PPP held in the mechanistic way suggested by some commentators in 1979, the two lines in Figures 10.4 and 10.5 would never have diverged. In fact the divergence between them over the ten years of the EMS has not shown a tendency to widen, except for fairly brief periods of time, at the end of which they converge again. Some interpret this as evidence that PPP is in fact working. But we should be careful to ask why this tendency is evident. It is quite clear that in 1986, for example, it represents the effect of the decision to devalue the Irish pound. This is shown by the sharp fall in the exchange rate line in Figure 10.5. This is not the train of events that the proponents of EMS membership suggested would happen. They believed that the price ratio line would tend to move towards the exchange rate line, due to the rapid feed-through of German inflation into Irish inflation. In other words, in 1986 Irish inflation should have come to a halt under the influence of our rising exchange rate, and the price line should have risen to meet the exchange rate line. This was not happened and the resultant loss of competitiveness forced the authorities to devalue. The two lines moved closer together, but this hardly vindicates the reverse PPP theory of inflation!

*Note:*

*Earlier we mentioned that PPP could be used to predict exchange rate movements. Figures 10.4 and*

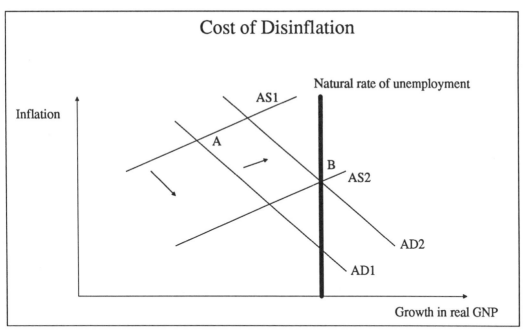

Figure 10.6

10.5 indicate that Ireland has gained in competitiveness relative to the UK and lost competitiveness relative to Germany. The implication is that the UK has lost competitiveness relative to Germany. PPP theory predicted that the DM/sterling exchange rate would depreciate, as indeed happened in late 1989.

# The EMS and the cost of disinflation

Earlier we mentioned that the EMS could be viewed as a powerful disinflation device. If firms and workers believed that Ireland's commitment to the EMS was credible, wage and price expectations would be revised downwards and low inflation would be combined with low unemployment. The more credible our EMS commitment, the quicker expectations would be revised downwards and the lower the cost of disinflation in terms of lost output and employment.[20]

*Note:*
*In addition to price and wage convergence it was also expected that Irish interest rates would converge to German rates. We defer a discussion of this aspect of Ireland's EMS experience until Chapter 12. This enables us to discuss in greater detail some of the theoretical issues underlining interest rates.*

To see why the EMS might confer a "credibility bonus" on the Irish economy consider the AS/AD model given in Figure 10.6. It will be recalled from Chapter 8 that the location or position of the AD curve depends, in part, on government expenditure, the money supply and net exports (exports minus imports). An expansionary fiscal or monetary policy or an increase in net exports shifts the AD curve up to the right and vice versa. The position of the AS curve depends in large part on the cost of producing output. An increase in the price of raw materials, wages or a fall in productivity will shift the AS curve upwards to the left and vice versa.

Suppose that point A in Figure 10.6 represents the average position of the Irish economy in the 1970s. At this point, relatively high inflation was combined with a slow growth rate in real GNP and an unemployment rate above the natural rate of unemployment. If Ireland's commitment to the EMS had been credible, prices and nominal wage rates (and indeed interest rates) would have converged to the German level. The reason for this is that if Irish employers and workers had been convinced that the DM/Irish pound exchange rate would have remained fixed *then it follows from PPP theory* that Irish prices would have converged to the German price level. If Irish prices had fallen then the way would have been open for a fall in nominal wages.

The decrease in nominal wages is reflected in Figure 10.6 as a movement down to the right of the AS curve. Inflation falls along the vertical axis and the growth rate in real GNP increases along the horizontal axis. There is however a further dimension to this process. The fall in inflation and wage rates should improve the competitive position of Irish firms on international markets particularly against non-EMS countries. This improvement in competitiveness should increase net exports. In other words, the fall in prices and wages should lead to a "crowding-in" of net exports. In Figure 10.6, the AD curve shifts up to the right. With the AS curve moving down to the right and the AD curve shifting upwards, the economy moves quickly towards a point such as B where low inflation is combined with a fast growth rate in real GNP and unemployment converges to the natural rate of unemployment.

The more credible Ireland's commitment to the EMS the faster the movement from the point A to the point B in Figure 10.6 and the lower the cost of disinflation. Compare this policy with, for example, the deflationary fiscal and monetary policy implemented in the UK in the late 1970s. In terms of Figure 10.6, UK economic policy would be illustrated as a shift down to the left of the AD1 curve (not shown). As we discussed in section 10.8 and in Chapter 8, the resulting fall in output and the increase in unemployment would lead to lower wage demands and eventually the AS curve would move down to the right. The economy would move towards the natural rate of unemployment but not before the economy experienced a prolonged recession which involved considerable costs in the form of lost output and an increase in unemployment. In contrast, the EMS policy adopted by the Irish government would achieve the same result, namely full employment, but would involve lower disinflation costs.

While the EMS policy seemed in theory to be very attractive the outcome, at least in the period 1979-87, was more or less the opposite to what was expected. It would appear that Ireland's EMS commitment was *not* credible due in large part to the expansionary fiscal policies pursued by successive governments in the late 1970s and early 1980s. As we discussed in Chapters 3 and 4, during this period there was a significant increase in the EBR and in the debt/GNP ratio and a very large deficit on the current account of the balance of payments. This expansionary fiscal policy was in contrast to the conservative policies pursued in Germany and therefore was not consistent with a fixed DM/Irish pound exchange rate. The lack of credibility in Ireland's EMS commitment is evident from the failure of wages, prices and interest rates to converge to German levels. First, Table 10.6 shows that between 1979 and 1987, average hourly earnings in Ireland increased by 150% compared to a 40% increase in West Germany. (We confine our analysis to the period up to 1987 for reasons that will become clear towards the end of this section.)

*Table 10.6*
**Average hourly earnings**

| Year | Ireland | UK | US | Germany | Main trading partners |
|------|---------|-----|-----|---------|-----------------------|
| 1979 | 100 | 100 | 100 | 100 | 100 |
| 1987 | 252 | 223 | 148 | 140 | 193 |

*Source*: Central Bank of Ireland, *Quarterly Bulletin*

Secondly, Irish prices did not converge to the German level. We saw, for example, in Figure 10.5 that the German/Irish price ratio consistently fell over the period 1979 to 1987. Thirdly, Irish interest rates did not converge to German interest rates. We discuss this aspect to the Irish experience in the EMS in Chapter 12. A glance at Figure 12.2 will, however, indicate the extent of the interest rate differential.

With regard to competitiveness, price inflation in Ireland did decrease between 1979 and 1987 but this did not result in any gain in competitiveness as inflation fell by an even greater amount in other countries. Because the nominal exchange rate was tied in the EMS (with the exception of 1983 and 1986 devaluations) and Irish wage and price inflation remained higher than elsewhere, the *real* exchange rate appreciated. Figure 9.6 in Chapter 9, for example, shows that the real trade-weighted exchange rate index for Ireland appreciated by approximately 12% between 1979-87. As a result there was no "crowding-in" of net exports.

In terms of the AS/AD model given in Figure 10.6, the increase in wage rates and the appreciation of the real exchange rate, could be illustrated as a shift to the left of both the AS and AD curves. In this case the Irish economy would experience the worst of all worlds as an increase in inflation would be combined with a fall in the growth rate in real GNP and an increase in unemployment. The EMS policy which seemed so attractive in 1979 had turned badly wrong. The commitment to the EMS resulted in real exchange rate over-valuation and this made the cost of disinflation very expensive in terms of lost output and employment. Commenting on Ireland's experience in the EMS Dornbusch (1988)[21] concludes:

A policy that uses a fixed exchange rate to disinflate and that requires at the same time fiscal consolidation can easily run into difficulties. The fixed exchange rate policy stands in the way of a gain in competitiveness and in fact easily becomes a policy of over-valuation. The over-valued currency then needs to be defended by high real interest rates. The combination of budget cutting, high real interest rates and an overly strong currency creates unemployment at each score. There is no offsetting crowding-in mechanism unless money wages are strongly flexible downwards or productivity growth is high. Neither was the case in Ireland and hence the country is locked into a high unemployment and high debt trap. (Dornbusch, 1988, p. 45.)

With regard to the above discussion we wish to emphasise that we are presenting one side of a debate on Ireland's experience in the EMS and that the evidence to-date is not unanimous. For example, Kremers (1989) presents econometric evidence which indicates that wage and price expectations *did* adjust to the new exchange rate policy within the EMS and that this adjustment took place in different stages in the 1980s.[22] There are also a number of specific issues on which there is little agreement. For example, if average hourly earnings are adjusted for productivity and the exchange rate, it can be shown that Ireland experienced a *gain* in competitiveness relative to Germany and the EMS countries over the period 1979 to 1987. However it can be argued that capital intensive multi-national companies setting up in Ireland have exaggerated the productivity data and that if hi-tech industries are excluded Ireland has experienced a loss of competitiveness relative to the EMS countries. We discuss this point in detail in the next section. Whatever the ins and outs in this issue it is important to bear in mind that prices and wages did not converge to German levels as was envisaged at the time of EMS entry.

We made the point of confining our discussion to the period 1979-87 because it is very possible that the economy only turned around after 1987. Since 1987 there has been a dramatic improvement in the Irish economy as cuts in government expenditure (rather than tax increases) led to a significant fall in the EBR and a stabilisation of the debt/GNP ratio. The improvement in the government finances has been associated with a fall in both prices and wages and, as we will see in Chapter 12, with a decrease in the Irish, German interest rate differential. The growth rate in real output has increased and there has been a marginal reduction in the unemployment rate.[23] Although it is still to early too derive any firm conclusions, it could well be that Ireland began to experience the benefits of EMS membership only after 1987 when the government was seen to redress the fiscal imbalances. If this is the case, the benefits of EMS entry were delayed for over eight years largly because of the failure of successive governments to adopt policies consistent with the EMS commitment.

Ireland's experience in the EMS continues to raise interesting issues and the on going debate will continue to provide valuable insights on why Ireland's unemployment rate is so high. The discussion in this section points to problems in the labour market and in exchange rate over-valuation. We discussed the Irish labour market in Chapter 7. We discuss the effectiveness of devaluation in improving competitiveness in Chapter 11.

# 0.11 Competitiveness: A Digression

We have tended to use the phrases "real exchange rates" and "competitiveness" to refer to the same phenomenon. However, there are a number of issues relating to the measurement of competitiveness that need to be discussed explicitly. First, "competitiveness" can be used in a wide sense to mean all the characteristics of Irish goods and services that make them good (or bad) value on international markets. Viewed from this perspective, price competitiveness is only one, and not perhaps the most important, dimension of competitiveness. But the important thing about price competitiveness is that it can change quite dramatically over relatively short periods of time, especially in a period of widely fluctuating exchange rates. A ten or fifteen percent movement in the sterling/Irish pound exchange rate within a year can clearly have a crucial impact on the profitability of, for example, the Irish subsidiary of a British food or clothing firm. It is unlikely that any other component of competitiveness in the broader sense would vary so widely so quickly.

The measurement of cost and price competitiveness raises several issues. Firms that lose competitiveness may go out of business and disappear from the statistics. The demise of these firms will therefore boost productivity. During the 1980s there was a 25% decline in employment in Irish manufacturing industry. Whole sectors virtually disappeared and these tended to be the most labour-intensive ones. At the other extreme, a small number of sectors (pharmaceuticals, various electronic engineering industries and some food processing sectors) recorded exceptional growth in output without much increase in employment. These developments have together led to such an increase in labour productivity that unit labour costs, expressed in a common currency, fell by 33% relative to those of our main trading partners between 1978 and 1988. In other words, by this standard there was an enormous gain in competitiveness. Table 10.7 shows that between 1979 and 1987 there was a considerable gain in competitiveness against the UK, the US and Germany and a smaller gain against the EMS average.

*Table 10.7*

**Real exchange rate based on unit labour costs: Index, 1979=100**

| Year | UK | US | Germany | EMS average |
|------|------|------|---------|-------------|
| *Irish pound real exchange rates based on unit costs* | | | | |
| 1979 | 100.0 | 100.0 | 100.0 | 100.0 |
| 1987 | 81.0 | 73.0 | 80.0 | 85.0 |
| *Irish pound real exchange rates based on unit costs excluding certain "hi-tech" industries* | | | | |
| 1979 | 100.0 | 100.0 | 100.0 | 100.0 |
| 1987 | 98.0 | 89.0 | 97.0 | 103.0 |

*Source:* Patrick Massey,"Exchange Rates and Competitiveness", *Quarterly Economic Commentary*, October 1988, p. 45-57
*Note*: A fall in the real exchange rate implies a competitive gain

However, if the high growth industrial sectors which we referred to above are excluded, then the data relating to unit labour costs expressed in a common currency is very different. Table 10.7 shows that when the "hi-tech" industries are excluded, the 19% gain in competitiveness against the UK is reduced to 2%. The 27% gain against the US is reduced to 11% and the 20% gain against Germany is reduced to 3%. The 15% gain in competitiveness against the EMS countries now works out as a loss in competitiveness.

# 10.12 Conclusion

We have learned from ten years' experience as full members of the EMS that membership does not, of itself, guarantee that our rate of inflation or interest rates will converge to the level prevailing in Germany. We have a much more sophisticated understanding now of the working of the purchasing power parity theory, and its limitations as an explanation of inflation, than we did in 1979. We are also conscious now, in a manner that was not true in 1979, of the importance of expectations about the future course of exchange rates, and how these in turn depend on markets' perceptions of domestic economic policies. The hoped-for benefits of EMS membership only began to flow when Irish economic policy became consistent with maintaining our commitment not to devalue relative to the low-inflation currencies in the EMS. Once this was the case, membership of the ERM became credible and the convergence that had been expected much earlier began to occur.

Looking forward to the 1990s, it is clear that there will be further developments on the road to full EMU in Europe. Ireland has, in effect, already surrendered control over its money supply by joining the EMS. (We never controlled it anyway under the sterling link, but now we have to observe the discipline of German, rather than British, monetary policy.) We have also in effect renounced the use of the rate of exchange as an instrument of economic policy. These restrictions on our economic policy-making are likely to become more formalised as the trend towards closer economic integration in Europe continues. We shall continue to argue that we require additional financial aid from the richer countries of Europe to assist us in adjusting to the new environment, but the ultimate justification for going along with these changes is that the potential benefit from using the instruments we are renouncing is small compared to that which will follow from the stable macroeconomic environment we hope to enjoy in the Europe of the 1990s.

In this chapter we have:

- Outlined the history of international financial systems such as the gold standard, Bretton Woods Agreements, the European Snake and the EMS

- Explained the background to the Irish decision to join the EMS even at the price of breaking the sterling link. Examined in detail Ireland's experience as a full member of the ERM of the EMS since 1979 . We emphasised that credible commitment to a system of fixed exchange rates involves a sacrifice of autonomy of economic policy-making

- Further progress towards European Economic and Monetary Union is likely to occur during the 1990s. This will involve a further reduction in the autonomy of Irish economic policy-making. In return for this, we can look forward to the benefits of a more stable macroeconomic environment.

Notes
1 M. Fullerton, "Emus". in Douglas Stewart (ed.), *Poetry in Australia*, Vol. 1, University of California Press, 1965, p. 193.

2. The National Economic and Social Council (NESC) in its recent report *Ireland in the European Community: Performance, Prospects and Strategy*, No. 88, August, 1989, discuss in great detail (five hundred and fifty seven pages) Ireland's prospects in an integrated market. The report points to economic gains from market integration. For example, firms will benefit from economies of scale and a more competitive environment should lower costs and increase efficiency. However,

it is argued that the gains from market integration are unlikely to be evenly distributed so that regional divergence rather than regional convergence would take place. The report evaluates a number of different alternatives for a future Europe including Customs Union, Common Market and European Monetary Union (EMU) and concludes that EMU would be the superior arrangement. It is suggested that Ireland is much more likely to achieve economic convergence with the rest of Europe through EMU than through our own productive efforts. However, the EMU system envisaged by NESC includes a substantial Community budget which would transfer resources to the regions and bring about regional convergence. Hence, the report is in favour of EMU so long as there is a provision in the form of a Community budget for regional redistribution. Without this provision, the NESC recommendation for full blown EMU largely falls away.

3. J. Fels, "The European Monetary System 1979-1987: Why has it worked?" *Intereconomics*, September/October, 1987, p.219. See also P. De Grauwe, "International Trade and Economic Growth in the European monetary System", Paper presented to the European Economics Association, Vienna, Austria, 1986.

4. F. Giavazzi, "The European Monetary System: Lessons from Europe and Perspectives in Europe", *The Economic and Social Review*, Vol. 20, No. 2, January 1989, p. 73-90.

5. H.M.S.O., "The European Monetary System", Cmnd. 7405, 1978.

6. C. Murray , "The European Monetary System: Implications for Ireland", Central Bank of Ireland, *Annual Report*, 1979.

7. C. McCarthy, "The European Monetary System and Irish Macroeconomic Policy", Central Bank of Ireland, *Annual Report*, 1979, p. 102-21.

8. For a detailed account of PPP theory see, R. Dornbusch, "Purchasing Power Parity", *The New Palgrave: A Dictionary of Economics*, J. Eatwell, M. Milgate and P. Newman (eds), Macmillan Press, 1987.

9. If we are to empirically estimate PPP, equation (1), the price indexes used in both countries should be very similar. That is, the goods and the associated weights used to compile the index should be identical in different countries. If the indexes are not the same then the "law of one price" looses its logic. But even then we can fall back on the hypothesis of money neutrality. This hypothesis states that an increase in the money supply will lead to an equal increase in the price level (including a depreciation of the exchange rate) and real variables will remain unchanged. Changes in the money supply have a neutral effect on the real economy. Hence given a monetary disturbance, an increase in the price level will be matched by an equal depreciation of the exchange rate and PPP will hold. We can empirically evaluate this hypothesis by using any price index including a price index for non-traded goods. We no longer have to be concerned about how the price index was compiled.

10. The choice of base year is of some importance. Refer back to Figure 9.5 in Chapter 9 and consider the trend in the $/IR£ real exchange rate. Between 1970 and 1989 the exchange rate has risen. However, between 1979 and 1989 there has been little change. This means that if 1970 is used as the base year the Irish pound is "over-valued". If 1979 is used as the base year the current exchange rate is "about right". Because of the choice of base year (and for other reasons), PPP does not provide a simple benchmark for the "true" value of the exchange rate.

11. For a discussion see, R. Dornbusch, "Exchange Rate Economics: 1986", *Economic Journal*, March 1987. The reasons for divergences from PPP are however difficult to identify. See for example,

258

I. Kravis, and R. Lipsey, *Towards an Explanation of National Price Levels*, Princeton Studies in International Finance, No. 52, Princeton University Press, 1983. L. Officer, *Purchasing Power Parity and Exchange Rates*, JAI Press, Greenwich, Conn. 1984.

12. Early empirical evidence on the inflation process is given in P.T. Geary, "World Prices and the Inflationary Process in a Small Open Economy: the Case of Ireland", *The Economic and Social Review*, Vol. 7, No. 4, p. 391-400, July, 1976. P.T. Geary, "Lags in the Transmission of Inflation: Some Preliminary Estimates", *The Economic and Social Review*, Vol. 7, No. 4, p. 383-389, July, 1976. P.T. Geary, and C. McCarthy, "Wage and Price Determination in a Labour Exporting Economy: The Case of Ireland", *European Economic Review*, Vol. 8, No. 3, p. 219-234, 1976. J. Bradley, "Lags in the Transmission of Inflation", *The Economic and Social Review*, Vol. 8, p. 149-154, 1977.

13. D.A.G. Norton, *Economic Analysis for an Open Economy: Ireland*, Dublin: The Irish Management Institute, 1980, p. 190.

14. This quote was cited in P.T. Geary, "Ireland's Policy Options", in *European Monetary Union and the Sterling Link*, Irish Council of the European Movement, Dublin, 1975.

15. R.C. Geary, E.W. Henry and J.L. Pratschke, "The Recent Price Trend in Ireland", *The Economic and Social Review*, April 1970, p. 345-356.

16. A. Leddin, "Interest and Price Parity: The Irish Experience in the European Monetary System", Paper presented at the Central Bank of Ireland, June, 1988.

17. T. Callan and J. FitzGerald, "Price Determination in Ireland: Effects of Changes in Exchange Rates and Exchange Rate Regimes", *The Economic and Social Review*, January, p. 165-188, 1989.

18. R. Thom, "Real Exchange Rates, Co-Integration and Purchasing Power Parity: Irish Experience in the EMS", *The Economic and Social Review*, January, p. 147-163, 1989.

19. T. O'Connell and J. Frain, "Inflation and Exchange Rates: A Further Empirical Analysis", Central Bank of Ireland, Research Paper 1/RT/89, April 1989.

20. One problem in identifying an EMS "credibility bonus" is that since 1979 inflation rates have fallen in most industrialised countries. How then do we determine whether or not the EMS has conferred any special benefits to member countries? Dornbusch (1988) examines different measures of the cost of disinflation. One measure is the *sacrifice ratio*, defined as the number of extra unemployment years for a one per cent reduction in inflation. Compared to non-EMS countries, the sacrifice ratio is high for EMS countries and in particular for Ireland, Germany and the Netherlands. Taken in conjunction with other evidence, Dornbusch concludes that the EMS does not confer any special disinflation benefit to member countries. See R. Dornbusch, *Credibility, Debt and Unemployment: Ireland's Failed Stabilization Policy*, National Bureau of Economic Research, Working Paper, WP/89/36, April, 1988, p. 32-33).

21. Dornbusch, *op. cit.*

22. J.M. Kremers, *Gaining Policy Credibility in the EMS: The Case of Ireland*, International Monetary Fund, Working Paper, wp/89/36, April, 1989, See also F. Giavazzi and A. Giovannini, *Limiting Exchange Rate Flexibility: The European Monetary System*, MIT Press, Cambridge, Mass., 1989.

23. See for example, D. McAleese, "Ireland-The Economy Is Doing So Well, There Is Talk Of An Irish Miracle", *Europe - Magazine of the European Community*, January/February, 1989.

Chapter 11

# Fiscal, Monetary and Exchange Rate Policy in an Open Economy

## 11.1 Introduction

In Chapter 6 we developed the IS/LM model in the context of a closed economy. We begin this chapter by expanding the IS/LM model to include the balance of payments and the exchange rate. We then use this framework to examine the effect of fiscal and monetary policy on output under both fixed and flexible exchange rates. The discussion differs fundamentally from the earlier closed economy analysis of Chapter 6 in that the emphasis is on the effect of fiscal and monetary policy on the external reserves and the exchange rate and how this in turn impacts back on output and employment in the domestic economy.

Through out this chapter our concern is with how the policy maker can achieve simultaneously both full employment (*internal balance*) and balance of payments equilibrium (*external balance*) in an open economy. We highlight policy dilemmas that can arise due to conflicts between these objectives and suggest possible solutions. The final section of the chapter examine devaluation as a policy instrument and, in particular,we discuss the effectiveness of devaluation as a means of improving competitiveness and increasing output and employment in the Irish economy.

## 11.2 The IS/LM Model and the Balance of Payments

In Figure 11.1 we reproduce the IS/LM diagram developed in Chapter 6. The IS curve shows the GNP and interest rate combinations that give equilibrium in the goods and services market. The LM curve, on the other hand, shows the combinations of GNP and the interest rate that give money market equilibrium. At the point A in the diagram, the two curves intersect and there is a simultaneous

260

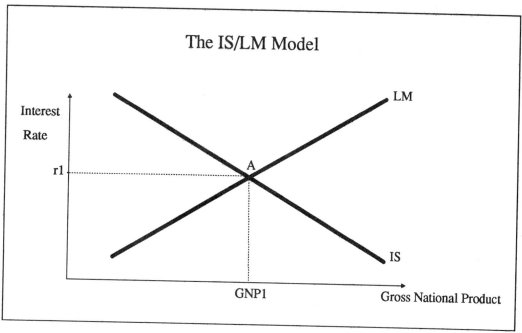

The IS/LM Model

Figure 11.1

equilibrium in both the goods and money markets. It will be recalled from Chapter 6 that changes in government expenditure or taxation (fiscal policy) are reflected in movements of the IS curve whereas changes in the money supply (monetary policy) are reflected in movements of the LM curve. An expansionary fiscal policy, for example, shifts the IS curve to the right and an expansionary monetary policy shifts the LM curve to the right.

The IS/LM model given in Figure 11.1 was developed for a closed economy and does not allow for the effect of fiscal or monetary policy on the balance of payments or the exchange rate. We now incorporate the balance of payments so that the model can be used for policy analysis in an open economy.

In Figure 11.2 we draw a reference line denoted as BP = 0 which shows the combinations of GNP and the interest rate which give balance of payments equilibrium. By balance of payments equilibrium is meant a situation where the Central Bank does not have to intervene in the foreign exchange market to stabilise the exchange rate. In other words, official intervention in the foreign exchange market is zero. If the economy is on the BP = 0 line, point A or B in the diagram for example, the balance of payments is in equilibrium.

To see why the BP = 0 line slopes upward, note that an increase in the interest rate on the vertical axis and an increase in GNP on the horizontal axis have opposing effects on the balance of payments. Consider first the effect of an increase in the interest rate on the balance of payments. If the exchange rate is fixed, an increase in domestic interest rates, relative to "world" interest rates, leads to a capital inflow

261

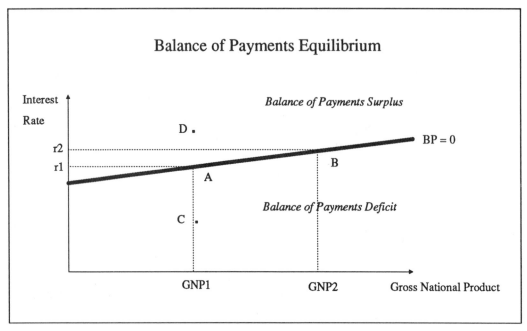

Figure 11.2

and therefore a surplus on the capital account of the balance of payments. The reason is that investors move funds to the country that offers the best return (highest interest rate). Conversely, a fall in domestic interest rates (relative to world interest rates) leads to a capital outflow and a capital account deficit.

In short:

1. $\uparrow r$ (relative to the "world" interest rate) $\rightarrow$ $\uparrow$ capital inflows $\rightarrow$ surplus on the capital account of the balance of payments.

*Note:*

*Capital flows largely consist of "internationally mobile funds" which can be moved by investors from country to country to take advantage of interest rate differentials. By the "world" interest rate we mean interest rates in the main industrial countries. In the Irish case, interest rates in the UK, Germany and the US are particularly relevant.*

Consider now how an increase in GNP on the horizontal axis affects the balance of payments. An increase in GNP leads to an increase in imports via the marginal propensity to import (MPM) and this results in a deficit on the current account of the balance of payments. Conversely, a decrease in GNP leads to a fall in imports and a current account surplus.

262

In short:

2. ↑ GNP → ↑ M → deficit on the current account of the balance of payments.

The BP = 0 line is drawn so that these opposing effects cancel and the overall balance of payments remains in equilibrium. In Figure 11.2, as the economy moves from point A to point B, the interest rate increases from r1 to r2 on the vertical axis and this leads to a capital account surplus. In contrast, the increase in GNP from GNP1 to GNP2 on the horizontal axis leads to a current account deficit. The BP = 0 line is drawn so that the positive effect of higher interest rates on the balance of payments offsets the negative GNP effect and the balance of payments remains in equilibrium.

If the economy is above the BP = 0 line, say at a point such as D in the diagram, there will be a balance of payments surplus. At the point D the interest rate is higher than necessary to give a balance of payments equilibrium and there is therefore a surplus. In contrast, if the economy is below the BP = 0 line, at the point C for example, there is a balance of payments deficit. In this case, the interest rate is lower than the equilibrium rate and there is an overall deficit.

The BP = 0 line is drawn for a given level of exports and imports, "world" interest rates and a fixed exchange rate. The *location* of the BP = 0 line will therefore change if any of these variables changes. An increase in exports, a fall in imports (not brought about by a change in GNP), a fall in world interest rates or an exchange rate depreciation will shift the BP = 0 line downwards to the right. Conversely, a fall in exports, a rise in imports (not due to GNP changes), an increase in world interest rates or an exchange rate appreciation, shifts the BP = 0 line upwards to the left.

The *slope* of the BP = 0 line depends on the (1) the *degree of capital mobility* and on (2) the *marginal propensity to import* (MPM). If there is a high degree of capital mobility (capital flows are very sensitive to interest differentials) then the BP line will be relatively flat. Only a small change in the interest rate (relative to the world rate) on the vertical axis is necessary to compensate for a given change in GNP on the horizontal axis. If there is *perfect capital mobility*, the BP = 0 line will be horizontal. A small change in the domestic interest rate leads to unlimited capital inflows or outflows. In this case, there is only one interest rate, the world rate, consistent with balance of payments equilibrium. On the other hand, if there is *imperfect capital mobility* (capital flows are relatively insensitive to interest rate differentials) because of, say, exchange controls, the BP = 0 line will be relatively steep. A large change in interest rates on the vertical axis is necessary to compensate for a given increase in GNP on the horizontal axis.

The larger the marginal propensity to import (MPM) the steeper will be the BP = 0 line. A large MPM means that a given increase in GNP on the horizontal axis will lead to a relatively large increase in imports. Interest rates will have to increase accordingly to compensate. Conversely, the lower the marginal propensity to import the flatter will be the BP = 0 line.

In general:

If there is a *high* degree of capital mobility and the MPM is *small* then the BP line will be relatively flat.

If there is a *low* degree of capital mobility and the MPM is *large* then the BP line will be relatively steep.

At the present time the Irish economy is probably best described by a horizontal BP = 0 line. This is because there is near perfect capital mobility between Ireland and the rest of the world. It is true that the Irish MPM is relatively large but the effect of this on the current account is likely to be completely dominated by the effect of an incipient rise in interest rates on the capital account. A horizontal BP = 0 line was certainly the case in Ireland up to 1979 when the Irish pound was rigidly fixed to sterling and capital could move freely between Ireland and the UK. Between December 1978 and December 1988 exchange controls restricted capital movements between Ireland and other countries and it is possible that during this period the BP = 0 line sloped upwards. However with the relaxation of exchange controls in 1988 and the stability of the Irish pound in the EMS in recent years, it is likely that there is near perfect capital mobility between Ireland and other countries at the present time.

*Note:*

*In Chapter 12 we examine the capital mobility issue in greater detail when we discuss interest rate policy in Ireland. In particular we explain how exchange rate expectations have an important effect on the degree of capital mobility.*

In Figure 11.3 a horizontal BP = 0 reference line is amalgamated with the IS/LM model. At the point A, the IS and LM curves intersect with the BP line. At this point the goods and money markets and the balance of payments are all in equilibrium. In what follows we will use this framework to analyse the effects of fiscal and monetary policy on output and the balance of payments in an open economy with both fixed and flexible exchange rates. Through out we assume perfect capital mobility so that the BP = 0 line is horizontal.

It is, of course, possible that the economy is not at a point on the BP = 0 line. We discuss this issue in section 11.4 when we identify an automatic adjustment mechanism which always moves the economy towards the BP = 0 line.

In what follows, it is important to bear in mind that under fixed exchange rates the Central Bank intervenes in the foreign exchange market to stabilise the exchange rate and as a result balance of payments deficits or surpluses are reflected in changes

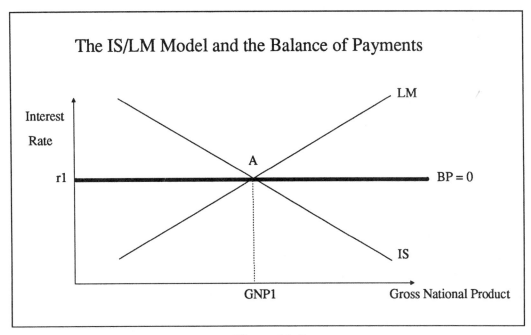

The IS/LM Model and the Balance of Payments

Figure 11.3

in the external reserves. Changes in the external reserves are, in turn, reflected in changes in the money supply. If, on the other hand, the exchange rate is flexible and the Central Bank does not intervene in the foreign exchange market, balance of payments deficits or surpluses are reflected in appreciation or depreciation of the exchange rate. As we will see, the effect of fiscal and monetary policy on output and employment is very different depending on whether the exchange is fixed or flexible.

# 3 Fiscal and Monetary Policy Under Fixed Exchange Rates

In order to simplify the analysis in this section, we will abstract from a number of the issues raised in earlier chapters. First, we assume that unemployment is above the natural rate of unemployment and that there are no supply constraints curtailing or restricting the growth in GNP. Secondly, we ignore "crowding-out" and the Ricardian Equivalence hypothesis and the effect of these on the effectiveness of fiscal policy. We also assume that an expansionary fiscal policy is financed in a non-monetary way and does not result in any increase in the money supply.

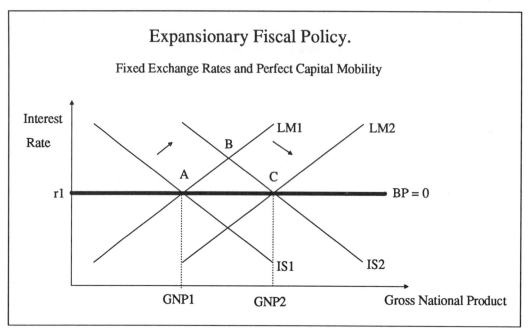

Figure 11.4

Thirdly, we assume that domestic prices are determined by world prices. That is we assume that in a small open economy (SOE) producers are "price-takers" rather than "price-makers" in international markets. This simply means that firms in small open economies cannot influence or determine world prices but instead must accept the going world price. This assumption was discussed in Chapter 9 and again in Chapter 10 under the heading of purchasing power parity (PPP) theory. The main implication of this assumption is that inflation is regarded as a reflection of exchange rate policy rather than domestic demand conditions. This is in complete contrast with the closed economy analysis of Chapter 8 where the emphasis was very much on the inflation/unemployment trade-off.

# Fiscal policy

In Figure 11.4 we illustrate the effect of an increase in government expenditure on output when the exchange rate is fixed. An increase in government expenditure shifts the IS curve outwards from IS1 to IS2 and the economy moves from the point A to the point B. At the point B, GNP has increased and there is a balance of payments surplus as the economy is above the BP = 0 reference line.

An expansionary fiscal policy results in a balance of payments surplus because:

1. The increase in GNP leads to an increase in imports via the marginal propensity to import and this results in a *deficit* in the current account of the balance of payments.

266

$\uparrow$ GNP  $\rightarrow$  $\uparrow$ M

2. However the increase in GNP also increases the demand for money and therefore the domestic interest rate. This results in a capital inflow and a *surplus* on the capital account of the balance of payments.

$\uparrow$ GNP  $\rightarrow$  $\uparrow$ Md  $\rightarrow$  $\uparrow$ r  $\rightarrow$  capital inflow.

Given perfect (or near perfect) capital mobility, effect (2) dominates effect (1) with the result that there is an overall balance of payments surplus. The deficit in the current account is more than offset by the surplus on the capital account.

The point B in Figure 11.4 is not a final equilibrium point. Given fixed exchange rates, the Central Bank must *intervene* in the foreign exchange market to stabilise the exchange rate. This intervention takes the form of supplying (selling) Irish pounds and accumulating foreign currencies. The increase in the external reserves in turn increases the money supply and the LM curve shifts outwards from LM1 to LM2. The economy now moves from point B to point C.

*Note:*
*Refer back to section 5.6 in Chapter 5 to see how an increase in the external reserves increases high powered money and, via the money multiplier, the money supply in the economy. If however the Central Bank engages in what is called "sterilisation", changes in the external reserves will not affect the money supply. We discuss sterilisation in detail in Chapter 12. We assume for the moment that the Central Bank does not engage in sterilisation.*

At point C, the domestic interest rate is again equal to the "world" rate and the balance of payments is in equilibrium. The current account of the balance of payments is in deficit but this is offset by the capital account surplus. As can be seen from the diagram, the effect of an expansionary fiscal policy is to increase GNP. Fiscal policy is therefore very effective when the exchange rate is fixed and capital is perfectly mobile (assuming, as we have, that the supply side of the economy does not act as a constraint).

*Note:*
*If there is imperfect capital mobility the BP = 0 line will slope upwards. Suppose that the degree of capital mobility is such that the BP = 0 line is steeper than the LM curve. The reader can verify that an expansionary fiscal policy will now result in a balance of payments deficit. The LM curve will now shift backwards reflecting a fall in the Central Bank's external reserves and the increase in GNP will be smaller than in the perfect capital mobility case. Hence the greater the degree of capital mobility, the more effective is fiscal policy.*

# Monetary policy

Figure 11.5 shows the effect of an expansionary monetary policy on GNP when the exchange rate is fixed. The increase in the money supply shifts the LM curve from LM1 to LM2 and the economy moves from point A to point B. At point B, GNP has increased but there is a balance of payments deficit as the economy is below the BP = 0 line.

The balance of payments deficit arises for two reasons.

1. The increase in the money supply leads to a fall in the domestic interest rate relative to the "world" interest rate and this results in a capital outflow and a deficit on the capital account of the balance of payments.

$\uparrow$Ms $\rightarrow$ $\downarrow$r (relative to the "world" rate) $\rightarrow$ capital outflow.

2. The increase in GNP leads to an increase in imports (via the marginal propensity to import) and a current account deficit.

$\uparrow$GNP $\rightarrow$ $\uparrow$M $\rightarrow$ current account deficit.

An expansionary monetary policy therefore results in a deficit in both the current and capital accounts of the balance of payments. In the case of an expansionary fiscal policy, a capital account surplus offsets the current account

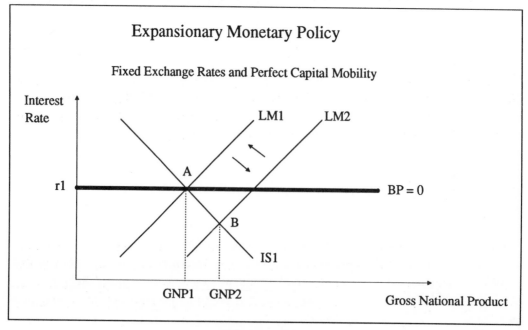

Figure 11.5

268

deficit giving an overall balance of payments surplus.

The economy will not however remain at point B in Figure 11.5 for very long. Given fixed exchange rates, the Central Bank must intervene in the foreign exchange market in order to stabilise the exchange rate. In particular, the Central Bank must create an artificial demand for Irish pounds and this will result in a fall in the external reserves and, via the money multiplier, a fall in the money supply. This is reflected in the diagram by the LM curve shifting backwards until the economy returns to its original position at point A. At this point, the domestic interest rate is again equal to the "world" rate and GNP returns to its initial level.

Because capital is perfectly mobile, the economy reverts back to point A in a very short space of time, days or weeks rather than months or years. The reason is that the fall in the interest rate leads to an immediate capital outflow and the money supply and the interest rate quickly return to their original levels. Given the speed with which capital flows out of the country, the interest rate does not remain below the "world" rate long enough to have any effect on GNP. The net result is that monetary policy is very ineffective when the exchange rate is fixed and capital is perfectly mobile.

*Note:*

*The degree of capital mobility does not change the result that monetary policy is ineffective when the exchange rate is fixed. The reader can verify that even if the BP = 0 line is upward sloping, an expansionary monetary policy will again result in a balance of payments deficit and the economy will eventually return to the initial level of output. With imperfect capital mobility, however, this will take longer to occur.*

## Summary
The above analysis suggests that fiscal policy is effective, and monetary policy ineffective, in influencing output and employment when the exchange rate is fixed and capital is perfectly mobile. Of course, the impact of fiscal policy depends on the slope of the IS/LM curves, as we discussed in Chapter 6.

# .4 Internal and External Balance

In the previous section we assumed that unemployment was above the natural rate and that there were no supply constraints on increasing GNP. In this section we expand that analysis by explicitly allowing for both unemployment and over-employment. We continue to assume fixed exchange rates and perfect capital mobility.

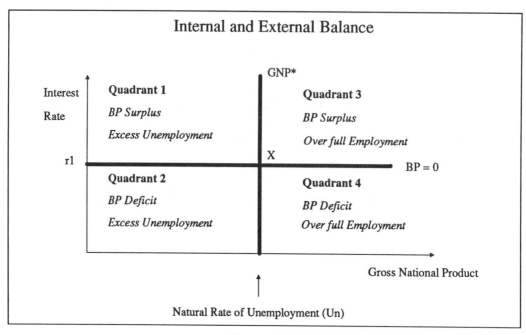

Figure 11.6

The economy is said to be in "internal balance" if there is "full" employment, that is, if the *actual* level of GNP is close to the *potential* GNP level or, which is the same thing, if the unemployment rate is equal to the natural rate of unemployment ($U_n$). In contrast, the economy is said to be in "external balance" if the balance of payments is in equilibrium, that is, if there is no Central Bank intervention in the foreign exchange market for Irish pounds. The balance of payments is in equilibrium if the economy is on the BP = 0 line.

In Figure 11.6, full employment GNP (which corresponds to the natural rate of unemployment) is indicated by the GNP$^*$ line and balance of payments equilibrium is indicated by the now familiar BP = 0 line. If the economy is to the left of the GNP$^*$ line, unemployment is greater than the natural rate (the actual level of GNP is less than potential GNP) whereas if the economy is to the right of the GNP$^*$ line there is "over-full employment", that is, actual unemployment is below the natural rate. As before, points above and below the BP = 0 line indicate a balance of payments surplus and deficit respectively. The *optimum position* for the economy is the point X where the GNP$^*$ line intersects the BP = 0 line. At this point, unemployment equals the natural rate of unemployment and the balance of payments is in equilibrium. In other words, the economy is in both internal and external balance.

*Note:*

*In the previous section we assumed the economy was in either quadrant 1 and 2 because we stated that unemployment was above the natural rate.*

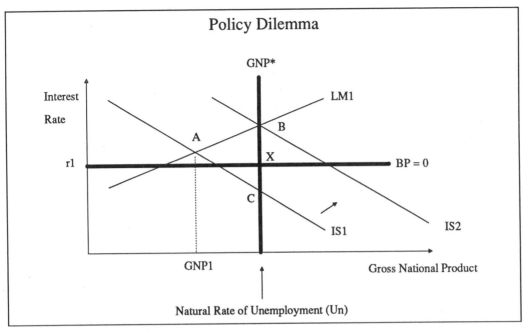

Figure 11.7

At any one time, the economy can be in one of four possible positions.

Quadrant 1: Excess unemployment and a balance of payments surplus.
Quadrant 2: Excess unemployment and a balance of payments deficit.
Quadrant 3: Over-full employment and a balance of payments surplus.
Quadrant 4: Over-full employment and a balance of payments deficit.

In Figure 11.7 we combine the internal and external reference lines with the IS and LM curves. We begin by assuming that the economy is at a point such as A in quadrant 1 and not at the overall optimum point for the economy. At this point, unemployment exceeds the natural rate of unemployment and there is a balance of payments surplus. If the government implements an expansionary fiscal policy the IS curve moves upwards from IS1 to IS2 and the economy moves to the point B. Unemployment now equals the natural rate but the balance of payments surplus has increased. On the other hand, if the government pursues an expansionary monetary policy the economy moves from point A to point C. Internal balance is again achieved but there is now a balance of payments deficit. This analysis suggests that a *policy dilemma* exists if the authorities attempt to achieve simultaneously internal and external balance. This is also true if the economy is in any of the other three quadrants and the authorities try to move to the point X. The nature of the dilemma consists in the following: it is possible to achieve one of the objectives (i.e. full employment) but not the other (balance of payments equilibrium). The authorities

271

are faced with the dilemma of choosing between these two objectives if they rely on one *policy instrument* on its own.

*Note:*
*The points B and C are temporary equilibrium points as the external reserves will be rising and falling respectively reflecting the balance of payments position.*

The policy dilemma of not being able to achieve both internal and external balance was first discussed by the Canadian economist Robert Mundell in the early 1960s.[1] He pointed out that it was necessary to use two policy instruments (fiscal and monetary policy) to achieve two policy objectives (internal and external balance). It was not possible to achieve two conflicting objectives with only one policy instrument. What is required to resolve the policy dilemma is a *policy mix*. In particular, he argued that monetary policy should be used to achieve external balance and fiscal policy to achieve internal balance. The reason for *assigning* instruments to objectives in this manner is that monetary policy, via changes in the interest rate, has an immediate and significant impact on the capital account of the balance of payments. On the other hand, fiscal policy, as we saw in the previous section, has a much greater impact on output and employment.

The rule suggested by Mundell therefore is:

Use an expansionary (deflationary) monetary policy to remove a surplus (deficit) on the balance of payments.

Use an expansionary (deflationary) fiscal policy to remove unemployment (over-employment).

This was Mundell's solution to the assignment problem. Referring back to Figure 11.7, suppose the economy is initially at point A and the objective is to move the economy to point X. The correct policy mix is to use an expansionary fiscal policy to shift the IS curve out to the right (reduce unemployment) and an expansionary monetary policy to shift the LM curve to the right (remove the balance of payments surplus). Both the LM and the IS curves now intersect at point X and internal and external balance has been achieved.

If the economy is at a point in any of the other three quadrants the correct policy mix is as follows.

Quadrant 2: Expansionary fiscal policy and a deflationary monetary policy.
Quadrant 3: Deflationary fiscal policy and a expansionary monetary policy.
Quadrant 4: Deflationary fiscal policy and a deflationary monetary policy.

This analysis illustrates that fiscal and monetary policy should, on occasions, be going in the opposite directions in order to achieve internal and external balance. This solution to the problem does however have a number of limitations. It has been pointed out that fiscal policy may not be sufficiently flexible to be used in conjunction with monetary policy. As the discussion in Chapters 3 and 4 suggested, both inside and outside lags can result in considerable delays before fiscal policy affects the level of output. We also have to bear in mind that in a small open economy fiscal multipliers are small. Both the timing and the impact of a fiscal policy on the economy can be very uncertain in practice.

Secondly, monetary policy achieves balance of payments equilibrium via capital inflows and outflows. At point X in Figure 11.7, a deficit in the current account of the balance of payments is offset by a capital account surplus so that external balance is achieved. The difficulty is that a country cannot run a capital account surplus indefinitely in order to cover a current account deficit. A capital inflow is equivalent to foreign borrowing and prolonged capital inflows increase a country's indebtedness. Eventually both the principal and interest will have to be repaid. This can only be done in the longer term by running a current account surplus. Hence, sooner or later further remedial action will have to be taken.

# 5  Fiscal and Monetary Policy under Flexible Exchange Rates

In this section we examine the impact of an expansionary fiscal and monetary policy on output and employment under flexible exchange rates. The analysis is similar to that in section 11.3 in that we again use the IS/LM diagram in conjunction with the balance of payments equilibrium line. The key difference between the situation under flexible exchange rates and under fixed exchange rates is that an incipient balance of payments surplus (deficit) causes the exchange rate to rise (fall) in the former case. As we will see, the results of section 11.3 are more or less completely reversed when the exchange rate depreciates or appreciates in response to a balance of payments deficit or surplus. In particular, we will demonstrate that fiscal policy is *ineffective* and monetary policy is *effective* in influencing output and employment under flexible exchange rates.

## Fiscal policy

In Figure 11.8, an expansionary fiscal policy shifts the IS curve outwards from IS1 to IS2 and the economy moves from point A to point B. At point B, GNP has increased and there is an overall balance of payments surplus. As in the fixed

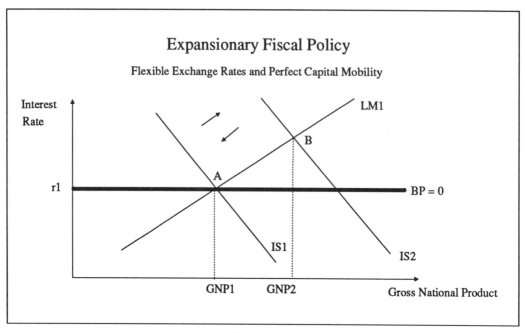

Figure 11.8

exchange rate case, the balance of payments surplus arises because with perfectly capital mobility the capital account surplus (brought about by higher interest rates) dominates the current account deficit (due to the increase in GNP).

However, if the exchange rate is flexible (no Central Bank intervention in the foreign exchange market), the balance of payments surplus will result in exchange rate *appreciation.* Exchange rate appreciation, in turn, reduces exports and increases imports and the IS curve now shifts backwards to the left. The economy reverts back to point A. The increase in GNP was therefore only temporary. In effect, under flexible exchange rates, an expansionary fiscal policy "crowds-out" net exports (exports minus imports) through exchange rate appreciation. Fiscal policy is therefore *ineffective* when the exchange rate is flexible and there is perfect capital mobility.

It should be noted that in the above analysis the LM curve is not affected because the Central Bank does not intervene in the foreign exchange market. This means that the external reserves and the money supply remain unchanged.

*Note:*

*If the BP = 0 line is steeper than the LM curve reflecting imperfect capital mobility, an expansionary fiscal policy will result in an increase in GNP and a balance of payments deficit. In this case, the exchange rate depreciates and this results in a further increase in GNP. The reader can verify that under these circumstances fiscal policy will have a greater effect on output and employment than in*

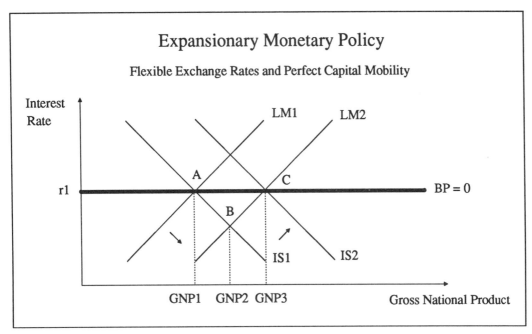

**Expansionary Monetary Policy**

Flexible Exchange Rates and Perfect Capital Mobility

Figure 11.9

*the fixed exchange rate and perfect capital mobility case. But note that we are assuming no supply side constraints and no domestic inflation as a result of the changes in output and the exchange rate.*

# Monetary policy

Figure 11.9 illustrates the case of an expansionary monetary policy under flexible exchange rates and perfect capital mobility. The increase in the money supply shifts the LM curve from LM1 to LM2 and the economy moves from point A to point B. At point B, GNP has increased and there is a balance of payments deficit as the economy is at a point below the BP = 0 line. In contrast with the outcome from an expansionary fiscal policy,    a deficit appears on both the current and capital accounts of the balance of payments.

The exchange rate now depreciates and this increases net exports. The IS curve shifts outwards from IS1 to IS2 and the economy now moves from point B to point C. GNP again increases and the balance of payments is in equilibrium. This result means that monetary policy is very *effective* under flexible exchange rates, perfect capital mobility and no supply-side constraints.

*Note:*
*This result is not changed very much if the BP = 0 line is upward sloping reflecting imperfect capital mobility.*

275

# Summary

Under flexible exchange rates with perfect capital mobility, monetary policy is very effective and fiscal policy ineffective in terms of achieving increases in output and employment. This is a complete reversal of the conclusions we reached when the

*Table 11.1*

**The effect of fiscal and monetary policy on output**

|  | Exchange rate | |
|---|---|---|
|  | *Fixed* | *Flexible* |
| *Monetary policy* | Ineffective | Effective |
|  | (regardless of degree of capital mobility) | |
|  | *Capital mobile* | |
| *Fiscal policy* | Effective | Ineffective |
|  | *Capital immobile* | |
| *Fiscal policy* | Effective | Effective |

exchange rate was fixed. Moreover, as we move from a fixed to a flexible exchange rate regime, the effectiveness of monetary policy unambiguously increases regardless of the degree of capital mobility. However, as we pointed out above, imperfect capital mobility can allow fiscal policy to be effective even with a flexible exchange rate. Table 11.1 summarises these conclusions.

# 11.6 Exchange Rate Policy

## Devaluation, output and employment

In Chapter 9 we examined the conditions under which exchange rate devaluation increased exports and reduced imports. Recall that:

Value of Exports = $P_x * Q_x$
Value of Imports = $P_m * Q_m$

where $P_x$ and $P_m$ are export and import prices and $Q_x$ and $Q_m$ are the quantities of exports and imports sold. Exchange rate devaluation should reduce $P_x$ thereby improving competitiveness and increasing $Q_x$. Similarly, devaluation should increase $P_m$, leading to a fall in $Q_m$. If the value of exports increases and the value of imports falls, the net effect will be an improvement in the trade balance and an increase in output and employment.

*Note:*
*Devaluation will improve the trade balance if the Marshall-Lerner condition holds. See Chapter 9.*

In Table 11.2 we show the basic open-economy Keynesian model. This model is very similar to that given in Chapter 6, section 6.2, except that exports and imports are now included as components of aggregate demand. It can be seen from the model that devaluation, by increasing exports and reducing imports, results in an increase in aggregate demand and this in turn should increase GNP and reduce unemployment.

In short:

Devaluation → ↑X and ↓M → ↑AD → ↑GNP → ↓U

Devaluation, by changing the price of exports relative to the price of imports, is in effect an "expenditure switching" policy. Expenditure is switched from imports to domestically produced goods and services (i.e. exports). However, it should be noted that the improvement in the home trade balance resulting from exchange rate devaluation must be matched by a trade deficit elsewhere. An increase in Irish exports must mean a rise in imports in some other country. Hence the gain in output and employment at home must be at the expense of a reduction in output and employment in some other country. This gives rise to the accusation that devaluation is a "beggar thy neighbour" policy in that the devaluing country is attempting to "export its unemployment" to other countries.

As happened in the 1930s, countries adversely affected by a devaluation are likely to retaliate by devaluing their currency in order to restore competitiveness. This can result in a series of "competitive devaluations" with each country devaluing so as to maintain output and employment. If this happens, there will be no net increase in aggregate demand in the countries concerned. It is frequently argued that if a number of countries are suffering from high unemployment, the best policy is not to go it alone with a competitive devaluation but instead to try to get countries to co-operate and implement a co-ordinated expansion in aggregate demand in each country. This would result in an overall increase in output and employment.

*Table 11.2*

**The open economy Keynesian model**

---

|  | *Fiscal policy*<br>↓ | *Exchange rate policy*<br>↓ |
|---|---|---|

$$U \leftrightarrow NI \leftrightarrow GNP = AD \equiv C + I + G + (X - M)$$

$$Ms: r :Md$$
$$\uparrow$$
*Monetary policy*

---

*Note:* Refer back to section 6.4, Chapter 6 for a glossary of terms. The symbol ↔ means that the two variables on either side are closely related. An increase in GNP, for example, will be followed by an increase in NI and a fall in unemployment. We use the identity symbol, ≡, to indicate that aggregate demand and expenditure are one and the same thing. We use a colon to indicate that the supply and demand for money determines the interest rate (r).

---

While devaluation can increase output and employment in one country it is not without its costs. In particular, devaluation involves a deterioration in the terms of trade. In section 9.1, Chapter 9, the terms of trade was defined as the ratio $P_x/P_m$. Devaluation decreases $P_x$ and increases $P_m$ so that there is an adverse movement in the terms of trade. This means that the home country must now export more goods and services to import a given amount of goods and services. Thus a devaluation works by reducing domestic living standards in the short term so as to raise output and employment in the longer run.

One fundamental difference between devaluation as a policy instrument and fiscal or monetary policy is that devaluation increases aggregate demand through an improvement in the trade balance. An expansionary fiscal or monetary policy reduces unemployment but in doing so creates a trade deficit (or reduces a trade surplus). Devaluation is therefore a particularly useful policy instrument if there is a trade deficit and unemployment is greater than the natural rate of unemployment. The policy dilemma that can exist between achieving a trade balance and full employment can be resolved by devaluation.

In Figure 11.10 we elaborate on this point by developing a net exports (exports minus imports ) reference line. We are now concentrating on the balance of trade, as opposed to the balance of payments, because capital flows, transfers etc. do not enter into aggregate demand. (The analysis is the same as for the BP = 0 with zero

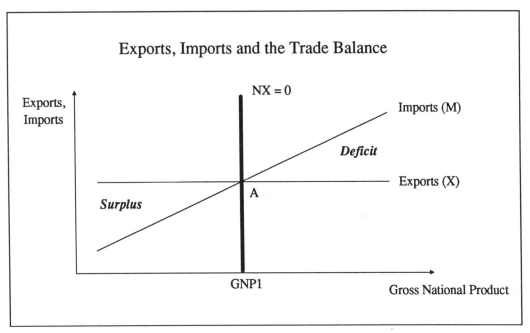

Figure 11.10

capital mobility case.) With GNP on the horizontal axis and exports and imports on the vertical axis, the imports schedule is shown as sloping upwards. This reflects the fact that imports increase as GNP rises. The slope of this line is determined by the marginal propensity to import (MPM). The greater the MPM the steeper will be the imports schedule. In contrast, the exports schedule is shown as a horizontal line indicating that changes in GNP do not affect the level of exports (exports are determined by "world aggregate demand" which we assume to be constant). At GNP1, exports equals imports and the trade account is balanced. We draw a horizontal $NX = 0$ reference line to indicate this level of GNP. To the right of the $NX = 0$ line, there is a trade surplus and to the left there is a trade deficit.

A devaluation of the exchange rate will shift the imports schedule downwards (imports are reduced for a given level of GNP) and shift the exports schedule upwards. The $NX = 0$ line will now shift to the right and the equilibrium level of GNP will move to the right along the horizontal axis.

With the interest rate along the vertical axis and GNP along the horizontal axis, Figure 11.11 shows a $NX = 0$ line which corresponds to trade balance at GNP1 and a full employment reference line denoted by $GNP^*$. As drawn, the $NX = 0$ line is situated to the left of the $GNP^*$. The economy can be in area I, II or III. These areas are characterized as follows:

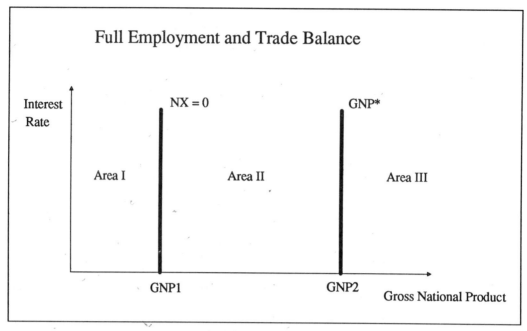

Figure 11.11

Area I.   Trade surplus and unemployment.
Area II.   Trade deficit and unemployment.
Area III. Trade deficit and over-employment.

If the economy is in area I or III there is no dilemma between achieving trade balance and full employment. For example, if the economy is in area I, an expansionary fiscal or monetary policy can be used to reduce unemployment and reduce the trade surplus. Similarly, if the economy is in area III a deflationary fiscal or monetary policy can be implemented to reduce over-employment and remove the trade deficit. A policy dilemma does however exists if the economy is in area II. In the early 1980s, when the balance of trade deficit was about 15% of GNP and unemployment was high and rising, the Irish economy was clearly in area II.

If the economy is in area II, devaluation can be used to resolve the policy dilemma. In Figure 11.12, depreciation shifts the NX = 0 line towards the $GNP^*$ (not shown in the diagram) and the IS curve moves from IS1 to IS2 (the IS curve shifts because of the increase in net exports). The net result is that full employment is combined with a balance trade account.

Suppose however the economy is at a point such as A in Figure 11.13, where there is full employment and a trade deficit. Depreciation again moves the NX = 0 line towards $GNP^*$ (not shown in the diagram) but because of the shift to the right of the IS curve the economy moves to the point B. At the point B, there is over-full

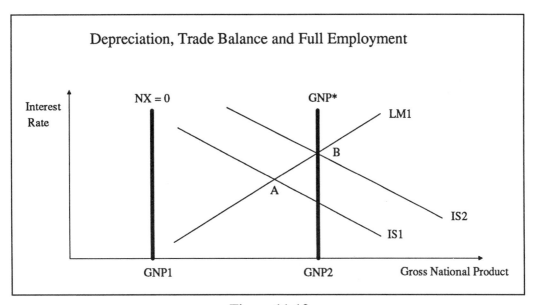

Figure 11.12

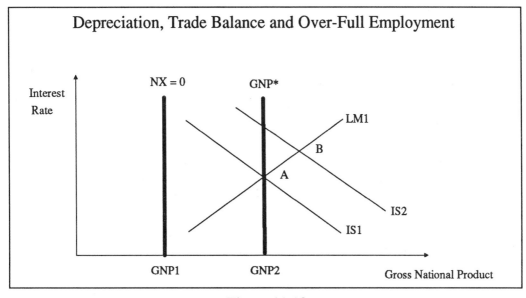

Figure 11.13

employment and a trade account deficit. The trade account continues to be in deficit because the expansionary effect of the depreciation on GNP leads to an increase in imports via the marginal propensity to import. Overall devaluation should improve a trade account deficit but the increase in imports associated with the rise in GNP offsets some of the effect of the change in the relative prices of imports and exports.

It is clear from the diagram that a deflationary fiscal or monetary policy is required to move the economy back to GNP$^*$. This example illustrates that if the

281

economy is close to GNP[*], devaluation will have to be accompanied by an *expenditure reducing* policy if the employment and trade account objectives are to be achieved. Put another way, if the objective of devaluation is simply to improve the trade account without increasing output and employment, an expenditure reducing policy will have to accompany it.

## 11.7 How Effective is Devaluation as a Means of Increasing Irish Output and Employment?

### Devaluation and competitiveness

Devaluation, by increasing import prices, leads to an increase in the domestic price level as measured, for example, by the consumer price index (CPI). This happens in two ways. First, the increase in prices of imports of finished goods and services has a direct effect on the CPI. Secondly, many of the raw materials used by Irish industry are imported and have few domestic substitutes. Oil and oil products are important examples. When their prices rise due to a fall in the value of the Irish pound, this inevitably increases the cost of producing final goods in Ireland. Firms will pass on these increases to consumers in the form of higher manufacturing output prices. Higher manufacturing output prices will, in turn, increase the CPI.

As domestic prices rise, the competitive gain which exporters and import-competing firms initially enjoyed after the devaluation will be eroded. If devaluation leads to an equal increase in the Irish price level, the trade balance, and therefore output and employment will not improve and the net result will simply be a higher price level and a lower exchange rate.

To see this recall from Chapters 9 and 10 the purchasing power parity (PPP) equation:

$$P_{irl} * E = P_f$$

where $P_{irl}$ and $P_f$ are the Irish and foreign price index respectively and E is the exchange rate measured as foreign currency/Irish pounds. If, as PPP theory predicts, the fall in E (devaluation) is matched by an equal rise in $P_{irl}$, the real exchange rate will remain unchanged and there will be no improvement in the competitive position of the economy. The fall in E is simply matched by an equal increase in $P_{irl}$. We reviewed the Irish literature on PPP in Chapter 10. Here we summarise the results of a paper that deals specifically with the impact of devaluation on the economy. Flynn (1986) found that a 10% devaluation of the exchange rate will be fully reflected in an increase in import, output and export prices within one to two years.[2]

According to this paper, in the short term, devaluation improves the trade balance but in the longer term this gain is eroded as prices rise.

*Note:*
*We use the word devaluation to refer to a conscious decision to lower the value of a fixed exchange rate. A depreciation refers to a fall in the value of a floating exchange rate. As Ireland has a fixed exchange rate in the EMS, but is floating against sterling, the value of our currency could fall either as a result of a decision to devalue in the EMS or if sterling rose against the EMS currencies (which would lead to a depreciation of the Irish pound).*

The increase in domestic prices may not stop when the real exchange rate has been restored to its original level. Devaluation can also create two types of vicious cycles which will result in further price increases. The first of these concerns the relationship between prices and wages. As the domestic prices rise, workers' real wages fall and trade unions demand higher nominal wages in order to maintain living standards. However the increase in wages will again increase prices and lead to further wage demands and so on. The longer this *price-wage spiral* continues, the greater will be the damage to the country's competitive position. In order to avoid this happening, exchange rate depreciation is frequently accompanied by an incomes policy which attempts to curtail wage increases. However unless there is prior agreement between the government and the trade unions, as, for example, was achieved in Australia in the 1980s, workers are unlikely to accept lower real wages and depreciation will not succeed in improving competitiveness.

The second type of vicious cycle concerns the relationship between devaluation and inflation. As we pointed out in Chapter 9 one of the main reasons why countries devalue in the first place is because they have a high inflation rate. However, if devaluation creates inflation and inflation can cause devaluation , the possibility of a *devaluation - inflation spiral* emerges. Why are we devaluing? Because we have high inflation! And why do we have high inflation? Because we are devaluing! There is a chicken and egg issue here but the point is that devaluation can result in a vicious cycle of rising inflation and a falling exchange rate. This spiral would be accentuated by the wage-price spiral mentioned above.

In discussing devaluation and competitiveness it is important to make a distinction between *occasional* and *frequent* devaluations of the exchange rate. The point is that the speed with which firms and consumers adjust to a devaluation will increase with the frequency of devaluation. Hence if the exchange rate is devalued fairly regularly, people will begin to anticipate its effects and prices will adjust more or less instantaneously. In this case, devaluation will not confer a competitive advantage on the economy even in the very short-run.

In the early 1980s, the Irish authorities did not regard devaluation as a feasible option in improving competitiveness. For example, the Governor of the Central Bank of Ireland stated:

... the competitive advantage survives only as long as domestic costs fail to adjust to the higher domestic prices which result from devaluation. If these costs adjustments are rapid, and the evidence suggests that they are, the competitive advantages of devaluation are of short duration, while the jump in inflation is permanent.
Murray C., "The European Monetary System: Implications for Ireland", Central Bank of Ireland, *Annual Report*, 1979, p. 99.

Following the decision not to devalue the Irish pound in the July 1985 EMS realignment, the Minister for Finance was quoted as follows:

Mr Bruton said it was "extremely short sighted" to consider devaluation as benefiting exports in a country that was so greatly dependent on importing raw materials. He said any price advantage from a devaluation "would be very quickly whittled away" by the increasing price of raw materials.
Irish Times, 21-7-1985, p. 9.

However valid these orthodox views are, there remains a real danger that a *misaligned* Irish pound could act as a drag on the economy's performance. We noted that PPP is a theory for the long-run. In the short and medium term there can be significant deviations from PPP. Countries can gain or lose temporarily if there exchange rate is under- or over-valued. If growth in output and employment has a high priority, the authorities should try to ensure that the currency is slightly under-valued in order to provide a competitive advantage for exporters.

# Exchange rate uncertainty and interest rates

In Chapter 12 we examine in detail how exchange rate expectations can affect the differential between domestic and foreign interest rates. Here we simply make the point that if investors expect a fall in the exchange rate, they will move funds out of the country in anticipation of making a capital gain. However as capital flows out of the country, the domestic money supply is reduced and the domestic interest rate increases relative to foreign interest rates. Hence, there is a link between exchange rate expectations, capital flows and movements in domestic interest rates.

As we pointed out in Chapter 9, it is extremely difficult to forecast exchange rate movements, particularly in the short-run. When the exchange rate is fixed, a decision by the government to devalue can be due to a number of factors. Some of the more likely reasons include:

1. A prolonged balance of payments deficit resulting in continued Central Bank intervention in the foreign exchange market and a fall in the external reserves.

284

2. An increase in the domestic inflation rate relative to foreign inflation rates resulting in a fall in competitiveness.

Holding a fixed exchange rate in the face of either of these developments would result in a *misalignment* which would distort the economy and would not be conducive to maximising economic growth. The *timing* and the *extent* of a devaluation is however a political decision. A decision to devalue would be taken ultimately by the Government, but the Central Bank and the Department of Finance would have very significant inputs to the debate. Speculators will naturally try to identify the reasons why the government decided to devalue and if these factors re-occur in the future, exchange rate uncertainty will increase.

This is essentially what happened in Ireland in the mid-1980s. As discussed in Chapter 10, the Irish government devalued the Irish pound on two occasions. The first was in March 1983, the second in August 1986. On both occasions it seemed that the decision to devalue was provoked by an appreciation of the Irish pound relative to sterling which had driven up our trade-weighted exchange rate index and led to a loss of competitiveness. This led to the view that the Irish government was operating a "dualistic exchange rate policy". The Irish pound was fixed in the EMS for as long as competitiveness with the UK was maintained. If Ireland's sterling exchange rate appreciated because of a weakness of sterling on foreign exchanges, the Irish government devalued the Irish pound in the EMS to restore competitiveness with the UK market.

This exchange rate policy obviously contributed to exchange rate uncertainty. In August 1986, the Irish pound was devalued by 8% when the sterling exchange rate rose to STG£0.96/IR£1. This level of the Irish pound has become a kind of bench-mark for speculators in the future. If the Irish pound approaches this level, speculators would fear a devaluation and the Irish pound would become subject to speculative pressure. This is indeed what happened in late 1989. As the exchange rate increased to STG£0.95/IR£1, capital flowed out of the country. In October 1989 the external reserves fell by 13% and in early December the Central Bank increased interest rates by 1%.

The basic point is that once speculators suspect that the government will resort to devaluation under certain circumstances, exchange rate speculation increases whenever these circumstances re-occur. The increase in uncertainty leads to capital outflows and higher domestic interest rates. Hence devaluation can result in an increase in interest rates in the longer term and this obviously has an adverse effect on investment, output and employment. It is not surprising therefore that the government in 1987, 1988 and 1989 continually emphasised that the Irish pound would not be devalued in any EMS realignment. The motive was to alleviate fears of a devaluation, reduce exchange rate uncertainty and advert an increase in interest rates. In effect, then, our desire to be regarded as a full member of the EMS virtually amounts to abandoning the use of the exchange rate as an instrument of economic policy. We have to find other ways of achieving external and internal balance than by resorting to devaluation.

## Devaluation and foreign borrowing

A devaluation increases the Irish pound value of foreign debt. In August 1986, Ireland's foreign debt stood at approximately IR£9,753 million. Hence the 8% devaluation in August 1986 automatically raised the foreign debt by IR£780 million. To put this in perspective, the total value of Irish exports in 1986 was IR£9,181m. This means we would have to increase exports by approximately 8.5% in order to pay off the rise in the foreign debt attributable to the devaluation. Only then would we be back to our initial position. However, the devaluation also increased the Irish pound value of our exports. One way of looking at our foreign debt service is to think of it as an import with a zero elasticity of demand. The less elastic the demand for imports, the less likely it is that a devaluation will be successful. Countries with large external debt should therefore be particularly careful about resorting to devaluation.

## Summary

In summary, the evidence suggests that devaluation is not likely to convey any long lasting competitive advantage on the Irish economy unless there is a strict incomes policy in place. After a period of approximately one year, the price level will increase by the amount of the devaluation and there will be no gain in competitiveness. In addition, devaluation can create both a wage - price spiral and a price - devaluation spiral with the result that there will be serious disruption of the economy in the longer term. The associated increase in exchange rate uncertainty can also lead to higher interest rates and foreign indebtedness will increase by the amount of the devaluation. Under these circumstances, it may be better to fix the exchange rate to a unit such as the ECU and then introduce fiscal and monetary policies that are consistent with that exchange rate. Of course, this recipe is likely to be more successful if we establish the appropriate exchange rate before the exchange rate is fixed. A misaligned exchange rate can act as a drag on the rate of growth of output and employment.

# 11.8 Conclusion

The main points of this chapter include:

- Fiscal policy is effective and monetary policy ineffective in terms of influencing GNP when the exchange rate is fixed and there is perfect capital mobility

- Under fixed exchange rates, fiscal policy should be used to achieve internal balance (full employment) and monetary policy to achieve external balance (balance of payments equilibrium)

- If the exchange rate is flexible and capital perfectly mobile, fiscal policy is ineffective and monetary policy effective in influencing output and employment

- Devaluation should increase output and employment by creating a trade surplus. However this type of policy is a "beggar thy neighbour" policy which is likely to lead retaliation by other countries

- If a country devalues in order to improve the trade balance, the depreciation will have to be accompanied by an "expenditure reducing" policy

- Devaluation is not without its costs. There will be an adverse movement in the terms of trade and inflation will increase. In the longer term, devaluation can push the economy into both a wage - price spiral and a inflation - devaluation spiral.

- Devaluation can also create exchange rate uncertainty and increase interest rates, as speculators anticipate that it will happen again

- Servicing external debt becomes more expensive because of a devaluation. It is like an import that cannot be reduced despite the increase in its cost. This reduces the chances of the devaluation achieving its objectives

- None the less, exchange rate policy should avoid misalignments which, can exact a high price in terms of slow growth and high employment.

# Notes

1. See R. Mundell, *International Economics*, Macmillan, 1967 and *Monetary Theory*, Goodyear, 1971.

2. J. Flynn, "A Simulation Model of the Effects of Exchange Rate Changes on Inflation and the Trade Balance", Central Bank of Ireland, *Quarterly Bulletin*, 2, 1986.

# Chapter 12

# *Interest Rates in a Small Open Economy*

## 12.1 Introduction

In this chapter we take up in greater detail some aspects of the determination of interest rates in a small, open economy. This topic was introduced in a general manner in Chapter 11 where we modified the traditional closed economy IS/LM analysis to allow for the fact that in a small, open economy the interest rate is largely determined by external forces. The way in which international financial considerations impinge on domestic money markets is of exceptional importance in Ireland. There are few other economies in the world where such a large proportion of GNP is internationally traded and where, at the same time, there is an independent currency that is not pegged to that of its main trading partner. For these reasons, in this and the following chapters, we devote considerable space to introducing the student to the workings of the Irish money market and the manner in which it is affected by foreign exchange flows.

## 12.2 Interest Rates in an Open Economy

As we noted in Chapter 11, world interest rates are highly interdependent. Money flows almost instantaneously from New York to Tokyo to Frankfurt in search of the highest rate of return. For this reason, in Chapter 11, we drew the BP = 0 line horizontally for a small, open economy under conditions of perfect capital mobility with a fixed exchange rate, indicating there was no scope for significant deviations between its interest rate and that prevailing in the "rest of the world".

We should bear in mind that when an investor is evaluating where in the world to place her money, what matters is the *total* rate of return on this money. The rate of return has two components. The first is the interest earned on the deposit in the currency of the country in which the money is placed, and the second is the effect of any change in the exchange rate between that currency and the investor's domestic currency. If the rate of exchange between two currencies is fixed, and there is no expectation that this link will be broken, then deciding in which country to deposit money comes down simply to a comparison of the rates of interest available in the two countries. Furthermore, if the money market in one of the countries is very small relative to the other, and there are no legal restrictions on the movement of capital from one country to the other, then any tendency for interest rates in the smaller country to diverge from those prevailing in the larger country would immediately lead to a capital inflow (if its rate rose) or outflow (if its rate fell). Hence, the small country's interest rate will tend to be determined by that prevailing in the large country.

*Note:*

*We ignore any differences between the countries' tax treatment of the interest earned, which may be an important consideration in the real world. A great deal of the money that flows across foreign exchanges is being moved to minimise tax liabilities!*

The situation described in the previous paragraph corresponds fairly accurately to the one that existed in Ireland until we joined the European Monetary System (EMS) in March 1979. Our currency was rigidly pegged to sterling and, despite occasional academic discussions of the merits of this arrangement, there was no serious expectation that this link would be broken. The Irish money market was infinitesimal relative to the UK market. It was therefore inevitable that Irish interest rates were very similar to those prevailing in London.

*Note:*

*We refer to rates of interest because there is a whole spectrum of interest rates in a country. Different rates are charged to different types of customers and on different types of loans. There is a term structure of interest rates, which means that short-term, medium-term and long term rates are different. (In appendix 5 we discuss the "yield curve", which summarises the relationship between interest rates on loans of different maturities.) Even with perfect capital mobility and fixed exchange rates, Irish interest rates always tended to be a little higher than those in London, reflecting the narrowness of the Irish market and allowing some premium for the greater riskiness, from an outsider's perspective, of investing in Ireland.*

This situation changed when we entered the EMS in 1979 and Britain did not participate in the exchange rate mechanism (ERM). As we saw in Chapter 9, after 1979 the Irish pound/sterling exchange rate fluctuated quite widely. An investor in Ireland or Britain now had to take account of the second component of the total return to investing mentioned above, namely, that part attributable to changes in the value of one currency in terms of the other.[1]

When deciding in which currency to invest money, the investor does not know what is going to happen to exchange rates over the period of the investment.

However, she will have expectations about the *future course of exchange rates* and these play a crucial role in the investment decision.

This point is illustrated in Table 12.1 where we compare Irish and UK interest rates under different assumptions of how the sterling exchange will move over the period. It is assumed that exchange rate expectations prove correct in all three cases. In case A, the Irish interest rate exceeds the UK rate by 5% but from an investor's point of view the returns in the two countries are equivalent as the Irish pound is expected to depreciate by 5%. For example, a UK investor could move funds to Ireland and receive an Irish pound return of 15%. However, when the funds are converted back into sterling at the end of the investment period, a loss of 5% is incurred on the foreign exchange market and the net (sterling) return is only 10%.

*Table 12.1*

**Interest differential adjusted for changes in the exchange rate**

|        | $R_{irl}$ | $(STG£/IR£)^{*}$ | $R_{uk}$ |
|--------|-----------|-------------------|----------|
| Case 1 | 15%       | -5%               | 10%      |
| Case 2 | 15%       | -6%               | 10%      |
| Case 3 | 15%       | -4%               | 10%      |

*Note*: $(STG£/IR£)^{*}$ is the expected change in the exchange rate over a year. Interest rates are per annum

Similarly, an Irish investor could move funds to the UK and get a return of 10%. When the funds are converted back into Irish pounds at the end of the year, a gain of 5% is made on the foreign exchange market and this gives a total Irish pound return of 15%. Given exchange rate expectations, investors will be indifferent between investing in Ireland and in the UK.

In Case 2, we assume that Ireland's sterling exchange rate is expected to depreciate by 6% rather than 5%. A greater return can now be obtained by investing in the UK. If, for example, an Irish investor moves funds to the UK he receives an interest rate return of 10%. However at the end of the period an additional gain of 6% in made on the foreign exchange market as the Irish pound has depreciated by this amount over the period. The total return, denominated in Irish pounds, is 16%. This exceeds the return available in Ireland by 1%. In this case, capital will flow out of Ireland to the UK. This will tend to raise the rate of return in Ireland until, at 16%, the return from lending money here is the same as that from moving it to the UK.

In case 3, the sterling exchange rate is expected to depreciate by 4%. Ireland now offers the better investment opportunity. A return of 10% is again available in the UK but on this occasion the depreciation of the exchange rate results in only a 4% gain on the foreign exchange market. This gives a total UK return (expressed in Irish pounds) of 14% which compares unfavourably with the return available in Ireland. This will attract money to Ireland and drive the Irish rate of interest down.

The above examples illustrate the importance of exchange rate expectations in comparing international interest rates. We shall return to the question of how exchange rate expectations are formed in appendix 5 when we discuss the "yield curve". In Chapter 13 we discuss the forward exchange rate and *interest rate parity theory (IRPT)*. This theory links the difference between forward and spot exchange rates to the differential between domestic and foreign interest rates.

# 3 Irish and UK Interest Rates Before 1979

Between 1826 and 1979, the Irish pound was rigidly fixed to sterling on a one-to-one, no margins, basis. Exchange rate expectations did not enter into the comparison of Irish and UK interest rates during this period because there was no possibility of this exchange rate link being terminated. In fact, as mentioned in Chapter 5, up until the Central Bank Act of 1971 the government did not process the legal authority to break the sterling link. From an investor's point of view, the expectation was, quite simply, that the sterling exchange rate would remain at parity and there was no possibility of incurring a capital loss or gain on the foreign exchange market. Some allowance for the greater riskiness of investing in the small Irish economy might have been made, but otherwise a straight forward comparison of Irish and UK interest rates was appropriate in deciding whether to invest in Ireland or the UK.

Figure 12.1 shows the trend in Irish, UK and German interest rates between 1970 and 1979. It is evident from the graph that Irish interest rates more or less mirrored UK rates over the period. On the other hand, there was a significant difference between Irish and German rates. The average difference between Irish and UK rates over the period was 0.31% compared with 2.14% between Ireland and Germany. This difference in interest rate differentials is, in large part, due to the fact that the Irish pound was pegged to sterling and flexible against the DM over this period.

The size of the UK money market relative to the Irish money market and the fixed exchange rate ensured that Irish interest rates were dictated by UK rates. Ireland was in effect in a monetary union with Britain in much the same way as Wales or Scotland. This meant that the Irish authorities had no control over domestic interest rates or indeed the money supply. If, for example, the Irish authorities reduced the money supply and domestic interest rates rose above UK rates, capital would flow into Ireland until such time that the domestic money supply and interest

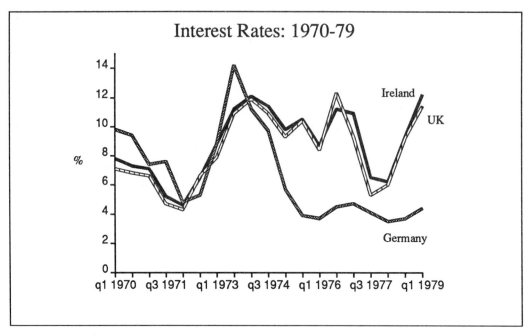

Figure 12.1

rates were back to their initial levels. Conversely, an increase in the money supply would lower interest rates and lead to an immediate capital outflow. Again the money supply and interest rates would quickly revert to their original levels.

*Note:*
*Monetary policy in Ireland in the pre-EMS period largely consisted of credit policy as a consequence of the considerations discussed in this section. We examine this policy in detail in Chapter 14.*

# 12.4 Irish and UK Interest Rates Since 1979

Following Ireland's entry into the EMS and the termination of the sterling link in 1979, exchange rate uncertainty became an extremely important consideration for an investor comparing Irish and UK interest rates. As discussed in section 12.2, the difference between Irish and UK interest rates now reflected exchange rate expectations. If the Irish pound was expected to appreciate over the period, Irish interest rates would be lower than UK rates. Conversely, if the exchange rate was expected to depreciate, Irish interest rates would exceed UK rates.

Figure 12.2 shows the behaviour of Irish, UK and German interest rates for the period 1979 to 1989. The gap between Irish and UK rates was very different from the pre-EMS period. On average, Irish interest rates exceeded UK rates by 1.1% and

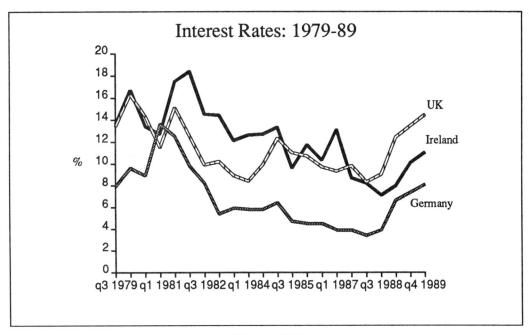

Figure 12.2

German rates by 5.6% over the period 1979q1 to 1989q2 (the average interest rate in Ireland was 12.4%).

One of the arguments put forward in favour of Ireland's entry into the EMS was that Irish interest rates would converge to the lower German rates. It was pointed out that given a fixed Irish pound/DM exchange rate, Irish interest rates could not remain above German rates without causing a capital inflow into Ireland. The outcome, as shown in Figure 12.2, was however very disappointing, at least until 1988. This reflects the fact that markets were not convinced that the Irish commitment to its central rate within the EMS was credible: they consistently anticipated devaluation. In fact, they were too pessimistic on this score. A German investor would have been more than compensated by the high rate of interest in Dublin for any foreign exchange rate loss suffered by moving funds from Frankfurt to Dublin over most of the period from 1979 to 1987.

*Note:*

*As mentioned, Irish interest rates were on average 0.31% higher than UK rates in the pre-EMS period and 1.1% higher than UK rates between 1979 and 1987. The higher differential after 1979 could be viewed as an implicit cost of EMS entry. If the sterling link had been maintained then it is likely that Irish interest rates would have continued to mirror UK rates and would therefore have, on average, been lower than was actually the case. The convergence of Irish interest rates to German rates evident from 1988 onwards, and the upsurge in UK rates, means that this cost has now disappeared.*

The behaviour of the Irish/UK interest differential since the end of 1985 deserves detailed examination (Figure 12.2). The sharp, but relatively short-lived, widening of the differential in the first quarter of 1986 was associated with leading and lagging of foreign exchange payments and receipts (see section 9.6, Chapter 9). This arose from the anticipation that the Irish pound might be devalued at the April 1986 EMS realignment. After the realignment, which left the value of the Irish pound virtually unaltered, there was a sharp fall in Irish interest rates and an improvement in liquidity in the Irish money markets as foreign exchange flowed back into the country. However, for reasons discussed in Chapter 11 it became increasingly clear that the Irish pound would have to be devalued. Interest rates rose again relative to the UK during the summer and after the August devaluation they climbed steeply due to a combination of continued weakness in sterling and the profound uncertainty provoked by the devaluation. The lack of progress towards correcting the public sector deficit, revealed in the autumn 1986 exchequer returns, and the growing political uncertainty generated a crisis atmosphere that was not dispelled until the second quarter of 1987, when the new government had successfully introduced a stringent budget and sterling had risen significantly relative to the EMS currencies.

Developments during 1987 were remarkable. Irish money markets ignored the surge in UK interest rates in the middle of the year. For the first time ever, the level of interest rates in Dublin was more influenced by trends in Frankfurt than in London. By 1989, the fact that London short-term interest rates were almost 5% higher than those in Dublin was no longer considered exceptional. The long-hoped-for decoupling of British and Irish money markets had become a reality due to the credibility of our commitment to maintain the value of our currency stable relative to the DM.

Note, however, that interest rate differentials are a reflection of exchange rate expectations. A relatively high UK interest rate is an indication that the market expects the sterling exchange rate to depreciate in the future. In July 1989, for example, the 5% differential between UK and Irish interest rates translated into an appreciation of the Irish pound from STG£0.87/IR£1 in July to STG£0.95/IR£1 in December 1989. As sterling fell, the interest rate differential narrowed; the Central Bank of Ireland was forced to raise domestic interest rates by 1% to stem the outflow of capital.

## Real interest rates

So far the discussion has been confined to nominal interest rates. In this section we distinguish between *nominal* and *real* interest rates. The real interest rate is the nominal interest rate adjusted for inflation.

(1)   $R_{real} = R_{nominal} - \text{Inflation rate}$

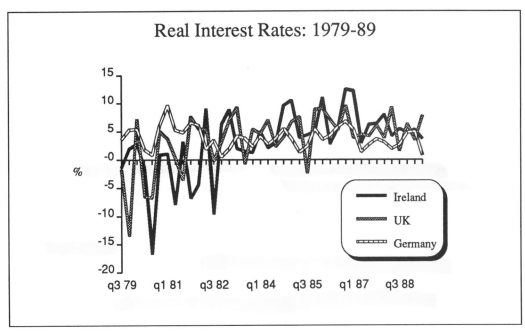

Figure 12.3

*Note:*

*In appendix 5 we discuss the "Fisher equation" which states that the nominal interest rate is equal to expected inflation plus the real interest rate. If it is assumed that inflation expectations are realised, equation 1 is equivalent to the "Fisher Equation".*

Between 1979q2 and 1989q2, the average real interest rate in Ireland was 3.11%. Real interest rates however varied quite considerably over the period. The maximum real interest rate was 12.5% (1986q4) and the minimum real rate was -16.7% (1980q3). This is in contrast to the situation in the 1950s and 1960s when real rates of interest were more stable.

Figure 12.3 shows the real rate of interest in Ireland, the UK and Germany between 1979 and 1989. It is evident from the graph that real interest rates were largely negative for all three countries in the period up to 1982. Since 1982, real interest rates have been positive. On average, real interest rates in Ireland were 0.55% and 0.73% *lower* than rates in the UK and Germany respectively over the period. This outcome is quite different from the nominal interest rate case and as such could be viewed as a benefit of EMS entry. However, real interest rates were lower in Ireland because Irish inflation exceeded UK and German inflation by even more than the nominal interest rate differential. While Ireland's nominal interest rates exceeded nominal rates in the UK and Germany, the differential has been more than offset by a relatively high Irish inflation rate.

295

# 12.5 Short-run Influences on Irish Interest Rates

In Chapter 6 we explained that interest rates were determined by the supply and demand for money. We discussed how the Central Bank controls the money supply and we examined the factors influencing the demand for money. This discussion however took no account of the institutional arrangements through which the control of the money supply is exercised. In this section we focus on the relationship between the Dublin inter-bank market, the Central Bank of Ireland balance sheet and the licensed banks' balance sheet. This perspective on interest rates provides the framework in which we examine the Central Bank of Ireland's interest rate policy in section 12.6.

We stress at the outset that in this section we are discussing the *short-run* (days and weeks) determinants of interest rates in Ireland. As previously mentioned, the main factors influencing Irish interest rates in the medium term (months and quarters) are foreign interest rates and exchange rate expectations.

Figure 12.4 shows the relationship between the Central Bank's balance sheet, the licensed banks' balance sheet and the Dublin inter-bank money market. Consider first the inter-bank market.

The *inter-bank money market* is a market where banks lend (supply) and borrow (demand) money from each other for periods ranging from a day to a year. We will explain later why banks find it necessary to borrow or lend from one another. What

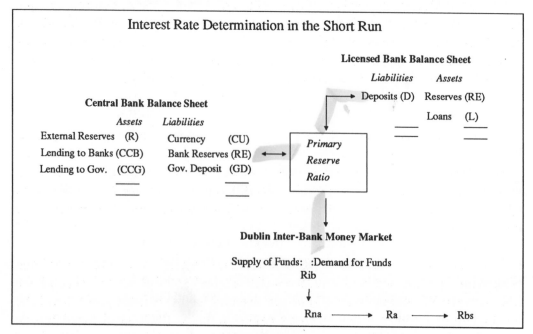

Figure 12.4

296

is important to note at this point is that the forces of supply and demand in this market determine the inter-bank interest rate ($R_{ib}$). Inter-bank interest rates range from the overnight interest rate to the one year rate and are published in national newspapers, usually with a brief comment on how rates moved the previous day. For our purposes the important interest rates are the one month and three month rates.

*Note:*

*Although the inter-bank market is frequently referred to as the "Dublin" inter-bank money market it has no exact location. It is a market conducted through computers, telephones and telex machines.*

The inter-bank interest rate ($R_{ib}$) is extremely important because it determines all other interest rates in the economy. The other important interest rates which take their lead from the inter-bank interest rate are the non-associated banks' interest rate ($R_{na}$), the associated banks' interest rate ($R_a$) and the building society interest rate ($R_{bs}$).

Normally, the non-associated banks will be the first to change their rates following a change in $R_{ib}$. This is because the non-associated banks are heavily dependent on the inter-bank market as a source of funds. Changes in the non-associated banks interest rate are usually followed, after a lag of approximately one to two weeks, by changes in the associated banks' interest rate. (Up to recently the associated banks had to consult with the Central Bank before they could change their rates.) After a further lag, which could range from one to two months, the building societies change their rate in response to the movement in the inter-bank rate. (Building societies are required to give borrowers at least one month's notice of interest rate changes.) This relationship between the various interest rates is shown in Figure 12.4 by the arrows linking $R_{ib}$, $R_{na}$, $R_a$ and $R_{bs}$.

*Note:*

*Arbitrage underlies the relationship between the various interest rates. If, for example, the non-associated banks increased their interest rates (in response to higher inter-bank rates) and the associated banks kept their interest rates constant, individuals and firms would switch their borrowing to the associated banks and switch their deposits to the non-associated banks. This would have the effect of reducing interest rates at the non-associated banks and increasing interest rates at the associated banks.*

In Figure 12.4 we draw two arrows to indicate first a link between the inter-bank market and the licensed banks' reserves (RE) at the Central Bank and, secondly, a link between RE and deposits (D) on the licensed banks' balance sheet. It will be recalled from Chapter 5 that licensed banks' reserves (RE) are dictated by the primary reserve ratio which is set by the Central Bank. A primary reserve ratio of 10% means that for every £1 in current and deposit accounts, the banks must keep

10p in reserves. The important point is that the supply and demand for money on the inter-bank market are in large part determined by the level of bank reserves (RE) in relation to the primary reserve ratio. If a bank has a "deficiency" of reserves (because of say an unexpected withdrawal of cash), that bank will attempt to *borrow* (demand) funds on the inter-bank market in order to replenish its holdings of reserves and thereby meet the primary reserve stipulation. Conversely, if a bank has "excess" reserves (because of say an inflow of cash), that bank will *supply* funds to the inter-bank market and earn interest on its excess reserves. If supply exceeds demand on the inter-bank market, $R_{ib}$ will tend to fall and conversely, if supply is less than demand, $R_{ib}$ will tend to rise. This change in $R_{ib}$ will in turn be reflected in all other interest rates in the system.

We can now go a stage further and ask what are the main factors influencing licensed banks' reserves? The main influences are:

1. changes in the external reserves (R).
2. changes in deposits (D) and bank lending (L).
3. changes in currency holdings (CU).
4. financing of the government's borrowing requirement (EBR).
5. Central Bank interest rate policy.

We now consider factors 1 to 4 in turn, deferring until section 12.6 a discussion of the role of the Central Bank.

## External reserves

Changes in the external reserves (R) on the asset side of the Central Bank balance sheet are a very important influence on domestic interest rates. In terms of the Central Bank balance sheet, a change in the external reserves on the asset side will be reflected in a change in licensed banks' reserves (RE) on the liability side. A fall in R will lead to a fall in RE and conversely an increase in R will lead to a increase in RE.

To see this relationship between R and RE, consider the case of a firm importing, say, £1m worth of wine from France. We wish to trace out on the Central Bank balance sheet the process whereby the importer withdraws £1m, in cash, from his deposit account and then converts this money into francs in order to pay his French supplier. The steps are as follows:

1. When the importer first withdraws the money from his account, licensed bank reserves (RE) decrease by £1m and currency in circulation (CU) increases by £1m.

2. The importer then goes to the foreign exchange desk in the bank and exchanges

298

£1m for francs. This is reflected in the Central Bank balance sheet as a fall in both CU and R.

3. Ignoring the temporary change in CU, the net effect is a decrease of £1m in RE and R.

The same analysis applies if there is an overall balance of payments deficit. If there is a surplus on the balance of payments, both R on the asset side and RE on the liability side of the Central Bank balance sheet increase.

Suppose now that prior to the withdrawal of funds the banks had the correct reserves/deposit ratio to meet the primary reserve ratio. Following the withdrawal of £1m from reserves the banks will have a *deficiency* of reserves and to redress the situation the banks will borrow the needed funds on the inter-bank market. This will result in an increased demand for funds on the inter-bank market and the interest rate ($R_{ib}$) will increase.

*Note:*
*Suppose a bank had £5m in reserve and £50m in deposit accounts and the required primary reserve ratio was 10%. In this case the bank has the correct amount of funds in reserve: reserve/deposits = £50/£500 = 10%. If an importer withdraws £1m, the bank will have a deficiency of reserves. Reserves/deposits = £4/£49 = 8.1%. In this case the bank will need to borrow £0.9m on the inter-bank market in order to meet the reserve requirement.*

The main point is that a balance of payments deficit will reduce licensed banks' reserves and this will lead to an increased demand for funds on the inter-bank market. Domestic interest rates will rise. Conversely, a balance of payments surplus will increase licensed banks' reserves and lead to an increase in the supply of funds on the inter-bank market. In this case, interest rates fall and this will be followed by a decrease in all other interest rates in the economy.

At any point in time, any transaction that affects the balance of payments (either the current or capital account) will affect R and RE and therefore interest rates. For example, a trade account surplus, transfers from the EEC, an increase in foreign borrowing by the government or purchases of land or securities in Ireland by foreigners will all tend to reduce domestic interest rates in the short-run.

As we pointed out in Chapter 9, the main factors influencing the balance of payments and therefore the external reserves are relative inflation rates, changes in world interest rates, relative growth rates in GNP and speculation. For example, if speculators expect a depreciation of the Irish exchange rate (for whatever reason), capital would be transferred from Irish pounds to some foreign currency in anticipation of making a capital gain. This will be reflected in the Central Bank balance sheet as a fall in R and RE and the banks will have a deficiency of reserves. The demand for funds on the inter-bank market will increase and domestic interest rates will rise. On the other hand, a fall in world (in particular, German) interest rates, a fall in Irish inflation and slower growth in Irish GNP would lead to a fall in inter-bank interest rates and therefore all other interest rates in the system.

## Savings and licensed bank lending

Because deposits (D) with banks are an important component of savings by the general public, an increase in private sector savings tends to lead to an increase in deposits on the liability side and an increase in licensed bank reserves (RE) on the asset side of the licensed banks' balance sheet. As a result, banks will now have excess reserves and the supply of funds to the inter-bank market will increase. Interest rates will tend to fall. Conversely, a decrease in savings will lead to an increase in interest rates on the inter-bank market.

An upsurge in bank lending (L) not accompanied by an increase in reserves will lead to an increase in inter-bank interest rates. Recall from Chapter 5 that when a bank makes a loan, the borrower's account is credited with the amount of the loan. The borrower then draws down the account at will. In terms of the banks' balance sheet, bank lending leads to an increase in bank deposits on the liability side and an increase in lending on the asset side. There is therefore a fall in the reserve/deposit ratio which will lead to a demand for funds on the inter-bank market. Interest rates will rise. Conversely, a fall in lending will lead to lower interest rates.

## Changes in currency holdings

Changes in currency holdings (CU) by the public tend to be seasonal and reasonably predictable. For example, there is always a significant increase in currency holdings in the weeks leading up to Christmas. In terms of the Central Bank's balance sheet in Figure 12.4, an increase in currency holdings will be reflected in an increase in CU and a decrease in RE on the liability side of the balance sheet. People simply withdraw money from their current and deposit accounts and hold it as currency. If the increase in CU was unexpected, and banks were maintaining only the exact amount of reserves in relation to deposits, the banks would be forced to borrow on the inter-bank market and interest rates would tend to increase. Conversely, a fall in currency holdings would tend to reduce inter-bank interest rates.

## Financing the government's borrowing requirement

There are a number of ways, both direct and indirect, that the government can influence interest rates. We will confine our discussion here to the effects of the financing of the exchequer borrowing requirement (EBR). We saw in Chapters 3 and 6 that the government can finance the EBR by borrowing from:

1. abroad.
2. the Central Bank.
3. the licensed banks.
4. the non-bank public.

Borrowing from the non-bank public does not directly affect domestic interest rates. Purchases of government stock will initially lead to a fall in licensed bank deposits as there is a transfer of funds to the government. However, when the government spends the money, a large part of it will find its way back into the banks and deposits will again increase. Overall there will be little change in bank deposits, bank reserves or interest rates.

If the government borrows from the licensed banks the situation is very similar to that when some firm or individual borrows from the banks. Bank lending increases on the assets side of the licensed banks' balance sheet and deposits rise on the liabilities side. If the banks were adhering exactly to the primary reserve ratio, there will be a deficiency in reserves following the increase in lending to the government. This in turn will lead to an increased demand for funds on the inter-bank market and interest rates will tend to rise.

Consider now the case where the government finances its borrowing requirement by borrowing abroad. Imagine the government borrowing, say, a certain amount in DMs from a bank in Frankfurt. When the money is transferred to Ireland, the government exchanges the DMs for Irish pounds at the Central Bank. The Central Bank will add the DMs to its external reserves (R) and credit the government's account at the Central Bank (GD) with the Irish pound equivalent. In terms of the Central Bank's balance sheet in Figure 12.4, R increases on the assets side and GD increases on the liabilities side.

That however is not the end of the process. When the government runs down its Central Bank deposit account by increasing expenditure, the money will, in part, result in an increase in licensed bank deposits and reserves. For example, if the government spent the funds on a new road, the various contractors involved in the project will receive cheques from the government drawn on its Central Bank account. The contractors will deposit the cheques in commercial banks and their reserves will increase. In terms of the Central Bank balance sheet, GD decreases and RE increases. The banks will now find that they have excess reserves and the supply of funds on the inter-bank market will increase. Domestic interest rates will tend to fall.

In brief, an increase in government foreign borrowing will lead to an increase in the external reserves (R) on the assets side of the Central Bank balance sheet and an increase in licensed bank reserves (RE) on the libilities side (the increase in GD is only temporary). The result will be a decrease in domestic interest rates.

The final source of funds available for financing the EBR is borrowing from the Central Bank. This amounts to the Central Bank printing money and making it available to the government. In terms of the Central Bank balance sheet in Figure 12.4, Central Bank lending to the government (CCG) increases on the assets side and government deposits (GD) increase on the libilities side. Essentially, the Central Bank credits the government's account by the amount of the loan. As in the case of government foreign borrowing, when the government spends the money, GD will decrease and licensed bank reserves (RE) will increase. This will lead to "excess" licensed bank reserves with the result that the supply of funds on the inter-bank market will increase and interest rates will tend to fall. The main difference between borrowing from abroad and borrowing from the Central Bank is that in the former case the external reserves increase. In the next section we will discuss the effects of the Central Bank's policy of lending to the government in greater detail.

*Note:*

*In terms of the effect on the money supply, a distinction can be made between government borrowing from abroad and from the Central Bank, on the one hand, and government borrowing from the banks on the other. Government borrowing from the banks leads to a once-off increase in the money supply. However, when the government borrows from the Central Bank or abroad, there is a multiple increase in the money supply. The reason is that in the case of borrowing from abroad or from the Central Bank, there is an increase in bank reserves which allows for a further rise in bank lending.*

# Summary

The reader might get the impression from the foregoing discussion that Irish interest rates are affected by a great number of factors. In the short-run, this is indeed the case. We saw for example that any factor influencing the balance of payments will result in a change in the external reserves and this will tend to affect domestic interest rates. Similarly, changes in currency holdings, savings, bank lending and the government's borrowing requirement are all important short-run influences on interest rates. We wish to emphasise, however, the point made at the beginning of this section that these factors only have a short-term influence on domestic interest rates. If, as in the case of Ireland, the exchange rate is fixed and there is a high degree of capital mobility, domestic interest rates cannot deviate very much from foreign interest rates without provoking capital inflows or outflows. For example, if government foreign borrowing lowers Irish interest rates below foreign rates, this will result in a capital outflow until such time as domestic rates rise back to their initial level. The financing of the government's borrowing requirement thus has only a short-run effect on domestic interest rates. The same consideration applies to the other determinants mentioned above.

# .6 The Central Bank's Interest Rate Policy

In Chapter 6 we discussed monetary policy in the context of the Keynesian/monetarist debate. The discussion centred on whether or not the government should attempt to influence aggregate demand and GNP through the money supply. The Keynesian school argues that changes in the money supply have weak effects on aggregate demand because investment is insensitive to changes in interest rates. The monetarists, on the other hand, argue that changes in the money supply may have harmful effects on GNP. They argue, for example, that excessive growth in the money supply is likely to lead to higher inflation. For this reason they argue that the money supply should be allowed to grow at a constant rate each year (enough to meet the predicted growth in real GNP) and that there should be no discretionary monetary policy.

In Ireland, monetary policy is dominated by a narrower range of issues than that debated in the international literature. In this country there are two components of monetary policy: interest rate policy and credit policy. We discuss interest rate policy in this section and we defer until Chapter 14 our discussion of credit policy. The first point to note with regard to interest rate policy is that in Ireland the Central Bank does not attempt to control the money supply or to influence aggregate demand through interest rates. The objective of interest rate policy is simply to *stabilise* interest rates in the short-run. A former Central Bank Governor outlined the policy as follows:

Although the Bank may not attempt to affect the broad trend in interest rates, it does pursue ... the important function of smoothing, within reason, short-run fluctuations and predictable seasonal patterns in interest rates.

O Cofaigh T. F., "Observations on Interest Rates", Central Bank of Ireland, *Annual Report*, 1983, p. 102.

To see how the policy works, recall from section 12.5 that a change in the external reserves (R) will lead to a change in the licensed banks' reserves (RE) and inter-bank interest rates ($R_{ib}$). The external reserves fluctuate as the Central Bank intervenes in the foreign exchange market to stabilise the Irish exchange rate in the European Monetary System. This variation in the external reserves is reflected in changes in inter-bank interest rates. The Central Bank's interest rate policy attempts to break this link between the external reserves and inter-bank interest rates by using the CCB variable (Central Bank lending to the banks) and by changing the primary reserve ratio. The Central Bank "sterilises" the effects of changes in R.

In terms of the Central Bank balance sheet in Figure 12.4, a decrease in R on the assets side leads to a fall in RE on the libilities side and forces the banks to borrow on the inter-bank market in order to maintain the primary reserve ratio. If the Central Bank lends the required funds to the licensed banks (increase in CCB) and/or reduces the primary reserve ratio, the need for the banks to borrow on the inter-bank market would be avoided and interest rates would remain unchanged.

Conversely, if the banks had "excess" reserves because of, say, an unexpected inflow of cash, this would lead to an increase in the supply of funds to the inter-bank market and interest rates would tend to fall. If the Central Bank was of the opinion that the increase in reserves was only temporary and that the fall in domestic interest rates was not warranted by fundamentals, it could increase the primary reserve ratio or sell government stock to the banks to remove the "excess" reserves. In this case, the supply of funds on the inter-bank market would remain unchanged and interest rates would remain stable. In practice, changes in the primary reserve ratio are very infrequent, and the Central Bank relies mainly on changing its lending to the banks to stabilise interest rates.

*Note:*

*The Central Bank may also withdraw liquidity from the market by "quoting for funds". From time to time the Bank quotes a specified interest rate for term deposits of specified periods. This instrument works only to withdraw funds from the market as the Central Bank does not keep deposits with the licensed banks.*

## Central Bank lending to the banks

There are five ways the Central Bank can make resources available to the commercial banks.[2]

1. *The short term facility (STF)*. This credit facility is similar to an individual having an "overdraft" facility at a bank. Normally, banks borrow on an overnight basis (against agreed securities) but they can borrow for a period of up to seven days. Each of the licensed banks is given a quota which is determined by the size of the bank and by its participation in the inter-bank market. Aggregate quotas in 1989 amounted to approximately £167m. The banks are charged a "short term facility interest rate" on borrowing and this interest rate increases the more the bank makes use of this facility. For example, if a bank borrows five or six times within a fortnight, the interest charged is the STF interest rate plus half of one percent. Frequent drawings lead to higher interest rate charges.

2. *Secured advances.* This is longer-term borrowing against the security of government stocks. Banks tend to avail of this facility after they have reached their short-term facility quota.

3. *Sale and Repurchase Agreements.* Licensed banks sell government stock to the

Central Bank in order to obtain cash. There is however an agreement for the licensed banks to buy back (repurchase) the stock at a later date. This agreement enables the Central Bank to provide funds (liquidity) to the market for specified periods. Conversely, the Central Bank could agree to sell government stock to the banks and thereby remove liquidity from the market.

4. *Foreign Currency Swaps*. This facility is similar to a sale and repurchase agreement except that foreign exchange rather than government securities is exchanged for an agreed period at the end of which the transaction is reversed. Licensed banks' holdings of foreign exchange (which incidentally are subject to exchange controls) are not defined as "primary reserves" and cannot be used to meet the primary reserve ratio. If a licensed bank has holdings of foreign exchange (which is intended for use at a later date) and is short of primary reserves, the foreign exchange can be temporarily exchanged for primary reserves at the Central Bank, allowing the bank to meet its reserve requirements. This facility can be used both to inject liquidity into the market (Central Bank exchanges Irish pounds for foreign currency) or remove liquidity (Central Bank swaps foreign currency for Irish pounds). It is important to note that the Central Bank does not publish information on swap transactions and as a result data for CCB does not reflect movements in this type of credit.

5. *Re-discounting government stock*. In this case, the banks simply sell government stock to the Central Bank in order to obtain funds.

All these channels of lending are known as "support for the inter-bank market". As a means of managing liquidity in the system, each of these instruments has its own uses. The STF is normally sufficient to meet day-to-day shortages of liquidity. Swaps and term deposits, on the other hand, are used to provide or withdraw liquidity for periods of time determined by the Central Bank. The primary reserve requirement is used when the shortage or surplus of liquidity is perceived to be of significant duration. In what follows we will define instruments 1, 2, 3 and 5 above as being equal to CCB. (There is no published information on instrument 4.) We then use this definition of CCB to evaluate interest rate policy.

# Central Bank intervention in the money markets

As an example of Central Bank intervention in the money market, consider the data in Table 12.2.

The data shows a clear inverse relationship between changes in the external reserves (R) and changes in Central Bank credit to the licensed banks (CCB). In the first two quarters of 1978, R fell and CCB increased as the banks borrowed from the Central Bank. This situation was reversed in the last two quarters as R increased

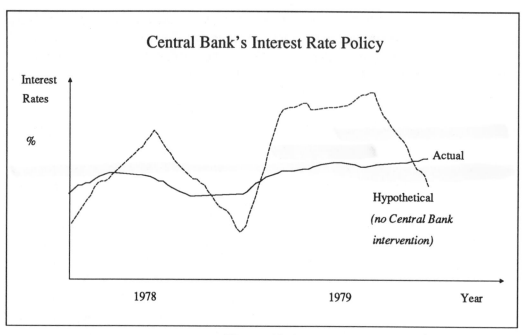

Figure 12.5

and the banks repaid the Central Bank. In 1979, R fell over the first three quarters and the Central Bank provided funds to the banks. The banks reduced their indebtedness to the Central Bank in the final quarter.

Figure 12.5 illustrates the hoped-for effect of changes in CCB on interest rates. First we draw the hypothetical trend in interest rates if the Central Bank did *not* provide funds to the banks. The second curve shows the trend in interest rates when support is provided through changes in CCB.

*Table 12.2*

**Changes in the external reserves and Central Bank credit: IR£ million**

|        |    | ΔR   | ΔCCB |      |    | ΔR   | ΔCCB |
|--------|----|------|------|------|----|------|------|
| 1978   | q1 | -45  | 34   | 1979 | q1 | -283 | 128  |
|        | q2 | -194 | 115  |      | q2 | -43  | 177  |
|        | q3 | 150  | -61  |      | q3 | -44  | 16   |
|        | q4 | 140  | -45  |      | q4 | 118  | -252 |

*Note*: The CCB variable does not include swap transactions
*Source*: Various Central bank of Ireland, *Quarterly Bulletins*

In the hypothetical situation where CCB is constant, interest rates rise as R falls and vice versa. This is shown in Figure 12.5 as interest rates rising in the first two quarters of 1978 and falling in the last two quarters. Similarly, reflecting the fall in R, interest rates rise over the first three quarters of 1979 and fall in the final quarter. As can be seen from Figure 12.5, when the Central Bank provides liquidity to the banks, the trend in interest rates is much smoother because the banks are not completely dependent on the inter-bank market for funds. This type of policy, in so far as it attempts to smooth predictable and temporary changes in interest rates, would seem to be desirable as it eliminates unnecessary, soon to be reversed, changes in interest rates. Fluctuations in interest rates can create uncertainty and possibly have an adverse effect on investment and output.

There is however a rather thin line between stabilising temporary changes in interest rates on the one hand, and attempting to influence the long-run trend in interest rates (at the cost of a fall in the external reserves) on the other. For example, we saw in Table 12.2 that the external reserves fell in the first three quarters of 1979. This was largely due to a sustained deficit on the current account of the balance of payments. The Central Bank increased lending to the banks in response to this fall in the external reserves and by the end of November 1979, the associated banks' indebtedness to the Central Bank had risen to IR£390m.

A number of points can be made with regard to this intervention by the Central Bank. First, a period of approximately nine months seems to stretch the term "temporary" somewhat. Secondly, as the period was extended it became clear that if the licensed banks were compelled by the Central Bank to repay their debts, interest rates on the inter-bank market would have increased significantly. The Central Bank was not prepared to allow this to happen and reacted to the situation by reducing the associated banks' primary reserve ratio from 13% to 10% and the secondary reserve ratio from 30% to 25%. By a stroke of a pen, the associated banks now had "excess" reserves which were used to reduce the banks' indebtedness to the Central Bank. This reduction in the required reserve ratios facilitated the repayment of £252m to the Central Bank in final quarter of 1979.

*Note:*

*As we will see in Chapter 14, this reduction in both the primary and secondary reserve ratio and the subsequent reduction in bank indebtedness to the Centrak Bank was associated (coincidental?) with a major improvement in the associated banks' compliance with the credit guidelines. Up to that point, the associated banks had consistently breached the credit guidelines and the Central Bank was unable to enforce its credit policy.*

The third point we wish to make is that this level of intervention had the effect of lowering the external reserves. If the Central Bank had not provided liquidity, domestic interest rates would have increased and capital would have flowed into the country. This capital inflow would in effect have financed the deficit on the current account of the balance of payments and the external reserves would have remained relatively stable. As the Governor of the Central Bank commented at the time:

... there was a conscious decision to take action to prevent (interest) rates going even higher, in recognition of the burden this would have placed on the economy; it was, however, at the cost of a larger fall than we would have liked in the external reserves..

C.M. Murray, "Monetary Policy", Central Bank of Ireland, *Annual Report*, 1980, p. 117.

## Evaluation

Econometric techniques can be used to indicate both the degree of Central Bank involvement in domestic money markets and the effectiveness of stabilisation policy. Consider first equation 1:

(1) $\Delta CCB = \alpha - \beta \Delta R$

where $\alpha$ and $\beta$ are coefficients and $0 < \beta < 1$. The coefficient $\beta$ is known as the *sterilisation* coefficient. It indicates how the Central Bank *reacts* to changes in the external reserves (R). A $\beta$ coefficient of, say, 0.7 means that for every £1m fall in the external reserves, the Central Bank injects (notice the negative sign in the equation) £0.7m into the money market. The sterilisation coefficient indicates the degree of Central Bank involvement in the money markets.

In equation 2, the variables are reversed:

(2) $\Delta R = \chi - \delta \Delta CCB$

where $0 < \delta < 1$. The coefficient $\delta$ which is known as the *offset* coefficient. It indicates what proportion of any injection or withdrawal of funds by the Central Bank is offset by a fall or rise in the external reserves. If, for example, $\delta$ equalled 0.4 this would mean that for every £1m injected into the money market by the Central Bank, the external reserves fell by £0.4m. The offset coefficient indicates the effectiveness of Central Bank policy. A low offset coefficient suggests an effective interest rate policy. Conversely, a high offset coefficient suggests that injections of funds by the Central bank will quickly disappear through changes in the external reserves.

If $\beta$ and $\delta$ equal 1 and 0 respectively, then this would indicate complete sterilisation and no offset. In this case, interest rate policy would be very active and very effective. If, on the other hand, $\beta$ and $\delta$ equalled 0.6 and 0.4, this means that for every £1 fall in the external reserves, the Central Bank injects 60 pence into the market. Of this 60 pence, 40% will be immediately offset through changes in the external reserves.

Two studies have estimated sterilisation and offset coefficients for the Irish economy. The first of these studies,[3] based on *quarterly* data, found for the pre-EMS period (1972-79) sterilisation and offset coefficients of 0.01 and 1.0 respectively. This means that prior to EMS entry the Central Bank did not engage to any significant extent in an interest rate policy but when it did the policy was entirely ineffective due to complete offset through changes in the external reserves.

In contrast, the results for the post-1979 period suggest sterilisation and offset coefficients of 0.75 and 0.79 respectively. This means that for every £1m fall in the external reserves, the Central Bank injected £0.75m into the money markets by the end of the quarter. However the offset coefficient indicates that 79% of the £0.75m injection was offset through further changes in the external reserves. These figures indicate that, in contrast to the pre-EMS period, the Central Bank has pursued an active interest rate policy since we joined the EMS. The reduction in the absolute value of the offset coefficient in the post-EMS period is probably a reflection of the exchange controls issued by the Central Bank in 1979.

The second study[4] based on *monthly* data over the period January 1980 to April 1985 found a sterilisation coefficient of 0.6. This means that for every £1m fall in the external reserves, the Central Bank injected (withdrew) £0.6m within the same month. However, over a period of five months, the offset coefficient was found to equal 1. In other words, any injection (or withdrawal) of funds by the Central Bank was *completely* offset by changes in the external reserves.

The results of these two studies are broadly consistent and suggest that there is a high degree of integration between Irish money markets and foreign money markets both before and since we joined the EMS, with the result that there is very little scope for an independent interest rate policy in Ireland. Attempts to sterilise changes in the external reserves so as to stabilise domestic interest rates in the longer term could prove ineffective and costly. Interest rate policy should therefore be confined to smoothing day-to-day variations.

# 7 Conclusion

In this chapter we examined the determinants of interest rates in Ireland and discussed the Central Bank of Ireland's interest rate policy. The main points covered in the chapter include:

- Domestic interest rates should equal foreign interest rates plus the expected change in the exchange rate. If the Irish pound is expected to depreciate in the future, domestic interest rates will exceed foreign interest rates

• Since entry into the EMS in 1979, Irish interest rates have, on average, exceeded both UK and German interest rates. However, recently there is evidence that Irish interest rates are at last converging to German rates as was expected at the time of EMS entry

• Bank and building society interest rates take their lead from inter-bank interest rates. Changes in the one- and three-month inter-bank interest rates will be quickly followed by changes in the non-associated banks', associated banks' and eventually in building societies' rates

• The short-run determinants of Irish interest rates include changes in the external reserves, changes in bank lending, changes in savings and currency holdings by the public and the financing of the government's borrowing requirement

• The Central Bank's interest rate policy attempts to smooth short-run fluctuations in interest rates by providing funds to the banks or withdrawing funds from the money market. If the banks borrow reserves from the Central Bank this reduces the pressure for funds on the inter-bank market and interest rates will remain relatively stable.

# Notes

1. Another complication was the fact that exchange controls were extended to apply to dealing between Dublin and London in 1979, whilst UK exchange controls were completely abolished in 1980. Investors were also affected by the introduction in Ireland of deposit interest retention tax (DIRT) in 1986.

2. For a detailed discussion see K. Barry, "The Central Bank's Management of the Aggregate Liquidity of Licensed Banks", Central Bank of Ireland, *Annual Report*, 1983.

3. A. Leddin, "Portfolio Equilibrium and Monetary Policy in Ireland", *The Economic and Social Review*, Vol. 17, No. 2, January, 1986.

4. F. X. Browne, "A Monthly Money Market Model for Ireland in the EMS", Central Bank of Ireland, *Annual Report*, 1986.

# Chapter 13

# Aspects of International Financial Theory

## .1 Introduction

In this chapter we introduce the student to some aspects of international financial theory. We begin by explaining how the forward exchange rate can be used to hedge against exchange rate risk. In section 13.2, we examine, from the perspective of an importer and an exporter, the experience with the sterling, dollar and DM forward exchange rate since 1979. This is followed in section 13.3 by a discussion of interest rate parity theory. This theory relates the difference between the forward and spot exchange rate (the premium or discount) to the differential between foreign and domestic interest rates. In section 13.4 we outline some of the more important internal hedging techniques for reducing exposure to exchange rate risk. We conclude the chapter by a discussion of financial futures and we explain how futures contracts can be used to hedge against both interest rate risk and exchange rate risk.

## .2 The Forward Exchange Market

Individuals or firms engaging in commercial or investment transactions find it desirable to minimise *foreign exchange risk* through some *hedging* technique. As an example of exchange rate risk consider the case of an exporter who expects to receive STG£1m in one months time and anticipates that the exchange rate at that time will be STG£0.82/IR£1. At this exchange rate, Irish pound receipts will be IR£1,219,512 (STG£1m * 1/0.82) and the exporter calculates that he will make a "normal" profit on the transaction. Suppose, however, that the Irish pound unexpectedly appreciates relative to sterling to a level of STG£0.94/IR£1. The exporter's sterling receipts of STG£1m will now translate into IR£1,063,829. This is IR£155,683 lower than was originally anticipated and it is possible that the exporter now incurs a loss on the transaction. This example serves to illustrate that changes in exchange rates can very easily reduce or eliminate profits.

A number of different hedging techniques have been developed to avoid or eliminate exchange rate risk. These techniques may be broadly categorised as *internal* and *external* hedging techniques. In a later section in this chapter we outline a number of internal hedging techniques. In this section we concentrate on one of the most widely-used external hedging techniques, the forward exchange market. It is important to note at the outset that while a hedging strategy minimises exchange rate losses, it also removes any potential (windfall) profits that might arise from exchange rate movements. In the above example, if the exchange rate had depreciated, the exporter would have gained. Hence while a hedging strategy removes the risk of loss it also removes any potential gain that might arise from exchange rate movements. In practice, firms' treasury managers and other individuals concerned with international cash flows do not always attempt to eliminate exchange rate risk as, on occasions, risk-taking can be very profitable. However, most firms are content to try to make money out of their trading activities and prefer to leave speculation on the foreign exchange markets to the experts!

## Forward exchange contract

A forward contract consists in buying or selling a specified amount of foreign currency for delivery some time in the future at an exchange rate agreed today. Payment and delivery are not required until the maturity date. For example, consider the case of an Irish firm importing cars from Germany. The cars will arrive in three months' time and the Irish importer will be required to pay, say, DM2,670,000 at that time. If the current *(spot)* exchange rate is DM2.67/IR£1, the importers bill will be exactly IR£1m. The importer however anticipates that over the next three months the Irish pound will depreciate against the DM and he is not prepared to take the exchange rate risk. (If the exchange rate moved to, say, DM2.5/IR£1, the importer's bill would increase to IR£1,064,000.) The importer can enter into a contract today to have DM2,670,000 delivered in three months' time at an exchange rate *(the forward rate)* agreed today. Once the importer enters into a forward agreement he is no longer exposed to any exchange rate risk.

Forward exchange rates are normally quoted for one, two, three, six and twelve months but contracts can be arranged for other periods. The rates are available from the banks and are now published in some of the national newspapers. In Table 13.1 we compare the spot and six month forward exchange rates for the Irish pound against sterling and the dollar.

Recall from Chapter 9 that the "bid" rate is the rate at which banks buy Irish pounds (or sell foreign currency) and the "offer" rate is the rate at which the banks sell Irish pounds (buy foreign currency). The spot rates given in Table 13.1 indicate that a bank dealer will sell sterling for STG£0.87 per Irish pound and buy sterling for STG£0.871 per Irish pound. The difference between the bid and offer rates is referred to as the "spread" and it provides the banks' profit from foreign exchange transactions.

The six-month forward rates given in Table 13.1 show the rates at which sterling and the dollar can be purchased or sold forward. Suppose for example an Irish importer wished to obtain sterling six months from now. The bank will sell sterling forward to the importer (delivery is in six months' time) at a exchange rate of STG£0.8848/IR£1. Similarly, an exporter who is due to receive a certain amount of dollars in six months' time can eliminate exchange rate risk by selling dollars to the bank at a forward exchange rate of $1.3955/IR£1.

*Table 13.1*

**Spot and forward exchange rates: July 1989**

|  | STG£/IR£ | | $/IR£ | |
|---|---|---|---|---|
|  | Bid | Offer | Bid | Offer |
| Spot | .8700 | .8710 | 1.4000 | 1.4020 |
| 6 month forward | .8848 | .8873 | 1.3915 | 1.3955 |

*Source:* AIB International Department

The forward exchange rate is normally at a *premium* or a *discount* relative to the spot exchange rate. Using indirect quotes, (i.e. STG£/IR£), which is the convention in Ireland, if the forward exchange rate is lower than the spot rate the Irish pound is said to be at a discount relative to the foreign currency. Conversely, if the forward rate is higher than the spot rate, the Irish pound is said to be at a premium relative to the foreign currency.

*Note:*

*If the Irish pound is at a discount relative to sterling then that is the same thing as saying that sterling is at a premium relative to the Irish pound. Conversely, if the Irish pound is at a premium, sterling is at a discount.*

In Table 13.1, the Irish pound is at a premium relative to sterling and at a discount relative to the dollar. Comparing the spot and forward rates, a greater amount of sterling can be obtained per IR£ in the future and hence the Irish pound is at a premium. Fewer dollars can be obtained in the future per IR£ and hence the Irish pound is at a discount relative to the dollar. If, as sometimes happens, the spot and forward rates are exactly the same, the forward price is said to be "flat".

A variation on the forward currency contract is the *forward currency options contract*. This gives the holder the right but not the obligation to buy or sell currency in the future. For this right, the holder will be charged a fee expressed as a percentage of the total amount of money involved. The right to sell a particular currency is referred to as a *put option* and the right to purchase a certain currency is known as a *call option*. The important point about option contracts is that while the holder can avoid exchange rate losses (downside risk) she can benefit from any favourable movements in the exchange rate (upside potential). For example, take the case of an Irish exporter who expects to receive $1m in three months' time. To avoid exchange rate risk the exporter enters into an options contract to convert dollars to Irish pounds at an exchange rate of, say, $3/IR£1. If the spot dollar exchange rate depreciates (Irish pound appreciates) to $4/£1, the exporter should exercise her option contract in order to avoid incurring an exchange rate loss. If however the spot dollar exchange rate appreciates (Irish pound depreciates) to, say, $2/IR£1, the exporter should allow the options contract to lapse and instead convert the dollars receipts to Irish pounds on the spot market. In this case she will gain from the exchange rate movement. If the exporter had used a normal forward currency contract, she would have avoided any exchange rate loss but would also have foregone any gains.

## Speculation and forward exchange rate

While the forward exchange rate is normally used to eliminate exchange rate risk, it can also be used for speculative purposes. This is because the forward exchange rate and the *future spot exchange rate* are rarely the same. Suppose for example that the six month sterling forward rate is currently STG£0.8848/IR£1 and that a speculator anticipates (for whatever reason) that the spot exchange rate in six months time will be STG£0.80/IR£1.

On the assumption that in six months' time the speculator's expectations with regard the future spot exchange rate prove correct, she could profit from the situation. The speculator could:

1. Contract to buy, say, STG£5m forward at STG£0.8848/IR£1. The Irish pound cost is IR£5,650,994.

2. Then in six months time sell the STG£5m on the spot market at STG£0.80/IR£1 and receive IR£6,250,000.

3. Profit on the transaction is IR£599,006.

In general, if the expected future spot exchange rate is less than the forward exchange rate, the speculator should buy the foreign currency forward and then sell it on the spot market. If the expected future spot exchange rate is greater than the forward exchange rate, the speculator should contract to sell the foreign currency on the forward market and purchase it on the spot market.

Let us suppose that a speculator could anticipate *perfectly* the three-month future spot exchange between sterling and the Irish pound. If, over the period 1979 quarter 2 to 1987 quarter 2, the speculator entered into a contract every three months to either buy or sell IR£1m forward, her profits at the end of the period would have been IR£1.123m. This profit cannot be expressed in percentage terms as no capital is actually invested when the speculator enters into the forward contract. The profit is simply the return from risk taking. There is, therefore, considerable scope for very profitable speculation on the foreign exchange markets, but the key question is; "Is there any rule on which a speculator could act and profit or is speculation in the foreign exchange market as random as playing blackjack in a casino?" We examine the Irish experience with regard to sterling, the DM and the dollar in the following section.

It is important to note that the type of speculation discussed above is not permitted under Irish exchange controls. Up to January 1988 firms could only buy or sell currency forward if the transaction was "trade related". Service industries had to use some alternative hedging technique or accept the exchange rate risk. As and from January 1988 the exchange controls were relaxed to allow service industries access to forward cover. However capital transactions and in particular debt repayments and speculative capital flows continue to be excluded. The exclusion of service industries from forward cover encouraged the development of alternative hedging techniques. One method of circumventing the controls was to use a "forward contract between two foreign currencies". Consider the case of an exporter who expects to receive a certain amount of dollars in the future but who cannot obtain forward cover because of the exchange controls. The exporter might observe that the Irish pound is much more stable relative to the DM than it is to the dollar because of Ireland's participation in the European Monetary System (EMS). Hence the exporter could enter into a forward contract to convert dollars to DMs and then convert the DMs to Irish pounds on the spot market. The stability of the EMS would remove most of the exchange rate risk.

# 3 The Forward Exchange Market for Irish Pounds: 1979-89

In Figures 13.1, 13.2 and 13.3 we compare the three month forward exchange rate ($F_t$) and the *future* spot exchange rate ($E_{t+1}$) for sterling, the DM and the dollar respectively. In other words, the forward rate today is compared with the spot rate

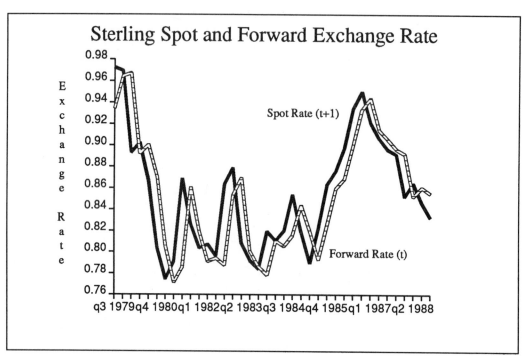

Figure 13.1

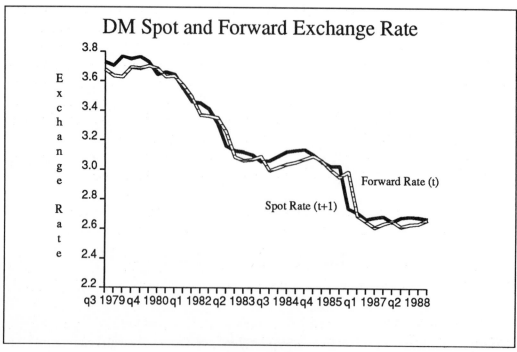

Figure 13.2

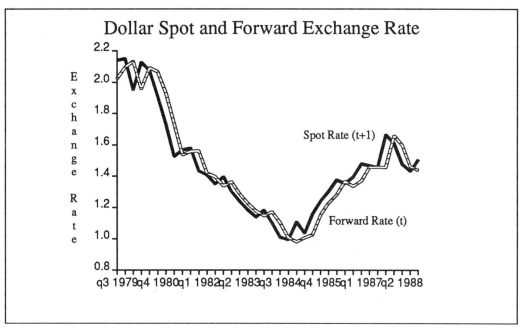

Figure 13.3

three months from now. It is evident from the three graphs that the two curves do not coincide. In particular, it is noticeable that, for all three currencies, the forward rate consistently *fails to predict turning points* in the future spot exchange rate.

As mentioned in the previous section, if the forward exchange rate and the future spot exchange rate are not equal, it is possible to profit from forward market speculation. In this section, however, we will examine $F_t$ and $E_{t+1}$ from the perspective of exporters and importers. Consider first the case of an exporter who expects to receive STG£1m in three months' time. The exporter has a choice as to whether to sell sterling forward and avoid exchange rate risk or sell sterling spot in three months' time and accept the exchange rate risk. Consider for example the situation in 1980 quarter 4. The alternative outcomes would have been as follows:

1. If the exporter had sold STG£1m three months earlier at a forward exchange rate of $(1/F_t) = (1/.8710)$, Irish pound receipts would have been IR£1,148,106.

2. If the exporter accepted the exchange rate risk and sold STG£1m on the spot market at $(1/E_{t+1}) = (1/.8038)$, Irish pound receipts would have been IR£1,244,091.

It is clear from this example that because $F_t$ is not equal to $E_{t+1}$, the exporter's receipts can differ significantly depending on which option he chooses. If the exporter had decided to hedge, his receipts would have been IR£95,984 *lower* (per STG£1m transaction) than if he had accepted the exchange rate risk and sold sterling

317

on the spot market. This is a very sizeable difference and it illustrates just how expensive hedging can be. For this reason, exchange rate exposure management is an integral part of treasury management in any large firm whose business involves extensive foreign exchange dealings. We repeat the point made earlier that exchange rate risk should not be avoided as a matter of course. Sometimes significant benefits can be obtained from accepting the exchange rate risk.

In the above example the exporter would make a loss if he contracted forward. However, an importer would have gained by entering into a forward contract. The reason is that the importer is buying foreign currency when the exporter is selling so that the two cases are mirror images of the same transaction.

It turns out that over the period 1979 quarter 2 to 1988 quarter 4, exporters would have gained (and importers lost) from a strategy of consistently covering forward. Table 13.2 summarises the results for an exporter who received STG£1m and the equivalent in DMs and dollars at the end of each quarter and who consistently sold these foreign receipts on the forward market.

*Table 13.2*

**Exporters' gains (+) and losses (-) per quarter from a strategy of covering forward: 1979 q2 - 1988 q4**

**Figures are expressed in IR£**

|  | *Sterling* | *Mark* | *Dollar* |
|---|---|---|---|
| Maximum profit | 121,988 | 43,175 | 161,567 |
| Mean profit | 1,959 | 10,026 | 374 |
| Maximum loss | -95,439 | -88,9051 | -150,084 |
| Standard deviation | 49,003 | 23,124 | 74,968 |

The data show that while an exporter would have made considerable profits and losses in certain quarters, on average a strategy of consistently covering forward would not only have removed the worry associated with exchange rate exposure but would actually have increased his profits. The opposite holds true for the importer.

Is there a reason for this outcome? Note from the previous example that the exporter loses from a hedging strategy if $E_{t+1}$ is less than $F_t$. Referring now to Figures 13.1, 13.2 and 13.3 note that when the Irish pound is depreciating, $E_{t+1}$ is less than $F_t$ and when the Irish pound is appreciating $E_{t+1}$ tends to be greater than $F_t$. This is particularly evident for sterling and the dollar. The exporter therefore would have gained from a hedging strategy when the Irish pound appreciated on foreign exchanges and lost when the Irish pound depreciated. Conversely, the importer gains from a hedging strategy when the Irish pound depreciates and loses when the Irish pound appreciates.

*Note:*

*The main explanation why $E_{t+1}$ is less than $F_t$ when the Irish pound depreciates and greater than $F_t$ when the Irish pound appreciates is interest rate parity theory, which we discuss in the following section.*

The above analysis suggests that when the Irish pound is appreciating, exporters would profit from covering forward. However, when the exchange rate is depreciating, exporters may find it beneficial to accept the exchange rate risk. The opposite holds for importers. The difficulty, however, is predicting sustained periods of Irish pound appreciation or depreciation. Put another way, the problem is to forecast turning points in exchange rate movements. As we have already emphasised in Chapters 9 and 10 this is by no means an easy task.

# .4 Forward Market Efficiency

The forward exchange rate is said to be an "unbiased" predictor of the future spot rate if, over time, the forward rate is equal to the future spot rate plus or minus a random error. Mathematically, the unbiasedness hypothesis may be written:

(1)  $E_{t+1} = \alpha + \beta F_t + u_t$

where $E_{t+1}$ is the spot exchange rate in time $t+1$, $F_t$ is the forward exchange rate in time $t$ and $u_t$ is a random error (i.e. the mean of the errors is zero and the errors fluctuate randomly about this mean). The terms $\alpha$ and $\beta$ are coefficients. If $F_t$ is an unbiased predictor of $E_{t+1}$, the coefficients $\alpha$ and $\beta$ will equal 0 and 1 respectively. In other words, $F_t$ will equal $E_{t+1}$ on average.

If the unbiased hypothesis holds, the forward rate published in the national newspapers today is the "best" indicator of what the spot exchange rate will be in the future. By the term unbiased we do not mean accurate. It simply means that the forecast error (or prediction error) tends to be random and cannot easily be explained. For example, refer back to Table 13.1 and note that in July 1989, the six month dollar forward rate was 1.3915. This can be taken as a forecast of what the dollar spot rate will be in December 1989. In fact, the spot rate in December turned out to be 1.4795, giving a forecast error of 8.8%. Not very impressive. Similarly, refer back to Figures 13.1, 13.2 and 13.3 and note that the $E_{t+1}$ and $F_t$ curves rarely coincide and that $F_t$ consistently fails to predict the turning points in $E_{t+1}$. In fact, the series $E_t$ (the current spot rate) and $F_t$ are much more closely related than $E_{t+1}$ (the future spot rate) and $F_t$ which seems to suggest that $F_t$ merely embodies information on current spot rates and as such contains little or no predictive power.

319

However, even under these circumstances, $F_t$ can still be an unbiased predictor of $E_{t+1}$. This is because the unbiased hypothesis does not require $F_t$ to be a good predictor of $E_{t+1}$, it simply requires that $F_t$ is not consistently wrong in its predictions. However the unbiasedness criteria does imply that all other forecasting techniques are even worse predictors of the future spot rate!

Related to the unbiasedness hypothesis is the issue of *forward market efficiency*.[1] A market is said to be efficient if prices fully reflect all available information. For example, a company's share price should reflect all publicly available information about the company. If this is not the case, unexploited profit opportunities are available and the stock market is said to be inefficient.[2] The same idea can be applied to the forward exchange market. Forward market efficiency requires that investors are *rational* in that he or she can process currently available information and use this information to forecast the future exchange rate (this is known as the rational expectations hypothesis). Again the investor's forecasts do not have to be correct all the time. Market efficiency simply requires that, on average, the forecast errors are unrelated or uncorrelated about a mean of zero.

To see how market efficiency relates to the forward exchange rate refer back to the discussion on speculation in section 13.2. There we assumed that expectations prove correct and that the *expected* future spot rate in six months time ($E^*_{t+1}$) was equal to STG£0.80/Ir£1. If the current forward rate ($F_t$) was equal to STG£0.8848/IR£1, a speculator could make a profit by purchasing sterling forward and then, in six months' time, selling sterling on the spot market. However, if a sufficient number of speculators share this view about the future spot exchange rate, the situation cannot persist. The sales of Irish pounds (purchases of sterling) on the forward market will drive $F_t$ downwards towards $E^*_{t+1}$ and, as profit opportunities disappear, speculation will tend to diminish. In summary, if the market is efficient, all available information will be accurately processed by investors in formulating the expected future spot rate so that $E^*_{t+1}$ will equal $E_{t+1}$. Because of arbitrage, the forward rate converges towards $E^*_{t+1}$ and will, in effect, embody all of the currently available information about the future spot exchange rate. It is in this sense that the forward market is said to be efficient. The *simple* market efficiency hypothesis may therefore be stated as:

$$E^*_{t+1} = E_{t+1} \text{ and } F_t = E^*_{t+1}$$

Exchange rate expectations prove correct on average (the rational expectations hypothesis) and the forward exchange rate equals the expected future spot rate. If the simple market efficiency hypothesis proves correct then $F_t = E_{t+1}$. But this is precisely the unbiasedness hypothesis given in equation (1) above. Hence, the *simple* market efficiency hypothesis and the unbiasedness hypothesis are one and the same thing.

*Note:*

*Associated with the unbiasedness and market efficiency hypothesis is the concept of a "random walk".*
*A variable is said to follow a random walk if changes in the variable from one period to the next are*
*unpredictable or random. An example is a drunk wandering along the street. His next step could be*
*to the left, to the right, straight ahead or even backwards! In effect, his next step is unpredictable*
*(i.e. random). There is some evidence that the Irish pound exchange rate follows a random walk.*[3]
*The implication is that historical exchange rate data cannot be used to forecast the future exchange*
*rate. This tends to bring into question techniques such as "chartism" which attempt to identify patterns*
*in exchange rate movements as a means of predicting the future exchange rate. It can be shown that*
*the random walk is perfectly consistent with the unbiasedness and market efficiency hypotheses but*
*that there is nothing in the unbiasedness and market efficiency hypotheses that requires the exchange*
*rate to follow a random walk.*

However, market efficiency allows for a *risk premium* on forward contracts. In the previous example, speculators, in an attempt to make profits, drive $F_t$ towards $E^*_{t+1}$. In practice, $F_t$ need not exactly equal $E^*_{t+1}$ because at some point speculators may demand a risk premium in order to compensate them for the possibility of being wrong. Market efficiency now requires that

$$E^*_{t+1} = E_{t+1} \quad \text{and} \quad F_t = E^*_{t+1} + RP_t$$

where $RP_t$ is the risk premium demanded by investors. This is known as the *general efficiency hypothesis* and it requires that the forward rate embody all publicly available information on the future exchange rate (given by $E^*_{t+1}$) as well as the market's attitude towards risk (given by $RP_t$). The important point to emerge from this discussion is that the relationship between $F_t$ and $E_{t+1}$ is no longer unambiguously defined. If a researcher estimates equation (1) and finds that $F_t$ is a *biased* predictor of $E_{t+1}$, it does not necessarily follow that the forward market is inefficient. It can be argued that the *general* rather than the *simple* market efficiency hypothesis holds and that the researcher did not properly account for the risk premium. Even if the researcher estimates an equation of the form:

(2) $\quad E_{t+1} = \alpha + \beta F_t + \chi Z_t + u_t$

we still cannot reject the efficient market hypothesis unless we are sure the additional variable $Z_t$ is a good proxy or indicator of the risk premium. Unfortunately, current research indicates that the risk premium can change signs over time and this makes it extremely difficult to measure.

*Note:*
*The simple market efficiency hypothesis assumes that investors are risk neutral so that the risk premium does not enter into the analysis.*

In the Irish context, very little work has been published to-date on the above issues. Leddin (1988), using quarterly data, found that the forward exchange rate for the Irish pound was an unbiased predictor of the future spot rate in the case of sterling and the DM but not the dollar. This result tended to concur with earlier findings in the international literature. For example, Cornell (1977) and Levich (1979) find evidence to support the simple market efficiency hypothesis and Levich (1981) finds that the forward exchange rate out-performs forecasting agencies in predicting the future exchange rate. However, using improved techniques, Hansen and Hodrick (1980) reject the simple market efficiency hypothesis and Frankel (1982) finds that a time varying risk premium is important in explaining why the simple market efficiency hypothesis is rejected. At the present time, the consensus in the international literature seems to be that the unbiasedness hypothesis does not hold. The implication is that if a rule can be developed to out-perform the forward exchange rate in forecasting the future spot rate, profits can be made from forward market speculation. The results relating to market efficiency are less decisive and, because of the estimation difficulties involved, will probably never be satisfactorily resolved. More recently, Taylor (1988) presented results which indicated that investors were *irrational* in processing information about the future exchange rate and this result tends to conform with the earlier findings in Dooley and Shafer (1983) that rules found to be profitable in one period continued to be profitable in later periods even after the rule became publicly known. The implication is that profits are available from forward market speculation.[4]

A word of caution is however necessary. In practice, forecast errors tend to be small and random so that it is very difficult to develop a "forecast rule" that out-performs the forward rate as a predictor of the future spot rate. This means that speculators in the foreign exchange market have very little chance of working out a formula that would guarantee them profits.

# 13.5 Interest Rate Parity Theory

Interest rate parity theory (IRPT) states that the forward premium or discount on the foreign exchanges is determined by the differential between domestic and foreign interest rates. In order to illustrate IRPT, we compare the return from an investment in Ireland with the return from an investment in the US. It is important to note that the investor is assumed to cover forward in order to avoid exchange rate risk. This use of the forward exchange rate guarantees the return on a foreign investment and for this reason the theory is often referred to a "covered interest rate parity" theory.[5] At the end of the period, the total amount of money received (principal plus interest) from a pound investment in Ireland equals:

(3)  $(1 + R_{irl})$

For example, £1,000 invested in Ireland at an interest rate of 10% (or 0.1) would give a total return of £1,100 at the end of the period:

£1,000$(1 + 0.1)$ = £1,100.

The return from, say, a US investment is more complicated. First we must convert Irish pounds into dollars using the exchange rate E. Secondly, we must invest the dollars in the US and receive interest at the rate $R_{us}$. Thirdly, we must contract forward so as to convert the total US return (principal plus interest) back into Irish pounds at the end of the investment period. By using the forward exchange rate, F, the investor is not exposed to any exchange rate risk. The total return from a US investment, denominated in Irish pounds, is given by:

(4)  $(1 + R_{us})E/F$

*Note:*
*The exchange rate E is first used to convert Irish pounds to dollars. The total US return is $(1 + R_{us})$. The forward rate, 1/F, is used to convert the dollars back into Irish pounds.*

As an example, suppose that an Irish investor wishes to invest £1,000 in the US and the following data apply:

| | | |
|---|---|---|
| E | = $1.416/IR£1 | Spot exchange rate. |
| F | = $1.3934/IR£1 | 1 year forward exchange rate. |
| $R_{us}$ | = 8.25% (or 0.0825) per annum. | US interest rate. |

First convert, say, IR£1,000 into dollars using the spot exchange rate, E. $1,416 = 1.416 * IR£1,000.

Secondly, invest $1,416 in the US at an interest rate of 8.25% and receive $116.8 ($1,416 * 0.0825) at the end of the investment period. This gives a total return (principal plus interest) of $1,532.8.

Thirdly, contract forward to convert $1,532.8 back into Irish pounds. This gives an Irish pounds return of IR£1,100, ($1,532.8 * 1/1.3934 = IR£1,100).

The same result could have been obtained by inserting the relevant data into equation (4):

IR£1,000(1 + 0.0825)1.416/1.3934 = IR£1,100

While the interest rate in the US is only 8.25%, the overall return from a US investment denominated in Irish pounds, is 10%. The reason for this difference is that the Irish pound forward exchange rate is at a discount relative to the spot exchange rate so that the investor gains on the foreign exchange market.

*Arbitrage* should now ensure that the return from an Irish investment and a US investment should be the same. Equating equation (3) with equation (4) gives:

$$(1 + R_{irl}) = (1 + R_{us})E/F$$

Rearranging

$$F/E = (1 + R_{us})/(1 + R_{irl})$$

Subtracting 1 from both sides and rearranging:

(5)   $(F - E)/E = (R_{us} - R_{irl})/(1 + R_{irl})$

Equation (5) is the most common way of expressing the IRPT. The equation states that the forward premium or discount (left hand side) should equal the interest differential (right hand side). If the Irish pound is at a premium (F > E), the foreign interest rate will exceed the domestic interest rate. Conversely, if the Irish pound is at a discount (F < E), the Irish interest rate will exceed the foreign interest rate. The reader can verify by inserting the relevant data into equation (5) that IRPT holds. An investment in Ireland or the US gives a return of 10%.

We now turn to the case where IRPT does not hold and we explain how arbitrage works to equate the forward premium or discount to the interest differential.

*Note:*
*We have used the dollar in the above example to develop the basic IRPT equation, but the theory can be generalized to include any currency and foreign interest rate. Hence in equation (5), the US can be replaced by the more general term of "interest rate in the rest of the world".*

# Arbitrage
We mentioned that arbitrage should ensure covered interest rate parity. In order to illustrate how arbitrage brings about convergence, consider what would happen if equation (5) did not hold. In particular assume the following data apply:

| E | = | STG£0.942/IR£1 | Spot exchange rate. |
|---|---|---|---|
| F | = | STG£0.951/IR£1 | 1 year forward exchange rate. |
| $R_{irl}$ | = | 10% per annum. | Domestic interest rate. |
| $R_{uk}$ | = | 14% per annum. | UK interest rate. |

Inserting this information into equation (5) it is clear that covered interest rate parity does not hold. The interest differential on the right hand side of the equation exceeds the Irish pound forward premium on the left hand side. A speculator could benefit from this situation.

One option is to borrow, say, IR£5m in Ireland for a period of one year. The steps involved are then as follows.

*Today*
1. Convert the IR£5m into UK pounds using the spot exchange rate, E, and receive STG£4,710,000.
2. Invest STG£4,710,000 in the UK for one year at an interest rate of 14% and receive STG£659,400 at the end of the period. Total UK receipts at the end of the year (principal plus interest) equals STG£5,369,400.
3. Contract to sell (deliver) STG£5,369,400 forward at 1/F and receive IR£5,646,057 one year from now.

*One year from now*
4. Fulfil the forward contract by selling STG£5,369,400 and receive IR£5,646,057.
5. Repay the Irish pound loan of IR£5m and the interest rate charges of 10% or IR£500,000. Total repayments equals IR£5,500,000.

*Overall*

| | |
|---|---|
| Proceeds | IR£5,645,057 |
| Repayments | IR£5,500,000 |
| Profit | IR£146,057 |

This example illustrates that if the interest rate parity equation does not hold then it is possible to profit from the situation with little or no risk to the speculator. We have simplified the analysis by ignoring transaction costs, different taxation rates on deposit interest and restrictions on investments imposed by governments. In practice these factors are important. Furthermore we have assumed that interest rates remain constant in both countries for the duration of the transaction period. This is unlikely to be the case, but investors could avoid this uncertainty by entering into fixed interest rate contracts.

In the above example it was profitable to borrow in Ireland and invest in the UK because the UK interest rate exceeded the Irish interest rate by more than the

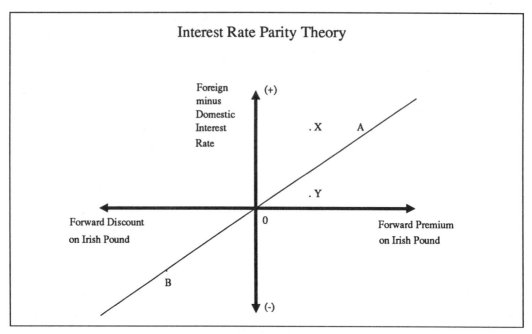

Figure 13.4

forward premium on the Irish pound. Figure 13.4 shows a graphical representation of the situation. The interest differential (foreign minus domestic) is given on the vertical axis and the premium (+) or discount (-) on the Irish pound is given on the horizontal axis. The line running upwards from left to right is the parity line. A point on this line indicates covered interest rate parity because the forward premium or discount is equal to the interest differential. The points A and B are two such points. In the previous example the interest differential exceeded the Irish pound premium. This situation is represented by the point X. As we saw, it was profitable in this case to borrow in Ireland and invest in the UK. In fact if we are at any point above and to the left of the parity line this investment rule will prove profitable. This is also true for the south-west quadrant.

Suppose now that the premium on the Irish pound exceeds the interest differential. This situation is given by the point Y in Figure 13.4. It is now profitable to borrow in the UK and invest in Ireland. In general, this rule will prove profitable for any point below and to the right of the parity line.

The available evidence for the Irish economy and elsewhere suggests that covered interest parity does hold.[6] In fact, banks tend to set the forward foreign exchange rate by looking at interest rate differentials. That is, we are normally at a point on the parity line. The reason is that the actions of speculators in attempting to profit from divergences bring about convergence. Recall that in the previous example it was profitable to borrow in Ireland and invest in the UK because the interest differential exceeded the Irish pound premium. Consider now how this investment rule might bring about interest parity.

First, borrowing in Ireland increases $R_{irl}$ and investing in the UK lowers $R_{uk}$. The term on the right hand side of the IRPT equation, $(R_{uk} - R_{irl})/(1 + R_{irl})$, therefore decreases. Simultaneously, the conversion of Irish pounds into sterling means that the supply of Irish pounds on the foreign exchange market increases and E tends to depreciate (fall). The purchase of Irish pounds forward means that the forward exchange rate, F, will appreciate (rise). Hence the value of the left hand side of the IRPT equation, $(F - E)/E$, tends to increase. With the value on the left hand side increasing and the value on the right hand side falling, convergence comes about. Allowing for transaction costs, profits will no longer be available and covered interest rate parity is restored. It is in this sense that arbitrage ensures that IRPT will hold.

*Note:*

*It is possible that exchange controls might prevent arbitrage restoring the values on the left and right hand sides of the IRPT equation. However, the leading and lagging by exporters and importers respectively (see Chapter 9) cannot be prevented by exchange controls and this would have the effect of re-establishing any divergence from IRPT.*

# Exchange rate expectations

In this section we draw together some of the main theories developed in this and previous chapters with a view to explaining how exchange rate expectations can be formed. Recall the theory of purchasing power parity (PPP), which we claimed in Chapters 9 and 10 provided the only firm basis on which we could build a theory of exchange rate determination. The PPP equation can be written as:

(6)   $P_{irl} * E = P_{world}$

where $P_{irl}$ and $P_{world}$ are prices in Ireland and the "rest of the world" respectively. According to PPP, exchange rates must, in the long-run, tend to levels that equalise the purchasing power of currencies internationally. We saw that, at its simplest, this implied that price differentials would tend to be reflected in movements in exchange rates. For example, re-arranging equation (6) as, $E = P_{world}/P_{irl}$, an increase in Irish prices relative to "world" prices would lead to a devaluation of the Irish pound in the EMS. In general, high inflation countries would tend to have depreciating currencies, low inflation countries appreciating currencies. This generalisation provides us with a basis on which to build *expectations* about movements in exchange rates. If the statistics show that recent trends in inflation in Ireland have led to the situation where the Irish pound is above its long-run PPP level, then markets will begin to anticipate a fall in the value of the Irish pound. Logically, this should cause a rapid outflow of funds from Ireland, in order to avoid the capital losses that will be incurred when the Irish pound falls.

Thus, we can see that, according to PPP theory, price differences or differential rates of inflation (if the analysis is conducted in terms of rates of change) are the driving force behind exchange rate expectations.

We can go a stage further and ask why inflation rates differ from country to country? Monetarists would answer, "because countries expand their money supplies at different rates". Increases in the money supply, via the quantity theory of money, lead to increases in inflation. According to this view, everything is ultimately driven by the rate of monetary expansion in each country. Schematically, these interrelationships can be summarised as follows:

Differentials in rate of money expansion $\rightarrow$ (Quantity Theory) $\rightarrow$ differentials in rates of inflation $\rightarrow$ (PPP) $\rightarrow$ expected changes in exchange rate.

We now examine exchange rate expectations from a slightly different perspective. We discuss the chain of events running from PPP theory to the "Fisher Equation", Interest rate parity theory (IRPT) and the forward exchange rate. The relevant equations are summarised as follows:

(6). $P_{irl} * E = P_{world}$          PPP theory.

(7). $R_n = P^e + R_r$          Fisher equation.

(8). $(F - E)/E = (R_{world} - R_{irl})/(1 + R_{irl})$    IRPT.

(9). $E_{t+1} = \alpha - \beta F_t$          Forward exchange rate as an unbiased predictor of the future spot exchange rate.

where

| | | | | | |
|---|---|---|---|---|---|
| $P_{irl}$ | = | Domestic price level. | $R_r$ | = | Real interest rates. |
| $P_{world}$ | = | "World" price level. | $P^e$ | = | Expected price level. |
| $E$ | = | Exchange rate, defined as STG£/IR£. | $F_t$ | = | Forward exchange rate. |
| | | | $R_{irl}$ | = | Nominal interest rate in Ireland. |
| $R_n$ | = | Nominal interest rate. | | | |
| $R_{world}$ | = | Nominal "world" interest rate. | $E_{t+1}$ | = | Future spot exchange rate. |

In the previous example we pointed out that if the Irish pound is above its long-run PPP level, markets will anticipate a devaluation of the Irish pound and investors will move money out of Ireland in order to avoid incurring capital losses. This outflow could, however, be staved off by a rise in Irish interest rates which would compensate investors for the eventual fall in the Irish pound and persuade them to leave their money in Ireland. Hence, an increase in inflation leads to higher domestic nominal interest rates.

This point is also evident from the "Fisher Equation", equation (7), which states that the nominal interest rate is equal to the expected inflation rate plus the real interest rate. Assuming that inflation expectations are realised (next period's inflation is what was expected this period) and assuming constant real interest rates, it is clear from equation (7) that an increase in inflation leads to an increase in nominal interest rates.

However, if equation (8), the IRPT relationship holds, an increase in the nominal interest rate in Ireland must be matched by a fall in the forward exchange rate and/or a devaluation of the spot exchange rate. In other words, the reduction in the foreign/domestic interest rate differential leads to a lower premium on the forward exchange rate of the Irish pound.

To complete the circle, equation (9) states that the forward exchange rate is an unbiased predictor of the future spot exchange rate. That is, over time, the forward exchange rate is a reasonably good predictor of the future spot exchange rate. A decrease in the forward exchange rate is therefore an indication that the future spot exchange rate of the Irish pound will be devalued some time in the future.

*Note:*
*We are using the term devaluation rather than depreciation as the analysis relates to the Irish pound which is fixed in the EMS. If the Irish pound was in a freely floating exchange rate system, we would use the term depreciation.*

In summary, inflation differentials between countries lead, via the "Fisher Equation", to differentials in nominal interest rates. Nominal interest rate differentials in turn, via IRPT, lead to a change in the premium or discount on the forward exchange rate. The two most common methods of predicting or forecasting the future spot exchange rate are deviations from PPP and the forward exchange rate. Both of these methods should give consistent forecasts of future exchange rates. It is however important to bear in mind that when the exchange rate is in a fixed or managed exchange rate system the decision to devalue is, at least in the short or medium term, primarily a political decision. (Refer back to the discussion of devaluation in Chapter 9.) Central Banks can postpone devaluing the exchange rate at the cost of the fall in the external reserves. In this regard, short-term indicators other than PPP and the forward exchange rate may be useful supplements to a forecast of the exchange rate.

# 13.6 Internal Hedging Techniques

In this section we outline some of the more common internal hedging techniques. These techniques enable firms to hedge against exchange rate risk and are less costly than external hedging techniques.

*Use Domestic Suppliers.* One way of eliminating exchange rate risk is to switch from a foreign supplier to a domestic supplier. This may not however be possible. A great deal of the raw materials imported into Ireland have no domestic substitutes. The alternative is to use a supplier from a country participating in the EMS. The stability of the EMS in recent years offers some protection against exchange rate movements. If this is not possible, then a supplier operating out of a weak currency country is preferable to a strong currency country supplier. If the foreign currency depreciates, imports will cost less in Irish pounds.

*Invoice in Irish Pounds.* If a company can invoice in Irish pounds, then exchange rate risk is eliminated. In effect, the exchange rate exposure is transferred to the other party in the transaction. Whether or not this is possible will probably depend on the relative strength of the two parties. For example, a large buyer may be able to pressurise a small supplier into accepting the exchange rate risk. On occasions, both parties may agree to trade on the basis of a mutually acceptable hard currency such as the DM.

*Leading and Lagging of Payments or Receipts.* Earlier in Chapter 9 we discussed how importers and exporters can speculate on future exchange rate movements by leading and lagging. Importers and exporters can also minimise exchange rate losses through leading (paying before time) and lagging (delaying receipts for as long as possible). Under Irish circumstances, this technique is easy to resort to if one is convinced the Irish pound is going to rise or fall. As always, the problem is the enormous difficulty of predicting exchange rate movements. But given the very high exports/GNP and imports/GNP ratios in Ireland, a concerted use of this strategy can have a very significant impact on the level of external reserves. For example, in January 1985, despite the existence of exchange controls, the external reserves fell by approximately IR£1,000m in just over a week on the expectation that the Irish pound would be devalued in an EMS realignment. As it turned out, the Irish pound was not devalued on that occasion.

*Match assets (liabilities) against liabilities (assets) in the same currency.* Consider the case of an Irish firm with foreign assets, for example, a subsidiary company in France. All of the assets and liabilities of the company in France will have to be translated from francs to Irish pounds in order to prepare the balance sheet of the parent company in Ireland. If the Irish pound appreciates on the foreign exchange market, then the value of the French subsidiary will, in Irish pound terms, have fallen and this will lower the value of the parent company. This type of exchange risk is referred to as *translation exposure*. One way to avoid or minimise this risk is to match overseas assets with liabilities in the same currency by, for example, borrowing in French francs. Hence if the Irish pound exchange rate appreciates, this will reduce the value of both assets and liabilities.

*Match foreign currency payments (receipts) against receipts (payments) in the same currency*. Consider the case of an exporter whose receipts, denominated in Irish pounds, could be reduced by an appreciation of the Irish pound exchange rate. This type of exchange rate risk is called *transaction exposure* or economic exposure. One way of avoiding this type of exposure is to match foreign currency receipts (from the sale of output) against foreign currency payments to suppliers. That way a loss on receipts will be matched by a reduction in payments. This technique will not however be possible unless the firm has a reasonable two-way flow in the same foreign currency.

*Transfer Pricing*. As we saw in Chapter 10, transfer pricing is concerned with setting intra-firm prices so as to minimise tax burdens. It is also possible to use transfer pricing (allowing, of course, for customs duties and tax laws) to reduce exchange rate exposure. For example, suppose a company has two subsidiaries, one in strong currency country and the other in a weak currency country. If the subsidiary in the weak currency country sells at cost to the other subsidiary, profits are maximised in the hard currency country and minimised in the weak currency country. The company will then gain if currencies move in the expected direction.

# 7 Futures Contracts

The function of a financial futures contract is to enable companies and individuals with positions in money, securities and foreign exchange markets to reduce their exposure to risk. Financial futures trading is conducted on the floor of an organized exchange. The main futures exchanges include (the year indicates the starting date):

International Money Market (IMM) of Chicago: 1972.
Singapore International Monetary Exchange (SIMEX): 1979.
New York Futures Exchange: 1979.
London International Financial Futures Exchange (LIFFE): 1982.

There are also other exchanges in Sweden, New Zealand, France and Canada. In terms of trading volume, the IMM is by far the largest and most important exchange. In May 1989, the Irish Futures/Options Exchange (IFOX) commenced trading. IFOX trades in three different types of contracts:

Future on 20 year Irish gilt.
Future on 3 month DIBOR (Dublin inter-bank offer rate).
Future on Irish pound/dollar exchange rate.

Each of these contracts has its own specifications. The contracts are for a standardised amount and are delivered on a standardised date in the future. As an example of how a futures contract might be used in practice, consider first the 3 month DIBOR contract.

## Interest rate futures contract
The specifications of the DIBOR contract are:

| | |
|---|---|
| Contract size: | IR£100,000 |
| Settlement date: | Third Wednesday of March, June, September, December. |
| Quotation price: | 100 minus the rate of interest. |
| Tick size | 0.01% |
| Tick value | IR£2.50 |

The DIBOR contract is a standardised size of IR£100,000. The standardised settlement dates are the third Wednesday of March, June, September and December. The quotation price is calculated as 100 minus the interest rate (the Dublin inter-bank offer rate). Hence, if the interest rate is 10%, the quotation price is 100 - 10 = 90. If the interest rate is 8%, the quotation price is 100 - 8 = 92. This means that if interest rates decrease, the quotation price increases and the buyer of the futures contract gains. If, on the other hand, interest rates increase, the quotation price falls and the buyer incurs a loss.

The tick size is the minimum price movement and is set at 0.01%. The tick value is calculated as the value of the contract multiplied by the tick size multiplied by the duration of the contract (3 months or 90 days).

Tick value = IR£100,000 * 0.0001 * 90/360 = IR£2.50

The purchaser of a futures contract is required to put up a deposit, known as the "initial margin", as collateral. Each day the clearing exchange mark all accounts to the current market value and the purchaser is refunded or required to pay a maintenance margin (variation margin) in cash each day. The variation margin is

332

equivalent to the difference between yesterday's and today's closing price. This feature of futures contracts is known as "mark-to-market". If the purchaser cannot pay the variation margin, the clearing exchange will close out his position and make good any losses from the initial margin. In this regard, the clearing exchange guarantees the performance of the futures contract.

Consider now the case of treasury manager who, in July 1990, anticipates a cash surplus of IR£1m between mid-September and mid-December 1990. The treasury manager proposes to place this money in a bank deposit. The current interest rate is 10% but the treasury manager expects interest rates to fall to 8% sometime in September. If interest rates do fall, then the interest received on the deposit will be reduced. For example, if the interest rate equals 10%:

$$\text{Deposit interest} = \text{IR£1m} * 10/100 * 90/360 = \text{IR£25,000}$$

that is the deposit interest equals the sum deposited multiplied by the interest rate multiplied by the duration (90 days). If the interest rate falls to 8%:

$$\text{Deposit interest} = \text{IR£1m} * 8/100 * 90/360 = \text{IR£20,000}$$

Hence a reduction in interest rates from 10% to 8% leads to a loss of IR£5,000 on deposit interest.

To hedge against falling interest rates the treasury manager enters into a futures contract. The basic idea is to set up in the futures market an equal but opposite position to that in the deposit or cash market. In order to "lock-in" an interest rate of 10% on a deposit of IR£1m, the treasury manager must purchase 10 contracts of IR£100,000. If interest rates fall, the value of the futures contract will increase and the profits on the futures contracts will compensate for the loss of interest on the IR£1m deposit. Suppose that in September the treasury manager's expectations are realised and interest rates fall to 8%. The treasury manager now sells the 10 futures contracts. The profit is:

$$\text{Profit on futures contract} = (92 - 90)/100 * 10 * \text{IR£100,000} * 90/360 = \text{IR£5,000}$$

That is, the treasury manager purchased ten contracts of IR£100,000 at a price of 90 and sold at a price of 92. The profit on the futures contract exactly offsets the loss on the deposit interest. In effect, the treasury manager has achieved a "perfect hedge". We could also calculate the profit on the futures contract using the tick values. The difference between the sell price (92) and the purchase price (90) is equivalent to 200 ticks. The profit is equal to the number of ticks multiplied by the tick value multiplied by the number of contracts.

$$\text{Profit on futures contract} = 200 * £2.50 * 10 = \text{IR£5,000}$$

The treasury manager by "fixing" the interest on a floating rate deposit also trades-away any potential gains. If interest rates increased over the period, the gain made on deposit interest is offset by a loss on the futures contract. It should be borne in mind that it takes two parties to complete a transaction. If someone is purchasing a futures contract, someone else must be selling. This means that the two parties are taking opposing views on how interest rates will move in the future. If the buyer of the futures contract gains, the seller of the contract loses and vice versa. In fact, because of the "mark-to market" feature of futures contracts the gains and losses are actually paid and/or received during the course of the contract.

Because of arbitrage between the cash and futures markets, the interest rates on futures contracts are very closely related to the interest rates embodied in the yield curve (see appendix 5). Hence, if the yield curve is upward sloping indicating that interest rates will increase in the future, the interest rate on futures contracts will be greater than current interest rates. This means that futures contracts only offer insurance against unexpected changes in interest rates, that is changes in interest rates over and above changes reflected in the yield curve.

## Foreign currency futures contracts

A foreign currency futures contract is an agreement to buy or sell a standard amount of foreign currency at a specified date in the future and at an agreed price. In this regard, a foreign currency futures contract is similar to a forward exchange rate contract as both techniques can be used to hedge against exchange rate risk.

For example, consider the case of an exporting firm that expects to receive $1m in three months' time. At a current exchange rate of $1.40/IR£1, expected Irish pound receipts are IR£714,286. The firm is however concerned that the Irish pound exchange rate will appreciate to $1.60/IR£1, in which case Irish pound receipts will fall to IR£625,000. The expected appreciation of the Irish pound will reduce export receipts by IR£89,286.

The firm could hedge against this exchange rate risk by selling foreign currency futures contracts. On IFOX, the dollar/Irish pound future is for a contract size of $50,000. Hence, the firm should contract to sell 20 future dollar contracts at an exchange rate of £1.40/IR£1. If the Irish pound appreciates to $1.60/IR£1, the firm buys dollar futures. In Irish pound terms, the purchase price is less than the selling price and the firm makes a profit equivalent to the loss incurred in the cash market. In this regard, foreign currency futures contracts are very similar to forward contracts. The two types of contracts differ however in a number of respects.

1. Forward contracts are negotiated with a bank at any location. Futures trading is conducted by brokers on the floor of an organized exchange. The IFOX system is a computerised trading system where dealers are linked via screens to a central computer.

2. Banks will enter into a forward contract for any amount. Futures contracts are for a standard size contract for delivery at a standard maturity date in the future.

3. Forward contract prices are expressed by a bank in the form of bid and offer rates. Some futures prices are determined on the floor of the exchange by an "open outcry" system. The IFOX system is based on an electronic automated system rather than "open outcry" and there is no actual trading floor.

4. Futures contracts require the purchaser to put up an initial margin as a good-faith gesture. A variation margin is then required each day as the price of the contract is mark-to-market. Forward contracts require no margin prior to the settlement date. This is one of the most important differences between futures and forward contracts.

# 3 Conclusion

Some of the main points discussed in this chapter include:

- The forward exchange transaction is an agreement to buy or sell a specified amount of currency at an agreed date in the future

- The premium or discount on forward exchange rates is related to the difference between domestic and foreign interest rates. The theory underlying this relationship is known as "covered interest parity theory"

- Covered interest rate arbitrage is the process that ensures that "covered interest parity" holds even in the short-run

- The hypothesis that the forward exchange rate is an unbiased predictor of the future spot exchange rate states that, on average, over long periods of time the forward exchange rate is a good predictor of the future spot rate, that is the prediction error will be small and random

- Forward market efficiency

- Risk premium

- Purchasing power parity (PPP) theory and the forward exchange rate can be used to forecast the future spot exchange rate. PPP and the forward exchange rate are related through the "Fisher Equation" and "covered interest parity theory"

- There are a number of internal hedging techniques that can be used to reduce exposure to exchange rate risk

- Financial futures contracts can be used to reduce interest rate and exchange rate risk

- A foreign currency futures contract is similar to a forward contract. One of the main differences is that in a futures contract the purchaser is required to put up an initial margin as collateral.

# Notes

1. Surveys of forward market efficiency are given in R.J. Hodrick, *The Empirical Evidence on the Efficiency of Forward and Futures Foreign Exchange Markets*, Harwood Academic Publishers, 1987 and R.M. Levich, "Empirical Studies of Exchange Rates, Price Behaviour, Rate Determination and Market Efficiency", in R.H. Jones and P.B. Kenen (eds.), *Handbook of International Economics*, Vol. II, North Holland, 1985.

2. E.F. Fama, "Efficient Capital markets: A Review of Theory and Empirical Work", *Journal of Finance*, 25, 1970, p. 383-417, distinguishes between three forms of market efficiency. Weak form efficiency is where current prices reflect only the information contained in historical prices. Semi-strong efficiency is where current prices reflect all public information. Strong form efficiency is where current prices reflects all information, including insider information.

3. A. Leddin "Interest and Price Parity and Foreign Exchange Market Efficiency: The Irish Experience in the European Monetary System", *The Economic and Social Review*, Vol. 19, No. 3, April 1988.

4. B. Cornell "Spot Rates, Forward Rates and Exchange Market Efficiency", *Journal of Financial Economics*, 5, p. 55-65, 1977.

M.P. Dooley, and J.R. Shafer, "Analysis of Short-run Exchange Rate Behaviour: March 1973 to November 1981", In *Exchange Rate and Trade Instability*, D. Bigman and T. Taya, (eds), Cambridge Ma., Ballinger, 1983.

J.A. Frankel "In Search of the Exchange Risk Premium: A Six-Currency test Assuming Mean-Variance Optimization", *Journal of International Money and Finance*, 1, p. 255-274, 1982.

L.P. Hansen and R.J. Hodrick, "Forward Exchange Rates as Optimal predictors of Future Spot Rates: An Econometric Analysis", *Journal of Political Economy*, 88, p. 829-853, 1980.

A. Leddin, 1988, *op. cit.*

R.J. Levich "On the Efficiency of Markets for Foreign Exchange", in R. Dornbusch and J. Frenkel, (eds), *International Economic Policy: An Assessment of Theory and Evidence*, John Hopkins University Press, Baltimore, 1979.

R.M. Levich "How to Compare Chance with Forecasting Expertise", *Euromoney*, August, 1981.

M.P. Taylor "What do Investment Managers Know? An Empirical Study of Practitioners' Predictions", *Economica*, 54, p. 185-202, 1988.

5. For a review of the literature on interest rate parity, see R. M. Levich, *op. cit.*

6. See F. X. Browne "Departures from Interest Rate Parity", *Journal of Banking and Finance*, Vol. 7, 1983 and A. Leddin, 1988, *op. cit.*

# Chapter 14

# *Credit Policy in Ireland*

## 14.1 Introduction

The objective of this chapter is to examine the various issues underlying credit policy in Ireland. As we will see, credit policy basically involves the Central Bank issuing credit guidelines to constrain the growth in bank credit with a view to influencing the level of nominal GNP and/or the external reserves. In the course of our discussion, we outline the theoretical structures underlying credit policy and how the banks reacted to the credit guidelines and we evaluate credit policy in terms of its ultimate objectives.

We begin the chapter by examining the concept of a credit guideline and the problem of enforcement. This is followed by a discussion of credit policy between 1965 and 1977 and between 1978 and the mid-1980s. The reason for making a distinction between these two sub-periods is that a fundamental change took place in both the theoretical foundations and objectives of credit policy after 1978. We conclude the chapter with a discussion of the costs typically associated with credit guidelines.

## 14.2 Credit Guidelines

Credit guidelines are issued by the Central Bank as a means of curtailing the growth in bank credit over a period of time. As explained in Chapter 11 it is not possible to control the money supply when the exchange rate is fixed and there is a high degree of capital mobility. As an alternative to money supply control, Central Banks may attempt to restrict the growth in bank credit. The ultimate objective in nearly all cases is to influence the level of the external reserves or to curtail the inflation rate in the economy. The basic argument put forward is that "excessive" growth in bank credit can fuel inflation or facilitate an increase in imports which would reduce the external reserves. For this reason, Central Banks feel that it is appropriate , on occasions, to pursue a credit policy.

Bank credit is of course much easier to control than the money supply as the Central Bank simply tells the banks by how much they can increase credit over a particular period of time. As an example of how a credit guideline affects bank lending, consider the hypothetical data in Table 14.1. Let us suppose that the Central Bank issues a credit guideline of 10% for the forthcoming year and that total bank lending outstanding at the beginning of the period is £100m. The guideline in effect states that the banks can increase lending by £10m over the year. If a bank does not adhere to the guideline and increases lending to, say, £115m, then the bank is said to have "excess" lending of £5m. Similarly, if bank lending falls short of that specified by the guideline, then the bank is said to a have "deficiency" in lending relative to the guideline. In this case, the bank has not maximised its lending. Since loans are the principal component of the banks' assets, credit guidelines are equivalent to placing a ceiling on the assets of the banking system.

*Table 14.1*

**Credit guidelines and bank lending**

|  | January 1990 | December 1990 | Change |
|---|---|---|---|
| Bank Loans Outstanding | £100m | £110m | 10% |

Credit guidelines have been issued by the Central Bank of Ireland since 1965 as a means of curtailing licensed banks' credit. Up to 1973 lending to the government was subject to credit controls but after that date the controls applied only to private sector credit. Table 14.2 shows the composition of licensed bank private sector credit as at February 1989. It can be seen that lending to the personal sector (including housing) and the manufacturing sector are the two largest categories, whereas lending to building and construction and energy are the two smallest categories.

A credit guideline that attempts to control *total* credit is referred to as a *quantitative credit guideline*. At times, the Central Bank has also issued guidelines to control the growth in personal lending (excluding lending for housing) and lending to the financial sector. Guidelines which relate to sub-sectors of total credit are referred to as *sectoral credit guidelines*.

It is important to note that licensed bank private sector credit is not the only type of credit issued to the private sector. As at December 1988, building society mortgages amounted to £2,751m and instalment credit issued by licensed banks, hire-purchase finance companies and state-sponsored bodies amounted to £700m. In 1987, credit unions extended a further £346.8m in credit to the private sector, up from £10.5m in 1970. This means that credit guidelines do not apply to all categories of credit extended by banks and other financial institutions. As we will see this can be important because if a borrower is refused a loan at a licensed bank due to credit restrictions, then it may be possible to obtain a loan at a bank or finance house not affected by the guidelines. In effect the borrower circumvents the controls and this can undermine the effectiveness of credit policy. (Borrowers could also reduce savings or sell existing assets.) It should be noted that if a borrower is refused a loan because of a credit guideline, then the borrower is said to have experienced "credit rationing".

*Table 14.2*
**Distribution of licensed bank lending**
**Resident non-government credit: February 1989**

|  | £ million | % |
|---|---|---|
| Agriculture, fishing and forestry | 1,202.6 | 11.3 |
| Energy | 264.5 | 2.5 |
| Manufacturing | 1,799.8 | 16.9 |
| Building and construction | 262.8 | 2.5 |
| Distribution, garages, hotels and catering | 1,285.7 | 12.1 |
| Transport | 338.4 | 3.2 |
| Postal services and telecommunications | 330.3 | 3.1 |
| Financial | 1,600.7 | 15.0 |
| Business and other services | 1,046.4 | 9.8 |
| Personal | 2,526.8 | 23.7 |
| *of which* | | |
| Housing | 1,274.4 | 12.0 |
| *Total* | 10,658.1 | 100.0 |

*Source*: Central Bank of Ireland, *Annual Report*, 1989.
*Note*: The distinction between residents and non-residents is based on the address of the customer and not on the location of the bank account. People living within the State for at least one year are considered to be residents.

# Credit guidelines: problems of enforcement

As we saw in Chapter 5, bank lending is one of the most important sources of bank profits. Hence, if there is a persistent demand for credit from the public and the banks have the necessary reserves, there is a very definite incentive for banks to meet this demand even if it involves breaching the credit guideline. As a result, Central Banks are normally obliged to accompany credit guidelines with some form of enforcement measure. In Ireland, the Central Bank has, over the years, used a *special deposits* technique. The basic idea of the special deposits measure is to ensure that a bank makes a loss on "excess" lending and, in this way, to remove the incentive to breach the guideline.

As an example, refer back to Table 14.1 and suppose that the bank's total lending at the end of the period was £115m. Given a guideline of 10%, the bank has "excess lending" of £5 million. A special deposit of £5m must now be placed with the Central Bank. No interest will be paid on this deposit and the deposit will be retained until such time that the bank makes a loss on the "excess" lending. As might be expected, if banks cannot earn profits on "excess" lending, they tend to adhere more closely to the credit guidelines.

*Note:*
*Special deposits are a cumbersome method of removing profits on "excess" lending. A straight forward alternative to special deposits is simply to fine banks an amount significantly greater than the profits on "excess" lending.*

Special deposits are not a *sufficient* method of removing profits on "excess" lending. The difficulty is that "excess" lending increases a banks lending base which in turn is used to calculate next year's credit allocation. Banks that breach a credit guideline therefore have an unfair advantage.

As an example, suppose that in year 1, Bank A and Bank B both have the same lending base of £100m and that the guideline for the forthcoming year is 10%. Assume that Bank A complies exactly with the 10% credit guideline so that at the end of the year its lending base is £110m. Assume that Bank B has "excess" lending of £5m so that its year-end lending base is £115m. The point is that next year's credit guideline is based on these two lending bases. A credit guideline of 10% in the second year would mean that Bank A could increase lending by £11m whereas Bank B could increase lending by £11.5m. In terms of the amount of money it can lend, the bank which did not comply with the credit stipulation moves ahead of the bank which did adhere to the guideline.

In order to remove this incentive to breach the guideline, the Central Bank must make some adjustment to a bank's lending base in calculating the second year's credit allocation. This type of measure is referred to as a "market base deduction". The effect is that a bank returns to its "correct" lending base by the end of the second year. In this way, no advantage is gained over banks which comply with the guidelines.

# 14.3 Credit Policy in Ireland: 1965-77

In this section we examine credit policy in Ireland between 1965 and 1977. We confine our analysis to the pre-1978 period because, as pointed out in the introduction to this chapter, both the theoretical foundations and objectives of credit policy changed radically from 1978 onwards. We discuss post-1978 credit policy later in this chapter. We begin this section by examining how the banks reacted to the credit guidelines. This is followed by a critical appraisal of the theoretical foundations and the objectives of credit policy over the period.

## The evolution of credit controls: 1965-77

As a background to our discussion, Figure 14.1 shows the percentage change in licensed bank private sector credit over the period 1965-77. The variation in the growth in bank credit is the most obvious feature of the graph. This variation is however exaggerated by a bank dispute in 1970 and the pent-up demand for credit which manifested itself at the end of the dispute. However, as a general observation, the growth in bank credit seemed to follow closely the twists and turns in the business cycle and credit guidelines did not, on average, smooth the supply of credit over the period.

Credit guidelines were first introduced in Ireland in 1965 as a means of curtailing the growth in the associated banks' lending to the private sector and to the government. Up to 1970, the credit guidelines applied only to the associated banks and the Central Bank issued no restrictions relating to capital inflows or outflows.

In 1970, the credit guidelines were extended to cover non-associated bank total lending (excluding instalment credit). These banks had grown dramatically in previous years by finding profitable lending opportunities in Ireland and then financing the loans by borrowing on the London money market. Essentially, the non-associated banks borrowed abroad and then loaned the money in Ireland at higher interest rates. To curtail non-associated bank foreign borrowing, the Central Bank also imposed restrictions on their "net external liabilities" over the period 1967 to 1978.

From 1973 to 1976, the Central Bank abandoned credit guidelines as the means of curtailing bank credit. The new instrument of credit control on which they relied was the primary and secondary reserve ratios. (The Central Bank Act of 1971 gave the Central Bank the legislative power to issue reserve requirements.) For some time the Central Bank had indicated a certain disillusionment with credit guidelines and it was not altogether surprising that they were abandoned as an instrument of policy. For example as far back as 1971, the Central Bank had stated:

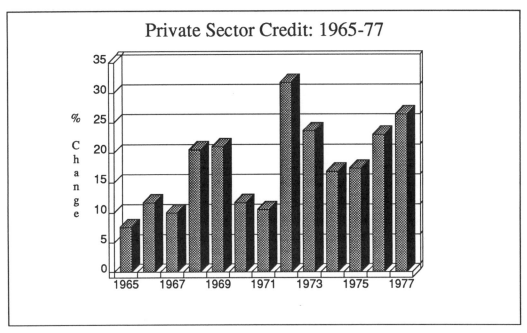

Figure 14.1

"Direct limits on bank lending ... if pursued for long periods of time, hamper competition between banks and lead to inequities and possible misallocation of resources. They also encourage attempts to circumvent the ceilings, thereby leading to pressures to extend the scope of the quantitative restrictions."
Central Bank of Ireland, *Annual Report*, 1970/1971, p. 32.

In 1973, the Central Bank also extended the restriction of capital flows to the associated banks. The new restriction required that "50% of any net inflow (other than for development purposes) be deposited with the Central Bank". The objective of this restriction was to reduce the degree of capital mobility between Irish and foreign financial markets and to increase the scope for an Irish monetary policy.

Finally, in 1977 credit guidelines were re-introduced to supplement the reserve requirements in curtailing bank lending to the private sector. The restriction on capital inflows, which had been terminated in 1976, was also re-introduced.

## Credit guidelines and the growth in bank credit

Table 14.3 compares the growth in bank credit with the guidelines issued by the Central Bank over the period 1965-77. Column 1 shows the *stipulated* growth in credit and column 2 the *actual* growth in bank credit. As an indicator of the banks' compliance with the guidelines, column 3 expresses column 2 as a percentage of column 1.

*Table 14.3*

**Credit guidelines and the growth in bank credit: 1965-77**

| Period | Credit guideline | | Actual change in credit | | Column (2) as a % of column (1). |
|---|---|---|---|---|---|
| | £m | % | £m | % | |
| | (1) | | (2) | | (3) |
| 1. Mar. '65-Dec. '65 | 33.4 | 10.5 | 20.0 | 5.7 | 59.9 |
| 2. Mar. '66-Mar. '67 | 43.0 | 11.8 | 40.5 | 11.1 | 94.2 |
| 3. Mar. '67-Mar. '68 | 40.4 | 10.0 | 68.2 | 16.8 | 168.8 |
| 4. Apr. '68-Apr. '69 | 64.2 | 14.1 | 106.3 | 23.3 | 165.5 |
| 5. Apr. '69-Apr. '70 | 80.0 | 14.2 | 82.0 | 14.6 | 102.5 |
| 6. Apr. '70-Apr. '71 | 75.0 | 11.6 | 130.0 | 20.0 | 173.3 |
| 7. Apr. '71-Apr. '72 | 118.0 | 11.7 | 49.3 | 4.8 | 41.8 |
| 8. Apr. '72-Apr. '73 | 200.0 | 19.0 | 321.3 | 30.3 | 160.6 |
| 9. Jan. '77-Dec. '77 | 359.0 | 18.0 | 439.0 | 22.0 | 122.3 |

*Source:* Central Bank of Ireland, *Quarterly Bulletins*

*Notes:*

1. Guidelines 1 to 6 relate to associated bank credit only. Guidelines 7 to 9 relate to licensed banks credit.

2. With the exception of 1977, the controls relate to bank lending to the private sector and the government.

3. The guideline in 1966/67 was revised upwards from 6% to 11% and in 1972/'73 from 15% to 19%.

While strict compliance with the guidelines is too harsh a criterion on which to evaluate credit policy, the data in column 3 do not indicate a high degree of adherence by the banks to the guidelines. Of the nine credit guidelines issued over the period, the growth in bank credit was within 40 percentage points of the guideline stipulation on only three occasions. In 1967, 1968, 1970 and 1972 the actual growth in bank credit exceeded the guideline by 68%, 65%, 73% and 60% respectively. By any reasonable criterion, the guidelines could not be said to have succeeded in curtailing bank credit over the period. The guidelines were not, at any time, enforced by the Central Bank. It was not until 1978 that special deposits were introduced. Before then the banks' compliance with the guidelines depended on moral suasion by the Central Bank or the goodwill of the banks. The outcome clearly indicates that these were not enough to ensure a moderate degree of compliance.

*Note:*
*A reading of the Central Bank statements accompanying the credit guidelines suggests that, on the whole, the credit guidelines were not particularly restrictive in the first instance (see appendix 6). It could therefore be hypothesised that if the guidelines were restrictive, the outcome would have been even more unfavourable.*

It is important to note that if the credit guidelines did not restrict or curtail bank credit over the period, then it was not possible for credit policy to achieve inflation or external reserves objectives. Furthermore, as already mentioned, the Central Bank relied on the primary and secondary reserve ratios as the means of regulating bank credit between 1973 and 1976. However between 1974 and 1977, the reserve ratios were never changed so that there was no "active" monetary or credit policy during this period.

## The objectives of credit policy

As we pointed out in Chapters 11 and 12, it is not possible to control the money supply in an open economy when the exchange rate is fixed and there is a high degree of capital mobility. Any policy-induced reduction in the money supply will increase domestic interest rates relative to foreign interest rates and capital will flow into the country. This capital inflow continues until such time as the money supply and interest rates return to their initial levels. Conversely, an increase in the money supply will lower interest rates and capital will flow out of the country. Again interest rates and the money supply revert to their initial levels. The process of re-adjustment takes very little time so that any change in the money supply is temporary.

Between 1965 and 1977, monetary policy in Ireland was formulated in two stages. The first stage involved using credit guidelines and reserve requirements to control bank credit and, in this way, regulating the money supply in the economy. The second stage involved estimating how changes in the money supply affected nominal output or the level of imports. The following quotes indicate that, at least up to 1977, control of the money supply was seen as an integral part of monetary policy. In 1966, the Central Bank stated:

In attempting to control the amount of money in the economy and in setting a target for bank lending for this purpose ....
Central Bank of Ireland, *Annual Report*, 1966/67, p. 30.

In 1971, the Governor of the Central Bank, T.K. Whitaker, discussing the issue of replacing credit controls with reserve requirements, stated:

Behind the innermost veil, there must still sit the notion of a Quantity! The Bank will still be aiming at controlling the aggregate lending of the banking system and, indirectly, the overall level of current and deposit accounts.

T.K. Whitaker, "The Central Bank and the Banking System", Lecture to the Cork Centre of the Institute of Bankers, November, 1971, p. 71.

Again in 1975, the Governor of the Central Bank commented:

The money supply (M3) we try to regulate....

T.K. Whitaker, "Monetary Policy", Central Bank of Ireland, *Quarterly Bulletin*, Geimhreadh, 1975, p. 76.

The Central Bank readily acknowledged that a number of variables influenced the growth in the money supply and that the credit guideline in any given year would have to be based on a forecast of the change in these variables. For example, the Governor of the Central Bank commented:

... the underlying projections for exports, deposits and net capital inflow may themselves be in error. In that case, other things being equal, the credit advice would need to be altered accordingly and in practice steps would be taken to ensure that this was done."

T.K. Whitaker, "Banking and Credit in Ireland Today, Central Bank of Ireland, *Quarterly Bulletin*, Geimhreadh, 1969, p. 114.

The second stage in formulating monetary policy involved estimating how changes in the money supply would influence prices and imports in the economy. In the early years, the objective of monetary policy was to curtail the level of imports. Following the rapid growth in real GNP in the early 1960s, the deficit on the current account of the balance of payments increased to 4.2% of GNP in 1965. Inflation, on the other hand, remained at a moderate level.

There is no concise statement outlining the theoretical foundations of monetary policy in these early years. We have to depend on indirect references in Central Bank publications in order to determine what theory provided the basis for monetary policy. In this regard, the governor of the Central Bank, in discussing why changes in the money supply may not have the desired effect on imports, commented:

... the assumption that the parameters - that is, income velocity and the marginal propensity to import - are constant may be falsified by events, so that expenditure in general and expenditure on imports in particular may differ from what was expected.

T.K. Whitaker, "Banking and Credit in Ireland To-Day", Central Bank of Ireland, *Quarterly Bulletin*, Geimhreadh, 1969, p.114.

The reference to income velocity (V) and the marginal propensity to import (MPM) seems to suggest that the theoretical foundation of monetary policy, at least in this early period, was a mixture of monetarist and Keynesian theories. A constant velocity of circulation of money is a monetarist assumption and the MPM is part of the Keynesian multiplier approach to the balance of payments. The reference to these two parameters suggests that changes in the money supply would, via the quantity theory of money, determine total expenditure in the economy. In turn, changes in total expenditure would, via the MPM, determine the level of imports.[1] Taking the two stages of monetary policy together, the process would be roughly as follows. The credit guideline would control the growth in bank credit which in turn would regulate the money supply. Policy-induced changes in the money supply would influence total expenditure which, in turn, would determine the level of imports. This is obviously a very long process involving a great number of estimates, forecasts and assumptions. The potential for error is clearly very great. Thus it is unlikely that any precise numerical target relating credit control to the growth of expenditure would be met. On the other hand, it is obviously reasonable to believe that a restrictive credit policy will, other things being equal, tend to slow down the growth of expenditure and thus help moderate inflationary pressures and curtail balance of payments deficits.

As inflation increased from 2.8% in 1966 to 8.8% in 1971 and 20.9% in 1975, statements on monetary policy seem to emphasise more and more the inflation objective. The Central Bank's view was that the growth in bank credit could contribute to inflationary pressures. For example, the Governor commented:

Net credit creation increases the flow of expenditure and, in a situation in which prices are already rising, such an increase makes a positive contribution to inflation. It makes it possible to spend more than we can afford on consumption purposes and to have cost increases passed on as price increases, to mention just two of the undesirable effects.
T.K. Whitaker, "The Role of the Central Bank", Lecture to the Economics Society, University College Dublin, 1970, p. 4.

This view of the causes of inflation conflicted with the increasingly influential small open economy (SOE) theory of inflation. We discussed this controversy in Chapter 10 under the heading of purchasing power parity. We note here however that in the mid-1970s the Central Bank was reluctant to accept the idea that inflation was beyond our control.

Imported inflation we have to accept. The overall rate of price inflation is not, contrary to the view of some of the more theoretical economists, entirely determined by the rate prevailing among our trading partners. We would be less unhappy if it were. Our domestic costs have recently been rising faster than we can legitimately blame on any external forces.

T.K. Whitaker, "Monetary Policy at Present", Talk to the Dublin Society of Chartered Accountants, February, 1975, p. 128.

The question remains as to what exactly was the *stance* of monetary and credit policy over the period. In other words, was the policy restrictive, neutral or expansionary? Our assessment is that policy was largely neutral over the period. In appendix 6, we give a list of quotes taken from Central Bank policy statements for each policy year. We acknowledge, of course, that the Central Bank's policy statements cannot be adequately summarised into single sentences or paragraphs but we believe we represent the Central Bank's policy fairly in these quotations.

A reading of the various statements indicates that monetary policy was in nearly all years geared towards accommodating the predicted growth in nominal GNP. There were only three years, 1965, 1969/70 and 1970/71, when policy could be said to have been clearly restrictive. (It might be argued that this was also the case in 1977.) Even when inflation and the balance of payments deficit were rising rapidly, as in 1974 and 1975, monetary policy still attempted to facilitate the projected growth in nominal GNP and employment. However, a policy that attempts to accommodate the change in nominal GNP is largely self-fulfilling. Nominal GNP, after all, is a major determinant of the demand for money and the demand for credit. This means, ironically, that monetary policy cannot be evaluated over the period in terms of its objectives because the policy comes close to saying that the target is the outcome.

# Personal lending guidelines

The assumption underlying the Central Bank's personal lending guidelines was that there is an important relationship between bank personal lending and consumer expenditure and, in particular, expenditure on finished imported consumer goods. On this basis, the objective of the personal lending guideline was to restrict personal lending with a view to curtailing consumer expenditure.

Over the period 1965-76 (no guideline was issued between 1976 and September 1978) personal lending guidelines issued by the Central Bank were, on the whole, broad, non-specific directives. For example, in 1966 the Central Bank stated:

(Banks should give) ... particular attention to the importance of encouraging productive activity and exports.

Central Bank of Ireland, *Annual Report*, 1966/67, p.22.

and in 1968:

... restraint should apply mainly to credit required for imports of finished consumer goods and other forms of personal consumption.

Central Bank of Ireland, *Annual Report*, 1968/69, p. 40.

However in 1970/71 and again in 1973, specific personal lending guidelines were issued. In both years, the banks were told that there should be "... no growth in the level of non-productive lending". Unlike all the other guidelines over the period, the 1974 personal lending guideline was enforced by a special deposit measure. This was the first time that such a measure was introduced.

*Note:*

*There were a number of ambiguities in the Central Bank's statements regarding the personal lending guidelines. Generally the statements referred to the licensed banks' personal loans but on occasions mentioned instalment credit. The guidelines were extended in 1970 to cover non-associated bank lending.*

A comparison of the personal lending guidelines and the actual growth in personal lending leads to no firm conclusions as to whether the guidelines constrained lending. It is possible that from time to time they did but on the whole personal loans would not seem to have been unduly restricted.

# Summary

As we pointed out at the beginning of the section, it is not possible to control the money supply in an economy when the exchange rate is fixed and there is near perfect capital mobility. However, over the period 1965-77, monetary or credit policy in Ireland largely consisted of issuing credit guidelines to control bank credit and, in this way, trying to regulate the money supply. This was not possible given the fixed exchange rate with sterling and the high degree of financial integration with the London money market. Moreover, the enforcement of monetary policy was flawed in that the credit guidelines did not succeed in constraining bank credit. If the Central Bank could not control credit it was not possible to control the money supply and credit policy could not have achieved its objectives.

On at least three occasions over the period, monetary policy was formulated with a view to influencing the level of imports or the rate of inflation in the economy. The transmission mechanism from changes in the money supply to total expenditure seems to have been assumed to be a stable velocity of circulation of money. This indicates that the quantity theory of money was the framework underlying monetary policy. However, for the most part monetary policy attempted to accommodate the predicted growth in nominal output so that, on balance, monetary policy facilitated a growth and employment objective at the expense of an anti-inflationary objective.

# 14.4 Credit Policy: 1978-84

In 1978, important changes occurred in the formulation of monetary or credit policy in Ireland. Firstly, the Central Bank acknowledged that it was not possible to control the money supply in the Irish economy.[2] The Governor of the Bank commented:

In an open economy such as Ireland's, it is generally accepted that the supply of money responds to the demand for it, so that monetary authorities cannot exercise a significant degree of control on the increase in money holdings ....
C.H. Murray, "Monetary Policy", Central Bank of Ireland, *Quarterly Bulletin*, 4, 1979, p. 71.

After 1978 monetary policy no longer involved using credit guidelines to control the money supply with a view to influencing nominal output. Monetary policy in Ireland after 1978 was based on a theory known as the *monetary approach to the balance of payments (MAB)*. This theory suggests issuing credit guidelines to achieve an external reserves target rather than attempting to influence the rate of inflation. We begin this section by outlining MAB theory and its implications for policy. This is followed by a discussion of whether or not the credit guidelines succeeded in achieving the intended external reserves target in Ireland. In the next section, we analyse how the banks reacted to both the quantitative and personal lending guidelines over the period 1978-84 and we give examples of the costs associated with credit guidelines.

## The monetary approach to the balance of payments

The monetary approach to the balance of payments (MAB)[3] theory is essentially the modern day version of the "automatic adjustment mechanism" that operated under the old gold standard (see the discussion in Chapter 10, section 10.2). The modern revival of the MAB dates from the work of the English Nobel prize winning economist James Meade (b. 1907) in the 1950s. Under the leadership of Jacques Polak, this analytical approach became the foundation of the International Monetary Fund's operational practices. Countries that are borrowing from the Fund are tied to policy programmes based on MAB.

The MAB is based on the following identity which can be derived from the *consolidated balance sheet* of the banking system:

(1) $\text{Ms} \equiv \text{DC} + \text{R}$

where: Ms = money supply, DC = domestic credit and R = external reserves.

This identity states that the money supply is equal to domestic credit (bank lending to the private sector and the government) plus the external reserves. In Chapter 5 we defined the money supply as being equal to currency plus banks' current and deposit accounts. The definition given in identity (1) simply shows the domestic assets and net foreign assets as counterparts of the money supply. We wish to stress that identity (1) is simplified for exposition purposes. In appendix 7 we derive the complete version of the MAB identity from the consolidated balance sheet of the Irish banking system.

Identity (1) can also be presented in terms of first differences. Hence:

$$(2) \quad \Delta \, Ms \equiv DCE + \Delta \, R$$

where DCE = domestic credit expansion, that is the change in domestic credit over the particular period.

Furthermore, because DCE equals bank lending to the private sector (Lp) plus bank lending to the government (BLG), identity (2) can be written:

$$(3) \quad \Delta \, Ms \equiv \Delta \, Lp + \Delta \, BLG + \Delta \, R$$

One of the important assumptions underlying MAB is that the money supply is determined by the demand for money (Md). That is, the money supply is assumed to be demand-led. For example, if the demand for money increases by 20% over the year, then so too will the money supply. A 40% increase in the demand for money will lead to a similar rise in money supply and so on. (At least, we have to assume that the *ex post* increase in the money supply cannot exceed the growth in the demand for credit.) This assumption is in keeping with the view that the Central Bank cannot control the money supply in a small open economy when the exchange rate is fixed. We will return to this point below.

Given that the Central Bank cannot control the money supply, MAB theory suggests that the Central Bank can influence the *composition* of the money supply by restricting domestic credit expansion. Given the growth in the money supply, the lower domestic credit expansion, the higher will be the external reserves and vice versa. In this way, a credit guideline can be used to achieve an external reserves target.

Referring to identity (3) above, the following steps illustrate how a credit guideline can be used to achieve an external reserves target.

(1). The first step is to estimate growth in the demand for money for the forthcoming year. Typically this estimate will be based on a forecast of the predicted change in nominal GNP and the interest rate. This estimate of the demand for money, by assumption, gives the target for the growth in the money supply.

(2). The next step is for the Central Bank to decide on the external reserves objective. The Central Bank decides whether an increase, decrease or unchanged external reserves is appropriate in the circumstances.

(3). The third step is to estimate the growth in bank lending to the government $\Delta$(BLG). (BLG consists of Central Bank and licensed bank lending to the government.) Licensed bank lending to the government is largely determined by the secondary reserve ratio. Central Bank lending to the government is at the Bank's discretion.

(4). Given the above estimates, the final step is to issue a credit guideline to ensure that the change in bank lending to the private sector ($\Delta$Lp) is consistent with the external reserves objective.

For example, suppose that the Central Bank predicts that the money supply will increase by £100m and that the change in bank lending to the government will be £25m. If the objective is to increase the external reserves by £25m, it is easy to see from identity (3) that the growth in licensed bank lending to the private sector should be restricted to £50m. Given the various estimates and the external reserves objective, the credit guideline is in effect calculated as a residual.

Suppose that the licensed banks did not adhere to the credit guideline and Lp increased by £100m, given the estimates for Ms and BLG, R would decrease by £25m over the period. Similarly if the credit guideline restricted the growth in Lp to £40m, the external reserves would increase by £35m. In summary, the Central Bank does not control the money supply but instead attempts to control licensed bank lending in order to achieve an external reserves target.

*Note:*

*MAB theory is often referred to as a theory of the balance of payments. The reason is that changes in the external reserves mirror the overall balance of payments. An overall deficit on the balance of payments leads to a fall in the external reserves. Conversely, a balance of payments surplus leads to an increase in the external reserves. Hence, an external reserves policy is tantamount to an overall balance of payments policy.*

In 1979 the Governor of the Central Bank outlined how credit policy was formulated as follows:

The first step in determining credit policy is the estimation of the demand for money for the year ahead. Then, taking into account such features as the desired relationship between the level of reserves and imports and the new obligations which face us as members of the EMS, the Bank decides on the desired level of official external reserves. Given the projected increase in the demand for money this, in turn, yields the increase in total domestic credit which would be consistent with the reserves objectives. Taking account of the public sector's demand for credit, the amount of credit available to the private sector ... is determined.
C.H. Murray, "Monetary Policy", Central Bank of Ireland, *Quarterly Bulletin*, 4, 1979, p. 72.

Given the predicted demand for money, the credit guideline restricts bank credit and therefore temporarily curtails the growth in the money supply. An excess demand for money emerges which raises interest rates and/or reduces aggregate expenditure. This in turn leads to a capital inflow and reduces expenditure on imports and the balance of payments improves. In effect, the Central Bank achieves an external reserves target by pursuing a "tight" monetary policy. If, however, the increase in the external reserves is due to capital inflows, this is equivalent to foreign borrowing by the private sector. This money will have to be repaid at a later stage so that further remedial action will be necessary in the future.

It is important to note that a key assumption implicit in the MAB theory is that the demand for money is a *stable* function of a few variables such as, for example, the change in nominal GNP and the interest rate. This is important because if the demand for money fluctuates unpredictably over time, so too will the amount of additional money that can be absorbed by the economy and the identity will be useless for policy purposes.[4]

*Note:*
*A further complication is that there may be a link between licensed bank credit to the private sector and the demand for money. In other words, there may be a behavioural relationship between Md and Lp. If this were the case, a decrease in Lp brought about by the credit guideline would lead to a decrease in Md. For example, suppose the credit guideline reduced the growth in Lp and, as a result, a certain proportion of people and firms refused loans at licensed banks abandon or postpone their expenditure plans. This would reduce the growth in GNP and decrease the demand for money. If a credit guideline succeeds in reducing both bank credit and the demand for money, the MAB identity cannot be used for policy purposes.*

# Credit guidelines and the external reserves target

As a background to what follows, Figure 14.2 shows the growth in licensed bank credit to the private sector from 1978 to 1988. The most obvious characteristic of the graph is the steady decline in the growth of bank credit from 1978 to 1987 and the pick-up in 1988. This is in keeping with the trends in the Irish business cycle. However, as the demand for credit decreased in the mid-1980s, the credit guidelines became redundant. The Central Bank cannot implement a credit policy if there is no demand for increased credit!

An important question is whether or not the credit guidelines achieved the desired external reserves target. Table 14.4 summarises the available data relating to the guidelines, the external reserves objective and the external reserves outcome. In 1978, the Central Bank objective was to *decrease* the external reserves by £200m. (This was the only year the Central Bank published a specific target for the external reserves.) It might seem odd that the Central Bank's objective was to lower the external reserves. However as the Central Bank pointed out at the time:

... the import cover afforded by the official external reserves is high at present by international standards and ... some reduction can be tolerated.
Central Bank of Ireland, *Annual Report*, 1978, p. 25.

By the end of the year, bank lending exceeded the credit guideline by £320m but, despite this, the external reserves *increased* by £50m. The reason for this

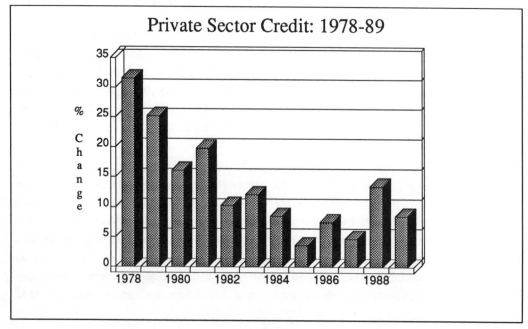

Figure 14.2

paradoxical outcome was that the Central Bank underestimated the demand for money by £348m. This outcome indicates a continuing problem in obtaining the banks' adherence to the credit guidelines and the difficulties in accurately predicting the demand for money.

*Table 14.4*
**Credit guidelines and the external reserves target**

| Period | Credit guideline | $\Delta R$ objective | $\Delta R$ outcome |
|---|---|---|---|
| Dec.'77- Dec.'78 | 20% | -£200m | +£50m |
| Feb.'79 - Feb.'80 | 18% | "little change" | -£262m |
| Feb.'80 - Feb.'81 | 13% | "small increase" | +£331m |
| Feb.'81 - Feb.'82 | 15% | "adequate level" | -£50m |

*Source:* Central Bank of Ireland, *Quarterly Bulletins*

*Note:*
*The Central Bank, in fact, abandoned the credit guideline in the middle of 1978 and replaced it with a new six-month guideline for the period to March 1979.*

There is little information on the external reserves target and the estimate of the demand for money for the 1979 credit policy year. However, a decrease in the external reserves of £262m does not seem to accord with the Central Bank's stated objective of having "... little change in the external reserves".

At the beginning of 1980 the economy was moving into a recession and the external reserves had decreased significantly over the previous year. The dilemma facing the Central Bank was to increase the external reserves but at the same time to "... avoid introducing a deflationary element into economic policy ..." (Central Bank of Ireland, *Annual Report*, 1980, p. 13). The Central Bank resolved this dilemma by encouraging the banks to borrow abroad. This was achieved by issuing a restrictive credit guideline of 13% and then exempting from the guideline any lending financed by foreign borrowing. In other words, if the banks borrowed abroad and then on-lent the money in Ireland, that lending would not be subject to the guideline.

This strategy proved particularly successful as the external reserves increased by £331m in 1980, almost exactly equal to the £323m borrowed abroad by the banks. The outcome may not however been entirely expected by the Central Bank as the intention was to achieve "... a small increase ..." in the external reserves and the growth in the demand for money was under-estimated by a significant £302m.

355

In 1981, credit policy aimed at maintaining the external reserves at "... an adequate level ...". Again little information is available for this year but it is likely that the outcome was more in line with intentions.

In 1982, the credit guideline was designed to "... not ... accommodate any slippage in the balance of payments" and, in 1983, to facilitate the "... expected growth in nominal GNP ...". Following the "adequate level" statement of 1981, the Central Bank became increasingly ambiguous with regard to the external reserves objective. However, in 1982 and 1983, the guidelines did not act as a constraint as the growth in bank lending was less than that stipulated by the guidelines. The reason for this was a fall in the demand for credit as the economy moved into recession. The guidelines therefore could not have contributed to an external reserves target in these two years.

*Note:*
*In 1984 an "indicative" credit guideline of 10% was issued. No credit guidelines have been issued by the Central Bank since then.*

In summary, the Central Bank would appear to have had only modest success in using credit guidelines to achieve an external reserves target. The main problems seem to be estimating the demand for money and obtaining the banks' compliance with the credit guidelines. A more fundamental criticism is that the MAB model is a long-run theory and as such it may not be an appropriate framework for short-run policy purposes. The MAB predicts that if the growth of domestic credit is consistently held below the predicted increase in the demand for credit, the external reserves will increase over time. This conclusion is much weaker than is required to justify using the MAB framework to achieve a specific external reserves objective each year.[5]

# 14.5 The Cost of Credit Guidelines

The analysis in the previous section suggested that the Central Bank had little success in using credit guidelines to achieve an external reserves target over the period since 1978. The problem is not that the Central Bank tried and failed to influence the external reserves but that credit guidelines can involve very definite costs with few related benefits. Hence, we are not dealing with a "costless" policy designed to achieve a worthwhile objective. In this section we discuss some of the costs associated with credit guidelines.

One type of cost is that competition between the various banks is stifled. An efficient bank which offers a very good service and is therefore successful in attracting deposits is not allowed to increase its market share at the expense of an

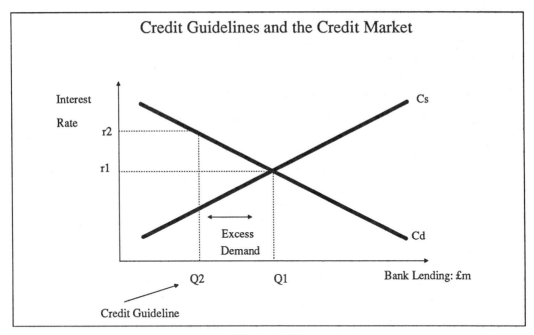

Figure 14.3

inefficient bank which offers a relatively poor service. Normally, the more deposits a bank can attract the more it can expand lending and the more profitable it becomes. Because of the guidelines, however, the efficient bank is constrained to expand at the same rate as the inefficient bank. The effect of credit guidelines on bank competition was one of the factors mentioned by the Central Bank in 1973 for abandoning credit guidelines.

Perhaps the major cost associated with credit guidelines is that the guidelines can cause a *misallocation of resources* in the economy. In Figure 14.3 we show two curves representing the supply of credit ($C_s$) and the demand for credit ($C_d$). On the vertical axis is the interest rate (r) and on the horizontal axis, bank lending (Q). At the point A, the two curves intersect at an interest rate of $r_1$ and bank lending of $Q_1$. Suppose now the Central Bank imposes a credit guideline which curtails bank lending to $Q_2$. At the interest rate of $r_1$, the private sector is demanding $Q_1$ but because of the guideline the banks can only lend $Q_2$. There is therefore an excess demand for credit equal to ($Q_1$ - $Q_2$) and the banks will have to "ration credit" to customers.[6]

*Note:*

*Referring to Figure 14.3, note that if the interest rate rises above r2, the demand for credit falls below that stipulated by the guideline. Similarly, if the demand for credit curve (Cd) shifts to the left due to, say, a decrease in nominal GNP, the credit guideline again becomes redundant. This is essentially what happened in Ireland after 1981.*

357

The difficulty is that bank managers must now decide which borrowers receive loans and which borrowers are refused. This can result in a misallocation of resources. For example, banks may be more inclined to lend to old established customers rather than new customers even if, after allowing for risk, the projects proposed by new customers offer a higher return. Similarly, loans may be allocated to individuals on the basis of "who they are" rather than on the basis of a feasibility study of the various project involved. The net result may be banks financing low productivity projects at the expense of high productivity projects. It should be noted that if there is no credit guideline, the interest rate acts as a price and rises or falls in order to establish equilibrium in the credit market. This price mechanism should result in an efficient allocation of resources because as the interest rate increases low productivity projects will become unprofitable and will not be undertaken.

In the next two sub-sections we explain, in the context of how the banks reacted to the Central Bank's quantitative and personal lending guidelines, how other forms of resource misallocation can occur.

## Stop/go in the availability of credit

In Table 14.5 we show how the associated banks reacted to the quantitative and personal lending guidelines over the period 1978 to 1981. We ignore the first guideline issued in 1978 as this was terminated by the Central Bank in September 1978 following a rapid growth in bank credit. We also ignore the guidelines issued in 1982 and 1983 as bank lending fell short of the stipulated amount in these years and the guidelines therefore did not act as a constraint. The data in Table 14.5 are presented as the cumulative percentage change from the introduction of each guideline. For example, the growth in bank credit of 17.5% in 1979 is directly comparable with the guideline of 18% issued in that year.

Consider first how the associated banks responded to the quantitative credit guideline. Following on from the failure of the first guideline in 1978, bank lending exceeded the six month guideline in 1978-79 by nearly 50%. In the first quarter of 1979, bank lending increased by 11.9% relative to an annual guideline of 18% and it appeared as if the guideline would again fail to curtail bank lending. Central Bank enforcement curtailed the growth in credit in the second quarter but by the end of the third quarter, bank lending marginally exceeded the guideline. The Central Bank now demanded special deposits from nine banks but also reduced the primary and secondary reserve requirements for the associated banks in order to reduce bank indebtedness. In the final quarter of 1979, the banks *decreased* lending to a level consistent with the guideline.

*Note:*

*The guidelines relate to the banks' net change in lending. Money repaid by the public on earlier loans can be loaned out without increasing net lending. If the banks do not lend any money over a particular period, the total amount of loans outstanding will decrease because of repayments by the public. The decrease in lending in the fourth quarter of 1979 indicates that the banks were not even lending money repaid to them on existing loans.*

*Table 14.5*

**Associated bank lending and the credit guidelines**
**Cumulative percentage change from the beginning of each period**

| Period | Total private sector credit | Quantitative credit guideline | Personal credit | Personal lending guideline |
|---|---|---|---|---|
| Sept'78 - March '79 | 14.7 | 10.0 | -3.0 | 5.0 |
| 1979 q1 | 11.9 | | 8.4 | |
| q2 | 14.6 | | 0.4 | |
| q3 | 18.6 | | -0.6 | |
| q4 | 17.5 | 18 | -1.4 | 10 |
| 1980 q1 | 2.4 | 3.1 | | |
| q2 | -0.5 | 3.6 | | |
| q3 | 5.1 | 11.9 | | |
| q4 | 12.7 | 13 | 5.7 | 6.0 |
| 1981 q1 | 6.8 | | 14.2 | |
| q2 | 6.8 | | 3.8 | |
| q3 | 14.5 | | 11.1 | |
| q4 | 16.3 | 15.0 | 13.5 | Directive |

*Source*: Central Bank of Ireland, *Quarterly Bulletins*

Over the first nine months of the 1980 credit policy year, the cumulative increase in credit was only 5% compared to a guideline of 13%. It was only in the final quarter that lending was maximized relative to the guideline. The Central Bank suggested that this slow growth in credit was partly due to the banks attempting to avoid a repeat of the situation in 1979.

The surge in the extension of credit towards the end of the ... year may have owed something to the scope for increased lending within the guideline; this, in turn, may have been attributable partly to

the pursuit by the banks of conservative lending policies earlier in the year in order to avoid the danger of breaching the guideline.
Central Bank of Ireland, *Annual Report*, 1981, p. 23, 24.

This analysis suggests a stop/go in the availability of credit as a result of the guidelines. When the banks expanded lending at a rate inconsistent with the guideline, the Central Bank enforced the guideline and this led to a fall in lending. For example, it would have been difficult to obtain credit in 1979 q2 and the period from 1979 q4 to 1980 q3 and much easier in the other quarters. The odds of successfully obtaining a loan would appear to depend crucially on the timing of the loan application rather than on the profitability of the project.

*Note:*
*As mentioned earlier, bank lending financed by foreign borrowing was exempt from the guideline in 1980. This "foreign currency based lending" would have considerably eased any excess demand for credit in this year.*

There are numerous other examples of where Central Bank policy resulted in a stop/go in the availability of credit. For example, the quantitative credit guideline, 1981 q2 and 1981 q4.

Turning to a comparison of the growth in personal lending and the sectoral guideline in Table 14.5, notice the decrease or slow-down in associated bank personal lending in 1980 q2, 1980 q4, 1981 q2, 1981 q4 and 1982 q2. All of these down-turns in personal lending were preceded by Central Bank statements to the associated banks requesting a curtailment of lending. For example, starting with 1980 q4:

... the increase (in personal lending) for the nine months to November was somewhat in excess of the 6% guideline ... The Central Bank *has been in communication* with banks in breach of the 6% guideline, with a view to taking appropriate action in the light of subsequent developments.
Central Bank of Ireland, *Quarterly Bulletin*, 4, 1980, p. 24

..the increase in (personal) lending ..was not consistent with the objectives of monetary policy. Accordingly, the banks concerned *have been contacted* with a view to securing compliance with the intent of monetary policy.
Central Bank of Ireland, *Quarterly Bulletin*, 2, 1981, p. 16.

... in view of this rapid increase (in personal credit), the Central Bank informed a number of banks that the intent of monetary policy was not being complied with *and advised these banks..*
Central Bank of Ireland, *Quarterly Bulletin*, 4, 1981, p. 24.

... growth in lending to the personal sector was relatively rapid and *banks have been contacted* with a view to securing compliance with the sectoral guideline of 7 per cent ...
Central Bank of Ireland, *Quarterly Bulletin*, 2, 1982, p. 15.

The close relationship between Central Bank enforcement of the personal lending guidelines and the decrease in bank lending does suggest that the banks rationed personal loans at certain times over the period.

# Discrimination

Refer back to Table 14.5 and note the decrease in associated bank personal lending between November 1978 and February 1980. In cumulative terms, personal lending *decreased* by 10.9%. However instalment credit, which is not subject to the personal lending guideline, *increased* by 25.9%.

These two figures are paradoxical because the interest rate on instalment credit is roughly *double* the interest rate on personal loans. The question is why would people borrow at high interest rates and not at low interest rates?

One explanation is that the banks discriminated against personal borrowers in order to maximise group profits. In Table 14.6 we divide "total credit subject to the quantitative credit guideline" into "productive credit" and "personal lending subject to the sectoral guideline". Below this we insert instalment credit which is exempt from both guidelines.

*Table 14.6*
**The relationship between the quantitative and sectoral credit guidelines**

| | |
|---|---|
| 1. "Productive" credit | (not subject to sectoral guidelines) |
| 2. Personal credit | (subject to the sectoral guideline) |
| | |
| 3. Total credit (3 = 1 + 2) | (subject to the quantitative credit guideline) |
| 4. Instalment credit | (exempt from both guidelines) |

Given that total credit is subject to the quantitative guideline (line 3), a reduction in personal lending (line 2) means that more money is available for "productive" lending (line 1). Borrowers refused personal loans at the associated banks could now be expected to switch to instalment credit which, although subject to higher interest rate charges, was at least available. Moreover, the associated banks have subsidiaries in the instalment credit market and these subsidiaries could be expected to receive a large proportion of the extra business. The net effect of this manoeuvring is to maximise the banks group profits because "productive" borrowers demands are met by the banks, and personal borrowers are catered for by their subsidiaries who charge higher interest rates. The banks, by forcing borrowers to switch to instalment credit, have in effect found a profitable way around the quantitative credit guideline.

An examination of the data indicates that associated bank personal lending was approximately £74.5m lower over the period November 1978 to February 1980 than it would have been if the banks adhered to the sectoral guideline. There is some evidence to suggest that a significant proportion of rationed borrowers were not prepared to pay the higher interest rates which instalment credit entailed and instead abandoned their expenditure plans.[7] In other words, borrowers who could not obtain a "cheap" associated bank personal loan decided to postpone or abandon their plans to purchase consumer goods rather than take out an instalment loan. If this is the case, then the objectives of the Central Bank's sectoral credit guideline to curtail consumer expenditure may have been partly achieved. However, because of the discrimination by the banks against personal borrowers, the growth in personal credit was approximately £74m lower than if the banks adhered perfectly to the guidelines. As such any reduction in consumer expenditure that might have occurred cannot be wholly attributable to the sectoral guideline but rather to discrimination by the banks.

# 14.6 Conclusion

In this chapter we examined credit policy in Ireland from 1965 to 1977 and from 1978 to 1982. We distinguished between these two sub-periods because of a fundamental change in credit policy after 1978. It should be borne in mind that credit policy in the earlier period could also be referred to, more generally, as monetary policy. This is not, however, the case after 1978. Monetary policy after this date consisted of both an interest rate policy and a credit policy. We discussed interest rate policy in Chapter 12.

With regard to the earlier sub-period some of the main points included:

- Credit guidelines were designed to control the money supply in the economy

- The objective of controlling the money supply was to influence imports or the inflation rate

- The theoretical model underlying monetary policy appears to have been the quantity theory of money and the assumption of a constant velocity of circulation of money

- For the most part, the credit guidelines attempted to accommodate the predicted growth in nominal GNP

- The credit guidelines did not curtail bank lending in the first instance but even if they had it would still not be possible to control the money supply because of the fixed exchange rate and perfect capital mobility between Ireland and the UK.

It is not possible to control the money supply in an economy when the exchange rate is fixed and there is perfect capital mobility. After 1978, the Central Bank acknowledged this point and, instead of attempting to control the money supply, credit policy attempted to influence the composition of the money supply. Some of the main points relating to the 1978-82 period include:

- The objective of the credit guidelines was to achieve an external reserves target

- The theory underlying credit policy was the monetary approach to the balance of payments (MAB)

- The evidence indicates that the Central Bank had only limited success in achieving its external reserves targets

- The quantitative credit guideline did not, on the whole, unduly constrain total private sector credit

- The Central Bank also issued sectoral credit guidelines to curtail banks' personal lending

- We presented some evidence which suggested that the credit guidelines involved costs in the form of a misallocation of resources.

# Notes

1. The governor of the Central Bank mentioned in one of his speeches that the research work of J. S. Oslizlok was used to formulate monetary policy. Although no formal model is outlined by Oslizlok in his published papers, the principal argument in his work is that the money supply could affect nominal output and that the Central Bank could exert some degree of control over the money supply. See: T.K. Whitaker, "Monetary Policy", Central Bank of Ireland, *Quarterly Bulletin*, Geimhreadh, 1969, p. 104. J.S. Oslizlok," Surveys of Sources of Monetary Supplies in Ireland", *Journal of the Statistical and Social Inquiry Society of Ireland*, 1962/63. J.S. Oslizlok, "Towards a Monetary Analysis of Aggregate Demand", Central Bank of Ireland, *Quarterly Bulletin*, November,

1967. J.S. Oslizlok, "Towards a Monetary Analysis of Aggregate Demand - 2: The Circulation of Active Money", Central Bank of Ireland, *Quarterly Bulletin*, February, 1968. It should also be noted that the paper by T.F. Hoare ("Money, Autonomous Expenditure and Aggregate Income", Central Bank of Ireland, *Annual Report*, 1972/73), was the first published attempt to model the monetary sector in Ireland. The model was based on the quantity theory of money and assumed that the velocity of circulation of money was constant. The paper illustrated how to calculate the expansion in credit consistent with a nominal output target.

2. It is possible that the change in the Central Bank's view with regard to money supply control was influenced by the results in F.X. Browne and T. O'Connell, "A Quantitative Analysis of the Degree of Integration between Irish and UK Financial Markets", *Economic and Social Review*, Vol. 9, No. 4, 1978. The evidence presented by these two Central Bank economists indicated that there was perfect integration between Irish and UK financial markets in the period up to 1978. Under these circumstances it is not possible to control the money supply in the Irish economy.

3. For a collection of essays on MAB theory see J.A. Frenkel and H. G. Johnson (eds.), *The Monetary Approach to the Balance of Payments*, London, Allen and Unwin, 1976. A useful survey of the early literature is given in M.E. Kreinin and L. H. Officer, *The Monetary Approach to the Balance of Payments: A Survey*, Princeton Studies in International Finance, No. 43, Princeton University Press, 1978.

4. The results presented in F.X. Browne and T. O'Connell, "The Demand for Money Function in Ireland: Estimation and Stability", *The Economic and Social Review*, Vol. 9, April, 1978 indicated that the demand for money in Ireland is a stable function of a few variables. This result is supported by the findings in M. Kenneally and M. Finn, "The Balance of Payments as a Monetary Phenomenon: A Review and Consideration of Irish Evidence, 1960 - 1978", *The Economic and Social Review*, Vol. 17, No 1, October 1985. The implication of these results is that MAB theory could be used in Ireland for policy purposes.

5. Both R. Kelleher, "Recent Trends in Monetary Policy", *Quarterly Economic Commentary*, ESRI, 1980 and the National Planning Board, *Proposals for Plan: 1984 - 1987*, National Planning Board, Dublin, 1984, point to the inappropriateness of the external reserves as a policy target. The point is that the external reserves doe not take account of foreign indebtedness and as such is an inadequate measure of the Central Bank's ability to maintain the Irish pound exchange rate in foreign exchange markets. Both papers argue that "external finance", defined as the change in the external reserves minus foreign borrowing, is the more relevant policy objective. It can be shown that if the Central Bank's objective was to stabilise "external finance" over the period, no additional credit would have been available to the private sector.

6. This type of rationing is referred to as "guideline credit rationing" as it is the credit guideline which causes the excess demand for credit. Other forms of rationing have been identified in the literature. For example, a theory of "equilibrium credit rationing" is given in J.E, Stiglitz and A. Weiss, "Credit Rationing in Markets with Imperfect Information", *American Economic Review*, Vol. 71, No. 3, 1981. A third type of credit rationing is known as disequilibrium (or dynamic) credit rationing. This type of rationing arises when the interest rate fails to move instantaneously to its equilibrium level following some disturbance to the supply or demand curves for credit. See for example, F. X. Browne, "Empirical Estimates of Dynamic Credit Rationing in the Market for

Associated Bank Private Sector Loans", Central Bank of Ireland, Technical Paper, 2/RT/84, January, 1984.

7. See, for example, A. Leddin, "The Impact of Credit Controls on Consumer Durable Expenditures and Fixed Investment in the Irish Economy", *Irish Business and Administrative Research*, Vol. 8, No. 2, 1986.

# Chapter 15

# *Economic Growth and Longer Term Policy Issues*

Little else is requisite to carry a state to the highest degree of opulence from the lowest barbarism, but peace, easy taxes, and tolerable administration of justice.
Adam Smith, *The Wealth of Nations*, 1776.

## 15.1 Introduction

Throughout most of this book we have been mainly concerned with the short-term performance of the economy. In Chapter 2 we examined in some detail the evolution of the components of national income during the 1980s. In other chapters we explored the impact of fiscal, monetary and exchange rate policies on cyclical fluctuations in the level of activity. In this chapter we turn our attention to the bigger picture. We examine the longer-term trends in Irish economic performance and broad issues of policy and development.

## 15.2 A Review of Irish Economic Performance in the Twentieth Century

This section contains a brief summary of the development of the Irish economy since Independence. We shall look at the main developments under a few key headings.

### Population and migration
In 1916 Padraic Pearse expressed the hope that in a

... free Ireland gracious and useful industries will supplement an improved agriculture, the population will expand in a century to 20 million and it may even in time go up to 30 million.[1]

In reality, large-scale emigration continued after Independence until interrupted by the great depression, and started up again during and after the second world war. The population continued to decline. A commission on *Emigration and Other Population Problems* was established in 1948. The reports, published in 1954, explored at length the reasons for emigration, and recommended policies which it was believed would help to reduce it. Their analysis focussed on the fact that emigration was heaviest outside the main urban areas and consisted to a large extent of a movement from rural Ireland to urban Britain and America. While some limited proposals were put forward to encourage industrial development, the main emphasis was placed on agricultural development with a view to retaining a larger population in the rural areas.

Ironically, in the years immediately following the publication of the Reports of this commission the annual rate of emigration soared to almost 3% of the population, the highest recorded since the 1880s, and the pace of rural depopulation accelerated. The total population fell to 2,818,000 in 1961. From a very long-run perspective, the fall in the population of what is now the Republic from over 6 million in 1841 to 2.8 million in 1961 is perhaps the most remarkable feature of Irish economic history. It provides a dramatic illustration of the openness of our economy and labour force.

During the 1960s, a lower rate of emigration led to a slight increase in the population. This accelerated during the 1970s when, for the first time in our history, a substantial net inflow of population occurred. The 1.5% rate of growth recorded during these years was the highest in Europe. This spurt of growth raised the total population to over 3.5 million by 1986. Projections prepared in the early 1980s, based on the assumption of a low rate of emigration, indicated that the population might pass 4 million by the end of the century. However, the resumption of large-scale emigration by the middle of the 1980s and the rapid drop in the birth rate after 1980 have made this very unlikely. Even if the outflow of population slows during the 1990s, it is likely that by the middle of the decade fertility will have fallen to the replacement level and the population of the Republic will stabilise in the region of 3.5 million.

Emigration is usually believed to have had a negative effect on the economy. It is obviously humiliating and dispiriting if almost half of each school-leaving cohort ends up living outside the country, as was the case during the 1950s. However, given the apparent inability of the Irish economy to absorb the potential growth of its labour force into worthwhile employment, emigration at least afforded young Irish people the opportunity of raising their living standards and relieved pressure on wage levels and welfare services in Ireland. We have seen how, early in the 1980s, when high unemployment throughout the western world virtually

367

closed off the safety valve of emigration, there was a sharp increase in unemployment and an unprecedented decline in living standards in Ireland. In fact, it is surprisingly difficult to find concrete evidence that high rates of emigration have a lasting adverse effect on the rate of economic growth.[2]

Persistent emigration has given Ireland an unusual population age distribution. While the proportion aged under 15 is high by comparison with other European countries, the proportion aged over 65 years old is not much lower than the average. Thus the combined level of young and old dependency is relatively high. (We drew attention to some implications of this in Chapter 7.) Furthermore, because emigration is concentrated among those aged 15-29, a high rate of emigration creates an indentation at this point in the age distribution. For example, in 1961, after the heavy emigration of the 1950s, there were only 145,000 people aged 25-29 left in Ireland, compared with 289,000 people aged 10-14. (This depleted cohort is now in its mid-50s.) However, the importance of this effect should not be exaggerated. Although emigration has raised the median age of the Irish population by about 3 years, we none the less have one of the youngest populations in western Europe.[3] The sharp fall in the birth rate since 1980 will result in a significant rise in the median age of the population between now and the end of the century. In general, the birth rate is a much more important influence on the population's age structure than is the emigration rate.

## Growth in GNP

We noted in Chapter 1 that in 1987 Irish GNP per person was the third lowest of the 24 countries in the OECD. Table 15.1 shows the long-term growth rate in real income in Ireland and Britain.

*Table 15.1*
**Annual average growth rates: 1926-80, %**

|  | *Real GNP/person* |
| --- | --- |
| Republic of Ireland | 2.2 |
| UK | 1.8 |

*Source*: Calculated from K.A. Kennedy and B.R. Dowling, *Economic Growth in Ireland: The Experience since 1947*, Dublin, Gill and Macmillan, 1975, Table 6.2 and K.A. Kennedy, T. Giblin and D. Mc Hugh, *The Economic Development of Ireland in the Twentieth Century*, London Routledge, 1988.

The slightly faster growth of real income per person in Ireland has resulted in some narrowing of the gap between the Republic and the UK, as may be seen from Table 15.2.

*Table 15.2*
**GNP/person: (1985 STG£ purchasing power parity)**

|  | 1926 | 1980 |
|---|---|---|
| Republic of Ireland | 1,016 | 3,297 |
| UK | 1,855 | 4,903 |
| Republic as % of UK | 55 | 67 |

*Source*: Kennedy *et al*. 1975 and 1988

However, despite the low level from which we started in 1922 and the sizeable loss of population up to 1961, the improvement in living standards in Ireland has been slow, and relatively little of the gap between Ireland and the UK has been closed. As a result many countries that were relatively underdeveloped at the start of the century overtook us after the second world war. However, this outcome is not surprising, given that our location and our history linked us so closely with the slowest-growing of the world's major economies, namely, the UK! Even the significant amount of foreign aid we obtained following our accession to the EEC and the EMS has not led to a noticeable narrowing of the gap between Ireland and the average of the European economies. It remains to be seen whether the closer integration of our financial markets with Europe and the completion of the EC internal market in the 1990s will lead to closer convergence of living standards than has been achieved to date.

In judging Ireland's growth record, account should be taken of the fact that between 1932 and 1966, over half the period included in this comparison, the Irish economy was one of the most heavily protected in the world. Prolonged reliance on generalised protectionism has not proved to be an effective way of promoting economic development anywhere in the world.[4] Whatever the merits of imposing tariffs on selected "infant industries" at the early stages of industrialisation, no example can be found of a country that has successfully used indiscriminate protectionism extending for over a generation to create a viable export-oriented industrial sector.

Finally, during the 1980s the Irish economy significantly under-performed Britain and other OECD economies. The reasons for this poor showing, which undid some of the gains made in early years, have been explored in previous chapters.

369

# 15.3 The Structure of the Economy

The decline of the rural population and the slow but steady growth of urban Ireland has resulted in a marked increase in the proportion of the population living in cities and towns. In 1926 only 32% of the population was classified as urban; by 1986 this had risen to 56%.[5] The growth in urbanisation has been accompanied by an even faster decline in the importance of agriculture. None the less this sector still contained 15% of the labour force in 1987, a percentage surpassed only in Greece, Portugal and Turkey in OECD countries. The proportion of the labour force employed in industry is relatively low (28%), as is the proportion in services (57%). In early-industrialising countries such as the UK, the US and Germany, the agricultural population moved to cities and towns to work in industry and the share of industrial employment in the total rose to a very high level. In recent decades, however, service employment has grown rapidly while industrial employment has stagnated. In Ireland, employment in industry increased relative to total employment throughout most of the period from 1926 to 1980.

There was a marked change in the composition of industrial employment as protectionism was dismantled during the 1960s and 1970s. Most of the employment in the industries that grew up under protectionism did not survive long under free trade. There was, however, a rapid expansion in the numbers engaged in new, export-oriented firms. This should be taken into account in interpreting the relatively modest net increase in total industrial employment during these years. However, during the recession of the 1980s almost one quarter of all employment in manufacturing was lost. This involved not only continued attrition from the old industries, but also a high closure rate among newer firms. It remains to be seen whether the renewed growth of the economy in the 1990s will lead to a recovery of the share of industry in the total or whether the service sectors will from now on be the main providers of additional jobs in Ireland.

We have repeatedly referred to Ireland as a small open economy. The export statistics show how open our economy is. As can be seen from Table 15.3, since the 1960s exports have consistently grown more rapidly than GNP, with the result that the ratio of exports to GNP is now one of the highest in the world.

The "smallness" of the economy can be illustrated by the fact that Irish GNP amounts to only 0.2% of the GNP of all of the OECD countries combined! Only Luxembourg and Iceland have smaller GNPs. But "smallness" in economic terms refers to a lack of market power or having to be a price-taker rather than a price-setter. It is unlikely that many Irish firms would have much influence over world prices, but in some industries (e.g. computers or pharmaceuticals) the concentration of firms in Ireland may be so large that, for example, a rise in Irish labour costs could have some effect on world prices. Even allowing for this possibility, it is none the less safe to regard Ireland as a clear example of a small, open economy (SOE).

*Table 15.3*
**Exports as a percentage of GNP**

|        | %  |
|--------|----|
| 1962   | 32 |
| 1970   | 52 |
| 1980   | 56 |
| 1988   | 74 |

*Source*: Central Bank of Ireland, *Quarterly Bulletins*, various issues

In interpreting the extraordinary growth in exports, and their exceptionally large share of GNP, account should be taken of our discussion of transfer pricing in Chapter 11 and of the gap between GNP and GDP in Chapter 2. There is a sense in which Irish exports are overstated by the inclusion of a significant amount of value added that eventually flows out of the economy as repatriated profits. (Similarly, Irish imports are inflated by the exceptionally high import content of our industrial exports.) None the less, even when allowance is made for these considerations, it remains true that the Irish economy is extremely open.

The large share of trade in GNP is not the only indication of the openness of the Irish economy. The importance of emigration to our labour market is also exceptional, while the influence of foreign interest rates on our financial markets illustrates that they, too, are highly integrated into the world economy.

The Irish economy has a relatively large public sector. We drew attention to the growth in the level of taxation relative to GNP in Chapter 4. In Chapter 7 we noted the rapid increase in public sector employment in the 1970s. Current government spending amounted to 50% of Irish GNP in 1986, a proportion surpassed only by the Scandinavian and the Benelux countries in the OECD. Public sector employment, spending and taxation are proportionately much higher in Ireland than in other OECD countries with comparable levels of income per person. During the 1960s and 1970s there was a proliferation of state agencies and state-sponsored bodies dealing with various aspects of the economy. A major structural adjustment was required during the 1980s to halt the growing dominance of the public sector in the country's economic life.

# 15.4 Economic Development and Policy

## Industrial policy

In the brief period between the demobilisation after the Civil War and the start of the Great Depression in 1930, Ireland pursued a strategy of limited state intervention in economic affairs in the hope that by concentrating on agriculture, where it was believed our comparative advantage lay, the foundations for economic development would be laid. Even during these years, however, the state was prepared to supplement private enterprise, as in the creation of the state monopoly Electricity Supply Board and the granting of a limited number of tariffs to help selected industries that made the case that they were facing unfair competition from abroad. It is not possible to draw any worthwhile conclusions about the potential success of this strategy, had it been continued longer, because of a dearth of data for the few years when it was in place.

In the 1930s the economic and political circumstances, both in Ireland and abroad, changed dramatically. The collapse of world trade in the Great Depression and the return flow of former emigrants to Ireland, probably resulted in a sharp fall in living standards. (There are, of course, no annual estimates of GNP for these years!) In response to the changed situation, the newly elected Fianna Fáil government embarked on a programme of generalised protectionism in 1932. Foreign investment was virtually excluded from Ireland and if anyone was willing to manufacture a product in Ireland a very high tariff was imposed on competing imports. As a result of these policies, the level of effective protection of Irish industry was extremely high throughout the next four decades. Even as late as 1966, the average rate of effective protection of Irish manufacturing industry was almost 80%, one of the highest in the western world.[6] All the firms that set up behind these high tariffs were Irish-owned, although in many cases British firms went into joint ventures with Irish residents to set up subsidiaries to cater for the Irish market. British car manufacturers, for example, put together special kits in England that were shipped to Ireland and assembled here by their subsidiaries. The limited number of semi-skilled jobs created in the Irish car assembly industry in this manner were paid for by the very high cost of cars in Ireland. Twenty years after protectionism gave way to free trade, none of these jobs survives.

After 1966, and the coming into force of the Anglo-Irish Free Trade Area Agreement, tariffs were rapidly dismantled, first for Britain and then for the rest of Europe after our entry in the EEC in 1973. Simultaneously, restrictions on direct foreign investment in Ireland were replaced by generous grants and tax incentives to attract export-oriented manufacturing firms to Ireland. This new "outward-looking" approach was designed to replace our reliance on Irish firms, or Irish-owned subsidiaries of British firms, catering for the small and stagnant domestic market with foreign (mainly US) owned firms that would grow through exporting.

The new firms that came to Ireland to avail of the generous incentives provided by the government, and to locate in a relatively low-cost environment inside the enlarged EEC, accounted for all of the growth of industrial employment, output and exports during the 1970s and 1980s. During the 1970s their growth offset the decline in the firms that had been established under protection. GNP grew at an average annual rate of about 4% during the 1960s, over twice the rate that had been recorded during the 1950s. The population stabilised and then began to grow rapidly. At least until the recession of the early 1980s, it was reasonable to view the new "outward looking" policy as a success.

By the 1980s the level of public sector support to Irish industry had reached a very high level. The Department of Industry and Commerce estimated that the value of all the state aids to industry (exclusive of foregone tax revenue) varied between £370 and £400 million over the period 1983-86.[7] Thus, by the early 1980s about 3% of GNP was being spent each year to promote industrial development. As shown in Table 15.4, data collected by the Commission of the European Community show that Ireland has one of the highest levels of industrial aid in the EC.

*Table 15.4*

**Financial resources devoted to industry as percentage of gross value added in industry (excluding shipbuilding and steel)**

|  | Average 1981-84 |
| --- | --- |
| Italy | 16.1 |
| Ireland | 13.8 |
| France | 8.3 |
| Denmark | 7.3 |
| Germany | 7.3 |
| UK | 6.8 |
| Belgium | 6.8 |
| Netherlands | 4.6 |
| Luxembourg | 3.5 |

*Note:* If shipbuilding and steel are included, all these proportions increase, and Luxembourg moves to the top of the list, followed by Italy and Ireland

*Source*: Commission of the European Community

The high level of state aid to industry shows that the contrast between the "protectionist" and "outward-looking" phases of Irish industrial policy is not as stark as is often made out. The array of grants and tax concessions offered to industries setting up in Ireland after the removal of the tariffs in effect replaced "commodity-based protection" with "factor-based protection". Just as a tariff on the price of a product allows a firm to incur higher costs than its competitors in the rest of the world, subsidies on its inputs also drive a wedge between domestic and world costs. It has been estimated that the industrial incentive package offered by the Irish government in the 1970s was equivalent to an effective protection rate of 24%.[8]

When many countries and even regions within countries resort to grants and tax concessions to attract footloose investment, there is a risk that the main beneficiaries will be the share-holders in international firms, rather than the local unemployed population. Firms search the world to find the most favourable package of incentives, playing one location off against another. This leaves a country such as Ireland, which hopes to benefit from the location of subsidiaries of foreign firms, in a difficult situation. If it continues to increase its incentives in response to competition from other countries, they may match the more generous aid offered, with the result that it costs all countries more to maintain their share of the available flow of investment. On the other hand, if we were to withdraw from the race, the result might be that no new foreign investment would come to Ireland.

For these reasons there is a growing awareness of the need for international action to curb the level of state aids to industry. The commission of the EC has powers, under the Treaty of Rome, to disallow new aids and it has had some success in reducing existing aids. However, as the figures provided above reveal, a vast amount of tax-payers' money is being spent in Europe in the competition for footlose industrial investment.

The nature of the aid offered appears to have had a significant effect on the type of industry that has been attracted to Ireland. We commented on the magnitude of the outflow of net factor income to the rest of the world in Chapter 9. Repatriated profits are a major component of this and their growth attracted considerable attention during the 1980s. We noted in Chapter 10 how these can be inflated by the practice of "transfer pricing". It can be argued that one of the consequences of offering generous tax concessions is that industries will show a very high rate of profit in this jurisdiction without giving a great deal of employment. Irish industrial growth in the 1980s has been dominated by a small group of sectors - pharmaceuticals and fine chemicals, electronic engineering and data processing equipment, and "other foods" - in which firms are able to take maximum advantage of the opportunities offered by the Irish corporate tax code to use transfer pricing to increase their world-wide after-tax profits. Net output per head in these "modern" sectors averaged £57,700 in 1984, compared with only £19,300 in the rest of Irish industry, but earnings per employee were actually slightly lower in the former

(£8,148 compared with £8,731), indicating the vastly greater profitability of the "modern" sector.[9]

Most Irish state aid to industry - capital grants, accelerated depreciation allowances, etc. - has the effect of lowering the cost of capital. On the other hand, as we have seen in Chapter 7, the rise in the effective rate of income taxation has raised the cost of employing labour. Thus the net result of public policy has been to change the factor price ratio in favour of capital and against labour.[10] While this strategy can be defended by claiming that it results in an inflow of technically sophisticated, high-growth firms, it is not a cost-effective way of trying to create employment in a relatively poor economy.

For these reasons, in addition to the desirability of reducing the level of aid, more attention should be paid to designing aid that will maximise the level of employment generated for a given level of state expenditure or foregone tax revenue. In particular, it is difficult to justify the artificial cheapening of capital that occurs when fixed assets are both grant-aided and given over-generous allowances in the tax code. This leads to the substitution of capital for labour, and attracts to Ireland firms that are more interested in acquiring fixed assets at the expense of the tax-payer than they are in creating sustainable employment.

# Economic planning

Many people were infatuated with French planning [in 1962]. The combination of intellectual rigour, as suggested by the word "planning", and romance, as suggested by the word "French" was extremely tempting. So a group of us went to Paris. We met with officials of the Commissariat du Plan, with French businessmen, and with economists. By the time we returned I had concluded, in a line that I could not get out of my mind: "Le Plan français, il n'existe pas". The French government had forecasts about the economy, it made certain interventions in the economy - but it had no plan.
Herbert Stein, former Chairman of the US Council of Economic Advisers, in *Fortune*, November 14th 1983.

We in Ireland were also fascinated with the idea that an economy could be "planned" or "programmed" in some gentle, indicative way that bore no relation to the horrors of soviet regimentation. From 1958 into the 1980s a stream of government publications attempted to chart a medium-term course for the Irish economy. In this section we shall review these documents and assess their contribution to the development of the Irish economy.

The *public capital programme*, as the public sector's capital budget was called after the war, reflected the government's priorities in the areas of "social overhead" and "productive infrastructure" investment, that is, spending on roads, schools, hospitals and capital grants to agriculture and industry. Its overall size could also be adjusted as a means of Keynesian-type demand management. In a sense, this annual programme was the first tentative step on the road to economic planning. Another factor that contributed to thinking in terms of more than just the annual budget was our participation in the *European Recovery Programme* (Marshall Aid) in 1949. Ireland, although neutral during the war, was offered some of this aid. The US authorities were anxious to see integrated proposals for spending the large amounts of aid that were made available. The Department of Finance opposed borrowing, even on very favourable terms, for ambitious new projects. In fact there were those who deplored the indignity of accepting US aid at all.[11] However, the Department of Foreign Affairs, where Sean MacBride was Minister, prepared a long-term recovery programme consisting mainly of schemes for the development of forestry and agriculture, and for spending on local authority housing and hospitals. The loans received under Marshall Aid were spent on these projects.

These tentative steps towards "planning" were overtaken by the stagnation of the early 1950s and the crisis of 1955 and 1956. Emigration soared to a record level as employment fell and unemployment rose. Living standards, which had not kept pace with expectations since the war, fell during the recession and an even sharper fall was only averted by the mass exodus from the country. T.K. Whitaker, who was Secretary of the Department of Finance at the time, has described the situation as follows:

The mood of despondency was palpable. Something had to be done or the achievement of national independence would prove to have been a futility. Various attempts were made to shine a beam forward in this dark night of the soul; they at least agreed on the need to devote more resources on an orderly basis to productive investment. Finally, over the winter and spring of 1958/59, a comprehensive survey of the economy, extending to its potentialities as well as to its deficiencies, was prepared in the Department of Finance. This was presented to the Government in May 1958 and was published under the title *Economic Development* in November of that year, simultaneously with the *First Programme for Economic Expansion*, which was acknowledged to be based largely upon it.

T.K.Whitaker, "Ireland's Development Experience", paper read to the Annual Conference of the Development Studies Association, Dublin, 1982.

The principal guidelines for economic policy set out in the *First Programme* were:

• To escape from stagnation "public and private development of a productive character must be stimulated and organised so as to overshadow the non-productive development which now bulks so largely in public investment and in national capital formation as a whole"

• To achieve this, capital spending on local authority housing and hospitals was to be reduced and additional resources invested in agriculture and industry

- Fiscal policy should give priority to a significant reduction in taxation, particularly income taxation, because "high taxation is one of the greatest impediments to economic progress because of its adverse effects on saving and on enterprise"

- The increase in wages and salaries should for a time lag behind that in Britain.

There followed pages of detailed recommendations designed to foster increased efficiency in agriculture, industry and services such as banking.

A number of features of this programme strike the reader today. In the first place, the hope was still that agriculture would provide the engine of growth for the development of the economy.[12] In this respect it reflected the views of the Emigration Commission. The conflict between trying to pursue our comparative advantage in agriculture while at the same time maintaining exceptionally high protective tariffs on industrial products was not discussed.[13]

In fact the *First Programme* did not explicitly address the question of the failure of protectionism and the need to move to an export-oriented strategy. In the brief section that touches on this issue, the achievements of the protected industries were listed (100,000 new jobs and a trebling of the volume of industrial production), but it was acknowledged that tariffs "might impair the incentive to reduce costs and increase efficiency". However, there was no clarion call to face up to the rapid dismantling of these tariffs. Instead it was rather blandly stated that "it is obviously essential not only that existing industries should become progressively more efficient, but also that new industries should be competitive in export markets and capable of withstanding the challenge presented by the Free Trade Area."

The *First Programme* attached little weight to Keynesian demand management. Instead, the emphasis was placed on the need to raise productivity in the individual sectors of the economy, what we should to-day call "supply-side" measures. It has been criticised for this,[14] but in view of the painful lessons that we learned from an inappropriate use of crude Keynesian policies in the 1970s, the *First Programme's* balance between supply and demand side measures was probably the right one as Ireland moved into the 1960s.

The *First Programme* was designed to give a fillip to the confidence of a nation demoralised by recession and the bankruptcy of the old protectionist strategy. In this it succeeded handsomely. *Economic Development*, and the *First Programme* which was based on it, captured the imagination of a much wider population than would normally be aware of a detailed discussion of economic policy. It has become the accepted wisdom to attribute the contrast between the economic stagnation of the 1950s and the expansion of the 1960s to the impact of these documents.

The contribution they made to economic policy and the performance of the economy is difficult to establish, however. Few of the recommendations they contained were implemented. The burden of taxation was not eased. Instead, as we noted in Chapters 2 and 4, income tax in particular rose inexorably. Moreover, as Kennedy and Dowling point out,

There is no evidence of a rise in the level of manufacturing investment, or its share in GNP, prior to the increase in the growth rate of GNP. Neither does it emerge that cutting back housing investment in any way helped to raise the level of manufacturing investment.
Kennedy and Dowling, *op. cit.*, p. 176.

Nor did agriculture prove to be the engine of growth as envisaged in the *First Programme*: even after entry into the EEC and a massive injection of subsidies from the Community, the share of GNP originating in this sector declined steadily. Instead, the role of economic locomotive was assumed by industry, as the scale of the inflow of foreign capital far exceeded that in the *First Programme's* projections. Finally, the projected target of 11% growth in the volume of GNP over the period 1959-63 was less than half the 23% growth actually recorded, so the statistical projections contained in the documents bore little resemblance to the outcome.

It is probably fair to say that neither the *First Programme*, nor whatever effect it had on policy, caused the increased growth after 1958. This was due largely to the buoyancy of the world economy in those years and the gradual opening up of the Irish economy to export-oriented investment, which allowed us to benefit more fully from favourable external developments.[15] Ireland's return to full participation in the international economic community after such a long absence was almost inevitable in the light of the failure of the inward-looking policies and the increasing importance of the EEC to both this country and to Britain. The *First Programme* recognised these developments and proposed they be confronted positively, but it did not place them at the centre of a new development strategy. The most puzzling aspect of Irish economic policy in the post-war period is that we waited 20 years after the end of the war before finally abandoning the policies that had been adopted as expedients in the 1930s.

However, it was inevitable that the dramatic improvement in the performance of the Irish economy in the years following the publication of the *First Programme* would be attributed to the programme itself, and, in view of the international vogue of "indicative planning" at this time (see the quotation at the beginning of this section), it is understandable that the planning exercise was repeated in a much more ambitious form in subsequent years. The *Second Programme 1964-70* was published in 1964 and the *Third Programme, Economic and Social Development, 1969-72* in 1969.[16] These contained much more detailed statistical analyses of the Irish economy than had been attempted in 1958. The national accounts framework used in the *First Programme* was supplemented by detailed sectoral projections based on an input-output model. As has been pointed out:

... the objective of both later programmes was to obtain a profile of the Irish economy at a specified later date (1970 for the Second, 1973 for the Third), which reflected the highest possible growth rates which could be achieved in the light of "policy possibilities, the probable development of the external environment and resource availability".

Bradley J., "Economic Planning: Lessons of the Past and Future Prospects", *Administration*, Vol. 36, No. 1, 1988.

Both of these programmes projected a growth rate of 4% a year in real GNP, which was the actual outcome during the recovery from the deep recession of the 1950s. However, projections of the growth of the economy, in aggregate and by sector, proved as wide of the mark during the *Second* and *Third Programmes* as they had been in the *First Programme*, with the added embarrassment that the greater detail contained in the later documents drew attention to their increasing lack of relevance as the planning periods progressed. The *Second Programme* was based on the assumption that Ireland would be a member of the EEC by 1970. As this was prevented by France's veto of British entry shortly after its publication, a rationale was provided for abandoning the programme in 1966. It also became clear very early on that the targets contained in the *Third Programme*, especially those relating to employment, would not be achieved.

The degree of disillusionment with the whole process of planning in the turbulent economic circumstances of the 1970s is reflected in the words of the Minister for Finance, Richie Ryan, in his 1975 budget speech:

... of all the tasks that could engage my attention, the least realistic would be the publication of a medium or long term economic plan based on irrelevances in the past, hunches as to the present and clairvoyance as to the future ...

quoted in Bradley, *op. cit.*

Irish economic planning would thus have seemed to have died amid the unrealized targets of the 1960s and the global economic uncertainty of the oil-price crisis of 1973. But it enjoyed renewed popularity after the formation of a new government in 1977. A Department of Economic Planning and Development was created.[17] A plan called *National Development 1977-80* was published, containing specific targets for the growth of output and employment, and above all the reduction in unemployment. It was envisaged that the public sector would provide an initial boost to the economy, after which the private sector would take up the running. This would require increased government spending and additional recruitment in the public sector as a job-creation measure. The adverse effects of implementing these policies on the public finances and the structure of the economy were outlined in Chapter 4. As we also noted, the projections contained in this plan proved to be far too optimistic and were rendered irrelevant by the second oil-price crisis in 1979.

In the end, this exercise in planning hindered, rather than helped, the implementation of an appropriate policy response as the country faced into the most protracted recession in its post-war history.

Subsequent statements on national development increasingly focussed on the constraints facing the economy and contained fewer specific targets. In 1981 the Coalition Government established a *Committee on Costs and Competitiveness*, which reported in October. The report set out calculations of a wage norm, taking into account the forecast increases in our competitors' wage costs and likely changes in exchange rates. The idea was that if this norm were adhered to there would be no deterioration in the country's competitiveness. Unfortunately, the norm proposed by the committee in October 1981 was rendered inappropriate almost as soon as it was published by a weakening of sterling. (The fall in sterling meant that greater wage moderation was called for in Ireland.) This episode provides a clear illustration of how difficult it is to frame policy in a small, open economy where even short-run forecasts of key variables can be very wide of the mark.

The next planning document was prepared by the Fianna Fáil government during 1982 and became the manifesto on which the party fought (and lost) the second General Election of 1982. This document, called *The Way Forward*, contained optimistic forecasts of economic growth based on a dramatic improvement in our international competitiveness. This was to be achieved by "moderate pay increases combined with increases in productivity".

In March 1983 the new Coalition Government established an independent National Planning Board to prepare a study that would form the basis for a new plan.[18] The result was *Proposals for Plan 1984-87*, published in April 1984. This document different fundamentally from its immediate predecessors, and in some ways returned to the spirit of the *First Programme*, by presenting very detailed sectoral policy recommendations. It contained in all no fewer than 241 recommendations, ranging over all aspects of economic and social policy. It advocated the need to reduce the level of public sector spending and borrowing, to bring down the level of taxation, and to increase the efficiency of the public sector, particularly of the monopolistic state companies whose services have to be bought by the rest of the economy. In many respects the package proposed resembled a "structural adjustment programme" of the type put in place by the International Monetary Fund in numerous heavily-indebted developing countries in the 1980s. It was clearly influenced by the philosophies of privatisation, deregulation and supply-side economics that were in the ascendancy in the US and Britain.

It is also notable that in *Proposals for Plan* the Keynesian emphasis on demand management that had been influential in the late 1970s was emphatically rejected. Its analysis of the unemployment problem focussed attention on the growing proportion of long-term unemployed in the total and called for special, targeted measures, rather than across-the-board demand stimulus, to alleviate this problem.

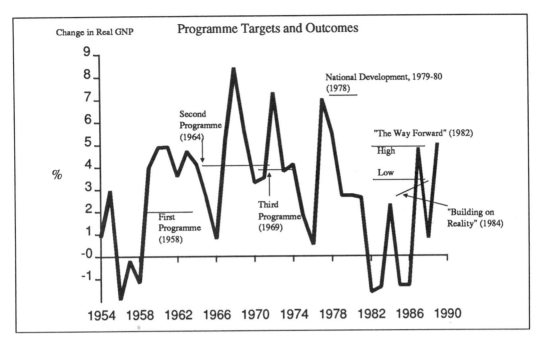

Change in Real GNP

Programme Targets and Outcomes

Figure 15.1

The Coalition Government's plan, *Building on Reality*, was published in autumn 1984. This generally endorsed the policy recommendations contained in *Proposals for Plan*. It emphasised the goal of stabilising the debt/GNP ratio and reducing the level of taxation. It forecast that total employment would increase over the next three years as employment in private sector services grew rapidly and industrial employment began to recover from the recession. These projections proved too optimistic. As we have seen in Chapter 4, the public finances continued to deteriorate until 1987 and employment did not begin to recover until 1988.

The minority Fianna Fáil government that was formed in 1987 published a *Programme for National Recovery 1987-90* in October 1987. This did not aspire to be a plan in the way earlier documents had. At its core was a national agreement between employers, trades unions and the government to adhere to a ceiling of 2.5% annual increases in wages and salaries over the period of the programme. A reduction in the rate of income taxation was promised and the prospect of increases in employment in state-sponsored enterprises was held out. A period of exceptionally low inflation facilitated adherence to the incomes policy agreed to in this document, but the rise in the inflation rate in 1989 has made it unlikely that this accord will be extended into the 1990s unless significant tax concessions can be used to raise disposable incomes.

What generalisations can be drawn from the profusion of planning documents published since 1958? First, it is instructive to compare the projections/forecasts of economic growth they contained with the actual out-turn. This is done in Figure

15.1.[19] It is evident that the targets/projections contained in all six programmes or plans that were published bore virtually no relationship to the outcome. The *First Programme*, as we saw, hoped for less than half the growth that occurred. At the other extreme, *National Development 1977-80* wildly overestimated the growth of the economy. *Building on Reality*, which was a sober document compared with *The Way Forward* published only two years earlier, was nevertheless very wide of the mark in its anticipation of a strong recovery in 1984/5.

At the time of writing, a medium-term forecast has just been published by the Economic and Social Research Institute. It projects an annual average growth rate in the region of 5% for the period 1989-94, with over 7% growth in 1990. It remains to be seen whether these projections prove to be any more accurate than the ones in Figure 15.1. It is possible that they are unduly influenced by the strong growth of the economy in 1989. The recovery from the under-performance of the 1980s should not be extrapolated for five years! These figures bring home the lesson that medium term economic forecasting in a small open economy is an extremely hazardous exercise, whose value is questionable.

One of the difficulties in evaluating the projections for the economy contained in the planning documents that have appeared in Ireland over the past thirty years is that they did not make clear what these numbers represented. Were they forecasts of how the economy was expected to perform or estimates of what might have been achieved if the policies proposed in the document had been implemented? With the increasing politicisation of the whole planning process, a third possibility has to be considered: were the projected growth figures simply public relations exercises designed to serve a political purpose by the government of the day?

One way of avoiding some of the scepticism that is bound to surround any projection of economic growth contained in a government White Paper is to explain in detail the assumptions on which it depends and to make available to independent economists the econometric model on which it is based. The UK Treasury uses a a large-scale econometric model in preparing the forecasts that are employed in the budget. Outsiders are allowed experiment with this model to see how it responds to different assumptions about the levels of the exogenous variables. This approach has not been used for any of the projections contained in official documents in Ireland.[20]

A more fundamental critique of the whole process of planning as it was attempted in Ireland is that it was based on a misunderstanding of the theory of economic planning as developed by economists such as Jan Tinbergen, Bent Hansen and Henri Thiel over the post-war period.[21] According to this theory, planning consists in setting values for the target variables (such as the growth in GNP) and trying to find values for the instrument or policy variables (e.g. government expenditure, taxes, the exchange rate) that will lead to the attainment of the targets, taking account of the structure of the economy and how it responds to changes in the values of the instrument variables. The central feature of the plan is finding the (unknown) values of the instrument variables that will do the job. However, as has been pointed out, we in Ireland "have tended to view economic policy with its head upside down: we have tended to focus on targets and projections as the ultimate unknowns, as though in many cases the instruments could be taken for granted".[22] Certainly many of the plans published over the past thirty years were extremely short on the details of which policy instruments were to be used to achieve the results that were sought. In some cases, for example the very high growth rates in *National Development 1977-80*, it is unlikely that any values of the instrument variables (taxes, government spending, the exchange rate) would have been capable of attaining the targets, given the structure of the Irish economy.

# 5 What Role for Planning?

The quotation from Adam Smith at the beginning of this chapter summarises one view of economic development. It is based on a laissez-faire philosophy which believes that market forces and the self-interest of the population will lead to rapid economic growth unless obstructed by war, high taxation or insecurity of property rights. This view, although it has enjoyed renewed popularity in Mrs Thatcher's Britain and Mr Reagan's America, has not been widely accepted in Ireland since Independence. This is not surprising because political nationalism tends to be linked with economic nationalism, which would see a much larger role for the state than is allowed under laissez-faire.

In fact many economists concerned with the study of economic development have tried to show that there are market failures and barriers to competition which make it unlikely that private enterprise in an underdeveloped, late-industrialising country will be able to build up a strong, export-oriented industrial sector or close the gap in living standards with richer countries. In Ireland this point of view has been dominant in various guises since the 1930s. A recent restatement of it is contained in a book on the unemployment problem by economists at the Economic and Social Research Institute:

It is necessary to challenge the simplistic view that all that needs to be done is to unshackle the private sector from state interference and that this sector will then deliver the jobs [required to attain full employment]. This belief, which is now highly influential, but it is not supported by the evidence of ... Irish history or by the experience of most OECD economies since the end of the war. On the other hand, there is plenty of evidence of a weak response by private indigenous enterprise to the same environment in which foreign enterprise was able to generate large profits.
*Employment and Unemployment Policy for Ireland* by staff members of ESRI, edited by Denis Conniffe and Kieran A. Kennedy, Dublin: The Economic and Social Research Institute, 1984, p.326.

It follows from this diagnosis of the problem that there should be a "substantially increased commitment of public funds" to help Irish firms overcome the structural barriers to competing successfully on world markets.

A number of points may be made about this view of the Irish economy. In the first place, while there was an increasing emphasis on the merits of laissez-faire in public debate during the 1980s, interventionism had been in the ascendency for the previous fifty years. In particular, advocates of a "substantial" increase in state expenditure on aid to industry should bear in mind that the level of such spending in Ireland is already the second highest in EC relative to value added in industry (see Table 15.4).

This school favours directing additional spending towards domestic or "indigenous" industries. But as members of the EC it would be legally impossible to direct aid by nationality of ownership. In any event, it is not very convincing to claim that the vast amount that has been spend on aid to industry since we adopted an "outward-looking" stance in the late 1950s has not achieved its objectives because it was misdirected to foreign-owned instead of being spent on indigenous firms. The grants and tax concessions that have been availed of by multinational firms have always been available to local firms.

There is another problem with this account of the failure of the Irish private sector. It is, in part at least, based on a sociological or psychological view to the effect that there is a lack of a dynamic enterprise in the Irish business community. Whatever the validity of this view, and it is certainly not supported by the behaviour of the Irish abroad, it is paradoxical to argue that such a deficit could be overcome by increased public sector involvement in business. A country that has failed to produce dynamic private sector entrepreneurs after seventy years of independence is unlikely to contain a significant reservoir of entrepreneurship in its public sector[23]. It is more likely that the reasons for the failure of private industry to develop rapidly since independence lie in the incentives it has faced and the environment it has to operate in, rather than in psychological or sociological factors. The debilitating effects of prolonged protectionism were not overcome by an excessive reliance on state aid that contained a strong bias in favour of fixed assets and transfer pricing. The availability of secure and relatively well-paid employment opportunities in the public sector during the 1960s and 1970s absorbed the most talented young people. Risk-taking and profit-seeking in the private sector were not fostered by the reward system.

A particular view of economic history, including the economic history of successful "late industrialising countries" from Sweden to Japan and Taiwan, is often used to bolster the case for more state spending on industry[24]. It is beyond the scope of this chapter to explore this issue in detail, but so frequently is Japan cited as an example of the success of state aid to industry that it is worth looking at this instance. The Ministry of International Trade and Industry (MITI) played an active role in fostering Japan's outstanding economic performance after the second world war. But MITI's role was primarily one of creating a favourable environment for Japanese industry at home and for its exports abroad. There was very little in the way of direct subsidies and grants to manufacturing industries. For example, it is estimated that in only one out of thirteen major industrial sectors did subsidies exceed 0.1% of gross value added (compared with the average of 15% in Irish industry!) In the late 1970s the Japanese government funded no more than 1.9% of all industrial research and development, far less than was the case in Europe and the US. Moreover, where MITI intervened and tried to control industrial development, it did harm, as well as good. It tried to "rationalise" the automobile industry by concentrating production in a few giant companies and discouraged Honda from entering! It wasted billions of dollars in trying to establish a Japanese aircraft industry, which went out of business after producing one prototype! More generally, it has been said that "... the main role of the [Japanese] government was to provide an accommodating and supportive environment for the market, rather than providing leadership or direction."[25]

Finally, in view of the importance of the employment issue in Ireland, a discussion of the country's disappointing long-run economic performance should be related to the wider debate on why the economies of western Europe have tended to generate so little additional employment for the past two decades, whilst employment in the US has increased by an average of 1.5% a year over the same period. This contrast has received relatively little attention in the debate on Irish economic policy, despite the impact it has had on the level of emigration from Ireland to the US. Some of the lessons that may be learned from the US experience were discussed in Chapter 4.

A general lesson that might be learned from attempts at planning over the last thirty years is the need to pay greater attention to macroeconomic issues, and in particular to removing distortions and barriers to competition and providing greater incentives to enterprise, thrift and diligence and to spend less time trying to "plan" or "project" macroeconomic variables which, in the nature of a small, open economy, are largely outside our control.

# 5 Conclusion

The medium-term prospects for the Irish economy as we face into the 1990s are very favourable. The major structural adjustment required by the excessive growth of public spending during the 1970s has been more or less accomplished. The economy is leaner and more competitive than it has been for many years although the burden of taxation remains high. The commitment of our exchange rate to the EMS is now credible and belatedly bearing the fruit that was expected on entry in 1979.

Ireland is well-placed to benefit from the dynamic gains that are expected to follow the completion of the European internal market and from the increased flow of regional and social aid that are being provided to help the weaker economies adjust to the new environment. However, we have seen how repeatedly in the past medium-term forecasts have borne very little resemblance to the outcome. It would be remiss of us not to warn the reader of how uncertain is any attempt to look forward over a period of years.

The scope for independent macroeconomic policy by the Irish authorities is small and has diminished steadily over the post-war period. Macroeconomic policy will probably now become less active and more attention will be focussed on microeconomic issues, such as making sure that markets work as efficiently as possible, and where there are clear market failures, identifying the appropriate interventions. "The romantic phase is over", as Keynes said when England left the gold standard in 1932, "and we can now set about doing what is right for the economy". This modest ambition should guide Irish economic policy in the years ahead.

# Notes

1. Cited in J.F.Meenan, *The Irish Economy Since 1922*, Liverpool University Press, 1970.

2. See B. M. Walsh, "Testing for Macroeconomic Feedback from Large-Scale Migration based on the Irish Experience, 1948-87: A Note", *The Economic and Social Review*, Vol. 20, No. 3, April 1989, p. 257-266.

3. The median age of the population is the age above and below which half the population falls. In 1986 the median age of the Irish population was 28 years.

4. For estimates of the costs of protectionism to developing countries, see Pan A. Yotopoulos and Jeffrey Nugent, *Economics of Development: Empirical Investigations*, New York, 1976, Chapter 7.

5. These are Census data relating to the population living in cities and towns with 1,500 or more inhabitants.

6. Dermot McAleese, *Effective Tariffs and the Structure of Industrial Protection in Ireland*, Dublin: The Economic and Social Research Institute, Paper No. 62, 1871.

7. *Review of Industrial Performance 1986*, Dublin: The Stationary Office, 1987.

8. Stephen E. Guisinger, "Do Performance Requirements and Investment Incentives Work?", *The World Economy*, Vol. 9, No. 1, March 1986, pp. 79-96.

9. See T.J.Baker, "Industrial Output and Wage Costs 1980-87", *Quarterly Economic Commentary*, October 1988.

10. See Frances P. Ruane and Andrew A. John, "Government Intervention and the Cost of Capital to Irish Industry", *The Economic and Social Review*, Vol. 16, No. 1, October 1984.

11. See Ronan Fanning, The Irish Department of Finance, Dublin: The Institute of Public Administration, 1978.

12. Out of a total of 212 pages of text, 100 were devoted to a detailed discussion of agriculture, forestry and fisheries. The headline in the *Irish Independent* proclaimed "Easier credit schemes for farmers proposed"!

13. A rationale for tariffs is to try to change a country's comparative advantage over time. The authors of the Emigration Commission Reports and of the *First Programme* did not seem to believe that this hope was being realised, yet they did not recommend that tariffs be dismantled.

14. "It is our contention that the desire to lay a basis for long-term, growth - in particular by changing the composition of the Public Capital Programme - involved an excessive emphasis on supply aspects at the expense of demand considerations." (Kennedy and Dowling, *op. cit.*, p. 226.)

15. See J.P.Neary, "The Failure of Irish Nationalism", in "Ireland: Dependence and Independence", *The Crane Bag*, 8/1, 1984.

16. After a decade of fairly rapid growth there was a feeling that more emphasis should be placed on social issues. The objectives listed under "social development" included "the better use of leisure"!

17. It is of interest to note that T.K.Whitaker, then a Senator, spoke against this step.

18. The reader should be aware that Brendan Walsh was a member of both the Committee on Costs and Competitiveness and the National Planning Board!

19. The idea of compiling this Figure, and the data for the earlier years, were provided by J. P. Neary.

20. The Economic and Social Research Institute, however, made explicit the assumptions they used in preparing their medium term forecasts for 1989-94 and they present a range of projections based on different assumptions.

21. See Desmond Norton, *Problems in Economic Planning and Policy Formation in Ireland, 1958-74*, Dublin: The Economic and Social Research Institute, 1975.

22. Norton, *op. cit.*, p. 30.

23. This is in fact acknowledged by Kennedy *et al.* when they refer to a "general entrepreneurial deficiency affecting both the public and private sectors" (*op. cit.* p. 247).

24. For an example of this type of reasoning applied to the Irish case see Eoin O'Malley, *Industry and Economic Development, The Challenge for the Latecomer*, Dublin: Gill and Macmillan, 1989.

25. Hugh Patrick quoted in C L Schultze, *The Brookings Review*, Fall, 1986, p. 6.

# *Appendices*

## Appendix 1     *Inflation and Real GNP*

The growth rate in nominal GNP can be broken down into the growth rate in real GNP and the inflation rate. Consider, for example, the following data relating to the Irish economy:

|       | Nominal GNP (£m) | Change in nominal GNP | Inflation |
|-------|------------------|-----------------------|-----------|
| 1987  | 18,032           |                       |           |
|       |                  | (4.17%)               | (2.1%)    |
| 1988  | 18,784           |                       |           |
|       |                  | (7.8%)                | (4.2%)    |
| 1989  | 20,250           |                       |           |

The objective is to calculate the real growth in GNP given nominal GNP and the inflation rate. The first step is to calculate an index for inflation. Set year 1 (the "base" year) equal to 100. The figures for the remaining years are obtained by adding on the percentage increase. Hence, 1987 = 100, 1988 = 102.1 and 1989 = 106.4 (in the third year the increase is 4.2% of 102.1 and not 100). The second step is to divide

|       | A Nominal GNP (£m) | B Price index | C Real GNP (£m) | D % change in real GNP |
|-------|--------------------|---------------|-----------------|------------------------|
| 1987  | 18,032             | 100.0         | 18,032.0        |                        |
|       |                    |               |                 | (2.0)                  |
| 1988  | 18,784             | 102.1         | 18,397.6        |                        |
|       |                    |               |                 | (3.4)                  |
| 1989  | 20,250             | 106.4         | 19,031.9        |                        |

the nominal GNP figures by the price index and multiply by 100. Note that column C = (A/B) * 100. A similar calculation applies in calculating real changes in wages. The distinction between nominal and real GNP is important because employment (or unemployment) moves with changes in real GNP. Firms do not need to hire workers to put up their prices!

---

# Appendix 2    Deriving the multiplier formula when savings is the only leakage

The basic model consists of an equilibrium condition and the consumption function:

(1)    GNP   =   C + I + G

(2)    C     =   $\alpha$ + MPC * NI

where $\alpha$ is the intercept term and MPC is the marginal propensity to consume. Substitute (2) into (1).

(3)    GNP   =   ($\alpha$ + MPC * NI) + I + G

Assume GNP = NI (recall from the circular flow diagram that only depreciation and indirect taxes separate these two variables).

(4) GNP = (MPC * GNP) + $\alpha$ + I + G

Bring the term in brackets over to the left hand side.

(5)    GNP - (MPC * GNP) = $\alpha$ + I + G

or

(6)    GNP(1 - MPC) = $\alpha$ + I + G

Divide both sides by (1 - MPC).

(7)    GNP = [1/(1 - MPC)] * ($\alpha$ + I + G)

The term, [1/(1 - MPC)], is the multiplier. Given that MPS = 1 - MPC, the multiplier formula could also be written as [1/MPS]. An increase in $\alpha$ (the intercept term in the consumption function which represents an increase in consumption not brought about by an increase in income), I or G will raise GNP by the multiplier. Conversely, a fall in α, I or G will reduce GNP by the multiplier.

## Appendix 3  *Deriving the multiplier formula with savings, taxation and import leakages*

The equilibrium condition is:

(1)    GNP  =  C + I + G + X - M

The behavioural relationships underlying the equilibrium condition are:

(2)   C   =   $\alpha$ + (MPC * NI) - T        Consumption function
(3)   T   =   $\beta$ + MPT * NI              Taxation function
(4)   M   =   $\chi$ + MPM * NI              Import function

The letters $\alpha$, $\beta$ and $\chi$ denote the intercept term in the consumption, tax and import equations respectively. The coefficients MPC, MPT and MPM are the marginal propensities to consume, tax and import respectively and they show how C, T and M react to changes in NI. The consumption function here differs from the over-simplified multiplier formula given in appendix 2 in that consumer expenditure is determined by gross income and by taxation. In appendix 2, consumer expenditure depended only on gross income. Here the consumption function states that a change in gross income affects consumer expenditure via the MPC whereas a change in taxation has a direct affect on consumer expenditure. In appendix 4 we examine the case where consumer expenditure depends on disposable income, that is, gross income minus taxation.

Substitute equation 3 into equation 2.

(5)   C   =   $(\alpha + MPC * NI) - (\beta + MPT * NI)$

or

(6)   C   =   $(MPC - MPT)NI + \alpha - \beta$

Substitute equations (6) and (4) into the equilibrium condition (1).

(7)    GNP = (MPC - MPT)NI + $\alpha$ - $\beta$ + I + G + X - $\chi$ - (MPM * NI)

Bring the terms involving NI over to the left hand side and assume GNP = NI.

(8)    GNP - (MPC - MPT - MPM)GNP = $\alpha$ - $\beta$ - $\chi$ + I + G + X

or

(9)    GNP(1 - MPC + MPT + MPM) = $\alpha$ - $\beta$ - $\chi$ + I + G + X

Recall that MPS = 1 - MPC

(10)   GNP(MPS + MPT + MPM) = $\alpha$ - $\beta$ - $\chi$ + I + G + X

Divide both sides by the term in brackets:

(11)   GNP = [1/(MPS + MPT + MPM)] * ($\alpha$ - $\beta$ - $\chi$ + I + G + X)

The term [1/(MPS + MPT + MPM)] is the multiplier formula when savings, taxation and import leakages are allowed for. Note that the minus sign on the tax and import intercept terms, $\beta$ and $\chi$ respectively, indicate that an increase in taxation and imports, not brought about by a change in national income, will decrease GNP via the multiplier formula. As before, an increase in $\alpha$, $\beta$ (the consumption and taxation intercept terms) I, G or X or a fall in $\chi$ (the import intercept term) will increase GNP via the multiplier formula and vice versa.

---

# Appendix 4    Deriving the multiplier formula when consumer expenditure depends on disposable income

The equilibrium condition is:

(1)    GNP  =    C + I + G + X - M

The behavioural relationships underlying the equilibrium condition are:

(2)  C  $=$  $\alpha + \text{MPC(NI - T)}$          Consumption function
(3)  T  $=$  $\beta + \text{MPT} * \text{NI}$          Taxation function
(4)  M  $=$  $\chi + \text{MPM} * \text{NI}$          Import function

As in appendix 3, the symbols $\alpha$, $\beta$ and $\chi$ denote the intercept term in the consumption, taxation and import equations respectively. The coefficients MPC, MPT and MPM are the marginal propensities to consume, tax and import respectively and they show now C, T and M react to changes in NI. The consumption function indicates that consumer expenditure is determined by disposable income, NI - T. Unlike the consumption function in appendix 3, changes in taxation now affect consumer expenditure via the MPC.

Substitute equation 3 into equation 2.

(5)     $C = \alpha + \text{MPC(NI} - \beta - \text{MPT} * \text{NI)}$

or

(6)     $C = \text{MPC(1 - MPT)NI} + \alpha - (\text{MPC} * \beta)$

Substitute equations (6) and (4) into identity (1).

(7)  GNP  $=$  $\text{MPC(1 - MPT)NI} + \alpha - (\text{MPC} * \beta) + I + G + X - \chi - (\text{MPM} * \text{NI})$

Bring the terms involving NI over to the left hand side and assume GNP = NI.

(8)     $\text{GNP} - \text{MPC(1 - MPT)GNP} + (\text{MPM} * \text{GNP}) = \alpha - (\beta * \text{MPC}) - \chi + I + G + X$

Rearrange

(9)    $\text{GNP[1 - MPC} + (\text{MPC} * \text{MPT}) + \text{MPM]} = \alpha - (\beta * \text{MPC}) - \chi + I + G + X$

Recall that MPS = 1 - MPC

(10)   $\text{GNP[MPS} + (\text{MPC} * \text{MPT}) + \text{MPM]} = \alpha - (\beta * \text{MPC}) - \chi + I + G + X$

Divide both sides by the term in square brackets:

(11)   $\text{GNP} = [1/(\text{MPS} + (\text{MPC} * \text{MPT}) + \text{MPM})] * [\alpha - (\beta * \text{MPC}) - \chi + I + G + X]$

The term [1/(MPS + (MPC * MPT) + MPM)] is the multiplier formula when savings, taxation and import leakages are allowed for and when the consumption function depends on disposable income. Note that the minus sign on the tax and import intercept terms, $\beta$ * MPC and $\chi$ respectively, indicate that an increase in taxation and imports, not brought about by a change in national income, will decrease GNP via the multiplier formula. Changes in taxation also affect consumer expenditure via the MPC. As before an increase in $\alpha$, the consumption intercept term, I, G or X will increase GNP via the multiplier formula.

Many more complex multiplier formulae can be derived. One that is of some interest is the *balanced budget multiplier* which shows that an equal increase in tax revenue and government expenditure has a multiplier of 1, and not zero as might be expected. Some textbooks elaborate multiplier formulae, presumably in the belief that a bit of algebra is good for the soul! However, it is far more important that the student understands the basic concepts, and the issues at stake, in the application of the Keynesian model, than that he or she spends a lot of time refining the multiplier formulae.

---

# A*ppendix 5*    *The yield curve*

The yield curve shows the yields from fixed rate debt securities of different maturities. Each of the securities should have similar or constant credit risk in order to facilitate comparison. Typically, the yield curve is calculated for government stock as the credit risk remains constant (for practical purposes, zero) over long periods of time. In the following table we show the yields on a range of Irish government stock for particular dates in 1988 and 1989. A graph of the different yields represents the yield curve.

The yield curve as at November 1988, is humped at the one year maturity. The yield curve as at October 1989, on the other hand, is inverted or negatively sloped. A positively sloped yield curve is often referred to as the "normal" type of curve because longer maturities contain more price risk than short maturities and, as a result, investors demand a risk premium to compensate.

The yield curve is of considerable interest to portfolio managers and investors as it can provide clues as to how interest rates and inflation may change in the future. The first piece of information incorporated in the yield curve is the future direction of interest rates. For example, suppose the yield curve is upward sloping and that the yield on a one year bond is 7% and the yield on a two year bond is 8%. This upward sloping yield curve can be taken as an indication that interest rates will increase in the future.

**Irish government securities' yields: % per annum**

| Maturity | Yield | |
|---|---|---|
| | *November 1988* | *October 1989* |
| 6 month | 8.33 | 10.95 |
| 1 year | 8.81 | 10.30 |
| 5 years | 8.68 | 9.63 |
| 10 years | 7.97 | 9.20 |
| 20 years | 7.62 | 8.73 |

*Source*: Department of Finance

To see why, consider two different investment strategies. Strategy A involves investing in a two-year government bond, the yield on which is 8%. Strategy B is a "roll-over" strategy in that the investment is for two separate one year periods. Funds are invested in government bonds of one year maturity on which a yield of 7% is paid and then re-invested for a further one year period. Arbitrage should now ensure that the yields from strategy A and strategy B are the same. If this is the case, the yield in year two of the "roll-over" strategy must be slightly over 9% (it is not correct to simply average the year one and year two yields because of the compounding of interest). An upward sloping yield curve therefore embodies the expectation that interest rates will increase in the future. Conversely, a negative yield curve suggests that interest rates will fall in the future.

We may now go a stage further and ask what provides the basis for the expectation that interest rates will rise or fall in the future? One possible explanation is provided by the "Fisher equation". This states that the nominal rate of interest ($R_n$) equals inflation expectations ($Inf^e$) plus the real interest rate ($R_r$).

$$(1) \quad R_n \quad = \quad Inf^e + R_r$$

Assuming that the real interest rate is constant (refer back to Chapter 12, section 12.4 for a discussion of the validity of this assumption), an increase in inflation expectations leads to an increase in nominal interest rates and, conversely, a fall in inflation expectations leads to lower nominal interest rates. Hence, on the assumption that the real interest rate is constant, an upward sloping yield curve embodies the expectation that inflation will rise in the future. On this basis, the inverted yield curve for Irish government stock as at October 1989 suggests that inflation is expected to decrease in the future.

But what provides the basis for inflation expectations? In the context of a large, relatively closed, economy like the US, the Quantity Theory of Money is perhaps the most important theory underlying inflation expectations (see Chapter 6). This theory states that the growth in the money supply will eventually be reflected in the inflation rate. Hence, an increase in the growth rate of money indicates an increase in inflation sometime in the future. Conversely, a fall in the rate of growth of money indicates a fall in the inflation rate. However, in Ireland, as we discussed in Chapters 8, 9 and 10, "purchasing power parity" (PPP) theory may be the most influential long run theory of the formulation of inflation expectations. This theory states that domestic inflation is determined by exchange rate movements and by foreign inflation rates. Hence, if the exchange rate is fixed, a decrease in the inflation rate in our main trading partners could, over time, be expected to lead to a lower Irish inflation rate. Conversely, an increase in foreign inflation would lead to higher domestic inflation. The yield curve for Irish government securities as at October 1989 could be taken to indicate that the exchange rate of the Irish pound will remain stable and/or be revalued in the EMS and that foreign inflation rates will fall in the longer term. In this regard, the yield curve paints an optimistic picture for the Irish economy over the next twenty years!

# Appendix 6    *The objectives of monetary policy: 1965-77*

*Mar. '65 - Dec. '65.* "... the Central Bank has had regard to the many difficulties both for the banks and for the economy in the way of slowing down the expansion in credit".
Central Bank of Ireland, *Annual Report*, 1964/65, p. 17.

*Mar. '67 - Dec. '68* "... any slackening in the growth of bank credit is neither desirable or necessary ...".
Central Bank of Ireland, *Annual Report*, 1966/67, p. 22.

*April '68 - April '69.* "... the Board ... have formed the opinion that a moderately liberal attitude towards the growth of credit is appropriate ...".
Central Bank of Ireland, *Annual Report*, 1967/68, p. 20.

*April '69 - April '70.* "... the aim of credit policy must be to reduce the pressure of inflation ... A lower rate of increase in total bank lending ... than actually occurred last year ... is indicated".
Central Bank of Ireland, *Annual Report*, 1968/'69, p. 47.

*April '70 - April '71.* In 1970 monetary policy was designed to exert "some degree of internal demand restraint" (Central Bank of Ireland, *Quarterly Bulletin*, Spring, 1970, p. 11) with the objective of reducing the balance of payments deficit from a projected £80-90m to £50m. This entailed reducing the growth in nominal GNP from a projected 13% to 10.5% and the real growth rate from 5% to 3%. The Central Bank's view was that "both public expenditure and credit can be powerful inflationary forces through their influence on the level of expenditure and ... there is no doubt that excessive income and price increases are facilated by liberal fiscal and monetary policies."
Central Bank of Ireland, *Quarterly Bulletin*, Spring, 1970, p. 9.

*April '71 - April '72.* "In providing for the year ahead, it would not be advisable to envisage a degree of credit restriction which would adversely affect business liquidity and therefore, investment, production and employment".
Central Bank of Ireland, *Annual Report*, 1970/'71, p. 31.

*April '72 - April '73.* "... monetary policy ... is not restrictive. It is designed to facilitate the maximum sustainable growth in output and employment ...".
Central Bank of Ireland, *Annual Report*, 1971-72, p. 31.

*April '73 - April '74.* "It would be most undesirable that credit expansion should itself generate inflationary spending ...".
Central Bank of Ireland, *Quarterly Bulletin*, 2, 1973, p. 17.

*1974* "The general effect is to allow bank credit ... to be increased at about the same rate as the prospective increase in Gross Domestic Expenditure".
Central Bank of Ireland, *Quarterly Bulletin*, 2, 1974, p. 14.

*1975* "It is expected that Gross Domestic Expenditure will increase by about 22 percent in 1975. To support this increase, it is the intention of the Central Bank that the growth in the money supply should be of the same order ... (and) ... bank lending should increase at a somewhat higher rate ...".
Central Bank of Ireland, *Annual Report*, 1975, p. 3.

*1976* "... monetary policy will aim at accommodating the reasonable demands of the private sector".
Central Bank of Ireland, *Annual Report*, 1976, p. 10.

*1977* " ... monetary policy should contribute to the achievement of a further reduction in the rate of inflation ...".
Central Bank of Ireland, *Annual Report*, 1977, p. 24.

# Appendix 7    The monetary approach to the balance of payments (MAB)

**Consolidated balance sheet of the banking system**

| *Liabilities* | *15 Feb. 1989* |
|---|---:|
| 1.  Capital employed | 2,229.2 |
| 2.  Government deposits at the Central Bank | 384.3 |
| 3.  Currency | 1,109.9 |
| 4.  Current accounts | 1,335.7 |
| 5.  Deposit accounts | 7,742.4 |
| 6.  Accrued interest | 184.1 |
| M3 = 3+4+5+6 (Money supply) | 10,372.1 |
| 7.  Net external liabilities of licensed banks | 3,889.5 |
| 8.  Acceptances | 130.5 |
| 9.  Other liabilities | 1,006.4 |
| *Total liabilities* | *18,012.0* |

| *Assets* | |
|---|---:|
| 10. Non-government credit | 10,658.1 |
| 11. Accrued interest | 235.8 |
| 12. Government credit | 2,921.1 |
| 13. Official external reserves | 3,244.9 |
| 14. Fixed assets | 429.6 |
| 15. Other assets | 522.5 |
| *Total assets* | *18,012.0* |

*Source*: Central Bank of Ireland, *Annual Report*, 1989, Table C1.

*Note*: Capital employed is calculated as a residual.

Assets = Liabilities. Hence:

$$M3 \equiv 10 + 11 + 12 + 13 + 14 + 15 - (1 + 2 + 7 + 8 + 9)$$
$$\equiv (10 + 11) + (12 - 2) + 13 - 7 - (1 + 8 + 9 - 14 - 15)$$
$$\equiv NGL + BLG + R - NEL - NNDL$$

*where*

| | | |
|---|---|---|
| NGL | = | Bank lending to the non-government sector |
| BLG | = | Bank lending to the government |
| R | = | External reserves |
| NEL | = | Net external liability of domestic banks |
| NNDL | = | Net non-deposit liabilities of domestic banks |

Consider changes over a period of, say, one year.

(1) $\Delta M3 \equiv \Delta NGL + \Delta BLG + \Delta R - \Delta NEL - \Delta NNDL$

Now from the balance of payments (see Chapter 9, Table 9.1):

(2) $\Delta R = BOP + GEB + PCI + \Delta NEL$

*where*

| | | |
|---|---|---|
| BOP | = | Balance of payments on current account (deficit -, surplus +) |
| GEB | = | Government external borrowing |
| PCI | = | Private capital inflow |
| $\Delta NEL$ | = | Change in net external liabilities of banks |

Substitute (2) into (1):

$$\Delta M3 \equiv \Delta NGL + \Delta BLG + BOP + GEB + PCI + \Delta NEL - \Delta NEL - \Delta NNDL$$
$$\equiv \Delta NGL + \Delta BLG + GEB - \Delta NNDL + BOP + PCI$$
$$\equiv DCE - \Delta NNDL + BOP + PCI$$

where DCE is domestic credit expansion in the economy i.e. the increase in bank lending to the private sector, ($\Delta NGL$), plus monetary financing of the government ($\Delta BLG + GEB$). If $\Delta NNDL$ and PCI are both assumed to be zero, this accounting identity states that:

$$\Delta M3 \equiv DCE + BOP \quad \text{or}$$

$$\Delta M3 - DCE \equiv BOP$$

If we consider M3 to be equivalent to the growth in resources in the banking system, this states that if resource growth is less than claims on resources (DCE) there will be a balance of payments deficit and vice versa.

# *Index*

Domestic credit expansion, 351, 398
Dooley, M P and Shafer, J R, 322
Dornbusch, R, 254
double counting, 2, 10
Dukes, Alan, 65, 68

EBR *see* exchequer borrowing requirement
economic activity
    Irish performance measured, 8-28
    and medium term policy issues, 366-85
Economic and Social Research Institute (ESRI), 50
    on employment, 179, 383-4
    evaluation of fiscal policy, 70-71
    forecasts, 26
    medium-term forecast, 382
*Economic Development*, 376, 377
economic planning, 375-83
    future role, 383-5
    misunderstanding of, 382-3
Economic Planning and Development,
  Department of, 379
economic policy, 372-83
    goals of, 31
    medium term issues, 366-85
    and rate of unemployment, 136
*Economic Review and Outlook* (Dept of Finance), 25
economy
    goal of macroeconomics, 5-7
    internal and external balance, 269-73
    Irish economic performance
    measured, 366-9
    international comparisons, 369
    planning, 375-83
    structure of, 370-2
    measurement of, 1-3
Educational Building Society, 100
Electricity Supply Board, 372
emigration, 78, 133, 385
    effects of, 7, 17, 129, 133-4
    remittances, 12
    20th-c., 366-8
Emigration and other Population Problems,
  commission on, 367, 377
employment, 133-6. *see also* internal balance

and AS curve, 41
and devaluation, 276-81, 282-4
and exchange rate policy, 276-82, 251-5
full employment and unemployment, 177-81
full employment budget, 52-3
state aid in creating, 374-5
entrepreneurs, 384
equilibrium
    balance of payments, 261-3
    exchange rate, 204, 242
    foreign exchange market, 204-5, 261-3
    money market, 109-11
    price, 39
    unemployment, 143-4
European Communities, Commission of the,
  151, 373, 374
European Community, 1992, 102
    currencies, 191
    Ireland in, 378-9
    subsidies, 12
    transfers to Ireland, 187
European Currency Unit (ECU), 213, 225-6, 227-9
    exchange rate, 227-30
European Monetary Co-operation Fund, 213, 230
European Monetary System (EMS)
    British attitude to, 225, 226, 227, 232, 234
    conflicting fiscal/monetary policies, 217
    convergence in, 232-4
    cost of disinflation, 251-55
    credibility bonus, 251-55, 259
    ERM, 196, 224-5, 233, 289
    exchange rates, 182, 188, 246-50
    inflation, 181
    Ireland in, 25, 95, 220, 237-44, 244-53,
     289, 303, 315
    pattern of trade, 245-6
    purchasing power parity, 240-44
    realignments, 230-2, 294
    role of, 212
    since 1979, 227-30
    "snake" system, 229n
    speculation in, 232n
    stabilisation effect, 303, 315
    White Paper on, 239

European Monetary Union, 223-6
   future of, 256-7
   "snake" system, 224, 226-7, 229n
European Recovery Programme (Marshall Aid), 376
European Regional Fund, 239
European Social Fund, 239
exchange rate mechanism (ERM), 196, 224-5, 233, 289
exchange rates, 3-4, 196-99 *see also* foreign exchange market; purchasing power parity
   "adjustment problem", 217
   and balance of payments, 185-217
   Central Bank policy, 188, 264-5
   competitiveness, 253-6
   depreciation and appreciation, 31
   determination, 202-9
   EMS, 182, 188, 246-50
   equilibrium exchange rate, 242
   expectations, 327-9
   factors influencing long-term, 209-12
   fixed exchange rates, 188, 212-16, 234, 264-5, 265-9
   fixed v floating, 216-17
   flexible exchange rates, 217, 273-6
   foreign exchange market, 192-3
   future course of, 290
   hedging techniques, 330-1
   importance in SOE, 152
   and interest rates, 284-5
   Irish policy, 220-56
   nominal, in EMS, 246-8
   nth country problem, 233n
   over-valuation, 252-3
   policy, 260-86, 276-81
   real, 199-202, 210, 241, 248, 253
   trade-weighted exchange rate index, 196-9
exchange transactions, 312-13
exchequer borrowing requirement (EBR), 55-6, 253-5
   and GNP ratio, 59-60
expected price inflation, 168
expenditure, flow of, 16
exports, 11 *see also* trade
   effect of decrease in, 209

Irish growth, 255-6
   prices, 14-15
external balance, 260, 269-73
external costs, 2-3
external reserves, 93, 188
   and borrowing, 214-16
   defined, 212
   influence of, 298-300
   target, 354-6

factor cost, 2, 9
factor payments, 9
factors of production, 155-6
FAS, 139
Fianna Fáil, 372
   economic policy, 64-7, 380, 381
final demand, 11
Finance, Department of, 25, 376
   budget data, 61
   and devaluation, 284
   forecasts, 26, 50n
   regulation of financial institutions, 102
finance, sources of, 113-16
Finance Act 1986, 102
financial institutions, 99-102
   credit guidelines, 339-40
financial theory, international, 311-35
Fine Gael, 64-7, 118
firms
   deficiency of aggregate demand, 150
   definition of profit, 38
   prices and equilibrium, 38-9
   role of, 1, 33-5
   savings, 23-4
First National Building Society, 100
*First Programme for Economic Expansion*, 376-7, 378-9, 380, 382
fiscal drag, 52n
fiscal indexation, 71
fiscal neutrality, 71
fiscal policy, 36-42, 70, 73-4, 111, 266-7 *see also* Keynesian Model
   and aggregate demand, 50-52
   effectiveness questioned, 46

405

public capital programme, 67, 375-6
public sector, 371
    consumption forecast, 26
    contribution to AD, 68
    dissavings, 22
    and labour market, 77-8, 134, 180-81
    recruitment ban, 65
public sector borrowing requirement (PSBR),
  66-7, 68, 76
purchasing power parity, 201n, 217, 238, 240-4,
  248-52, 266, 327, 395
    absolute, 240
    and devaluation, 282-3
    and exchange rates, 3-4, 327-9
    and inflation in SOE, 181, 242-4
    relative, 241
    empirical evidence, 243-4
    theory of, 210, 240-2, 242-44

Quantity Theory of Money, 84n, 123-6, 234, 395
Quarterly Economic Commentary (ESRI), 26
Quesnay, Francois, 33

Random walk, 321n
rational expectations, 175-6
Registrar of Friendly Societies, 102
household savings, 23
reverse crowding-out, 68, 118
Ricardian Equivalence Effect, 75-6, 265
Ricardo, David, 51
Ryan, Richie, 64, 68, 379
Ryan, Prof W J L, 194-5

Sacrifice ratio, 259
sale and repurchase agreements, 305
Samuelson, Paul, 166
Sargent, Thomas, 176
savings, *see also* marginal propensity to save
    and consumption, 44
    function, 44
    increase in, 75-6
    influence on interest rates, 300
    ratio, 26
    savings, national, 23-4

Schmidt, Helmut, 224
Schwartz, Anna, 125
Scotland, 138n
*Second Programme 1964-70*, 378-9
shares, 106-8
short-term credit facility, 304
Singapore International Monetary Exchange, 331
Single European Act, 224, 239
small open economy (SOE), 129, 155, 266, 271-2
    importance of rate of exchange, 152
    importance of trade, 189-91
    inflation, 242-4, 347-8
    and unemployment, 181-3
    interest rates in, 288-309
    Ireland as, 370-1
    NAIRU in, 182
Smith, Adam, 366, 383
snake system, 224, 226-7, 229n
Social Welfare, Department of, 136
social welfare system, 31, 53
    and unemployment, 139-42, 140-1
Solow, Robert, 166, 179
Spain, 5, 227
special drawing rights, 212
speculation, 106-09
    and balance of payments, 299
    demand for money, 106-9
    EMS realignments, 232n
    and exchange rate, 210-11, 314-15
    leading and lagging, 211
speculative demand for money
  *see* money, demand for
spillover effects, 2-3
stabilisation policy, 47-52, 50, 65-6
    difficulties in implementing, 48-52
    effect of, 50-52
    EMS as stabiliser, 251
    evaluation of, 308-9
    inside and outside lags, 49
stagflation, 40, 166-7
state-sponsored bodies, 339-40, 381
state-sponsored financial institutions, 99, 100
Stein, Herbert, 375
sterilisation, 267, 304, 308-9